Happiness in Economics

The International Library of Critical Writings in Economics

Series Editor: Mark Blaug

Professor Emeritus, University of London, UK
Professor Emeritus, University of Buckingham, UK
Visiting Professor, University of Amsterdam, The Netherlands
Visiting Professor, Erasmus University of Rotterdam, The Netherlands

This series is an essential reference source for students, researchers and lecturers in economics. It presents by theme a selection of the most important articles across the entire spectrum of economics. Each volume has been prepared by a leading specialist who has written an authoritative introduction to the literature included.

A full list of published and future titles in this series is printed at the end of this volume.

Wherever possible, the articles in these volumes have been reproduced as originally published using facsimile reproduction, inclusive of footnotes and pagination to facilitate ease of reference.

For a list of all Edward Elgar published titles visit our site on the World Wide Web at
http://www.e-elgar.co.uk

Happiness in Economics

Edited by

Richard A. Easterlin

University Professor
University of Southern California, USA

THE INTERNATIONAL LIBRARY OF CRITICAL WRITINGS IN ECONOMICS

An Elgar Reference Collection
Cheltenham, UK • Northampton, MA, USA

Published by
Edward Elgar Publishing Limited
Glensanda House
Montpellier Parade
Cheltenham
Glos GL50 1UA
UK

Edward Elgar Publishing, Inc.
136 West Street
Suite 202
Northampton
Massachusetts 01060
USA

A catalogue record for this book is available from the British Library.

ISBN   1 84064 754 X

Printed and bound in Great Britain by MPG Books Ltd, Bodmin, Cornwall

Contents

Acknowledgements

The editor and publishers wish to thank the authors and the following publishers who have kindly given permission for the use of copyright material.

Academic Press, Inc. for excerpt: Richard A. Easterlin (1974), 'Does Economic Growth Improve the Human Lot? Some Empirical Evidence', in Paul A. David and Melvin W. Reder (eds), *Nations and Households in Economic Growth: Essays in Honor of Moses Abramovitz*, 89–125.

American Economic Association for article: Rafael Di Tella, Robert J. MacCulloch and Andrew J. Oswald (2001), 'Preferences over Inflation and Unemployment: Evidence from Surveys of Happiness', *American Economic Review*, **91** (1), March, 335–41.

Blackwell Publishers Ltd for articles: Yew-Kwang Ng (1978), 'Economic Growth and Social Welfare: The Need for a Complete Study of Happiness', *Kyklos*, **31** (4), 575–87; R. Layard (1980), 'Human Satisfactions and Public Policy', *Economic Journal*, **90**, December, 737–50; Andrew E. Clark and Andrew J. Oswald (1994), 'Unhappiness and Unemployment', *Economic Journal*, **104** (424), May, 648–59; Andrew J. Oswald (1997), 'Happiness and Economic Performance', *Economic Journal*, **107** (445), November, 1815–31; Robert H. Frank (1997), 'The Frame of Reference as a Public Good', *Economic Journal*, **107** (445), November, 1832–47; Bruno S. Frey and Alois Stutzer (2000), 'Happiness, Economy and Institutions', *Economic Journal*, **110** (466), October, 918–38; Richard A. Easterlin (2001), 'Income and Happiness: Towards a Unified Theory', *Economic Journal*, **111** (473), July, 465–84.

Critical Review for articles: Jeffrey Friedman and Adam McCabe (1996), 'Preferences or Happiness? Tibor Scitovsky's Psychology of Human Needs', *Critical Review*, **10** (4), Fall, 471–80; Amartya Sen (1996), 'Rationality, Joy and Freedom', *Critical Review*, **10** (4), Fall, 481–94; Tibor Scitovsky (1996), 'My Own Criticism of *The Joyless Economy*', *Critical Review*, **10** (4), Fall, 595–605.

Arie Kapteyn for his own article: (2001), 'Relative Utility and Income Growth: An Example'.

MIT Press Journals for article: Huib van de Stadt, Arie Kapteyn and Sara van de Geer (1985), 'The Relativity of Utility: Evidence from Panel Data', *Review of Economics and Statistics*, **LXVII** (2), May, 179–87.

Russell Sage Foundation for excerpt: Bernard M.S. van Praag and Paul Frijters (1999), 'The Measurement of Welfare and Well-Being: The Leyden Approach', in Daniel Kahneman, Ed Diener, and Norbert Schwarz (eds), *Well-Being: The Foundations of Hedonic Psychology*, Chapter 21, 413–33.

Every effort has been made to trace all the copyright holders but if any have been inadvertently overlooked the publishers will be pleased to make the necessary arrangement at the first opportunity.

In addition the publishers wish to thank the Marshall Library of Economics, Cambridge University and the Library of Indiana University at Bloomington, USA for their assistance in obtaining these articles.

Introduction

Richard A. Easterlin

With scarcely a shot fired, economics is in danger of surrendering the empirical study of subjective well-being to other disciplines. Since the 1940s, surveys reporting personal happiness or life satisfaction have been accumulating steadily. These data have been a gold mine to scholars in disciplines other than economics, and a recent research bibliography reports over 3000 contributions. Economic research on subjective welfare, however, has been stifled by the heavy hand of a disciplinary paradigm stipulating that what people say is irrelevant to understanding their feelings or behavior. Meantime, a number of distinguished psychologists – who do listen to what people say – have, in an imposing and encyclopedic volume, now laid claim to a new field they term hedonic psychology, which virtually writes off the relevance of economics to individual well-being (Kahneman, Diener, and Schwarz, 1999). Among their tentative conclusions is that "happiness ... is a personality trait with a large heritable component" (ibid., p. 14). "External factors" such as economic circumstances are, at best, second or lower order determinants of subjective well-being, and, because of the dominance in determining happiness of genetics and personality, economic policy can have only a small long-term effect on well-being (p. 227).

Only a small number of economists have ventured into the fray, and most of these, only recently. The present volume assembles some of the most cited contributors, in the hope of mustering interest among fellow economists, perhaps even recruits.

Like my graduate school colleagues, I was taught that meaningful interpersonal comparisons of well-being could not be made. No one ever demonstrated this empirically; it was taken as axiomatic. It came as something of a surprise to me, therefore, and perhaps will also to some of my fellow economists, that subjective testimony reveals a number of regularities, some of which accord with economists' *a priori* expectations about welfare:

1. At a point in time, subjective well-being varies directly with income.
2. The so-called "misery index," which assumes that well-being varies inversely with both the unemployment and inflation rates, is supported empirically, albeit with somewhat different relative weights of the components than are usually assumed.
3. Throughout the life cycle, the well-being of better-educated persons is greater than that of less-educated, and that of whites is greater than blacks.

If subjective testimony is meaningless, it is hard to explain why such findings turn up in one data set after another. Indeed, psychologists conclude, contrary to economic orthodoxy, that measures of well-being based on subjective testimony "contain substantial amounts of valid variance" (Diener, 1984, p. 551). Their research finds significant positive correlations between an individual's self-reported well-being and a variety of non-self-report measures, such as evaluations by professional psychologists, peers, and relatives (ibid.; cf. also Sandvik, Diener, and Seidlitz, 1993).

True, the self-reported well-being of an individual might have substantive content, but that does not mean that the well-being of one person can be compared directly to that of another. As already indicated, however, empirical regularities are found repeatedly in comparisons among groups in the population. How can one account for such persistent results? Again, research – this time on the sources of subjective well-being – suggests the answer: the personal concerns that shape happiness evaluations are much the same for most people everywhere most of the time – living conditions, family, and health (Cantril, 1965). Hence, most people in evaluating their well-being are using quite similar criteria. This conclusion may not satisfy the purist, and it does not mean that welfare comparisons can readily be made on a person-to-person basis. But if it is groups or classes of the population in which one is interested, the general similarity of concerns suggests that meaningful comparisons can be made, and this similarity helps account for the regularities repeatedly observed.

If economic research on subjective testimony merely confirmed what we think we already know, then we might shrug it off with a "so what." But there are other findings on subjective well-being that either run counter to *a priori* expectations, or pose puzzles challenging explanation:

1. Economic growth – rapid or otherwise – does not raise subjective well-being, even though the cross-sectional relation between well-being and income is positive.
2. Over the life course, a cohort's average subjective well-being remains constant – this, despite the fact that people typically say they were less happy in the past and expect to be happier in the future.

To suggest that economic growth does not increase individual welfare is nothing short of economic heresy. Yet this finding has now turned up in time series for quite a few countries. And if individuals' *ex ante* expectations of improved well-being turn out not to be true *ex post*, could it be that economic decisions are made on the basis of false expectations of the extent of welfare improvement?

Perhaps these few observations are enough to provoke a few stalwarts to read on. In the hope that this is so, let me sketch in the remainder of this introduction, the evolution of economic research on subjective well-being as I understand it, and how the various papers collected here fit in.

In 1970–71 it was my good fortune to be a fellow at the Center for Advanced Study in the Behavioral Sciences at Stanford. My economic preconceptions had already been tainted by prior association with demographers, to the extent that in research on the determinants of childbearing I had abandoned absolute for relative income. As a result, I was vulnerable to the influence of several prominent sociologists and psychologists who were also at the Center. I think it was reference to social psychologist Hadley Cantril's *The Pattern of Human Concerns* (1965) that first got me started looking at data on self-reported happiness. The outcome is the first chapter in this volume, "Does Economic Growth Improve the Human Lot?" published in 1974 in a collection honoring Moses Abramovitz. The empirical analysis in this paper posed what Harvey Leibenstein subsequently called the "paradox of happiness": within a country at a point in time happiness varies directly with income, but over time happiness does not increase as a country's income increases.

Working independently and drawing heavily on the literature of physiological psychology, Tibor Scitovsky, the most eminent welfare economist of the time, arrived at essentially the same agnostic conclusion about the impact of economic growth on well-being. His book presenting his analysis, *The Joyless Economy*, was published in 1976. Recently there was a well-deserved commemoration of *The Joyless Economy* in a special issue of the journal *Critical Review*, which I have drawn on here. The article by Jeffrey Friedman and Adam McCabe (Chapter 2) admirably summarizes the high points of Scitovsky's reasoning. Also presented are Scitovsky's own reflections on the book some two decades later (Chapter 3).

In the 1950s and 1960s the famous income-savings paradox had posed a cross-section/time series puzzle much like the paradox of happiness. Explanations had usually invoked two types of social comparison – one with prior experience (now called "habit formation" models), the other with relevant others ("relative income" or "interdependent preference" models) (Duesenberry, 1949; Modigliani, 1949). These two lines of explanation have also come to the fore as determinants of subjective well-being. In my early work I speculated that Duesenberry's relative income argument explained why economic growth did not raise subjective well-being; Scitovsky, in contrast, stressed comparison with past experience. Initially, the relative status argument tended to predominate. In his 1976 book, *The Social Limits to Growth*, Fred Hirsch stressed the growing importance as consumer income rises, of the demand for positional goods – goods whose value depends not on how much you have, but how much you have relative to others. His argument is encapsulated here in an early paper by Yew-Kwang Ng (Chapter 4). Ng was perhaps the first economic theorist to take seriously the empirical findings on subjective well-being, and has produced over the years a number of thoughtful contributions on the economics of happiness (Ng, 1996; 1997).

Another prominent contributor to the relative income explanation was Robert Frank, who in his 1985 book, *Choosing the Right Pond*, demonstrated the pervasiveness of relative status considerations in a wide variety of behavior, as well as in feelings of subjective well-being. Frank's interests have also consistently encompassed policy implications of a relative income model. I have taken advantage here of a recent paper of his on happiness that states concisely his argument that "a progressive consumption tax would greatly enhance every citizen's opportunity to pursue his or her vision of the good life" (Chapter 5, p. 1845). I have also included the first paper to focus specifically on the policy implications of empirical research on happiness, one by Richard Layard published in the *Economic Journal* in 1980. Among other things, Layard opens the door to manipulating utility functions via education (Chapter 6). Layard's paper makes clear that serious attention to happiness research can lead to conclusions that threaten the economic precept of the sanctity of individual preferences, a point to which I shall return in the end.

Part I concludes with three papers from the Leyden School, a group of Dutch economists who have made a series of important research contributions following the pioneering work in 1968 of Dutch economist Bernard van Praag. While this work does not deal with happiness or life satisfaction as such, it focuses on a critical determinant of subjective well-being, the "income norm," that is, the scale registering the adequacy of income. The Leyden School employs an ingenious technique to measure this norm, and their findings on the nature and determinants of income norms and the policy implications of this work are summarized here in a recent overview article by van Praag and Frijters (Chapter 7). Among other things income norms are found to vary directly with actual income, and economic decisions, as hinted above, consequently turn out to be based on false expectations of the extent of welfare improvement. I have also included a much neglected 1985 paper by several members of this school, which includes both habit formation and interdependent preferences in a model of economic welfare (Chapter 8). Estimation of the parameters of this model suggests that in combination the two determinants imply that economic growth does not increase economic welfare. One of the co-authors of the 1985 paper, Arie Kapteyn, has been kind enough to provide a brief addendum, illustrating this specific point (Chapter 9).

Since around 1990 there has been a small upsurge in economic research on subjective well-being. Considerable credit for this is due to British economist Andrew J. Oswald and his collaborators. Part II of this volume opens with Oswald's 1997 overview of some major findings of happiness research (Chapter 10). The approach followed in much of the work by Oswald and his colleagues has been empirical, centering on statistical analysis of happiness (or life satisfaction) as a dependent variable and, as independent variables, an array of personal and demographic characteristics. The authors are careful to caution that they are identifying statistical associations, not necessarily cause and effect. They find a marked similarity in the structure of happiness relationships in the United States and a number of European countries. Controlling for a variety of factors, those who are happier are married, white, higher income, better educated, and employed (Chapter 10; cf. also Blanchflower and Oswald, 1999; 2000). By translating dry statistical coefficients into dollars and cents terms, they have made the results of happiness research much more accessible to the general public. Thus they suggest that "to 'compensate' men for unemployment would take a rise in income at the mean of approximately $60,000 per annum, and to 'compensate' for being black would take $30,000 extra per annum. A lasting marriage is worth $100,000 per annum when compared to being widowed or separated" (Blanchflower and Oswald, 1999, p. 15).

Unemployment is an economic factor whose negative effect on subjective well-being is exceptionally high, a point developed explicitly in the next article, by Andrew E. Clark and Oswald (Chapter 11). Based on an "unhappiness" measure summarizing responses to 12 questions on symptoms of mental distress, they find that the unemployed are significantly more unhappy among both men and women, young and old, and the more and less educated, though there are differences in the size of the effect among the various subgroups. The adverse impact of unemployment on well-being may lessen somewhat with the length of unemployment, though the effect is still large among those unemployed for over a year. A recent study using panel data for German working men and a standard happiness question, confirms the Clark and Oswald results, and provides support for their speculation that the psychological distress due to unemployment is not caused merely by the loss of income associated with job loss (Winkelmann and Winkelmann, 1998). Indeed, the adverse effect on happiness of unemployment due to the non-income component exceeds that due to the loss of income. The panel data exclude the possibility that time-invariant individual characteristics, such as poor health, cause both unemployment and depressed life satisfaction, and strongly suggest that causation runs from unemployment to life satisfaction, and not vice-versa.

Economists' advocacy of full employment policies is typically premised on the income/output loss associated with lapses from full employment. The finding just noted makes clear that the welfare argument for full employment policies is considerably stronger. This comes out explicitly in the next article, by Rafael Di Tella, Robert J. MacCulloch, and Andrew J. Oswald (Chapter 12). Macro economic policy aims to forestall serious inflation as well as promote full employment, and the so-called "misery index" assumes that in terms of social welfare a one percentage point cut in the unemployment rate is equivalent to a one point cut in the rate of inflation. The article does indeed demonstrate that subjective well-being varies inversely with both the unemployment and inflation rates. But the impact on well-being of a one point change in the unemployment rate is substantially greater (1.7 times) than that of a one point change in the inflation rate. Recent decades have seen the increasing subordination of employment to price-level concerns as a goal of monetary and fiscal policy. This article implies that policy makers, if their ultimate interest is social welfare, have got it backward.

The evidence is fairly persuasive that in developed countries subjective well-being does not increase as income increases over time, though there may be longer term up or down movements around the trend, as well as short term fluctuations (Blanchflower and Oswald, 1999; Diener and Oshi, forthcoming; Easterlin 1995; Kenny 1999). It is sometimes argued that things are different in developing countries – that income growth does increase happiness, at least up to a point, after which happiness levels off as income rises. As appealing as this proposition is, I have seen no time series evidence to support it. Fragmentary time series data for today's developing countries are only now starting to become available and most of these data are not comparable over time because of variations in question wording. The only country for which a long time series is available encompassing income levels below those of many of today's developing countries is Japan. Consistent with the results for developed countries there is no improvement in subjective well-being, despite a five-fold growth in per capita income (Easterlin, 1995).

There are, however, sizeable differences in subjective well-being among nations at a point in time. Over the period from 1974 to 1983, for example, the Dutch and Danes consistently ranked higher than the French, Germans, and Italians. Political scientists Ronald Inglehart and Jacques-Renier Rabier have suggested that these differences in life satisfaction may be due to cultural differences, "in the extent to which it is permissible to express unhappiness and dissatisfaction with one's life," but no evidence is offered in support of this hypothesis (Inglehart and Rabier, 1986).

Economists have had little to say about such differences. But a recent analysis of cross-sectional happiness differences among Swiss cantons by Bruno S. Frey and Alois Stutzer points the way to more systematic analysis (Chapter 13). They find that individual well-being is higher in cantons with more direct democracy, as measured by access to initiatives and referenda, and perhaps also in cantons with greater local autonomy. This result holds after controlling for income differences among cantons, including the possible effect on income of the use of democratic procedures to reduce tax burdens. This analysis is a significant step toward trying to pinpoint specific cultural factors affecting happiness differences.

Considerable attention has been devoted by economic theorists to the life cycle saving hypothesis, which is premised on assumptions about how individuals structure their well-being over the life cycle. However, aside from the subjective well-being literature, no work has been done to assess life cycle welfare as such. Based on statistical analysis of cross-sectional data for several countries, Blanchflower and Oswald conclude that subjective well-being is U-shaped with age with a trough occurring around age 40 (Chapter 10; Blanchflower and Oswald, 1999). The panel data for German working men does not confirm this finding, nor does a longer panel study by psychologists covering about 10 years (Costa, Zonderman, et al., 1987; Winkelmann and Winkelmann, 1998). In Chapter 14 of this volume, I apply the demographic technique of cohort analysis to follow the course of subjective well-being over 24 years of the life span for cohorts starting at young adult, mid-life, and older ages. The outcome, consistent with the panel studies, is no significant change in subjective well-being, positive or negative, over the adult life cycle. I also present evidence for a number of countries that people typically assess their past happiness as less than their present, and expect to be happier still in the future, and I propose a model with supporting evidence to explain the disparity between *ex ante* expectations of welfare change – what psychologists call "decision utility" – and *ex post* subjective well-being, "experienced utility." A centerpiece of this model is the changing nature of consumption norms. The results are much like those obtained in the analysis of income norms in Chapter 9, namely, that on average norms change to the same extent as actual income. But my model assumes a change over the life cycle in the role of habit formation versus interpersonal comparison in determining the consumption or income norm – an assumption that remains to be tested.

As previously mentioned, research by psychologists is increasingly tending to emphasize as determinants of subjective well-being genetic and personality factors and to downplay the role of external social and economic conditions. The finding of life cycle stability in the subjective well-being of a cohort might be taken as support for the psychologists' position. But such an inference would be premature. Some of the evidence already noted, such as the impact of unemployment and inflation on well-being, runs counter to the psychologists' view. Additional support for the importance of "external factors" in shaping well-being is the persistently higher well-being over the life cycle of more-educated compared with less-educated persons (Chapter 14). It seems likely that differential access to education may channel individuals into higher and lower income tracks and, in so doing, create persistent long-term differences in well-being. Further support is provided by the even larger excess of white over black subjective well-being (Blanchflower and Oswald, 1999; Easterlin 2001). Contrary to the agnostic policy implications of the psychological literature, these results point to the potential relevance to individual welfare of policy interventions.

Research on subjective well-being ultimately raises much more fundamental policy issues, issues that challenge the foundations of the economic and political system under which we live. As Friedman and McCabe point out, this system is premised on the "assumption that individual freedom automatically leads to happiness by virtue of the individual's knowledge of her own best interests" (Chapter 2, p. 475). They draw attention to Scitovsky's argument, however, that individuals do not necessarily know their own best interests, and that "an untutored desire need *not* serve the interests of its possessor" (ibid.). This conclusion is also implied by recognition of the mechanism accounting for the lack of impact on subjective well-being of economic growth – the positive effect of income growth is wholly undercut by an equivalent rise in income norms engendered by that income growth. If our present economic system is, in fact, little more than what psychologists Brickman and Campbell (1971) call an "hedonic treadmill," a system where ever-growing abundance is matched by ever-growing material aspirations, then we are not the governors of the system in which we live, as we would like to think, but are, in fact, governed by that system – a system that has set us on a course of economic growth *ad infinitum*. Is it possible to break out of this bind without sacrificing our cherished goal of individual freedom? To conclude this volume, I have used a short essay on Scitovsky's work by Nobel Laureate Amartya Sen, who with characteristic wisdom wrestles with this critical issue (Chapter 15). Sen would no doubt be the first to acknowledge that his is not the last word on the subject. But one may hope that it is, for economists, at least a first word. As economists, we have been taught that it is not scientific to talk about the "good life," and we feel uncomfortable any time such issues surface. But what is one to do when science points us in that direction? Perhaps it is time for social scientists to consider that they might learn something from humanists.

References

Blanchflower, David G. and Andrew J. Oswald (1999), 'Well-Being Over Time in Britain and the USA', unpublished manuscript, November.

Blanchflower, David G. and Andrew J. Oswald (2000), 'The Rising Well-Being of the Young', in David G. Blanchflower and Richard B. Freeman, *Youth Employment and Joblessness in Advanced Countries*, Chicago: University of Chicago Press, 289–328.

Brickman, Philip and D.T. Campbell (1971), 'Hedonic Relativism and Planning the Good Society', in M.H. Appley (ed.), *Adaptation Level Theory: A Symposium*, New York: Academic Press.

Cantril, Hadley (1965), *The Pattern of Human Concerns*, New Brunswick, NJ: Rutgers University Press.

Costa, Paul T. Jr., Alan B. Zonderman, Robert R. McCrae, Joan Cornoni-Huntley, Ben Z. Locke and Helen E. Barbano (1987), 'Longitudinal Analyses of Psychological Well-Being in a National Sample: Stability of Mean Levels', *Journal of Gerontology*, **42** (1), 50–55.

Diener, Ed (1984), 'Subjective Well-Being', *Psychological Bulletin*, **95** (3), 542–75.

Diener, Ed and S. Oshi (forthcoming), 'Money and Happiness: Income and Subjective Well-Being Across Nations', in E. Diener and E.M. Suh (eds), *Subjective Well-Being Across Cultures*, Cambridge, MA: MIT Press.

Duesenberry, James S. (1949), *Income, Savings, and the Theory of Consumer Behaviour*, Cambridge, MA: Harvard University Press.

Easterlin, Richard A. (1995), 'Will Raising the Incomes of All Increase the Happiness of All?', *Journal of Economic Behavior and Organization*, **27**, 35–47.

Easterlin, Richard A. (2001), 'Life Cycle Welfare: Trends and Differences', *Journal of Happiness Studies*, **2**, 1–12.

Frank, Robert (1985), *Choosing the Right Pond*, New York and Oxford: Oxford University Press.

Hirsch, Fred (1976), *The Social Limits to Growth*, Cambridge, MA: Harvard University Press.

Inglehart, Ronald and Jacques-Rene Rabier (1986), 'Aspirations Adapt to Situations – But Why are the Belgians so Much Happier Than the French?', in Frank M. Andrews (ed.), *Research on the Quality of Life*, Ann Arbor, MI: Survey Research Center, Institute for Social Research, University of Michigan, 1–56.

Kahneman, Daniel, Ed Diener and Norbert Schwarz (eds) (1999), *Well-Being: The Foundations of Hedonic Psychology*, New York: Russell Sage Foundation.

Kenny, C. (1999), 'Does Growth Cause Happiness or Does Happiness Cause Growth?', *Kyklos*, **52** (1), 3–26.

Modigliani, Franco (1949), 'Fluctuations in the Saving–Income Ratio: A Problem in Economic Forecasting', in Conference on Research in Income and Wealth, *Studies in Income and Wealth*, Vol. XI, New York: National Bureau of Economic Research, 371–443.

Ng, Yew-Kwang (1996), 'Happiness Surveys: Some Comparability Issues and an Exploratory Survey Based on Just Perceivable Increments', *Social Indicators Research*, **38**, 1–27.

Ng, Yew-Kwang (1997), 'A Case for Happiness, Cardinalism, and Interpersonal Comparability', *The Economic Journal*, **107**, November, 1848–58.

Sandvik, Ed, Ed Diener and Larry Seidlitz (1993), 'Subjective Well-Being: The Convergence and Stability of Self-Report and Non-Self-Report Measures', *Journal of Personality*, **61** (3), September, 317–42.

Scitovsky, Tibor (1976), *The Joyless Economy: An Inquiry into Human Satisfaction and Consumer Dissatisfaction*, New York: Oxford University Press.

van Praag, Bernard (1968), *Welfare Functions and Consumer Behavior: A Theory of Rational Irrationality*, Amsterdam: North Holland.
Winkelmann, Liliana and Rainer Winkelmann (1998), 'Why are the Unemployed So Unhappy? Evidence from Panel Data', *Economica*, **65**, February, 1–15.

Part I
Early Contributors

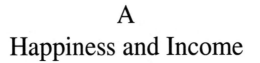

A
Happiness and Income

[1]

Does Economic Growth Improve the Human Lot ? Some Empirical Evidence

RICHARD A. EASTERLIN
UNIVERSITY OF PENNSYLVANIA

Over a decade ago, Moses Ambramovitz published an essay, "The Welfare Interpretation of National Income and Product," in a predecessor volume to this one, honoring another distinguished Stanford economist (Abramovitz, 1959). Abramovitz concluded that "we must be highly skeptical of the view that long term changes in the rate of growth of welfare can be gauged even roughly from changes in the rate of growth of output,"[1] and called for "further thought about the meaning of secular changes in the rate of growth of national income and empirical studies that can fortify and lend substance to analysis [pp. 21, 22]."*

This paper is offered in the spirit of this little-heeded call. It brings together the results of surveys of human happiness that have been conducted in

---

[1] A differing conclusion, perhaps more representative of the profession at large, is reached by Nordhaus and Tobin (1972): "Is growth obsolete? We think not. Although GNP and other national income aggregates are imperfect measures of welfare, the broad picture of secular progress which they convey remains after correction of their most obvious deficiencies [p. 24]."

* M. Abramovitz, "The welfare interpretation of secular trends in national income and product." In *The Allocation of Economic Resources: Essays in Honor of Bernard Francis Haley* (M. Abramovitz *et al.* eds.), Stanford, California: Stanford Univ. Press, 1959.

nineteen countries, developed and less-developed, during the period since World War II, to see what evidence there is of an association between income and happiness. Are the wealthy members of society usually happier than the poor? What of rich versus poor countries—are the more developed nations typically happier? As a country's income grows during the course of economic development, does human happiness advance—does economic growth improve the human lot?

Happiness is not confined, of course, to economic well-being. Abramovitz noted that "since Pigou ... economists have generally distinguished between social welfare, or welfare at large, and the narrower concept of economic welfare," with "national product ... taken to be the objective, measurable counterpart of economic welfare [p. 3]." Happiness corresponds to the broader of these two concepts, that of social welfare, or welfare at large. However, as Abramovitz points out, economists have normally disregarded possible divergences between the two welfare concepts, and operated on Pigou's dictum "that there is a clear presumption that changes in economic welfare indicate changes in social welfare in the same direction, if not in the same degree [p. 3]." It is this dictum, as applied to the study of economic growth, that is the central concern of this paper. Is there evidence that economic growth is positively associated with social welfare, i.e., human happiness?

The term "happiness" is used intermittently, albeit loosely, in the literature of economics.[2] To my knowledge, however, this is the first attempt to look at the actual evidence. The initial section of this paper is devoted to a somewhat lengthy discussion of the concept and measurement of happiness, as the term is used in this study. The second section presents the results of the empirical analysis, and the third, an interpretation of the findings. The conclusions, in brief, are that the evidence supports Abramovitz's skepticism of a positive correlation between output and welfare, and for a good reason. The increase in output itself makes for an escalation in human aspirations, and thus negates the expected positive impact on welfare.

1. The Concept and Measurement of Happiness

a. Concept

The basic data used here are statements by individuals on their subjective happiness. These self-reports are sometimes designated "avowed" or "reported" happiness to underscore the possibility that they may not accurately

---

[2] It is used, for example, in welfare economics by Mishan (1968): "If, for instance, welfare is used as a synonym for happiness ... [p. 504]." Similarly, Little (1950) comments: "And, according to our present definition of 'welfare' (='happiness') ... [p. 30]." In a recent economics text, Eckaus (1972) writes: "What is the economic system supposed to do? The answer that it should contribute to human happiness is as good a start as any [p. 7]."

reflect the true state of the respondents' feelings. This possibility will be examined shortly.

The data are of two types. The first consists of the responses to a Gallup-poll-type survey in which a direct question of the following sort was asked: "In general, how happy would you say that you are—*very* happy, *fairly* happy, or *not very* happy?" Sometimes this was preceded by a question asking the respondent to state "in your own words, what the word 'happiness" means to you."

The other set of data comes from a more sophisticated procedure, devised by Cantril (1965) in a pioneering study of the hopes, fears, and happiness of persons in 14 countries of the world. Since Cantril's study figures prominently in the following analysis, it is worth quoting him at some length. He starts with a general description of the technique he calls the "Self-Anchoring Striving Scale":

> A person is asked to define on the basis of *his own* assumptions, perceptions, goals, and values the two extremes or anchoring points of the spectrum on which some scale measurement is desired—for example, he may be asked to define the "top" and "bottom," the "good" and "bad," the "best" and the "worst." This self-defined continuum is then used as our measuring device.
>
> While the Self-Anchoring Striving Scale technique can be used on a wide variety of problems, it was utilized in this study as a means of discovering the spectrum of values a person is preoccupied or concerned with and by means of which he evaluates his own life. He describes as the top anchoring point his wishes and hopes as he personally conceives them and the realization of which would constitute for him the best possible life. At the other extreme, he describes the worries and fears, the preoccupations and frustrations, embodied in his conception of the worst possible life he could imagine. Then, utilizing a nonverbal ladder device [showing a scale from 0 to 10], symbolic of "the ladder of life," he is asked where he thinks he stands on the ladder today, with the top being the best life *as he has defined it*, the bottom the worst life *as he has defined it*.
>
> . . . .
>
> The actual questions, together with the parenthetical instructions to interviewers, are given below:
>
> 1. (A) All of us want certain things out of life. When you think about what really matters in your own life, what are your wishes and hopes for the future? In other words, if you imagine your future in the *best* possible light, what would your life look like then, if you are to be happy? Take your time in answering; such things aren't easy to put into words.
>   PERMISSIBLE PROBES: What are your hopes for the future? What would your life have to be like for you to be completely happy? What is missing for you to be happy? [Use also, if necessary, the words "dreams" and "desires."]
>   OBLIGATORY PROBE: Anything else?
>
> (B) Now, taking the other side of the picture, what are your fears and worries about the future? In other words, if you imagine your future in the *worst* possible light, what would your life look like then? Again, take your time in answering.

> PERMISSIBLE PROBE: What would make you unhappy? [Stress the words "fears" and "worries."]
> OBLIGATORY PROBE: Anything else?
> Here is a picture of a ladder. Suppose we say that the top of the ladder (POINT-ING) represents the best possible life for you and the bottom (POINTING) represents the worst possible life for you.
>
> (C) Where on the ladder (MOVING FINGER RAPIDLY UP AND DOWN LAD-DER) do you feel you personally stand at the *present* time? Step number_____ [pp. 22–23, italics in original].*

This technique thus yields a rating by each individual of his personal standing on a scale from 0 (the worst possible life) to 10 (the best possible life), where "worst" and "best" are defined by each person for himself. The survey also asked for current evaluations of past and prospective personal standings, plus a similar set of evaluations by each individual of the situation of the nation as a whole. In the present analysis, use will be made only of the rating by each individual of his personal happiness at the time of the survey, since this is relevant to subjective well-being, and reports on one's feelings at the moment are likely to be more accurate than those on how one might feel or did feel in other situations.

Although the procedures differ in the Gallup poll and Cantril approaches, the concept of happiness underlying them is essentially the same. Reliance is placed on the subjective evaluation of the respondent—in effect, each individual is considered to be the best judge of his own feelings. He is seen as having a frame of reference that defines for him the range from unhappy to happy states of mind. His summary response—whether in terms of broad categories of happiness, as in the Gallup poll, or in terms of a numerical rating from 0 to 10, as in Cantril's approach—is a statement of his present position within that frame of reference.

The approach has a certain amount of appeal. If one is interested in how happy people are—in their subjective satisfaction—why not let each person set his own standard and decide how closely he approaches it? The alternatives of obtaining evaluations by outside observers or seeking to use objective indicators of happiness inevitably run into the problem of what observers or what indicators one should rely on. Moreover, despite the use of ratings based on a scale that varies from one individual to the next, it is possible to make meaningful comparisons. For example, consider two population groups. These might be two segments of a national population at a given time, say rich and poor, or the populations of an entire country at two different times, or the populations of two different countries at a given time. Whatever the

* *Patterns of Human Concerns* by Hadley Cantril. Rutgers University Press, New Brunswick, New Jersey (1965).

case, it is of interest to ask whether on the average individuals in the first population differ significantly from those in the second in how high they rate themselves in terms of personal happiness, even though the scale being applied differs within each population and between the two. After all, in opinion surveys on the relative merit, say, of presidential aspirants, the criteria used by respondents in forming their evaluations doubtless differ. Indeed, it is of interest to ask whether there are systematic differences in the criteria used for the evaluations (a point we shall look into later). It may be argued, of course, that political opinion polls are of value because of their implications for prospective behavior of the respondents. But perhaps the same may be said of opinions on personal happiness—might not individuals with a low personal happiness rating be expected to behave differently from those with a high personal rating?

At the same time, a number of reservations on the meaningfulness of the data come to mind. There is first the question of the relevance of the happiness concept to populations differing widely in cultural characteristics. It is true that the present approach allows each individual to define his own standard of happiness. But is the idea itself present in all cultures? One indication that it is is the observation by Inkeles (1960) that happiness, in contrast to certain other concepts relating to emotional states, "may be translated fairly well from one language to another ... [p. 15]." Cantril (1965) devoted considerable effort to this translation issue:

> One of the problems that had to be overcome was translating the original questions from English into the various languages used. In some cases this was by no means an easy task, and considerable time was spent with experts to be sure the translation contained the precise nuances wanted. One of the methods often utilized in this translation process was to have someone who knew the native language, as a native, for example, an Arab, and who also was completely fluent in English translate our questions into Arabic. Then someone whose native language was English but who had a perfect command of Arabic would translate the Arabic back into English so a comparison could be made with the original question and, through discussion and further comparisons, difficulties could be ironed out.
>
> Translations from English had to be made into the following twenty-six other languages which we list here alphabetically: Arabic, Bengali, Cebuano, German, Gujarati, Hausa, Hebrew, Hindi, Ibo, Ilocano, Ilongo, Malayalam, Marathi, Oriya, Polish, Portuguese, Serbo-Croatian, Slovenian, Spanish, Tagalog, Tamil, Telugu, Urdu, Waray, Yiddish, and Yoruba [p. 26].*

Apparently the effort paid off, for the nonresponse rate was generally low. To judge from this experience, happiness is an idea that transcends individual cultures.

* *Patterns of Human Concerns* by Hadley Cantril. Rutgers University Press, New Brunswick, New Jersey (1965).

Moreover, the considerations affecting personal happiness in different cultures turn out to be quite similar. In his survey, Cantril found that typically certain hopes and fears were more frequently expressed than others. Here, for example, is a tabulation he prepared of the things mentioned most frequently by Americans in discussing their hopes, and the proportion of the sample mentioning each item (Cantril, 1965, p. 35):*

Own health	40%
Decent standard of living	33
Children	29
Housing	24
Happy family	18
Family health	16
Leisure time	11
Keep status quo	11
Old age	10
Peace	9
Resolution of religious problems	8
Working conditions	7
Family responsibility	7
To be accepted	6
An improved standard of living	5
Employment	5
Attain emotional maturity	5
Modern conveniences	5

To facilitate handling such data, Cantril (1965, p. 36) further classified the items listed above into nine "general" categories of personal hopes:

Economic	65%
Health	48
Family	47
Personal values	20
Status quo	11
Job or work situation	10
International situation, world	10
Social values	5
Political	2

Hopes relating to economic matters appear to be foremost in the minds of Americans, but clearly do not exhaust the content of happiness.

Similar classification of the replies for other countries enabled Cantril to compare the personal hopes of people in widely differing national and cultural circumstances (Table 1). What stands out is that hopes regarding economic,

* *Patterns of Human Concerns* by Hadley Cantril. Rutgers University Press, New Brunswick, New Jersey (1965).

TABLE 1

PERSONAL HOPES BY COUNTRY, CA. 1960[a,b]

Country	Economic	Family	Health	Values and character	Job/work	Social	International	Political	Status quo	Total
Brazil	68	28	34	14	8	1	1	—	1	155
Cuba	73	52	47	30	14	4	3	15	1	239
Dominican Republic	95	39	17	15	25	2	—	9	—	202
Egypt	70	53	24	39	42	9	2	4	—	243
India	70	39	4	14	22	8	—	—	2	159
Israel	80	76	47	29	35	10	12	2	4	295
Nigeria	90	76	45	42	19	14	—	—	—	286
Panama	90	53	43	26	26	3	—	1	1	243
Philippines	60	52	6	9	11	5	—	—	—	143
United States	65	47	48	20	10	5	10	2	11	218
West Germany	85	27	46	11	10	3	15	1	4	202
Yugoslavia	83	60	41	18	20	4	8	—	2	236

[a] From *Patterns of Human Concerns* by Hadley Cantril, Rutgers University Press, New Brunswick, New Jersey (1965).
[b] Percentage of population mentioning hopes that fall in indicated category. Sum of percentages exceeds 100 percent because some respondents mention hopes falling in more than one category.

family, and health matters repeatedly dominate the perceptions of happiness by individuals in the various countries, with economic concerns typically the most frequently mentioned. Needless to say, the specific nature of these concerns often differs (some evidence on this regarding economic aspirations is presented toward the end of this essay), and there are undoubtedly variations among people within countries as well. If one looks at a like tabulation for personal fears rather than hopes, a similarity among countries again appears, though the relative importance of the categories changes somewhat (e.g., typically health increases in relative importance). On reflection, the similarity in the results for different countries is plausible. In all cultures the way in which the bulk of the people spend most of their time is similar—in working and trying to provide for and raise a family. Hence the concerns that they express when asked about happiness are similar.

b. Measurement Problems

Let us turn to some technical issues regarding the data. For one thing, there is the question of the stability of the replies. Are emotional states so highly variable that the replies to questions about personal happiness tend to fluctuate widely over short periods of time, with the ups and downs of daily life? This problem has been studied by comparing the results of surveys of the same population run at short intervals. The conclusion, reported by Robinson and Shaver (1969, p. 17), is that "[o]ne of the most impressive features of the questions ... is the stable test–retest reliabilities they exhibit." This result is confirmed by the data used here. Two surveys by the American Institute of Public Opinion (AIPO) containing a happiness question were taken within two weeks of each other in September 1956. The results were virtually identical. A third poll taken six months later still showed very little change (see Table 8 below).

Another important issue is the validity of self-reports on happiness. Are people capable of assessing their own emotional states? One test, though hardly a definitive one, is to examine the consistency of self-reports with evaluations by outside judges—peers, professional psychologists, and so on. The results of such tests are summarized as follows by Wilson (1967):

> Data from these several studies suggest that judges agree poorly among themselves, that judges vary in the extent to which they agree with self-ratings, and that few judges agree closely with self-ratings. At the same time, the data show that most judges agree with self-ratings to some extent and that the pooling of judges' estimates increases the agreement with self-ratings. These facts would seem, if anything, to support the validity of self-ratings [p. 295].*

* From W. Wilson, "Correlates of avowed happiness," *Psychological Bulletin* **67**, 1967, 294–306. Copyright 1967 by the American Psychological Association and reproduced by permission.

DOES ECONOMIC GROWTH IMPROVE THE HUMAN LOT?   **97**

Comparisons have also been made between self-reports on happiness and measures presumed to be indicative of happiness, e.g., indicators of physical health, and between self-reports on happiness and measures of other psychological states such as depression and self-esteem (Bradburn, 1969, p. 39; Robinson and Shaver, 1969, pp. 26–31). In both cases the self-reports show significant correlations with the other measures of the type expected. In all of these comparisons, there is inevitably the question of what is to be taken as the ultimate arbiter of "happiness." Perhaps the most that can be said is that the general consistency of self-reports with the other bases of evaluation bolsters one's confidence in the ability of people to assess with some validity their own feelings.

The result bears also on another issue—whether a person is likely to report his true feelings to an anonymous interviewer. The fact that the self-reports check out fairly well with other bases of evaluation suggests that the replies are reasonably honest. Indeed, in view of the considerable success in obtaining reports on such matters of intimate concern as personal income and sex, it might be felt that there would be no serious problem in getting people to state how happy they are. However, one possibly important source of bias exists. In formulating replies to survey questions, respondents are influenced by considerations of what they believe to be the proper or socially desirable response (Davis, 1965).[3] Thus, if the social norm is that happiness is a good thing, there might be a tendency toward an upward bias in the replies due to considerations of social desirability.

Again, there have been attempts to test for this factor. Comparisons have been made between replies given to an interviewer and the responses on a self-administered questionnaire, the presumption being that one is likely to be more honest in the latter situation. Also, correlations have been run between people's statements of their happiness and their tendencies toward social conformity, as measured by standard psychological tests. Sometimes the tests suggest some influence of social desirability in the replies; sometimes they do not (Bradburn, 1969, p. 38; Wilson, 1967, p. 295).

Of course, if all responses were similarly biased, there would be no real problem for the present study. The concern here is with the relation of happiness to income, and the real question is whether there may be differential bias in the replies by income level. Is it likely, for example, that rich people would feel that they were expected to reply that they are "very happy," and conversely for poor people? On reflection it is not wholly certain what reply people might think was expected of them. While most respondents might feel that the social norm is that "money makes one happy," there is the

---

[3] Cf. Edwards (1957). Recent work by Block (1965) and Rorer (1965) suggests that the importance of this factor in biasing survey results has been exaggerated.

possibility that others would be influenced by the notion of the "carefree, happy poor." The expected bias in the replies would clearly be different depending on which is perceived as the social norm. Beyond this there is the question of the universality of the norm. Has "the" norm been the same in the United States since 1946, or has it perhaps been altered by public attention in the 1960s to the "poverty problem"? Is the norm the same in 19 different countries ranging over the various continents of the world?

It is also pertinent to consider the context in which the happiness question is asked. If one were asked his income and then, immediately following, how happy he was, the respondent might link the two questions, and his awareness of a social norm might bias his reply. In the Gallup poll surveys used here, however, the happiness question is intermixed with 50 or more survey questions, most of which deal with current events, usually political. The question on economic status comes at the end of these surveys along with other inquiries as to personal characteristics. Under these circumstances, the respondent, in formulating his reply to the happiness question, is not likely to feel the interviewer is regarding him as a "rich person" or as "a poor person" and to answer the way he thinks such a person "ought" to answer. The Cantril survey is specifically focused on people's feelings—their hopes, fears, and how happy they are. Even in this case, however, the question on economic status comes at the end of the survey. It is far from clear that in considering questions a respondent would feel himself especially cast in the role, say, of a poor person, as distinct from that of one who is young or married or has any one of a number of other personal characteristics.

Finally, it is instructive to note the effect of variations in the wording of the happiness question. The National Opinion Research Center (NORC) has asked a question similar to that in the AIPO surveys, but the happiness categories differ as follows:

	(1)	(2)	(3)
AIPO	Very happy	Fairly happy	Not very happy
NORC	Very happy	Pretty happy	Not too happy

The first and third categories are virtually alike. It seems reasonable to suppose, however, that many individuals would consider the NORC's rating (2), "pretty happy," closer to (1) and farther from (3) than the AIPO's rating "fairly happy." Hence, one might expect that some respondents who chose category (1) in the AIPO poll would have chosen (2) in the NORC poll, and some who chose (2) in the AIPO poll would have chosen (3) in the NORC poll. The results of polls taken at similar dates confirm this expectation— the percentage in group (1) tends to run lower and the percentage in group (3) runs higher in the NORC polls (see Table 8, panels A and B). Moreover, a shift of this type is common to all income classes, with no systematic difference in magnitude.[4] The direction of the shift and the consistency by income level suggest that respondents throughout the population are placing similar interpretations on the question asked and are answering, at least to some extent, in terms of their real feelings.

However, when all is said and done, the possibility of differential bias in the replies by income level cannot be ruled out, though the magnitude remains uncertain, and this qualification must be borne in mind in interpreting the findings presented here. My own feeling is that while such bias may exist, it is not significant enough to invalidate the conclusions on the association between income and happiness. Perhaps the most important basis for this judgment is the impressive consistency of the results in a variety of times and places with widely differing cultural and socioeconomic circumstances.

2. The Evidence

a. Within-Country Comparisons

Does greater happiness go with higher income? Let us look first at the comparative status of income groups within a country at a given time.

Table 2 presents the data from the most recent survey of the American population, conducted in December 1970. Of those in the lowest income group, not much more than a fourth report that they are "very happy." In the highest income group the proportion very happy is almost twice as great. In successive income groups from low to high the proportion very happy rises steadily. There is a clear indication here that income and happiness are positively associated.

How typical is this result? Tables 3–5 summarize the results of 29 additional surveys. Sixteen of these surveys are of the Gallup-poll type; 13, of the Cantril type. Ten of the surveys relate to the United States between 1946 and 1966; 19 to other countries, including 11 in Asia, Africa, and Latin America. The classifications by socioeconomic status tend to differ among the surveys and are typically broad and nonnumerical, consisting of designations such as

---

[4] This statement is based on a comparison of the 1963 AIPO data, shown here in part in Table 10, with the NORC data (from a somewhat more restricted population) in the work of Bradburn (1969, p. 45). I am grateful to William H. Kruskal for suggesting this comparison.

100 RICHARD A. EASTERLIN

"poor," "wealthy," "lower class," and "upper class." But the results are clear and unequivocal. In every single survey, those in the highest status group were happier, on the average, than those in the lowest status group.

TABLE 2

PERCENTAGE DISTRIBUTION OF POPULATION BY HAPPINESS, BY SIZE OF INCOME, UNITED STATES, 1970[a,b]

Income (in $1000)	(1) Very happy	(2) Fairly happy	(3) Not very happy	(4) No answer
All classes	43	48	6	3
15+	56	37	4	3
10–15	49	46	3	2
7–10	47	46	5	2
5–7	38	52	7	3
3–5	33	54	7	6
Under 3	29	55	13	3

[a] Data from AIPO Poll of December 1970.
[b] $N = 1517$.

TABLE 3

PERCENTAGE NOT VERY HAPPY IN LOWEST AND HIGHEST STATUS GROUPS, UNITED STATES, 1946–1970[a]

Date	Number of groups	Lowest status group Designation	N.V.H. (%)	Highest status group Designation	N.V.H. (%)	N
Apr. 1946	4	Poor	11	Wealthy	3	3151
June 1947	4	Poor	9	Wealthy	0	3088
Dec. 1947	4	Poor	12	Wealthy	3	1434
May 1948	4	Poor	10	Wealthy	0	1800
Aug. 1948	4	Poor	15	Wealthy	4	1596
Nov. 1952	3	Poor	12	Average +	8	3003
Jan. 1960	3	Low income	6	Upper income	2	2582
July 1963	6	Income < $3000	10	Income = $15,000 +	0	3668
Oct. 1966	6	Income < $3000	6	Income = $15,000 +	0.3	3531
Dec. 1970	6	Income < $3000	13	Income = $15,000 +	4	1517

[a] Data from Table 2 and AIPO polls 369, 399, 410, 418, 425, 508, 623, 675, and 735. In No. 623 (Jan. 60), the responses were on a scale ranging from −5 to +5. For the present purpose, all negative values were classified as "not very happy (N.V.H.)." Comparisons among surveys are of uncertain reliability because of variations in the specific question asked and in the group designations.

TABLE 4

PERCENTAGE NOT VERY HAPPY IN LOWEST AND HIGHEST STATUS GROUPS, SEVEN COUNTRIES, 1965[a]

Country	Number of groups	Lowest status group		Highest status group		
		Designation	N.V.H.[b] (%)	Designation	N.V.H.[b] (%)	N
Great Britain	3	Very poor	19	Upper, upper middle, middle	4	1179
West Germany	3	Lower middle, lower	19	Upper, upper middle	7	1255
Thailand	2	Lower/middle	15	Middle/upper	6	500
Philippines	2	Lower middle, lower	15	Upper, upper middle	5	500
Malaysia	2	Lower/middle	20	Middle/upper	10	502
France	3	Lower	27	Upper	6	1228
Italy	3	Lower middle, lower	42	Upper, upper middle	10	1166

[a] Data from World Survey III, 1965.
[b] Not very happy.

101

TABLE 5

PERSONAL HAPPINESS RATING IN LOWEST AND HIGHEST STATUS GROUPS, THIRTEEN COUNTRIES, CA. 1960[a,b]

(1) Country	Date	(2) Number of groups	(3) Lowest status group Designation	(4) Rating	(5) Highest status group Designation	(6) Rating	(7) Difference, high minus low [(6)−(4)]	(8) N
United States	Aug. 1959	5	Lower economic	6.0	Upper economic	7.1	1.1	1549
Cuba	Apr.–May 1960	3	Lower socioeconomic	6.2	High, upper middle socioeconomic	6.7	0.5	992
Israel	Nov. 1961–June 1962	3	Lower income	4.0	Upper income	6.5	2.5	1170
West Germany	Sept. 1957	3	Lower economic	4.9	Upper economic	6.2	1.3	480
Japan	Fall 1962	3	Lower, middle lower socioeconomic	4.3	Upper, upper middle socioeconomic	5.8	1.5	972
Yugoslavia	Spring 1962	4	Lower, farmer	4.3	Upper, nonfarmer	6.0	1.7	1523
Philippines	Spring 1959	4	Lower economic	4.1	Upper economic	6.2	2.1	500
Panama	Jan.–Mar. 1962	2	Lower socioeconomic	4.3	Upper socioeconomic	6.0	1.7	642
Nigeria	Sept. 1962–spring 1963	2	Lower socioeconomic	4.7	Upper socioeconomic	5.8	1.1	1200
Brazil	Late 1960–early 1961	5	Lower socioeconomic	3.9	Upper socioeconomic	7.3	3.4	2168
Poland	Spring 1962	5	Unskilled	3.7	White-collar	4.9	1.2	1464
India	Summer 1962	4	Income < R75	3.0	Income > R301	4.9	1.9	2366
Dominican Republic	Apr. 1962	2	Lower socioeconomic	1.4	Upper socioeconomic	4.3	2.9	814
Average				4.2		6.0	1.8	

[a] Data from Cantril, 1965, pp. 365–377.
[b] Minimum: 0; maximum: 10.

102

This finding is corroborated by the results of other studies of happiness and related emotional states. In an article published 10 years ago, Inkeles (1960) concluded:

> Those who are economically well off, those with more education or whose jobs require more training and skill, more often report themselves happy, joyous, laughing, free of sorrow, satisfied with life's progress. Even though the pattern is weak or ambiguous in some cases, there has not been a single case of a *reversal* of the pattern, that is, a case where measures of happiness are inversely related to measures of status, in studies involving fifteen different countries—at least six of which were studied on two different occasions, through the use of somewhat different questions. There is, then, good reason to challenge the image of the "carefree but happy poor" [p. 17, italics in original].*

Similar conclusions are reached by Bradburn (1969), Robinson and Shaver (1969), Wilson (1967), and Gurin *et al.* (1960). In a comprehensive study surveying the literature on mental health, Davis (1965, p. 68) reported that "study after study shows that mental health is positively related to socio-economic status in a variety of measures of mental health and SES."

In addition to classification by income level, data on happiness are sometimes available by characteristics such as sex, age, race, education, and marital status. While the association of happiness with income is the most pervasive, some other patterns are apparent, though not without exception. Perhaps the firmest is a positive association between happiness and years of schooling. There is also some suggestion that the young are happier than the old, married persons than unmarried, and whites than blacks. Where the data permitted multivariate analysis, the independent association of income and happiness has been confirmed (Bradburn, 1969, p. 294; Gurin *et al.*, 1960, p. 221; Robinson and Shaver, 1969, pp. 19–23). Also, the available evidence indicates low happiness levels among the unemployed and those on relief.

Inevitably, a question arises as to the direction of causality. Does higher income make people happier? Or are happier people more likely to be successful, i.e., receive higher income? It would be naïve to suppose that the issue is an either/or one. But emotional states are noticeably absent among the many factors usually cited by economists in explaining income differences. Factors such as education, training, experience, innate ability, health, and inheritance are among those principally mentioned. It might be felt that emotional well-being is implicit in the ability factor, or perhaps in that of health, though health is usually taken to refer to physical well-being. But it is doubtful that one would expect the influence of emotional well-being on earnings to stand out as clearly as in the simple bivariate comparisons shown

* A. Inkeles, "Industrial man: The relation of status to experience, perception and value," *American Journal of Sociology* **66**: 1960, 1–31. Published by the University of Chicago Press; Copyright 1960, 1961 by the University of Chicago.

here. Moreover, for some countries, some of the status designations, such as "upper class," are essentially hereditary. To argue that happiness causes such class differences is akin to arguing that, where happiness is correlated with age, happiness causes the age differences. Finally, as we have seen, when people are asked about the things that make them happy or unhappy, personal economic concerns are typically foremost [Table 1; cf. also Gurin *et al.* (1960, pp. 22–28)]. The worries of less-happy respondents differ most from those who are more happy in their emphasis on financial security [(Gurin *et al.*, 1960, p. 29; Wessman, 1956, pp. 213, 216); cf. also Table 11 below]. On the whole, therefore, I am inclined to interpret the data as primarily showing a causal connection running from income to happiness.[5]

b. International Comparisons

What happens when one looks at cross-sectional differences among countries? Are richer countries happier countries? Let us examine the Cantril data first, since that study made the greatest effort to assure comparability of approach among the various countries.

Table 6 presents the average personal happiness ratings for each of fourteen countries, along with figures on real GNP per capita. Cantril's own reading of these data is that they show a positive association between income and happiness and he presents correlation results to this effect (Cantril, 1965, p. 194).[6] He generalizes this into a five-stage scheme, reminiscent of Rostow's stages of growth, to describe the phases of emotional well-being through which a country passes in the course of economic development (Rostow, 1960; Cantril, 1965, Chapter XV). However, as with Rostow's classification, countries do not fall neatly into one or another stage. One's confidence in the generality of the scheme is further undermined by the following passage, which concludes the presentation of the stage scheme:

> It should be noted in passing, however, that people in some cultures or subcultures may seem to qualify for placement in this fifth [highest] stage of "satisfaction and gratification" who have not gone through earlier stages of development but appear to outside observers to be stuck at relatively primitive levels. The Masai of Kenya and Tanganyika might be regarded as such a pocket of contentment within their microcosm. There is, of course, every likelihood that once the boundaries of such a microcosm are penetrated by "advanced" cultures with the aspirations they intrude into people's minds, then the people within such a microcosm will alter the standards by means of which they judge satisfaction *and revert to an earlier stage of development* [*ibid.*, p. 310, italics added].*

[5] In interpreting the association between mental health and socioeconomic status, Davis (1965, pp. 74–77) leans in this direction also.

The point that for some countries some of the status designations are essentially hereditary also indicates that we are dealing here in substantial part with "permanent income" differences, and that the results cannot be dismissed on the grounds that they are dominated by transitory influences.

DOES ECONOMIC GROWTH IMPROVE THE HUMAN LOT?   **105**

TABLE 6

PERSONAL HAPPINESS RATING AND REAL GNP PER HEAD,
FOURTEEN COUNTRIES, CA. 1960[a, b]

Country	Period of survey	(1) Rating of personal happiness (min: 0; max: 10)	(2) Real GNP per head 1961 ($U.S.)
United States	Aug. 1959	6.6	2790
Cuba	Apr.–May 1960	6.4	516
Egypt	Fall 1960	5.5	225
Israel	Nov. 1961–June 1962	5.3	1027
West Germany	Sept. 1957	5.3	1860
Japan	Fall 1962	5.2	613
Yugoslavia	Spring 1962	5.0	489
Philippines	Spring 1959	4.9	282
Panama	Jan. –Mar. 1962	4.8	371
Nigeria	Sept. 1962–spring 1963	4.8	134
Brazil	Late 1960–early 1961	4.6	375
Poland	Spring 1962	4.4	702
India	Summer 1962	3.7	140
Dominican Republic	Apr. 1962	1.6	313
Average		5.0	

[a] Data in column (1) from Cantril, 1965, p. 184; data in column (2), except for West Germany, from Rosenstein-Rodan, 1961, pp. 118, 126, 127; data in column (2) for West Germany from Table 7.
[b] For sample sizes see Table 5.

To judge from this paragraph, some cultures or subcultures may "have it made" before they are touched by, or as long as they can remain free from, economic development.

Actually the association between wealth and happiness indicated by Cantril's international data is not so clear-cut. This is shown by a scatter diagram of the data (Fig. 1). The inference about a positive association relies heavily on the observations for India and the United States. [According to Cantril (1965, pp. 130–131), the values for Cuba and the Dominican Republic reflect unusual political circumstances—the immediate aftermath of a success-ful revolution in Cuba and prolonged political turmoil in the Dominican

---

[6] Actually Cantril (1965, pp. 193–194) uses a somewhat different measure of socio-economic development, of which the GNP data shown here are one component.

* *Patterns of Human Concerns* by Hadley Cantril. Rutgers University Press, New Brunswick, New Jersey (1965).

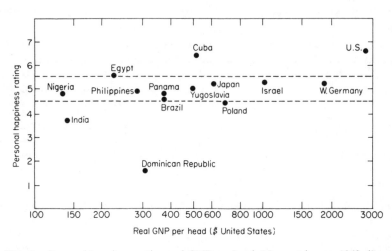

FIG. 1.   Personal happiness rating and GNP per head, 14 countries, ca. 1960. (Source:
Table 6.)

Republic].[7] What is perhaps most striking is that the personal happiness
ratings for 10 of the 14 countries lie virtually within half a point of the mid-
point rating of 5, as is brought out by the broken horizontal lines in the
diagram. While a difference of rating of only 0.2 is significant at the 0.05
level, nevertheless there is not much evidence, for these 10 countries, of a
systematic association between income and happiness. The closeness of the
happiness ratings implies also that a similar lack of association would be
found between happiness and other economic magnitudes such as income
inequality or the rate of change of income.

Of course, picking and choosing among points is a dubious practice.
What one can perhaps safely say is this: In the within-country data shown in
Table 5, the difference in happiness rating between low- and high-status
groups averages almost 2 points, and for only 1 of the 13 countries is the
difference less than 1 point. In contrast, in the comparison of national averages
shown in Table 6, the ratings for 10 of 14 countries lie within a range of 1.1
points. The tenfold range in per-capita income covered by these countries
almost surely exceeds the typical income range between low- and high-status
groups covered in the within-country data. The happiness differences between
rich and poor countries that one might expect on the basis of the within-

---

[7] The comparability of the Cuban data is further qualified by the fact that the survey
was confined to the urban population. For Egypt, the coverage of the rural population was
quite limited, and the survey is labeled by Cantril (1965, pp. 346–347) as a "preliminary
pilot investigation".

DOES ECONOMIC GROWTH IMPROVE THE HUMAN LOT? **107**

country differences by economic status are not borne out by the international data.

The other principal sources of international data are of the Gallup-poll type. In this case, the effort to secure comparability in asking the happiness question, which was only one of many questions, was less than in Cantril's study. In 1965, however, a survey obtained responses to a uniform inquiry in seven different countries. The results of this, plus that of a 1958 survey in Japan and a 1966 survey in the United States, are reported in Table 6.

There are four countries represented in both Tables 6 and 7—the United States, West Germany, Japan, and the Philippines. One's confidence in the data is bolstered by the striking similarity in the results. In both cases the United States appears much happier than West Germany, and West Germany slightly happier than the Philippines. The Japanese data in Table 7 are least

TABLE 7

PERCENT DISTRIBUTION OF POPULATION BY HAPPINESS,
NINE COUNTRIES, 1965[a]

Country	Very happy	Fairly happy	Not very happy	Other	N	Real GNP per head 1961
Great Britain	53	42	4	1	1179	$1777
United States[b]	49	46	4	2	3531	2790
West Germany	20	66	11	3	1255	1860
Thailand	13	74	12	1	500	202
Japan[c]	—	81 —	13	5	920	613
Philippines	13.5	73	13.5	0	500	282
Malaysia	17	64	15	4	502	552
France	12	64	18	5	1228	1663
Italy	11	52	33	4	1166	1077

[a] Happiness data are from World Survey III, 1965, except those for the United States and Japan, which are from Table 8 and the 1958 survey of Japanese national character, respectively. GNP data are from Rosenstein-Rodan, 1961, except those for Great Britain, France, West Germany, and Italy. For these countries GNP was estimated to bear the same proportion to the United States figure as that shown by the geometric mean estimates by Gilbert *et al.*, 1958, p. 36, extrapolated from 1955 to 1961 by the per-capita volume indexes in OECD, 1970, p. 11.

[b] 1966.

[c] 1958. (Question read "not happy" rather than "not very happy.")

comparable with those of the other countries, but even the relative position of Japan vis-à-vis the other three is not much different in Table 7 from that in Table 6.

108   RICHARD A. EASTERLIN

What association between happiness and income is indicated by the Table 7 data for all nine countries? The results are ambiguous. The four lowest income countries are neither at the top nor at the bottom of the Table, but are clustered in the middle. This result cannot be attributed to the younger age of the populations in these countries, for it shows up in comparisons for individual age classes. (This is true also of the data in Table 6.) If there is a positive association between income and happiness, it is certainly not a strong one. In contrast, in the within-country comparisons by economic status, shown in Tables 3 and 4, the happiness differences are clear and consistent. The conclusion indicated by the Gallup-poll data is thus consistent with that shown by the Cantril data.

International happiness comparisons for 1946 and 1949 are given by Cantril (1951, p. 281), Wessman (1956, p. 166), and Inkeles (1960, p. 13). These are confined to a few Western European countries and their overseas descendants. The comparability of the questions is uncertain, but for what it is worth, the results are similar to those shown above—if there is a positive association among countries between income and happiness it is not very clear.

The international data are intriguing in various respects. For example, notice the high position of Great Britain compared with the United States in Table 7. This result is a persistent one, to judge from the polls mentioned in the preceding paragraph. Also, in those polls Canada and Australia show levels of happiness comparable in magnitude to Great Britain and the United States. There is also a noteworthy closeness in the results for the four Asian countries shown in Table 7. Perhaps there are cultural influences in the international happiness data, though one should hesitate before lumping together Thailand, Malaysia, the Philippines, and Japan as having a common culture. Of course, even if there are cultural influences, they would not necessarily systematically bias the relation of happiness to income indicated by the international data. Suppose, for example, one were to argue that cultural biases are obscuring a strong positive relation between income and happiness among countries. This implies that, *ceteris paribus*, in poorer countries cultural influences operate systematically to elevate happiness as compared to richer countries, an implication which seems doubtful in view of the cultural heterogenity among countries within both the rich and poor categories.

c. National Time Series

What one would like most, of course, is historical series on happiness as countries develop. The crucial question is: "Will raising the incomes of all increase the happiness of all ...?" (Inkeles, 1960, p. 18). Unfortunately, as is too often the case, time series data are in short supply. In addition, comparability over time is impaired by variations in the wording of the happiness

DOES ECONOMIC GROWTH IMPROVE THE HUMAN LOT?   **109**

question. It was possible, however, to put together a series for one country, the United States, covering intermittent dates from 1946 through 1970. (Three of these dates, in 1956–1957, are only six months apart, and demonstrate the point made earlier regarding the short-run stability of the survey results.) In the first seven surveys the happiness classification was the same— "very happy," "fairly happy," or "not very happy." In the last three, "not happy" was used instead of "not very happy." This more negative designation of the lowest happiness category resulted, for the lowest happiness class, in a downward bias compared with the earlier data, and for the middle "fairly happy" category, in a corresponding upward bias. However, the "very happy" class seems comparable over all 10 surveys and reliance is therefore placed on the trend shown by this category. Fortunately, it is possible to utilize as a check happiness data obtained by NORC and Cantril, which overlap the AIPO data in the period when the change in AIPO question wording occurred.

TABLE 8

PERCENT DISTRIBUTION OF POPULATION BY HAPPINESS,
UNITED STATES, 1946–1970[a]

A. AIPO Polls

Date	Very happy	Fairly happy	Not very happy	Other	N
Apr. 1946	39	50	10	1	3151
Dec. 1947	42	47	10	1	1434
Aug. 1948	43	43	11	2	1596
Nov. 1952	47	43	9	1	3003
Sept. 1956	53	41	5	1	1979
Sept. 1956	52	42	5	1	2207
Mar. 1957	53	43	3	1	1627
July 1963	47	48	5[b]	1	3668
Oct. 1966	49	46	4[b]	2	3531
Dec. 1970	43	48	6[b]	3	1517

B. NORC Polls

Date	Very happy	Pretty happy	Not too happy	N
Spring 1957	35	54	11	2460
Dec. 1963	32	51	16	1501
June 1965	30	53	17	1469

[a] Data from Table 2 and AIPO Polls 369, 410, 425, 508, 570, 571, 580, 675, and 735. NORC data from Bradburn, 1969, p. 40.
[b] Question read "not happy" rather than "not very happy."

110   RICHARD A. EASTERLIN

The upper panel of Table 8 presents the results of the 10 AIPO surveys covering 1946–1970. From 1946 through 1956–1957, the proportion "very happy" drifts slowly but steadily upward. There is then a noticeable decline between 1957 and 1963, and a second one from 1966 to 1970. By 1970 the proportion "very happy" is just about the same as in 1947. If one views the period as a whole, there is a noticeable swing, but little indication of any net trend up or down.[8]

The finding of a downturn between 1957 and 1963 runs into the difficulty that the question wording changed between these two dates, though as indicated this should not have affected the "very happy" replies. However, three NORC polls were taken independently around this time. As noted earlier, the happiness categories in the NORC polls differ from those in the AIPO polls. Our interest, however, is in the change over time shown by the NORC polls (Table 8, panel B). The results confirm those shown by the AIPO polls—a decline in happiness between the late 1950s and mid-1960s. (The exact timing is obviously open to question because of the intermittent nature of both sets of survey data.) Further support is provided by two United States surveys reported by Cantril (1965, p. 43) which show a decline in the national average personal happiness rating between 1959 and 1963 from 6.6 to 6.2.

To a limited extent, it is possible to follow the trends for individual income groups. Table 9 presents the data for the first four surveys, which appear to

TABLE 9

PERCENT VERY HAPPY BY SIZE OF INCOME,
UNITED STATES, 1946–1952[a]

Date	All classes	Average+ and wealthy	Average	Poor
Apr. 1946	39	47	43	34
Dec. 1947	42	52	46	37
Aug. 1948	43	54	50	37
Aug. 1948	43	51	51	37
Nov. 1952	47	51	51	42

[a] Data from AIPO Polls 369, 410, 425, and 508.

have had roughly consistent income classifications. (Unfortunately, no subdivision by income is available for the three 1956–1957 surveys.) To judge from the data in Table 9, there was a common advance in happiness in all major income groups through 1952.

[8] The Gallup article on the 1970 survey reported that there was an upward trend over the last quarter century, apparently because a comparison was made only between the first and last surveys shown in Table 8 above.

DOES ECONOMIC GROWTH IMPROVE THE HUMAN LOT? **111**

The surveys relating to the period of declining happiness show a rather interesting difference from this pattern (Table 10). Whereas the national average shows a slight rise between 1963 and 1966, the data by income class show a decline for the poorest groups. Thus the slight rise shown by the

TABLE 10

PERCENTAGE VERY HAPPY BY SIZE OF INCOME,
UNITED STATES, 1963–1970[a]

Date	All classes	$15,000+	$10,000–14,999	$5000–9999	$3000–4999	Under $3000
July 1963	47	59	50	50	46	40
Sept. 1966	49	67	62	50	42	34
Dec. 1970	38	56	49	43	33	29

[a] Data from Table 2 and AIPO Polls 675 and 735.

national average reflects an upward movement for the higher income groups which more than offsets the decline among the lower. (Could this be partly due to the national prominence given to the poverty problem at this time?) Between 1966 and 1970, however, all income classes show a noticeable decline, and in 1970 there is no class which is higher than it was in 1963.

Certainly, one must be cautious about drawing any strong conclusions from the limited United States time series studied here. As in the case of the international cross sections, however, it seems safe to say that if income and happiness go together, it is not as obvious as in the within-country cross-sectional comparisons.

3. Interpretation

a. Theory

Why do national comparisons among countries and over time show an association between income and happiness which is so much weaker than, if not inconsistent with, that shown by within-country comparisons? To economists, long accustomed to dealing with anomalies such as these, the possible relevance of Duesenberry's "relative income" explanation of the celebrated United States income–savings paradox will immediately spring to mind [(Duesenberry, 1952), cf. also Brady and Friedman (1947)]. The basic idea was stated quite simply by Karl Marx over a century ago: "A house may be large or small; as long as the surrounding houses are equally small it satisfies all social demands for a dwelling. But if a palace rises beside the little house, the little house shrinks into a hut."[9]

Suppose one assumes, following Duesenberry, that the utility a person obtains from his consumption expenditure is a function, not of the absolute level of his expenditure, but of the ratio of his current expenditure to that of other people, that is,

$$U_i = f\left[\frac{C_i}{\sum a_{ij} C_j}\right],$$

where U_i and C_i are the utility index and consumption expenditures, respectively, of the ith individual, C_j is consumption of the jth individual and a_{ij} is the weight applied by the ith consumer to the expenditure of the jth (Duesenberry, 1952, p. 32). In the simplest case, in which the expenditures of every other person are given equal weight, the utility obtained by a given individual depends on the ratio of his expenditure to the national per-capita average. The farther he is above the average, the happer he is; the farther below, the sadder. Moreover, if the frame of reference is always the current national situation, then an increase in the level of income in which all share proportionately would not alter the national level of happiness. A classical example of the fallacy of composition would apply: An increase in the income of any one individual would increase his happiness, but increasing the income of everyone would leave happiness unchanged. Similarly, among countries, a richer country would not necessarily be a happier country.

The data are presently too limited to warrant pushing this line of explanation very far, and the illustration above is certainly too simple. An intriguing research issue, for example, is the appropriate values of the a_{ij}'s [which can be viewed as a variant of the sociologist's problem of "reference groups" (Merton, 1968, Chaps. X and XI)]. Any given individual in the population does not give equal weight to all others in forming his reference standard; among other things, "peer group" influences play a part. Thus, the reference standard of a rich man probably gives disproportionate weight to the consumption of his well-to-do associates vis-à-vis persons living in poverty, and conversely for the reference standard of the poor man.

Nevertheless, the general form of the argument remains valid. Despite peer group influences, there is a "consumption norm" which exists in a given society at a given time, and which enters into the reference standard of virtually everyone. This provides a common point of reference in self-appraisals of well-being, leading those below the norm to feel less happy and those above the norm, more happy. Over time, this norm tends to rise with the

---

[9] As quoted by Lipset (1960, p. 63). I am grateful to Leonard Berkowitz for bringing this to my attention.

general level of consumption, though the two are not necessarily on a one-to-one basis.

Other possible interpretations of these data come to mind. For example, emphasis might be placed on external diseconomies of production. At a given time, it might be argued, the rich are better able to avoid these sources of "ill-fare" and hence are happier. But over time and across societies increases in income are largely or wholly offset by a corresponding growth in pollution, congestion, and so forth.

A radical interpretation of the data might emphasize power as the key factor in happiness. At any given time those who have more power (the rich) are happier. But over time and across societies, increases in income have not been accompanied by a wider diffusion of power among the various socio-economic strata (the Establishment persists), and hence happiness has not grown.

b. Evidence for a "Relative Income" Interpretation

There are a number of reasons why an interpretation based chiefly on "relativity" notions seems more plausible. First, a certain amount of empirical support has been developed for the relative income concept in other economic applications, such as savings behavior and, more recently, fertility behavior and labor force participation (Duesenberry, 1952; Easterlin, 1973, 1969; Freedman, 1963; Wachter, 1971a,b). Second, similar notions, such as "relative deprivation," have gained growing theoretical acceptance and empirical support in sociology, political science, and social psychology over the past several decades (Berkowitz, 1971; Davies, 1962; Gurr, 1970; Homans, 1961; Merton, 1968; Pettigrew, 1967; Smelser, 1962; Stouffer *et al.*, 1949). Indeed, to scholars vitally concerned with professional reputation in a competitive field of learning, it should hardly come as a surprise that relative status is an important ingredient of happiness. Third, historical changes in the definition of poverty attest to the importance of relative position in society's thinking on this matter. For example, Smolensky (1965, p. 40) has pointed out that estimates of "minimum comfort" budgets for New York City workers throughout the course of this century "have generally been about one-half of real gross national product per capita." [cf. also Fuchs (1967), Rainwater (unpublished paper), Tabbarah (1972).]

By no means least important are the statements in the surveys of the respondents themselves on what they take to comprise happiness. These statements overwhelmingly emphasize immediate personal concerns, such as adequacy of income, family matters, or health, rather than broader national or social issues such as pollution, political power, or even threat of war. Furthermore, economic worries appear to be especially important among lower income persons. Table 11, for example, reports on the "one thing"

TABLE 11

RELATION OF ECONOMIC STATUS AND MAJOR WORRIES,
UNITED STATES, 1946[a,b]

Major worry	Economic status (percent)		
	Upper	Middle	Lower
My family and children	20	20	24
Health (personal and family)	19	21	18
Financial worries, money	6	12	22
Security, job, future	13	17	12
World and national conditions	7	6	4
Work conditions	7	5	3
Personal traits	3	2	2
Housing	2	1	1
Miscellaneous	9	7	5
Nothing	13	10	10
No answer	5	7	5
	104	108	106
Sample size	195	637	1506

[a] From A. E. Wessman, A psychological inquiry into satisfactions and happiness. Ph.D. dissertation in psychology, Princeton Univ. Princeton, New Jersey, 1956.

[b] The question asked was "What one thing do you worry about most?" Percentages add to more than 100 because some respondents gave more than one answer.

worried about most by Americans of upper, middle, and lower economic status in a 1946 survey. For all three groups worries about economic, family, and health matters predominate. However, the item on which the three groups most markedly differ is that labeled "financial worries, money." Such concerns increase significantly as economic status declines.

Finally, there is evidence that consumption norms vary directly with the level of economic development. Here, from Cantril's survey (1965, pp. 205, 206, 222), are some statements by Indians on their material aspirations, and, for comparison, those of Americans:

INDIA: I want a son and a piece of land since I am now working on land owned by other people. I would like to construct a house of my own and have a cow for milk and ghee. I would also like to buy some better clothing for my wife. If I could do this then I would be happy. (thirty-five-year-old man, illiterate, agricultural laborer, income about $10 a month)

DOES ECONOMIC GROWTH IMPROVE THE HUMAN LOT? **115**

INDIA: I wish for an increase in my wages because with my meager salary I cannot afford to buy decent food for my family. If the food and clothing problems were solved, then I would feel at home and be satisfied. Also if my wife were able to work the two of us could then feed the family and I am sure would have a happy life and our worries would be over. (thirty-year-old sweeper, monthly income around $13)

INDIA: I should like to have a water tap and a water supply in my house. It would also be nice to have electricity. My husband's wages must be increased if our children are to get an education and our daughter is to be married. (forty-five-year-old house-wife, family income about $80 a month)

INDIA: I hope in the future I will not get any disease. Now I am coughing. I also hope I can purchase a bicycle. I hope my children will study well and that I can provide them with an education. I also would sometime like to own a fan and maybe a radio. (forty-year-old skilled worker earning $30 a month)

UNITED STATES: If I could earn more money I would then be able to buy our own home and have more luxury around us, like better furniture, a new car, and more vacations. (twenty-seven-year-old skilled worker)

UNITED STATES: I would like a reasonable enough income to maintain a house, have a new car, have a boat, and send my four children to private schools. (thirty-four-year-old laboratory technician)

UNITED STATES: I would like a new car. I wish all my bills were paid and I had more money for myself. I would like to play more golf and to hunt more than I do. I would like to have more time to do the things I want to and to entertain my friends. (Negro bus driver, twenty-four-years old)

UNITED STATES: Materially speaking, I would like to provide my family with an income to allow them to live well—to have the proper recreation, to go camping, to have music and dancing lessons for the children, and to have family trips. I wish we could belong to a country club and do more entertaining. We just bought a new home and expect to be perfectly satisfied with it for a number of years. (twenty-eight-year-old lawyer)*

It is a well-accepted dictum among social scientists other than economists that attitudes or "tastes" are a product of the socialization experience of the individual. What more eloquent testimony could be provided than the fore-going statements? Cantril (1965) puts it this way:

> People in highly developed nations have obviously acquired a wide range of aspirations, sophisticated and expensive from the point of view of people in less-developed areas, who have not yet learned all that is potentially available to people in more advanced societies and whose aspirations concerning the social and material aspects of life are modest indeed by comparison [p. 202].*

In a comprehensive survey of long-term trends in American consumption, Brady has pointed out that "today, the great majority of American families

* *Patterns of Human Concerns* by Hadley Cantril. Rutgers University Press, New Brunswick, New Jersey (1965).

live on a scale that compares well with the way *wealthy* families lived 200 years ago" [cf. Davis *et al.*, 1972, p. 84, italics added]. But, as the above statements show, the typical American today does not consider himself wealthy. His consumption standards are not those of his colonial pre-decessors; rather they are formed by his personal experience with the human condition as evidenced in contemporary America. The same is true of the typical Indian living in modern India. Material aspirations or tastes vary positively with the level of economic development. Moreover, these changes in tastes are caused by the process of income growth itself (though the cause–effect relation may run both ways). As a result of secular income growth, the socialization experience of each generation embodies a higher level of living and correspondingly generates a higher level of consumption stan-dards. Even within the life cycle of a given generation, the progressive accre-tion of household goods due to economic growth causes a continuous upward pressure on consumption norms. This upward shift in standards (tastes) tends to offset the positive effect of income growth on well-being that one would expect on the basis of economic theory. Dramatic supporting evidence is provided by the results of a survey of recent experience in Taiwan, analyzed by Freedman (unpublished paper):

> While economic growth has increased income levels, it has, at the same time, expanded consumption possibilities with the result that present incomes seem no more adequate relative to needs. Only 20 percent of the respondents said their financial position had improved during the last five years, although real per capita income increased about 40 percent during that period [p. 38].

It would be premature to assert that "everything is relative," but it is hard to resist the inference that relative considerations play an important part in explaining the evidence presented here.

c. An Analogy[10]

The present interpretation may be clarified by an analogy with compari-sons of height. Americans today are taller than their forebears and than their contemporaries in present-day India. Suppose, however, that representative samples of Americans and Indians in 1970 were asked the following question: "In general, how tall would you say that you are—*very* tall, *fairly* tall, or *not very* tall?" It seems reasonable to suppose that this question would elicit a similar distribution of responses in the two countries, even though on an objective scale most Americans are, in fact, taller than most Indians. The reason for the similar distributions would be that, in answering, individuals

---

[10] My colleagues, Stefano Fenoaltea and John C. Lambelet, have contributed impor-tantly to the development of the argument in this section.

in each country would apply a subjective norm of "tallness" derived from their personal experience. The reference standard in terms of which Americans would evaluate "tallness" would be larger than that applied by Indians, because Americans have grown up in and live in a society in which persons are generally taller. An American male 5 ft 9 in. in height living in the United States, though tall on an international scale, is not likely to feel tall. By the same token, Americans today are not likely to feel taller than their forebears, because today's standard of reference is higher.

What, then, are the "facts" of tallness? By an objective scale, current-day Americans are, indeed, taller. If, however, one is interested in *feelings* about height, the truth is quite possibly different. Today's Americans may not, on the average, feel any taller than do contemporary Indians or than their ancestors did. The reconciliation between the "objective facts" and "subjective states of mind" lies in the mediating role of the social norm for height, which enters together with one's actual height in determining feelings of tallness. This norm varies among societies both in time and space, and is a direct function of the heights typical of these societies.

The situation with regard to happiness is like that for height, but with one critical difference. It is similar in that each individual, in evaluating his happiness, compares his actual experience with a norm derived from his personal social experience. It is different in that there is no objective scale of measurement for happiness, independent of the individual. On the contrary, the concern is precisely with subjective states of mind. One may attempt to use "objective" indexes such as consumption, nutrition, or life expectancy to infer happiness. Or one may seek to gauge well-being from various behavioral indicators, for example, measures of the prevalence of social disorganization (delinquency, suicide, and so forth). Ultimately, however, the relevance of such measures rests on an assumed connection between external manifestations and internal states of mind—in effect, on a model of human psychology. And if it is feelings that count, there is a real possibility that subjective reports may contradict the "objective" evidence. To social scientists, and especially economists, this can be frustrating. As Mishan (1969) observes,

> [t]here is a temptation . . . to lose patience with human cussedness and to insist that if both the Smith family and the Jones family receive a 10 percent increase in their "real" income they are better off, even if they both sulk at the other's good luck. But while this may be salutary morals, if welfare is what people experience there is no escape for us in honest indignation [p. 82].*

On the contrary, there are good psychological reasons why people may not feel better off, even though they "should." This is because the standard with

* E. J. Mishan, *Welfare Economics: Ten Introductory Essays*, 2nd ed. New York: Random House, 1969. Copyright 1969 by Random House, Inc.

reference to which evaluations of well-being are formed is itself a function of social conditions. As these conditions "improve," the norm tends to advance along with people's actual experience. Economic analysis has been able, for a long time, to resist the uncomfortable implications of this mechanism, by assuming that tastes are given and/or are unmeasurable. For many of the short-term problems with which economists have traditionally been concerned, this may not be seriously damaging. But with the growth in concern about long-term economic growth, on the one hand, and in evidence on people's feelings and aspirations, and the factors governing them, on the other, one can only wonder whether this view will be much longer defensible.

4. Summary and Concluding Observations

The concern of this paper has been with the association of income and happiness. The basic data consist of statements by individuals on their subjective happiness, as reported in thirty surveys from 1946 through 1970, covering nineteen countries, including eleven in Asia, Africa, and Latin America. Within countries there is a noticeable positive association between income and happiness—in every single survey, those in the highest status group were happier, on the average, than those in the lowest status group. However, whether any such positive association exists among countries at a given time is uncertain. Certainly, the happiness differences between rich and poor countries that one might expect on the basis of the within-country differences by economic status are not borne out by the international data. Similarly, in the one national time series studied, that for the United States since 1946, higher income was not systematically accompanied by greater happiness.

As for why national comparisons among countries and over time show an association between income and happiness which is so much weaker than, if not inconsistent with, that shown by within-country comparisons, a Duesenberry-type model, involving relative status considerations as an important determinant of happiness, was suggested. Every survey that has looked into the meaning of happiness shows that economic considerations are very important to people, though by no means the only matters of concern. In judging their happiness, people tend to compare their actual situation with a reference standard or norm, derived from their prior and ongoing social experience. While norms vary among individuals within a given society, they also contain similar features because of the common experiences people share as members of the same society and culture. Thus, while the goods aspirations of higher status people probably exceed those of lower status people, the dispersion in reference norms is less than in the actual incomes

DOES ECONOMIC GROWTH IMPROVE THE HUMAN LOT? **119**

of rich and poor. Because of this, those at the bottom of the income distribution tend to feel less well off than those at the top. Over time, however, as economic conditions advance, so too does the social norm, since this is formed by the changing economic socialization experience of people. For the same reason, among different societies at a given time, there tends to be a rough correspondence between living levels and the social norm. As a result, the positive correlation between income and happiness that shows up in within-country comparisons appears only weakly, if at all, in comparisons among societies in time or space. Various pieces of evidence were noted in support of this interpretation.

In a sense, these results are a testimony to the adaptability of mankind. Income and aspirations in time and space tend to go together, and people seemingly can make something out of what appears, in some absolute sense, to be a sorry lot. At the same time, the conclusions raise serious questions about the goals and prospective efficacy of much social policy. As sociologist George C. Homans remarks (1961, p. 276) regarding similar findings on another subject, "[t]hings like this have persuaded some people who would prefer to believe otherwise that any effort to satisfy mankind is bound to be self-defeating. Any satisfied desire creates an unsatisfied one."

The present results do not necessarily imply that a redirection of attention is needed from economic growth to income redistribution as a vehicle for improving welfare. The data themselves give no indication that international differences in happiness are systematically related to inequality. And the theoretical relationship is uncertain—if relative positions were unchanged and income differences halved, would happiness be greater? It is at least plausible that sensitivity to income differences might be heightened, so that lower income people might suffer as much in the new situation from an income spread of 50% as they previously had from a spread of 100%. If this were so, then subjective welfare would be unchanged.

The only sure conclusion is that we need much more research on the nature and causes of human welfare. Bradburn (1969, p. 233) makes the point simply and effectively: "Insofar as we have greater understanding of how people arrive at their judgments of their own happiness and how social forces are related to those judgments, we shall be in a better position to formulate and execute effective social policies."

The present analysis also points to a clear need for research on the formation of preferences or tastes. Economists have generally insisted that the determination of tastes is not their business. But on this matter there are hopeful signs of change in economists' tastes themselves. Katona (1951, 1971), Morgan (1968), Strumpel (1973), and their associates at the Survey Research Center in Michigan have been doing pioneering studies on this subject [cf. also Pfaff (1973)]. In the 1950s, Siegel (1964) did some little-noticed work modeling the formation of aspirations. A central tenet of Galbraith's (1958, 1967) assault on economic theory has been the "dependence effect," that tastes are subject to substantial manipulation by the business system.[11] Recently, Houthakker and Pollak (to be published, Chapter 2) have initiated a formal inquiry into habit formation.

In the area of growth economics, the present findings raise doubt about the importance of the "international demonstration effect." If those in rich and poor countries shared a common scale of material aspirations, then countries higher on the scale of actual income should show a higher level of happiness. At the same time, the within-country cross-sectional findings, indicating a similarity in the aspirations of members of the same society, lend support to the concept of an internal demonstration effect.[12]

Economists' models of economic growth tend uniformly to exclude tastes as a variable.[13] But it is possible that not only are tastes affected by economic growth, but that taste changes serve as a spur to growth, in the manner suggested by Mack some years ago (1956). Thus one might conceive of a mutually reinforcing interaction between changes in tastes and changes in per capita income, which, *ceteris paribus*, drives the economy ever onward and per capita income ever upward.

Another interesting analytical possibility opened up by recognition of taste changes is in the relation of economic changes to political behavior. Recent work on the causes of political agitation and revolution has stressed the importance of disparities between the aspirations of the population and their fulfillment (Davies, 1962; Gurr, 1970). Since economic goods form such an important part of human concerns, a growth model which included material aspirations as a variable might incorporate also the political consequences of unfulfilled expectations, and possible feedback effects of any resultant political activity on the growth process itself.

Finally, with regard to growth economics, there is the view that the most developed economies, notably the United States, have entered an era of satiation. Economic growth, it is said, tends to eventuate in the "mass con-

---

[11] The present view of taste formation, while not precluding the mechanism stressed by Galbraith, is different and broader. This is shown clearly by the height analogy, where the norm is seen to change as a function simply of the social experience of individuals, without any overt attempt at manipulation by persons or organizations in the society.

[12] In a five-country study of attitudes toward ways of life, Morris found much greater differences among countries than among economic classes within countries. The study, however, was confined to college students, and economic status referred to the income group of parents (Morris, 1956, Chap. 4).

[13] An exception is Hagen's work (1962), based on McClelland's *n*-achievement motive (McClelland, 1961). It should be noted that achievement motivation, which relates to goal-striving, differs from level of aspiration, the concern here, which refers to goal-setting.

DOES ECONOMIC GROWTH IMPROVE THE HUMAN LOT? **121**

sumption society" (Rostow, 1960), the "affluent society" (Galbraith, 1958), the "opulent society" (Johnson, 1967), or the "post-industrial society" (Bell, 1970). The present analysis raises serious doubts whether the United States is in such an era, or, indeed, whether such a terminal stage exists. Long-term fluctuations aside, the present generation is not noticeably more advanced over its predecessor than has been the case for over a century—the long-run growth rate of per-capita income has been remarkably steady since at least the first half of the nineteenth century (Davis *et al.*, 1972, Chap. 2). The view that the United States is now in a new era is based in part on ignorance of the rapidity of growth in the past. Consider the following statement: "The advancement of the arts, from year to year, taxes our credulity, and seems to presage the arrival of that period when human improvement must end" [as quoted by Davis *et al.* (1972, p. 177)]. This was made by Henry L. Ellsworth, Commissioner of Patents, in 1843! Similarly, a writer in the Democratic Review of 1853 predicted that electricity and machinery would so transform life that fifty years thereafter: "Men and women will then have no harassing cares, or laborious duties to fulfill. Machinery will perform all work—automata will direct them. The only task of the human race will be to make love, study and be happy." [14] Brady's recent work catalogs in great detail the myriad advances in food, clothing, housing, transportation, and style of life in general that followed one upon the other throughout the nineteenth century (Davis *et al.*, 1972, Chap. 2). Is there any reason to suppose that the present generation has reached a unique culminating stage in this evolution, and the next will not have its own catalog of wonders, which, if only attained, would make it happy? An antimaterialistic cultural revolution may be in the making, but it seems dubious that a major cause is an unprecedented affluence which American society has recently attained. If the view suggested here has merit, economic growth does not raise a society to some ultimate state of plenty. Rather, the growth process itself engenders ever-growing wants that lead it ever onward.

ACKNOWLEDGMENTS

This paper was made possible by the opportunities and facilities offered by the Center for Advanced Study in the Behavioral Sciences, Stanford, California, where I was a Fellow in 1970–1971. It is not possible to acknowledge all those from whom I benefitted while at the Center, but special appreciation must be expressed to Elliot Aronson, Leonard Berkowitz, David Krantz, William H. Kruskal, Amos Tversky, and Stanton Wheeler. I am also grateful to Jack Meyer for statistical assistance. This research was partially supported by NSF grant GS-1563.

[14] As quoted by Ekirch (1944, p. 120). I am grateful to Joseph S. Davis for bringing this to my attention.

122   RICHARD A. EASTERLIN

A first draft of this paper was circulated during the academic year 1971–1972, and elicited' many valuable and instructive reactions. It has been possible to take account of only a few comments in this revision, and for these I am especially grateful to Paul A. David, Stefano Fenoaltea, Henry A. Gemery, J. Robert Hanson, Alex Inkeles, John C. Lambelet, and Melvin W. Reder.

REFERENCES

Abramovitz, M. (1959)   The welfare interpretation of secular trends in national income and product. In *The Allocation of economic resources: Essays in honor of Bernard Francis Haley* (M. Abramovitz *et al.*). Stanford, California: Stanford Univ. Press.

AIPO Poll (December 1970)   Reported in *San Francisco Chronicle*, January 14, 1971.

Bell, D. (1970)   Unstable America. *Encounter* **34**: 11–26.

Berkowitz, L. (1971)   *Frustrations, comparisons, and other sources of emotion arousal as contributors to social unrest.* Multilith.

Block, J. (1965)   *The challenge of response sets.* New York: Appleton.

Bradburn, N. M. (1969)   *The structure of psychological well-being.* Chicago, Illinois: Aldine.

Brady, D. S., and Friedman, R. (1947)   Savings and the income distribution. *Studies in income and wealth*, Vol. 10, pp. 247–265. New York: National Bureau of Economic Research.

Cantril, H. (1951)   *Public opinion, 1935–1946.* Princeton, New Jersey: Princeton Univ. Press.

Cantril, H. (1965)   *The pattern of human concerns.* New Brunswick, New Jersey: Rutgers Univ. Press.

Davies, J. C. (1962)   Toward a theory of revolution. *American Sociological Review* **37**: 5–18.

Davis, J. A. (1965)   *Education for positive mental health.* Chicago, Illinois: Aldine.

Davis, L. E., Easterlin, R. A., and Parker, W. N., (eds.) (1972)   *American economic growth: An economist's history of the United States.* New York: Harper.

Duesenberry, J. S. (1952)   *Income, saving and the theory of consumer behavior.* Cambridge, Massachusetts: Harvard Univ. Press.

Easterlin, R. A. (1969)   Towards a socio-economic theory of fertility. *In Fertility and family planning: A world view* (S. J. Behrman, L. Corsa, Jr., and R. Freedman, eds.), pp. 127–156. Ann Arbor: Univ. of Michigan Press.

Easterlin, R. A. (1973)   Relative economic status and the American fertility swing. In *Social structure, family life styles, and economic behavior* (E. B. Sheldon, ed.). Philadelphia, Pennsylvania: Lippincott for Institute of Life Insurance.

Eckaus, R. S. (1972)   *Basic economics.* Boston, Massachusetts: Little, Brown.

Edwards, A. L. (1957)   *The social desirability variable in personality assessment and research.* New York: Holt.

Ekirch, A. A. (1944)   *The idea of progress in America, 1815–1860.* New York: Columbia Univ. Press.

Freedman, D. S.   Consumption of modern goods and services and their relation to fertility: A study in Taiwan. Unpublished paper.

Freedman, D. S. (1963)   The relation of economic status to fertility. *American Economic Review* **53**: 414–426.

Fuchs, V. R. (1967)   Redefining poverty and redistributing income. *The Public Interest* **8**: 88–95.

Galbraith, J. K. (1958)   *The affluent society.* Boston, Massachusetts: Houghton.

Galbraith, J. K. (1967)   Review of a review. *The Public Interest* **9**: 109–118.

Gilbert, M. *et al.* (1958)   *Comparative national products and price levels.* Paris: OECC.

Gurin, G., Veroff, J., and Feld, S. (1960)   *Americans view their mental health.* New York: Basic Books.

Gurr, T. R. (1970)   *Why men rebel.* Princeton, New Jersey: Princeton Univ. Press.

Hagen, E. E. (1962)   *On the theory of social change: How economic growth begins.* Homewood, Illinois: Dorsey Press.

Homans, G. C. (1961)   *Social behavior: Its elementary forms.* New York: Harcourt.

Houthakker, H. S., and Pollak, R. A. (to be published)   *The theory of consumer's choice.* San Francisco, California: Holden-Day.

Inkeles, A. (1960)   Industrial man: The relation of status to experience, perception, and value. *American Journal of Sociology* **66**: 1–31.

Johnson, H. G. (1967)   *Money, trade, and economic growth.* Cambridge, Massachusetts: Harvard Univ. Press.

Katona, G. (1951)   *Psychological analysis of economic behavior.* New York: McGraw-Hill.

Katona, G., Strumpel, B., and Zahn, E. (1971)   *Aspirations and affluence.* New York: McGraw-Hill.

Lipset, S. M. (1960)   *Political man: The social bases of politics.* Garden City, New York: Doubleday.

Little, I. M. D. (1950)   *A critique of welfare economics.* London and New York: Oxford Univ. Press.

McClelland, D. C. (1961)   *The achieving society.* Princeton, New Jersey: Van Nostrand-Reinhold.

Mack, R. P. (1956)   Trends in American consumption and the aspiration to consume. *American Economic Review* **46**: 55–68.

Merton, R. K. (1968)   *Social theory and social structure,* 1968 ed. New York: Free Press.

Mishan, E. J. (1968)   Welfare economics. *International encyclopedia of the social sciences,* Vol. 16, pp. 504–512. New York: Macmillan.

Mishan, E. J. (1969)   *Welfare economics: Ten introductory essays,* 2nd ed. New York: Random House.

Morgan, J. N. (1968)   The supply of effort, the measurement of well-being, and the dynamics of improvement. *American Economic Review* **58**: 31–39.

Morris, C. (1956)   *Varieties of human value.* Chicago, Illinois: Univ. of Chicago Press.

Nordhaus, W., and Tobin, J. (1972)   Is growth obsolete? In *Economic growth,* 5th Anniversary Series, National Bureau of Economic Research, pp. 1–80. New York: Columbia Univ. Press.

OECD (1970)   *National accounts statistics: 1950–1968.* Paris: Organisation for Economic Cooperation and Development.

Pettigrew, T. F. (1967)   Social evaluation theory: Convergences and applications. *Nebraska Symposium on Motivation* (D. Levine, ed.). Lincoln: Nebraska Univ. Press.

Pfaff, M. (1973)   Economic life styles, values, and subjective welfare: A comment. *In Social structure, family life styles, and economic behavior* (E. B. Sheldon, ed.). Philadelphia, Pennsylvania: Institute of Life Insurance.

Rainwater, L.   A decent standard of living: Subsistence vs. membership. Unpublished paper.

Robinson, J. P., and Shaver, P. R. (1969)   *Measures of social psychological attitudes* (Appendix B to *Measures of political attitudes*). Ann Arbor, Michigan: Survey Research Center, Institute for Social Research.

Rorer, L. G. (1965)   The great response-style myth. *Psychological Bulletin* **63**: 129–156.

Rosenstein-Rodan, P. N. (1961)   International aid for underdeveloped countries. *Review of Economics and Statistics* **43**: 107–138.

124   RICHARD A. EASTERLIN

Rostow, W. W. (1960)   *The stages of economic growth*. London and New York: Cambridge Univ. Press.

Siegel, S. (1964)   Level of aspiration and decision making. In *Decision and choice: Contributions of Sidney Siegel* (A. H. Brayfield and S. Messick, eds.). New York: McGraw-Hill.

Smelser, N. J. (1962)   *Theory of collective behavior*. New York: Free Press.

Smolensky, E. (1965)   The past and present poor. *The concept of poverty* (First Report of the Task Force on Economic Growth and Opportunity), pp. 35–67. Washington, D. C.: Chamber of Commerce of the United States.

Stouffer, S. A., *et al.* (1949)   *The American soldier: Adjustment during wartime life*, Vol. I. Princeton, New Jersey: Princeton Univ. Press.

Strumpel, B. (1973)   Economic life styles, values, and subjective welfare—An empirical approach. In *Social structure, family life styles, and economic behavior* (E. B. Sheldon, ed.). Philadelphia, Pennsylvania: Lippincott for Institute of Life Insurance.

Tabbarah, R. B. (1972)   The adequacy of income: A social view of economic development. *Journal of Development Studies*. **8**: 57–76.

Wachter, M. L. (1971a)   A labor supply model for secondary workers. Discussion Paper No. 194, Revised. Wharton School of Finance and Commerce, Univ. of Pennsylvania.

Wachter, M. L. (1971b)   A new approach to the equilibrium labor force. Discussion Paper No. 226. Wharton School of Finance and Commerce, Univ. of Pennsylvania.

Wessman, A. E. (1956)   A psychological inquiry into satisfactions and happiness. Ph.D. dissertation in psychology, Princeton Univ. Princeton, New Jersey.

Wilson, W. (1967)   Correlates of avowed happiness. *Psychological Bulletin* **67**: 294–306.

World Survey III (1965)   International Data Library and Reference Service, Survey Research Center, Univ. of California, Berkeley.

ADDITIONAL BIBLIOGRAPHY

Arrow, K. J., and Scitovsky, T. (eds.) (1969)   *Readings in welfare economics*. Homewood, Illinois: Irwin.

Baumol, W. J. (1952)   *Welfare economics and the theory of the state*. Cambridge, Massachusetts: Harvard Univ. Press.

Bradburn, N. M., and Caplovitz, D. (1965)   *Reports on happiness*. Chicago, Illinois: Aldine.

Brenner, B. (1971)   Mental well-being: Conceptual framework. *Annual meeting of the American Sociological Association, 66th, Denver, Colorado, August 1971*, revised paper.

Dalkey, N. C., and Rourke, D. L. (1971)   Experimental assessment of delphi procedures with group value judgments. R-612-ARPA. Santa Monica, California: The Rand Corporation.

Dalkey, N. C., Lewis, R., and Snyder, D. (1970)   Measurement and analysis of the quality of life: With exploratory illustrations of applications to career and transportation choices. RM-6228-DOT. Santa Monica, California: The Rand Corporation.

Easterlin, R. A. (1968)   Economic growth: An overview. *International encyclopedia of the social sciences*, Vol. 4, pp. 395–408. New York: Macmillan.

Freedman, D. S. Consumption aspirations as economic incentives in a developing economy—Taiwan. Unpublished paper.

Graff, J. deV. (1957)   *Theoretical welfare economics*. London and New York: Cambridge Univ. Press.

Harsanyi, J. C. (1953–1954)   Welfare economics of variable states. *Review of Economic Studies* **21**: 204–213.

DOES ECONOMIC GROWTH IMPROVE THE HUMAN LOT? **125**

Inkeles, A. (1969)   Making men modern: On the causes and consequences of individual change in six developing countries. *American Journal of Sociology* **75**: 208–225.

Lewin, K., *et al.* (1944)   Level of aspiration. In *Personality and the behavior disorders* (J. McV. Hunt, ed.). New York: Ronald Press.

Linder, S. B. (1970)   *The harried leisure class*. New York: Columbia Univ. Press.

Lingoes, J. C., and Pfaff, M.   Measurement of subjective welfare and satisfaction. Unpublished paper.

Mishan, E. J. (1967)   *The costs of economic growth*. New York: Praeger.

Schnore, L. F., and Cowhig, J. D. (1959–1960)   Some correlates of reported health in metropolitan centers. *Social Problems* **7**: 218–226.

Veblen, T. (1934)   *Theory of the leisure class*. New York: The Modern Library.

Weisskopf, W. A. (1964)   Economic growth and human well-being. *Quarterly Review of Economics and Business* **4**: 17–29.

Wessman, A. E., and Ricks, D. F. (1966)   *Mood and personality*. New York: Holt.

B
Determinants of the Happiness–Income Relationship

[2]

Jeffrey Friedman and Adam McCabe

PREFERENCES OR HAPPINESS?
TIBOR SCITOVSKY'S PSYCHOLOGY
OF HUMAN NEEDS

Tibor Scitovsky's *The Joyless Economy*, first published in 1976, created only a small ripple of excitement.[1] It deserved better. With rigor and originality, Scitovsky managed to throw doubt onto the most important category of economic thought: the individual's "preferences." And this had ramifications far beyond economics. To doubt the value of individual preferences is to question not only the utility of wealth, but that of individual freedom.

Thus, *The Joyless Economy* was as much a challenge to the premises of modern politics as to those of the modern economy. It should have gotten a hearing from political philosophers as well as economists. To commemorate the twentieth anniversary of its appearance, we now present a symposium on *The Joyless Economy* in the hope that it might stimulate long-overdue discussion and reflection about the book's economic and political, as well as its cultural, philosophical, psychological, and educational implications.

Scitovsky's chief question was whether consumer capitalism makes people happy; his answer was largely negative. Radicals might have been expected to be pleased with this outcome, but as Amartya Sen notes below, Scitovsky's argument was not much better received on the left than on the right. *The Joyless Economy* was a revolutionary book, but that was the problem with it. It was

---

Critical Review 10, no. 4 (Fall 1996). ISSN 0891-3811. © 1996 Critical Review Foundation.

The authors thank Tibor Scitovsky for comments on previous drafts.

equidistant from both the "conservatism" of economics and the "radicalism" of most opponents of *Homo economicus*. For Scitovsky found fault with the exercise of individual economic choice even when it is *not* impeded by the constraints on individual freedom that concern the left. In attempting to end destitution, exploitation, the manipulation of desire, and alienation from our social nature, the left seeks a goal that is not so very different from that of the (libertarian) right: removing constraints on the achievement of our freely chosen ends. Against this shared preoccupation with liberty, *The Joyless Economy* suggested that our freely chosen ends may be the very source of our unhappiness. Scitovsky (1976, 4) wrote:

> We gradually dismantled the Laws of God and came to believe in man as the final arbiter of what is best for him. That was a bold idea and a proud assumption, but it set back for generations all scientific inquiry into consumer behavior, for it seemed to rule out—as a logical impossibility—any conflict between what man chooses to get and what will best satisfy him.

In challenging as "unscientific" the economist's assumption that individual choice reflects the pursuit of rational self-interest (ibid., viii), Scitovsky also challenged the central tenet of modern liberalism—of both the left- and right-wing varieties.

Drawing on research in physiological psychology (explored in detail in Michael Benedikt's contribution to the symposium), Scitovsky began with the familiar human tendency to avoid discomfort and seek pleasure; but he challenged the notion that these tendencies are merely two sides of the same utilitarian continuum. In Scitovsky's view, there are *two* sources of displeasure: not only too much stimulus—pain; but too little—boredom. Therefore, there are two wellsprings of pleasure: the reduction of stimulus that is above its optimal level, and its increase from suboptimal levels.

Affluent societies have, in Scitovsky's view, produced widespread *comfort* by reducing the sources of pain for most of their members; and by making available the food, shelter, clothing, medicine, and other resources that can be used to counteract the pain that persists. But *pleasure* stemming from the achievement of comfort is short lived. By lowering the level of stimulus, our comfort-seeking choices can lead directly to the other source of distress, ennui. Scitovsky is as concerned to alleviate boredom as to reduce pain. Indeed, in *The Joyless Economy* he is *more* concerned with the relief of boredom, because affluent societies are less adept at this than at the production of comfort. Affluence quells the uncomfortable stimulus of basic, unmet needs. But as creatures who evolved to take pleasure in striving to meet those needs, we are left unsatisfied when they are sated. "Being on the way to [our] goals and struggling to achieve them are more satisfying than is the actual attainment of the goals" (Scitovsky 1976, 62), for the struggle itself is stimulating and its conclusion creates a void: the need for new stimuli. "Too much comfort," Scitovsky writes, "may preclude pleasure" (ibid.); passivity induces boredom.

One way people may overcome boredom is by subjecting themselves to physical stimuli—exercise or sex, for example. (Here Scitovsky may have found a plausible explanation for many aspects of contemporary life commonly blamed on "narcissism" or the decline of "traditional values.") The alternative to physical stimulation is mental relief from boredom—new ideas or information. But information that is *too* novel is unpleasantly overstimulating. "Most of the time," therefore, "we absorb information by relating it to what we already know" (1976, 54). We draw on background information to render new stimuli more pleasant. Scitovsky goes so far as to define "culture" as "the preliminary information we must have to enjoy the processing of further information." Only "stimulus enjoyment" is, by this definition, "a cultural activity" (ibid., 226). Scitovsky's definition of culture, no matter how unpleasantly novel it may first appear, does map onto normal usage to some extent. "The word 'culture,'" Scitovsky points out, "usually makes people think of the ability to enjoy literature, music, painting, and other fine arts whose enjoyment takes effort and time to learn, although the appreciation and enjoyment of food, sports, games of skill and card games, political, economic, and scientific news, and so on are also learned skills and must therefore be included in the definition of culture" (ibid., 226–27).

Inasmuch as we require a cultural education to enjoy novel mental stimuli, perhaps the banal aspects of popular culture are explained by the fact that most of its consumers are not very highly educated, and thus would find sophisticated stimuli too novel to be pleasant.[2] Scitovsky also suggests that an overemphasis on the consumption of material comforts may trigger, in compensation, the "extraordinary interest in violence" —the ultimate banal stimulus—displayed by popular culture (1976, 283).

Scitovsky identifies two different respects in which people's untutored impulses may lead them to get less enjoyment out of life than they are capable of. First, they may pursue comfort over stimulation. Programmed, as it were, to meet basic needs that, until the recent arrival of affluence, were virtually never satisfied, we respond to material abundance by, for example, increasing the frequency of our meals and making them more sumptuous, perversely reducing the pleasure we used to derive from much-anticipated feasts. Previously savored pleasures now become necessities whose presence no longer makes us happy, but whose absence causes discomfort. "Affluence crowds out, for many people, the pleasures of want satisfaction" by addicting them to comforts (Scitovsky 1976, 79). Among the many pleasures sacrificed are those from stimulating work, which vanish when work becomes merely a means to the end of buying material comforts.

Scitovsky does believe that the problems of affluence can be overcome by seeking stimulation in activities other than want satisfaction. But as compared to Europeans, he argues, Americans are ill equipped to make this substitution because of their Puritan heritage, which opposes pleasures and education that are not instrumental to "a healthy and productive life" (1976, 207). Hence our preference for vocational training over "frivolous" learning, even in higher education; and the priority we give to "the earning of money ahead of the enjoyment of life" (ibid., 210).

Below, however, Ronald Inglehart provides evidence that the onset of affluence has effected a major shift toward "Postmaterialist" values, even in the United States. Might the Postmaterialist pursuit of novelty turn into a quest for ever-more stimulation that is, in the end, just as unsatisfying as the Materialist pursuit of ever-more comfort? Scitovsky does not think so. "The pleasures of stimulation," he maintains, "unlike those of want satisfaction, are not eliminated by their too persistent and too continuous pursuit" (1976, 77-78).

The second way our preferences can make us unhappy is by disposing us toward consuming relatively simple, ineffective stimuli rather than more difficult, "cultural" forms of excitement. Many people prefer watching television, driving for pleasure, and shopping to such stimuli as complex "music, painting, literature, and history" (Scitovsky 1976, 235). But while television, driving, and shopping "can all be very stimulating, up to a point," they "quickly become redundant, unsurprising, and monotonous," because they "are unable to keep our minds busy and unbored" (ibid., 232–33). Hence the often noted dissatisfaction of even the most avid television viewers with what they are watching. The problem, Scitovsky maintains, is not that the stimulus television and the like provides is "inherently inferior, which it is not, but that it is limited in quantity"; the more time one spends on these activities, the less one gains in incremental stimulation. Scitovsky suggests thinking of these "simple pleasures" as "channels through which novelty is transmitted. . . . Without an increase in novelty content, more time spent watching television, driving around, or shopping merely spreads the novelty thinner, increases redundancy, and reduces the intensity of enjoyment" (ibid., 234–35). "The remedy," he writes, "is culture," which gives us "access to society's accumulated stock of past novelty and so enable[s] us to supplement at will and almost without limit the currently available flow of novelty as a source of stimulation" (ibid., 235).

It is not difficult to find grounds for paternalism in Scitovsky's argument. "Since consumption skills are typically acquired by the young while they are in school, more mandatory liberal arts courses in the school curriculum are one alternative," he writes, "and since much of the training in consumption skills is learned by doing, subsidies to the arts are another" (1976, 247). One can also imagine more radical forms of coercion that might find justification in *The Joyless Economy*, since if valid, its argument decisively rebuts the convenient liberal assumption that individual freedom automatically leads to happiness by virtue of the individual's knowledge of her own best interests. The heart of Scitovsky's view is that an untutored desire need *not* serve the interests of its possessor.

Thus, if we step back from the question of what policies should be adopted within liberal societies and consider social systems as wholes, both the democratic and the capitalist dimensions of liberal society appear to be threatened by Scitovsky's analysis. Democracy and capitalism are similar in—ideally—giving people whatever they want, whether in the way of governance or of other "goods" (cf. Scitovsky 1976, 269).[3] Yet Scitovsky's argument emphasizes that what people want may be bad for them.

Liberals have traditionally (albeit not universally) sidestepped this

476   *Critical Review Vol. 10, No. 4*

possibility. They have preferred a priori defenses of democracy and capitalism as *intrinsically* just—defenses that are impervious to empirical falsification—over a posteriori defenses of the *results* produced by democracy and capitalism. If, a priori, each individual has the right to live her life as she sees fit, then it hardly matters whether the result of her freedom is satisfaction or misery; what is important is that she have the liberty, and what John Rawls calls the "primary goods," necessary to live in whatever manner she chooses, *regardless* of how satisfying that choice turns out to be. By the same token, if people collectively have the right to choose whatever governors they want, the wisdom of their choices becomes a matter of, at best, secondary concern. Much more important is the task of blocking power relations that might distort democratic choices. Accordingly, the task of most liberal philosophy has been to elaborate the grounds of individual and collective freedom, and the research agenda of modern political science and sociology has been to identify the sources of tyranny and inequality, and to design institutions and policies that would rectify these evils. Similarly, economists have been largely uninterested in the effects of capitalism on individual well-being, having defined the question out of existence by identifying (objective) well-being—"utility"—with the satisfaction of (subjective) individual preferences.

By denying that objective interests even exist, or by reducing interests to preferences, the defenders of democracy and capitalism cede the empirical ground to their opponents. Thus, most economists are inhibited, by the manifestly false doctrine that there can be no interpersonal comparison of utilities (a doctrine that would render the daily life of friends, lovers, and parents incomprehensible), from even debating the possibility that departures from capitalism might be beneficial—except when such departures would *further* the satisfaction of people's preferences by mitigating externalities or by providing public "goods." The door is therefore left open to any manner of interventionist panaceas for the problems Scitovsky identifies.

But those who might see in Scitovsky grounds for using state intervention to rectify the joyless economy face a paradox: the state they would enlist to remedy capitalism is democratic, and the justificatory principle of democracy is the same as that of capitalism—self-governance. A democratic state is thus a rather unlikely means of circumventing people's untutored desires; those desires are (supposedly) sovereign in a democratic polity as much as they are in a capitalist economy. Scitovsky's own defense of coercively imposed liberal-arts education for children, for example, would have to gain approval from the very electorate that, having failed to receive such an education, could hardly be expected to understand its benefits. His support of public funding for the arts requires ratification by the very public that, prior to the adoption of this policy, would be untrained in its value. Conversely, people who do appreciate such measures would, presumably, be willing to provide them without state involvement (where familiar collective-action problems did not interfere). One of the limitations of the tendency—endemic in democratic cultures of never-ending public-policy discussion—to think in terms of discrete "policy proposals" rather than systemic reform is that the former must be implemented by the very system that has often caused the problem one is trying to ameliorate. The problems caused by errant desires are likely to be exacerbated, not relieved, by the political system—democracy—that gives people what they desire.

The Joyless Economy thus raises some of the deepest theoretical issues in political economy and philosophy, as well as shedding light on a vast range of questions about the merits of popular and high culture, the organization of work, the nature of art, and the best way to live. In its concreteness it underscores the abstractness of contemporary economic and political thought, and it reveals the reason for this abstractness: the conviction that individual or collective freedom to choose how to live is intrinsically valuable. This conviction drains any urgency from the investigation of how we *should* live; indeed, it taints such investigation as suspect, because an open inquiry into whether freedom is good for people, rather than being good a priori, might lead to "elitist" conclusions (as discussed in Schor's contribution below). It is not surprising, then, that such investigation is rare, and that Scitovsky's example is a lonely one.

In light of the profound questions posed by Scitovsky's innovative book, the symposium presented below is but a first step. The implications of Scitovsky's view have not been thought through; the debate has not been joined. The same can be said more generally, however, of most debates about democratic capitalism, or what Karl Popper called the "open society." The putative empirical benefits of the open society—peace, prosperity, the advance of knowledge, the correction of error—are hardly ever discussed without the stultifying interference of a priori liberal precepts that render such discussions moot. The assumption that capitalism or democracy is intrinsically valuable makes the investigation of their actual effects nugatory.

Merely noting this is not, of course, sufficient to negate that assumption: we indeed should *not* be all that concerned with their empirical effects if democracy and capitalism *are* inherently (and superordinately) good. The argument that they are not inherently good must be made at another time. But one can, at this point, note the following inconsistency: although it is otiose if open societies are intrinsically valuable, discussion of their effects frequently *does* occur. Both the proponents and the opponents of laissez-faire capitalism, for example, dispute whether its consequences are beneficial, not just whether it is inherently just. The problem is that, hamstrung by their commitment to it *regardless* of its consequences, the defenders of the open society tend to reply lazily, dogmatically, or tautologically to its critics, and this allows simplistic paternalism to pass as supremely realistic by comparison.

If Scitovsky's theory stimulates the debate that it should, one can only hope it will avoid this pattern. There are signs, even in this "early" discussion of Scitovsky, that a more realistic approach is possible. Inglehart's contribution, for example, suggests that without paternalistic assistance, generations raised in affluence have already begun to question the hegemony of "comfort." Although it is unclear how congruent "Postmaterialism" is with the pursuit of higher pleasures, Inglehart's research shows that Scitovsky's argument does not necessarily entail paternalism: individuals can, at least when raised amidst material abundance, be relied upon to try to take care of their own need for stimulation as much as their need for comfort (cf. Scitovsky 1976, 78). On the other hand, it might be the case that the growth of state-funded higher education is responsible for the value changes Inglehart discusses. In that case, state paternalism might still be called for—if its systemic costs are not greater than its benefits, and if the paradox of its democratic approval can be resolved.

Albert Hirschman's consideration of the pleasures of "commensality" is another step toward a more nuanced consideration of the open society's effects on our well-being, since it illuminates a uniquely eudaimonistic[4] aspect of democracy. The association (first evident in classical Greek politics) between commensality, equality, and democracy that Hirschman describes raises the possibility that both democracy and equality have an instrumental element, rather than being (solely) ends in themselves. Democracy, in this view (which is not necessarily Hirschman's), should at least in part be evaluated empirically—but not merely for its success in procuring the objects of political action (any more than common meals should be evaluated solely on the basis of their success in feeding people). Rather, democracy should be judged by its ability to produce feelings of pleasure among its participants. This position is a step removed from the a priori insistence on freedom, equality, or democracy as ends in themselves, since it is always possible that these purported ends will turn out *not* to produce pleasure—or that, as Hirschman shows below, they may produce pain.[5]

The paternalistic implications of Scitovsky's work are most explicitly addressed in Sen's essay. Sen notes that Scitovsky's "spirit" is not paternalistic, since Scitovsky denies that people would continue their fruitless pursuit of ultimately boring comforts if they were sufficiently self-aware. What they "really" want is pleasure, but what they may "prefer," and end up pursuing, is comfort. But it remains possible that people will not or cannot achieve the self-awareness necessary to transcend their unhappy preferences. As soon as objective needs—the empirical conditions of happiness—are logically separated from subjective desires, there is conceptual space for people "really" to want what truly is not in their interest.

Conversely, if freedom is, as Sen argues, intrinsically (and very) valuable, it is difficult to see why we should be concerned with Scitovsky's, or anyone else's, empirical findings about freedom's potentially unhappy effects. It is this lack of concern, it seems to us, that has led to the neglect of *The Joyless Economy* that Sen, and we, deplore.

NOTES

1. But see *Times Literary Supplement* 1995, where a survey of prominent scholars lists *The Joyless Economy* as one of the 100 most important books of the second half of the century.
2. Perhaps the global appeal of American culture reflects the spread of affluence, which suddenly puts millions of people in need of mental stimuli that are pleasant to the uneducated eye and ear. American culture, being newer than competitors, may simply require less acculturation than the alterna-

tives, making it more universally accessible but, at the same time, less challenging and less satisfying.

3. One might argue that capitalism allows people's desires to be manipulated to favor comfort over pleasure through such devices as persuasive (rather than informational) advertising. But if so, democracy cannot very well be expected to counteract such manipulation, since a democracy's electorate will consist of consumers who, because of their exposure to advertising, will tend to favor government policies designed to encourage the production of wealth, with which they may purchase comforting consumer goods.

4. We use this term advisedly, to mean "happiness-oriented." We do not mean to call forth the Aristotelian connotations of *eudaimonia*, along with the much-disputed question of precisely what Aristotle meant by it. ("Utilitarian" is a better term, except that its association with preference satisfaction is even more misleading than the Aristotelian resonances of *eudaimonia*. It is a striking feature of contemporary philosophical discourse that no term seems available for referring to objectively existing states of psychological happiness, the fostering of which might form the object of social or political philosophy.)

5. In this connection, one of Hirschman's most famous contributions, his distinction between "exit" and "voice," is apposite. There are certainly many times when democracy, due to disagreement and other facets of human nature, is decidedly *un*pleasant. In these instances a market-like "exit" option may prove much more conducive to happiness than requiring those unhappy with their situation to remain engaged in using democratic "voice" to change matters. (Cf. Hirschman 1977.)

REFERENCES

Hirschman, Albert O. 1977. *Exit, Voice, and Loyalty*. Princeton: Princeton University Press.

Scitovsky, Tibor. 1976. *The Joyless Economy: An Inquiry into Human Satisfaction and Consumer Dissatisfaction*. New York: Oxford University Press.

Times Literary Supplement. 1995. "The Hundred Most Influential Books Since World War II." October 6: 39.

[3]

Tibor Scitovsky

MY OWN CRITICISM OF
THE JOYLESS ECONOMY

ABSTRACT: *The Joyless Economy* focused on the boredom of the idle rich *and neglected the boredom of the idle and idled poor. However, their bore-dom is much more serious than what the book dealt with, because it is chronic and often incurable. It usually begins with the neglect of destitute children who never learn how to concentrate on learning in school, become unruly and often end up unemployable, and have no better way than vio-lence to release their energies.*

I am overwhelmed by all the praise, statistical confirmation, con-structive criticism, and wealth of highly relevant new ideas sparked, 20 years after its publication, by my book, which originally received scant recognition and poor sales. This symposium greatly broadens and enriches our understanding of the many components of the goodness of life, of which I only analyzed a small segment in my book; and it is bound to stimulate further work on the subject and serve as a better basis for policy. I would like to pick out the few points I find easy to answer or develop a little further, and then fol-low Albert Hirschman's example and engage in self-censure by adding my own, more severe criticism of the book to that of my critics, based on my further and deeper understanding of the conse-

---

Critical Review 10, no. 4 (Fall 1996). ISSN 0891-3811. © 1996 Critical Review Foundation.

Tibor Scitovsky, 1175 North Lemon Avenue, Menlo Park, CA 94025, was a professor of economics at Stanford University; the University of California, Berkeley; Yale University; and the University of California, Santa Cruz.

quences of boredom and prompted by the social problems that have emerged in recent years.

Let me start with Hirschman's, Juliet Schor's, and Michael Benedikt's well-justified objections to my narrow focus on the private domain, to the almost complete neglect of the public one. I dealt only with the desire for status, the comfort of belonging, and the stimulus of conversation in pubs and cafés, but was remiss in overlooking all the pleasure and stimulation provided by many public goods and activities, ranging from beautiful landscapes and cityscapes to one's public activities and duties as a citizen.

Hirschman is very right in adding the stimulation of politics and participation in public life, and in showing that the company of others with whom one has something in common can be both stimulating and comforting, even without involving stimulating conversation. I find especially fascinating and important his discussion of having meals at the same table with other people as the origin of political union and Athenian democracy, as well as the habit of drinking in company, which creates similar though often less peaceful communities, as could be expected, considering that drink makes many people aggressive and violent.

Peaceful and friendly communal drinking, however, characterize English pubs, where the British, though great respecters of other people's privacy—who seldom even talk to a person to whom they have not been introduced—drop their customary reserve and exude peaceful sociability. What most impresses young Swedes in London is the pubs' relaxed, friendly, sociable atmosphere, which makes all customers feel as if they belonged to the same, large family—or so I was told at a London conference of Swedish youths. They complained of their country's lack of social life and wished that London pubs could be transplanted to Sweden.

Let me just add a few simple examples to Hirschman's very important ones. Forming part of an appreciative audience at a concert, theater, or movie is much more stimulating than hearing and seeing the same on radio or TV in the privacy of one's home; being in a crowded London pub or Paris café is comforting and stimulating even without knowing a soul to talk to; most people get a kick out of joining demonstrations or the actions of a crowd, as Gustave Le Bon pointed out in his *Psychologie des Foules*; and the huge memberships (estimated at 12 million)[1] of the more than 800 antigovernment militias may be similarly explained.

Schor also objects to my book's failure to deal with public goods; but even more serious is her criticism of my "failure to provide a structural critique of consumer society," by which she seems to mean an explanation of why the United States became a consumer society and is now so slow to emerge from consumerism, continuing to focus on the consumption and possession of private goods to the neglect of the environment, infrastructure, collective goods, family and social life, and various other stimulating activities.

I plead guilty to focusing too narrowly on showing the way out of consumerism and neglecting to list its causes. I mentioned only one cause, our Puritan tradition, but not American capitalism, where every action of businessmen aims at maximizing the sale of goods and services and thereby promotes consumerism. This may be largely responsible for environmental deterioration; for the schools' ever-greater emphasis on work skills, which increasingly crowd out the teaching of history, literature, music, and the arts; and for workers' long, 40-hour workweeks and short, two-week summer vacations, which leaves them little time to spend with their families, educate their children, and enjoy leisure activities.

In Germany, where the law requires employees' equal representation on the supervisory committees of business firms with 50 or more employees, workers have gained the country's 36-hour workweek and six weeks of paid vacation. In addition, quite a few German firms, including not only BMW but Volkswagen, Bayer, Hertie A.G. (a chain of warehouses), and the German plants of IBM, Pirelli, and Hewlett Packard, are experimenting with greater flexibility in their employees' work time and have already moved to a four-day work week, with workers and some office employees free to choose which days other than Sundays they want to have free and, often, how many hours, and at what times, they wish to work (Wagner 1995). This provides workers with more time for family life and enjoyable leisure activities and enables neighboring parents so to coordinate their worktime that an adult is always present to supervise their children, while maintaining and even increasing these firms' profitability. (The explanation is that while they reduce their employees' workdays and work hours, they increase their plants' overall workdays and work hours by introducing multiple shifts, thereby saving as much or more on fixed costs as the increase in their labor costs.)

Even more important, however, is Schor's argument that people's spending on positional goods is the main reason why we are stuck with consumerism, even though our rising incomes long ago assured virtually our whole population's comfortable survival. She correctly notes that competitive spending on positional goods is a zero-sum game that can never add to one's comfort or contentment as long as everybody else also spends on it. All this does is to use up hard-earned income and absorb resources that could better be used in the public domain, as Benedikt's graphic description of America's slumming amply demonstrates.

Moreover, spending on some positional goods also depresses the economy and so reduces income, thereby diverting expenditure from the public domain yet further (cf. Scitovsky 1987 and 1994).

Unfortunately, nothing can be done to keep people from the zero-sum game of positional competition, other than to acquaint them with, and lure them into spending their time and money on, the more stimulating and longer-lasting satisfactions of cultural activities. That, of course, was the purpose of my book. But I failed to mention that cultural activities not only cure boredom but are also likely to make the public more aware of the importance of such public goods as pleasing natural and architectural environments and the proper maintenance of our cities as ingredients in a full and enjoyable life.

Schor further blames consumerism for women's increased participation in the labor force, which diminishes the time they can spend with family and children for the sake of earning more of the income they want to spend on positional goods. I am sure she is right; but women's justified desire for economic independence must also be a motive for their increased entry into the labor force. For the resulting neglect of children and family I would rather blame partly the lopsided emancipation of women in the United States, where equal access to education and professional advancement is not yet matched by control over their own bodies; and partly the failure to allow workers more, and more flexible, free time, as in Germany.

I found Ronald Inglehart's paper most gratifying for its statistical support and elaboration of my views, and interesting for the new vistas it opens on the subject. But to discuss his data intelligently, I would have to study his other writings, of which this is a very condensed summary, in order to learn about the questions and answers on which he bases his findings concerning the shift in people's preferences from materialistic to postmaterialist values. Unfortunately, I have been unable to do that prior to the publication of this symposium.

Amartya Sen has done me the honor of seeing much more in my book than I put there. My only concern was to explain why many well-to-do people, able to afford everything they would need for a full and satisfactory life, nevertheless end up with a feeling of emptiness and boredom. This contradicted economists' traditional, simple-minded assumptions that each of us (1) knows what is best for him- or herself, and (2) aims rationally to achieve or at least approximate it within his or her available means. I tried to discover what was wrong with those assumptions, in the hope that the answer would also enable me to show how to avoid boredom.

The first assumption's flaw is that many people are unaware of their need for enjoyable activity, and in any case lack the skills that most such activities require to be enjoyable. The flaw in the second assumption is that most of us have many different desires that are often in conflict; and different people's various resolutions of that conflict amount to the existence of many different "rationalities." There are egoists and altruists, misers and spendthrifts, the ambitious and the unambitious, the scientifically and the artistically minded, etc., with innumerable gradations in between.

Once these simple facts explained boredom to my satisfaction, I pursued them no further, because I was always more interested in presenting my problem in the simplest possible language, unencumbered by unnecessary detail, and then proceed to find its remedy, rather than exploring the ramifications and philosophical implications of that problem. Only much later did I sometimes realize what important discoveries I missed, owing to my passion for simplicity in argument and presentation.

I am grateful therefore to Sen for enriching my austere argument by bringing in the unexamined life, explaining how the need for novelty to render mental activity enjoyable explains the desire for freedom, and generally for deepening our understanding of such concepts as rationality, utility, and revealed preference. I would only add to his paper—as well as to my book—that physical and mental activity, which are among our most basic needs, resemble sleep, another of our basic needs, in mostly having no economic cost at all. Indeed, many activities are both pleasurable and income-earning or -saving.

Benedikt's paper is bursting with interesting and important ideas, both his own and everybody else's who has written on all the different sources of human contentment. My book dealt with the single subject of boredom and its relief through stimulation; he discusses all sources of satisfaction, their relations, their interaction, and their changing intensity with iteration and through time. I could not agree more with his condemnation of the decline in our landscapes and cityscapes, which has resulted from our seeking satisfaction the wrong way. I hope he will sooner or later enlarge these insights into a great and important book.

His criticism of my volume for narrowly focusing on the problem of the happiness of the well-to-do leisure classes, without even mentioning the more serious problems of the poor, I find devastating but well deserved; I too, with the benefit of hindsight, have independently come to the same conclusion. The explanation, though no excuse for my omission, is that more than 20 years ago, when I conceived and wrote the book, our country's rich and poor inhabitants alike had enjoyed a long period of unprecedented prosperity, with very low levels of unemployment and poverty, few homeless people, and with workers' long work hours allowing them insufficient leisure to be bored, leaving only the affluent leisure classes disappointed with their lives.

Those exceptionally happy days, however, soon came to an end; and the last few years have witnessed not only greatly increased numbers of impoverished, unemployed, unemployable, and homeless people but also much more violence and murder, and the emergence of juvenile gangs and teenage vandalism in our midst. All of this made me repent having written a whole book just to explain and remedy the occasional yawns of the well-to-do, without a word about the much more serious problems of the poor.

Curiously enough, however, Benedikt, while noting my serious omission, suggests no way of correcting it, despite his great erudition and the innumerable other aspects and related problems he brings into the discussion. That, however, gives me a chance to imitate Hirschman and engage in self-subversion.

The poor among us suffer not only the humiliation of unemployment and the malnutrition, homelessness, and other privations of poverty, all of which are serious problems that need attention; but they also suffer from boredom, just like the idle rich; except that the boredom of the idle and idled poor is chronic, which makes it a deprivation as extreme as starvation, and with equally fatal consequences. Just as people with no money to buy food stoop to thieving to avoid starvation, so those with no work and lacking the skills for harmless activities to relieve their boredom will relieve it with violence and vandalism—the only stimulating activities that require no skill, only muscular strength or a weapon.

It is striking that young criminals, when interviewed in prison, always seem to mention the desire to escape their terrible boredom as one of the reasons for their criminality. This calls to mind Sir Roy Harrod's prediction that the continued rise in labor productivity would, in the long run, save so much labor that ordinary people with no special talents would face the problem of how to occupy all the leisure time that scientific progress will have won for them. He foresaw a return to the war, violence, and blood sports of the Middle Ages, when the idle rich had no access to schools to teach them harmless activities with which to keep busy and wile away their time (Harrod 1958).

Those two things made me realize for the first time that education's most important function is to civilize, i.e., instruct in the harmless activities of life so as to divert people from harmful, violent ones. Until little more than a hundred years ago, education, including the three R's, was the privilege of the leisure classes. The working classes' long, hard, tiring labor left them insufficient leisure to need relief from boredom.

But if education teaches the skills needed for the many harmless activities that relieve boredom, what explains all the violence in our midst today, when we have schools that are both free and compulsory for all? The answer, I belatedly realized, is that learning itself is one of the enjoyable activities whose skill has to be learnt to make them enjoyable enough to relieve boredom. It is also the most essential of enjoyable activities, because without being able to enjoy it, one would hardly be willing to make the effort of learning the skills necessary to also enjoy other stimulating activities. That is why *children must learn the skill of the very act of learning before they enter school*. Proper parenting is the best, perhaps the only way to teach them that skill, thereby making formal learning in school enjoyable and desirable activities.

Most of the juvenile crime, violence, and vandalism around us may be explained by the inadequate parenting of children in poor families where both parents work and there is no extended family to take their place; and by the circumstances of illegitimate children born into poverty to mothers with not enough time for parenting, and who are often too young to know its meaning and importance, being children themselves. When such neglected children enter school before having discovered that learning is fun and gives them a feeling of pride and satisfaction, they are usually afraid of school, are bored by it, find it hard to concentrate, and get poor grades they are ashamed of, leading them to be truants and ultimately dropouts; and all too many of them end up on the street, engage in gratuitous violence, and join juvenile gangs.

Parenting, therefore, which must already begin in infancy, is an essential and crucially important part of education; and its three phases, as child psychiatrist Warden H. Emory (1975) argues, deserve more attention than they have hitherto received. Its first, passive, so-called spectator phase, is when infants begin to learn their parents' and/or other grownups' behavior and speech by just observing them. Most parents who looked forward to having children perform the easy parenting appropriate to that phase instinctively. They (or at least one of them) must be present during most of the child's waking hours, talking among themselves and to the child, doing their chores and attending to the child's various needs while the child hears and observes them, saying what they are doing while doing it, so that the child can learn the meaning of words and the use of speech. The great importance of parenting even in this earliest phase was only recently recognized in Romania, where many of the orphans in overcrowded and understaffed orphanages suffered from severe and incurable retardation, the cause of which was traceable to their being left completely alone during most of their waking hours, with no adults present whom they could hear talking and see walking about and attending to the children's needs.

Another danger for children at that very early age is busy parents' habit of planting their children in front of a TV screen just to keep them quiet, which it does. If television is used for this purpose too much, however, it prolongs the child's stay in the passive, early spectator phase, postpones its reaching the next, more active phase, and thereby retards its entire development. In addition, too much television viewing of inappropriate programs often also provides children with the wrong behavioral models to imitate.

Children must proceed, at the latest by age two, to the second, so-called participator phase, where they learn to become active by imitating adult behavior and speech that they could only observe in the first phase. Parents now must encourage, help, correct, and praise children as they learn to speak, stand, move about, and perform various simple activities around the house, so they can discover the skills they have already acquired and their ability to learn new ones. This also enables them to take pride in showing off their abilities; in this way they learn to enjoy the fruits of learning as well as the very act of learning.

That leads to the third, "initiator" phase of children's pre-school development, where they take pleasure in initiating the actions and activities they learned by imitating them. At this stage, they discover their identity and learn what they look like, how they feel in various situations, what their possibilities and shortcomings are; they imagine what they could be and begin to develop their personality. Now adults must continue to encourage, help and correct their behavior and activities just as in the previous phase; but in addition they must praise or reward them for good and harmless behavior, and reprimand or punish them for bad and harmful behavior. This is essential for teaching them the difference between right and wrong, and for their learning to prefer the first and dislike the second, so they may grow up into upright, useful, and civilized human beings.

Children must go through all three of these phases before entering school, because only then will they look forward to going to school, enjoy and be willing to learn what it teaches, recognize their own potentialities and limitations, enjoy doing their homework, want to excel, and perform well. But many children continue to need parental supervision even during their school years. Children who go home from school into an empty house where they are left alone until their parents get home from work are often involved in street violence; according to a Justice Department report, "Arrests among juveniles . . . for violent crimes jumped 100 percent between 1983 and 1992 . . . and the peak time during which youths age 6 to 17 commit violent crimes was from 3 to 6 p.m.—from when school ends to when parents return from work" (*New York Times* 1995).

I go into this discussion of inadequate parenting and gratuitous violence by juveniles not so much because they are important social problems in the United States today, but because the first is the cause, the second a sure symptom of the most serious form of boredom. Neglected children are not only bored; when their boredom keeps them from learning in school, it becomes a chronic disease that can forever deprive them of the enjoyment of music, literature, the arts, interesting work—just about all the good things life has to offer, all of which require a skill to be learned beforehand to make them enjoyable. The discouraging experience of juvenile criminals in correctional institutions bears that out.

Gratuitous violence may be the ultimate relief from boredom for those who have no work and lack both the skills for engaging in enjoyable activities and the money to pay for entertainment. When youngsters unable to concentrate on learning drop out of school and cannot find work, they usually go into the street, where the coming and going of people and vehicles provides them with some entertainment to relieve their boredom for a while, until it loses its novelty and becomes monotonous. At that stage, they seek relief in vandalism and violence, which is why psychologists consider these to be sure symptoms of boredom in impoverished, uneducated people who cannot or need not find work to keep them busy. For work is the main antidote to boredom for the majority of mankind, not only because much work is itself enjoyable and satisfying, but also because even monotonous and unpleasant work keeps boredom at bay when it is tiring and exhausting enough to call for sleep and rest to recuperate.

Let me end by thanking the editor of *Critical Review* for organizing this symposium, which has greatly added to, enriched, and completed what my book said about boredom. As its author I am especially grateful for having been given this opportunity to fill in one of its serious omissions.

NOTES

1. The FBI refers callers to Southern Poverty Law Center 1996 as the best available source on the subject; but the estimate of 12 million members of the 809 militias (more than 14,800 per militia) is perhaps an exaggeration.

REFERENCES

Emory, Warden H. 1975. "The Military Experience." In *Boredom: Root of Discontent and Aggression,* ed. Franz E. Goetzl. Berkeley: Grizzly Peak Press.

Harrod, Roy F. 1958. "The Possibility of Economic Satiaty." In *Problems of United States Economic Development*. New York: Committee on Economic Development.

New York Times. 1995. News item, September 8:8.

Scitovsky, Tibor. 1987. "Growth in the affluent society." *Lloyds Bank Review* no. 163 (January). Reprinted in Scitovsky 1995.

Scitovsky, Tibor. 1994. "Towards a theory of second-hand markets." *Kyklos* 47(1). Reprinted in Scitovsky 1995.

Scitovsky, Tibor. 1995. *Economic Theory and Reality: Selected Essays on Their Disparities and Reconciliation*. Aldershot, U.K.: Edward Elgar.

Southern Poverty Law Center. 1996. *False Patriots: The Threat of Antigovernment Extremists*.

Wagner, Dietrich, ed. 1995. *Arbeitszeitmodelle*. Göttingen: Verlag für Angewandte Psychologie.

[4]

KYKLOS, Vol. 31 – 1978 – Fasc. 4, 575–587

ECONOMIC GROWTH AND SOCIAL WELFARE: THE NEED FOR A COMPLETE STUDY OF HAPPINESS

Yew-Kwang Ng*

Does economic growth increase social welfare? This question has been 'on the agenda', to use a modern phrase, for a long time. Recent attention to the problem by economists is particularly notable; see, *e.g.* Easterlin [1974], Beckerman [1975], Hirsch [1976], Scitovsky [1976], McDougall [1977], Mishan [1977]. However, we seem to be as divided and as far from a definite answer as ever. It seems to me that, in trying to answer this problem we must undertake a complete multi-disciplinary study. Before discussing the need for the complete study (*Section II*), I shall first introduce the readers to the discussion by presenting a geometrical analysis of the Harrod-Hirsch concept of positional goods and its implication on the problem under consideration.

I. GROWTH, ASPIRATION, AND FRUSTRATION:
THE HARROD-HIRSCH CONCEPT OF POSITIONAL GOODS

Not intended as a complete analysis, economics has its obvious limitations. However, many alleged limitations are actually familiar economic factors, though usually discussed under different names. For example, in discussing the 'tyranny of small decisions' Kahn [1966] explicitly noted that the undesirable results of 'small decisions' are associated with the presence of externalities, decreasing costs, *etc.* Similarly, many of the alleged costs of economic growth

* Monash University, Australia.

YEW-KWANG NG

can be seen to be no more than external diseconomies and can be treated as such. (For a 'spirited defence' of economic growth along this approach, see BECKERMAN [1975].) A basic limitation of traditional economics is the neglect of the subjective factors. Since welfare depends both on objective and subjective factors, this neglect makes purely economic analysis incapable of providing a complete answer to questions concerning welfare. Partly to illustrate this point and partly for its own interest, let us consider the HARROD-HIRSCH concept of positional goods.

HARROD [1958] uses the concept of oligarchic wealth in connection with the problem of satiety; HIRSCH [1976] develops it into the concept of positional goods and uses it to question the desirability of economic growth. Positional goods are those goods or aspects of goods, services, work positions and other social relationships that are (1) scarce in some absolute or socially imposed sense and (2) subject to congestion or crowding through more extensive use[1]. Included as positional goods are: (1) goods of more-or-less fixed physical supply such as natural landscapes, old masterpieces, and personal services on a per capita basis; (2) those valued mainly for its relative scarcity or status. For example, if we create a higher level of awards, it makes the existing awards less venerable. As more people get the bachelor degree one may need a Ph.D. to feel distinguished.

To concentrate on the contrast between positional goods and non-positional goods, let us assume that the relative prices of different positional goods do not change with respect to each other so that we may lump them into a single composite good. Similarly, all non-positional goods are lumped as Y. This permits us to work with the two-dimensional *Figure 1*.

Abstracting for the moment from the problems of possible differences and changes in tastes, we operate with the same set of indifference curves. Consider a person with average income facing the budget line AA'. He may consume an average amount of both positional goods (X^0) and non-positional goods (Y^0). (Persons of

1. Both conditions are mentioned by HIRSCH [1976, p. 27] who regards either condition as sufficient to make a good positional. But it fits his argument better to make both conditions necessary. If a good is subject to congestion (as most goods are) but can be expanded in supply to relieve the congestion, then obviously it cannot be classified as a positional good.

ECONOMIC GROWTH AND SOCIAL WELFARE

Figure 1

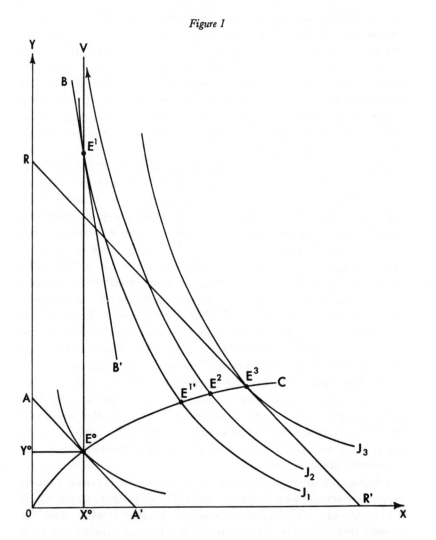

average income, even on average, may have above average consumption of Y and under average consumption of X or *vice versa*
depending on the consumption pattern of the whole society. This
divergence does not affect the main contention below.) Since positional goods are likely to be income elastic, his rich contemporary

577

YEW-KWANG NG

are likely to consume a disproportionately larger amount of X, *e.g.* at the point E^3. In other words, the income consumption curve OC is likely to be concave. However, this is not an essential assumption for the central argument here. With economic growth, our Mr.Average can expect his income to increase, eventually catching up with or even surpassing the original rich man income. Does this mean that he can eventually consume at E^3 on the indifference curve J_3? The answer is negative. Since positional goods cannot be increased with economic growth, their prices will increase relative to non-positional goods as the latter become abundant. Thus, the average-man's budget line will not move from AA' towards RR'. Rather, it will not only move out but also rotate in a clockwise direction to a position such as BB'. Hence, Mr.Average can never reach the point E^3, though he may reach the point E^1 or even some point vertically above E^1 with further growth. While E^1 is beyond the reach of even the rich man before economic growth, it may lie below the indifference curve J_3. It is even likely that, no matter how high one travels along the vertical line X^0V, one can never reach, say, the indifference curve J_2 which may approach X^0V asymptotically or eventually becomes vertical and/or even turn rightward. Nevertheless, as we travel along X^0V upward, we hit successively higher indifference curves before they become, if at all, vertical and turn rightward. This seems to suggest that economic growth improves the welfare of Mr. Average even though it cannot make him as well off as the rich. However, this may not be true if we take account of the likely effects of economic growth in raising the aspiration levels of Mr. Average. With economic growth, Mr. Average may aspire to attain the consumption point E^3 and then find that his aspiration is repeatedly frustrated. For example, he may work hard to earn an income sufficient to provide his children with good education, hoping that they will then get good jobs. But since other people are doing the same thing, his children may have better education than he had but no better than the average of their generation. They are likely to end up with no better than average jobs. The aspiration for 'good' jobs will likely be frustrated.

To digress a little on the problem of education, it seems likely that education has an important purely competitive aspect in addition to the commonly recognized productive and consumption aspects

ECONOMIC GROWTH AND SOCIAL WELFARE

(internal effects) and external benefits (a better educated person may
make a better citizen and neighbour). The purely competitive aspect
consists both in competition for (relative) distinction and for better
jobs. If competition for better jobs consists in better training, this has
a productive aspect as well. But to the extent that *relative* performance in educational achievement is important in getting better jobs,
it also has a purely competitive aspect. It is true that, in view of the
difficulty of employers in knowing the ability of applicants, educational performance is useful as an indicator. (See ARROW [1973], SPENCE
[1973], STIGLITZ [1975], WOLPIN [1977].) However, if all individuals
agree not to work too hard in scoring high marks in examination,
persons of highest intelligence will still come out best. Hence, to the
extent that the *relative* performance counts, there is an element of
external costs involved. Though the amount of the external costs is
a matter scarcely anyone can be sure of, it seems not impossible that
it may offset to a large extent the external benefits of education. The
massive government subsidy to education in many countries may
thus be quite excessive.

Returning to *Figure 1,* it can be seen that travelling along X^0V
upward, the successively higher indifference curves become closer
and closer to each other as measured along the income-consumption
curve OC. An increase in Y from E^0 to E^1 is equivalent to the movement
from E^0 to $E^{1'}$. But no matter how many times Y is increased above
E^1, the indifference curve does not lie above E^2. Thus, even if we do
not assume that the marginal utility of income is diminishing but
rather constant as we travel along OC, the marginal utility of Y as
we travel along X^0V must still be fastly diminishing. The small gain
in utility can therefore easily be overbalanced by the loss in frustrated
aspirations. Economic growth, to the extent that it increases socially
unrealizable expirations, may actually reduce social welfare.

It may, however, be argued that the cause of the reduction in welfare is the unrealistic aspiration rather than growth as such. What is
needed is not to stop growth but to realise that growth can make an
average person better off along X^0V but not along OC, *i.e.* more non-
positional goods but not more positional goods. If aspiration can
stick to this realistic path, no frustration need arise. Whether this is
possible cannot be answered here as it involves the psychological and
sociological problems of the formation of aspirations. In any case,

YEW-KWANG NG

it seems clear that the problem of aspiration is as important, if not more important than economic abundance, at least in the economically advanced countries.

An important consideration neglected in HIRSCH's argument presented above is that, apart from changes in aspiration, there may also be other possible changes in tastes, abilities to enjoy, *etc*. For example, as Mr. Average travels along X^0V, he may gradually learn how to enjoy non-positional goods more effectively. Thus, there may be changes in the shape of the indifference curves such that he may be consuming at a point along X^0V which, according to the new indifference map, lies above E^3. Let us put this in terms of *Figure 2*. With X being held constant at X^0, we may concentrate on changes in (non-positional) income Y. The curve RT measures the original marginal welfare of Y^2. With learning in consuming, it may move upward to $R'T'$. However, as the whole curve moves upward, the minimum level of income (denoted as M) sufficient to provide a non-negative level of (total) welfare may also increase to M'. This increase in M may be due to the following interrelated factors: a change in aspiration, an increase in one's customary standard of living, and increases in the prevailing social standards of living. Whether total welfare increases or not as income per capita increases depends much on the relative magnitudes of the above two movements. Welfare may thus be more a function of the *rates* of increase in income, in aspiration, *etc*. than in the absolute level of income. Economic growth may be important

2. To speak of *marginal* welfare, welfare (*i.e.* happiness) has to be *in principle* cardinally measurable. But this is obviously true though the practical difficulty of measurement is very real. An individual can not only meaningfully say that he is happier in *x* than in *y* but also that he is *much* happier in *x* than in *y* than he is happier in *w* than in *z*. If this is so, his happiness cannot be just ordinal. Since the innovation of the indifference curve analysis, economists have been very shy of talking about cardinal utility or welfare. For the positive theory of consumer behaviour, ordinal preference is sufficient for the purpose. It is then preferable to abstract from cardinal utility. But for questions as those we are dealing with in this paper, the concept of cardinal welfare is very helpful if not indispensable. To question the use of cardinal welfare in this connection is to commit the fallacy of misplaced abstraction. On cardinal measurability and interpersonal comparability, see NG [1975]; for an argument that interpersonal comparisons of utility are not value judgments, see NG [1972].

ECONOMIC GROWTH AND SOCIAL WELFARE

Figure 2

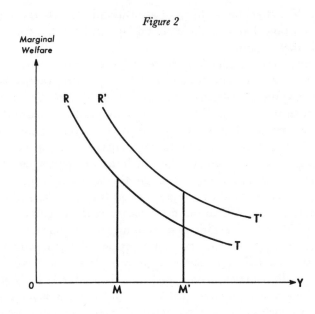

more in providing a positive rate of increase in income than in providing a high level of income.

It may also be argued that if a certain change in aspiration or what not leads to a reduction in happiness, then whatever external factor that causes this change should be deemed to produce an external diseconomy. On the other hand, if the factor is internal (*i.e.* under the control of the individual concerned), then its effect will be taken into account by the individual unless imperfect foresight or irrational preference is involved. On this view, problems such as changes in aspiration, *etc.* can all be handled by the traditional concept of externality, imperfect foresight, *etc.* In a formal sense, this is so. But this seems to overstretch the concept of external economy a little. Certainly no court in the world would grant compensation for 'damages' through a change in aspiration. Moreover, the individuals affected may not know of the existence of the effects, or whether the effects are beneficial or harmful. One may then say that this is a problem of imperfect foresight. Quite so. But when we take into account long-run effects including changes in aspiration, *etc.*, the as-

581

YEW-KWANG NG

sumption of perfect foresight becomes very dubious. Just by lumping everything into externality and/or imperfect foresight is not going to solve the problems. We have to begin analysing them.

II. TOWARDS A COMPLETE STUDY OF HAPPINESS

Whether a certain measure (in promoting economic growth or any other objective) will increase or decrease social welfare depends both on its effects on the objective world (a change in distribution, more production and/or more pollution, or a change in output-mix) and its effects on the subjective world (changes in knowledge, beliefs, aspirations, *etc.* of individuals). The subjective-objective classification is exhaustive. However, it is useful to think in terms of a third group of factors which have both subjective and objective elements and are products of the interaction of these elements. These are the institutional factors, including governments, laws, religions, families, customs, various organizations, *etc.* Institutions are formed by the interactions of individuals between themselves and with the objective environment. Once formed, they serve to regulate and constrain these interactions and hence affect the future course of the subjective and objective worlds. (See arrows in the right half of *Figure 3.*) All measures are originated from the subjective world (all initiatives are taken by some individuals), working through the institutional setting to affect the objective world, the institutional setting, and/or the subjective world itself. (See arrows in the left half of *Figure 3.*) In the process, it is almost certain that not only the objective world will be affected, but the institutional setting and the subjective world will change as well. Hence, a complete analysis of any significant policy or event has to take account of all its effects on the objective world, the institutional setting, and the subjective world.

   Economic analysis (including cost-benefit analysis, an application of welfare economics) is mostly confined to the study of the objective effects. Though this may include how these objective effects are evaluated by individuals, the effects on the institutional setting and on the psychology of individuals themselves are usually excluded. This is partly due to the fact that these effects are very difficult to identify (not to mention quantify) and partly due to the division

582

ECONOMIC GROWTH AND SOCIAL WELFARE

Figure 3

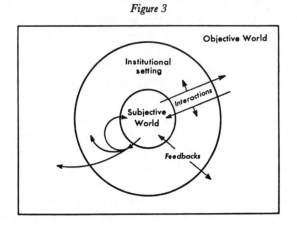

of the various fields of study largely isolated from one another. The confinement to the objective effects means that the analysis is useful mainly for relatively small changes whose institutional and subjective effects are negligible. For example, if the problem is to choose between two alternative routes for a freeway which will have similar social and environmental effects, a study of the direct costs and benefits is sufficient for the purpose. However, if the problem is whether the freeway should be built at all, the effects on the environment, *etc.* have also to be taken into account. For even larger problems like the desirability of economic growth, one needs a more complete analysis taking account of all significant objective, institutional, and subjective effects (using perhaps the concept of indirect externality; NG [1975a]).

Due to increasing complexity and interrelatedness of a modern society, it seems likely that more and more problems are going to involve all objective, institutional, and subjective effects. For example, in the freeway example above, it is likely that the two alternative routes may have different social and environmental effects. If this is so, then a more complete analysis is called for even for the small problem of the choice of alternative routes. However, since the institutional and subjective effects are very tricky to analyse, we have a dilemma. We know that the effects are there but they are very difficult to study. One way out of this dilemma is to say that, since the institutional and subjective effects are almost impossible to identify and may either be beneficial or harmful, in the absence of better information, we may disregard them and concentrate on the objective effects. This is a generalization of the theory of third best discussed in NG [1977]. This may be a valid approach for some problems at the moment but it does not mean that we should not pay more attention and resources to the study of the institutional and subjective effects, hoping to achieve a more complete analysis in the future.

To achieve a more complete analysis, it seems that an inter-disciplinary study is required. One of the relevant disciplines is psychology. EASTERLIN [1974] has recently brought together the results of various psychological studies of human happiness. The con-clusion of this survey is that while there is a clear and positive cor-relation between income and (self-reported) happiness within a country at a particular time, it is uncertain whether such a positive association exists across countries and over time. EASTERLIN also discusses some conceptual and measurement problems of using self-reports of happiness and concluded with a qualified approval. One basic difficulty is the problem of comparability. The same amount of happiness may be described as 'very happy' in a poor country or fifty years ago but described only as 'fairly happy' in a rich country now. There is a simple method to reduce this difficulty which does not seem to have been used. This is discussed below.

The most popular method used in happiness questionnaires is to ask a respondent to tick one of the following: very happy, fairly (or pretty) happy, not very (or not too) happy. This has the advantage of being very simple but it raises problems of comparability. CANTRIL [1965] devises a so-called 'self-anchoring striving scale'. A respondent is to register a number from 0 to 10 with 0 representing the worst possible life and 10 representing the best, as defined by the respondent himself. This method may be useful for certain comparative studies but it does not overcome the difficulty of comparability since the same number may represent different amounts of happiness for different people. While this difficulty is very difficult to overcome completely (see, however, NG [1975]), it can be reduced by the following simple method. Though different persons may select different adjectives or numbers to describe the same amount of happiness, there is one level of happiness that is more objectively identifiable, the level of zero

ECONOMIC GROWTH AND SOCIAL WELFARE

(net) happiness[3]. No matter how large or small gross happiness an individual may have, if it is roughly equal to, in the opinion of the individual, the amount of pain or suffering, the net amount of happiness is zero and has an interpersonal significance in comparability. Hence, an intertemporal and interregional comparable piece of information is the proportion of people having zero, positive, and negative net happiness. Such wordings as 'not too happy' may subsume both negative, zero, *and* relatively small amounts of positive happiness. Moreover, this relatively small amount is determined by the subjective judgment of the respondent and hence not interpersonally comparable. Thus a simple way to reduce the difficulty of comparability is to pin down the dividing line of zero happiness.

Different persons get happiness in different ways. Some feel happy serving God, some feel happy having a good family life, some feel happy being adventurous, *etc.* But virtually everyone like to have happiness for oneself, for his family and perhaps also for others. According to a major school of moral philosophy, happiness is the only acceptable ultimate objective in life. Yet the study of happiness is in such a primitive stage. At the risk of repetition, it may be said that more attention and more resources should be devoted to the study of happiness (Eudaimonology?) taking account of the objective, subjective, and institutional factors.

REFERENCES

ARMSTRONG N. E. [1950]: 'Utility and the Theory of Welfare', *Oxford Economic Papers*, Vol. 3, pp. 257–271.

ARROW KENNETH J. [1973]: 'Higher Education as a Filter', *Journal of Public Economics*, Vol. 2, July, pp. 193–216.

BECKERMAN WILFRED [1975]: *Two Cheers for the Affluent Society: A Spirited Defence of Economic Growth*, St. Martin's Press, New York.

3. 'There can be little doubt that an individual, apart from his attitude of preference or indifference to a pair of alternatives, may also desire an alternative not in the sense of preferring it to some other alternative, or may have an aversion towards it not in the sense of contra-preferring it to some other alternative. There seem to be (there certainly are) pleasant situations that are intrinsically desirable and painful situations that are intrinsically repugnant. It does not seem unreasonable to postulate that welfare is +ve in the former case and −ve in the latter (ARMSTRONG [1951, p. 269]).' Similarly, it is meaningful for someone to say, 'If I had to lead such a miserable life, I would wish not to be born into the world at all'.

YEW-KWANG NG

CANTRIL H. [1965]: *The Pattern of Human Concerns,* Rutgers University Press, New Brunswick, New Jersey.

DAVID PAUL A. and REDER MELVIN W. (Eds.) [1974]: *Nations and Households in Economic Growth,* Essays in Honor of Moses Abramovitz, Academic Press, New York.

EASTERLIN RICHARD A. [1974]: 'Does Economic Growth Improve the Human Lot? Some Empirical Evidence', in: DAVID and REDER.

HARROD ROY F. [1958]: 'The Possibility of Economic Satiety', in *Problems of United States Economic Development,* Vol. 1, Committee for Economic Development, New York.

HIRSCH FRED [1976]: *Social Limits to Growth,* Harvard University Press, Cambridge, Massachusetts.

KAHN ALFRED E. [1966]: 'The Tyranny of Small Decisions: Market Failures, Imperfections, and the Limits of Economics', *Kyklos,* Vol. 19, 2, pp. 23–47.

MACDOUGALL DONALD [1977]: 'Economic Growth and Social Welfare', *Scottish Journal of Political Economy,* Vol. 24, November, pp. 193–206.

MISHAN E. J. [1977]: *The Economic Growth Debate: An Assessment,* Allan and Unwin, London.

NG YEW-KWANG [1972]: 'Value Judgments and Economists' Role in Policy Recommendation', *Economic Journal,* Vol. 82, September, pp. 1014–1018.

NG YEW-KWANG [1975]: 'Bentham or Bergson? Finite Sensibility, Utility Functions, and Social Welfare Functions', *Review of Economic Studies,* Vol. 42, October, pp. 545–570.

NG YEW-KWANG [1977]: 'Towards a Theory of Third Best', *Public Finance,* Vol. 32, pp. 1–15.

SCITOVSKY TIBOR [1976]: *The Joyless Economy,* Oxford University Press.

SPENCE M. [1973]: 'Job Market Signalling', *Quarterly Journal of Economics,* Vol. 87, pp. 355–374.

STIGLITZ JOSEPH E. [1975]: 'The Theory of 'Screening', Education, and the Distribution of Income', *American Economic Review,* Vol. 65, June, pp. 283–300.

WOLPIN KENNETH I. [1977]: 'Education and Screening', *American Economic Review,* Vol. 67, December, pp. 949–958.

SUMMARY

Does economic growth increase social welfare (happiness)? Answers to such questions can only be provided by a complete analysis of all the objective, subjective, and institutional effects. All measures originate from the subjective world, working through the institutional setting to affect the objective world, the institutional setting and/or the subjective world. Due to the increasing complexity of the modern society, it is likely that more problems are going to involve significant institutional and subjective effects, making a complete multidisciplinary study more necessary. As an introduction to this argument, the HARROD-HIRSCH concept of positional goods and its implications on the desirability of economic growth are analysed geometrically and extended. A simple method to reduce the difficulty of comparability in happiness surveys is also suggested.

C
Policy Implications

[5]

The Economic Journal, **107** (*November*), 1832–1847. © Royal Economic Society 1997. Published by Blackwell Publishers, 108 Cowley Road, Oxford OX4 1JF, UK and 350 Main Street, Malden, MA 02148, USA.

THE FRAME OF REFERENCE AS A PUBLIC GOOD*

Robert H. Frank

Does consuming more goods make people happier? For a broad spectrum of goods, available evidence suggests that beyond some point the answer is essentially no. Much of this evidence is from the large and growing scientific literature on the determinants of life-satisfaction and psychological well-being.[1] Evidence from this literature also suggests, however, that there are ways of spending time and money that do have the potential to increase people's satisfaction with their lives, and herein lies a message of considerable importance for policy-makers.

The psychologist's conception of human well-being is somewhat different from the economist's. Economists speak of an individual's utility, which in traditional economic models is assumed to be an increasing function of present and future consumption of goods, leisure, and other amenities that people typically view as desirable. Faced with a limited income, the individual is assumed to choose among alternatives so as to maximise her utility. The analogous construct in the psychological literature is 'subjective well-being', a composite measure of life satisfaction, positive affect, and negative affect.

Operational measures of subjective well-being take one of several forms. By far the most popular approach in the psychological literature has been simply to ask people how happy or satisfied they are.[2] For example, people may be asked to respond, on a numerical scale, to a question like, 'All things considered, how satisfied are you with your life as a whole these days?' Or, 'Thinking of your life as a whole, would you consider yourself (a) very happy; (b) fairly happy; or (c) not happy.' Another approach measures the frequency and intensity of positive affect by asking people the extent to which they agree with such statements as: 'When good things happen to me, it strongly affects me.'

More recently, neuroscientists have also used brainwave data to assess positive and negative affect. Subjects with relatively greater electrical activity in the left prefrontal region of the brain are likely to indicate strong agreement with statements like the ones above, while those with relatively greater electrical activity in the right prefrontal region are much more likely to disagree with these statements.[3] The left prefrontal region of the brain is rich in receptors for the neurotransmitter dopamine, higher concentrations of which been shown independently to be correlated with positive affect.[4]

---

* I thank Jeremy Chua, Rajib Das, Nadja Marinova, Rupal Patel, Lisa Shenouda, and Andrea Wasserman for their able research assistance.
[1] For an excellent and accessible survey of this literature, see Myers (1993).
[2] See Easterlin (1974).
[3] Davidson (1992).
[4] Reported by Goleman (1996).

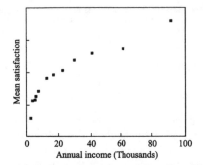

Fig. 1. Income *vs.* satisfaction in the United States, 1981–4. *Source*: Diener *et al.* (1993).

Satisfaction as identified by any of these measures is predictive of a variety of observable behaviours that most of us take to be indicative of well-being. For example, people who call themselves happy, or who have relatively high levels of electrical activity in the left prefrontal region, are more likely to be rated as happy by friends; more likely to initiate social contacts with friends; more likely to respond to requests for help; less likely to suffer from psychosomatic illnesses; less likely to be absent from work; less likely to be involved in disputes at work; less likely to die prematurely; less likely to attempt suicide; less likely to seek psychological counselling.[5] In short, it seems that what the psychologists call subjective well-being is a real phenomenon. Empirical measures of it have high consistency, reliability, and validity.[6] In what follows, it is not my claim that the only goal of a person or a society should be to achieve the highest possible levels of subjective wellbeing. (Would you prefer to be Socrates dissatisfied or a pig satisfied?) For the purposes of this discussion, I need assume only that an increase in subjective well-being counts as a good thing if it is achieved without having to compromise other important values.

My claim is that available evidence on the determinants of subjective well-being suggests a variety of ways this could be achieved. The basic idea is simple – namely, that, whereas across-the-board increases in many forms of material consumption goods have little discernible effect on subjective well-being in the long run, the same resources can be used in alternative ways that do give rise to lasting increases in subjective well-being.

THE DETERMINANTS OF SUBJECTIVE WELL-BEING

Richard Easterlin was the first to call economists' attention to survey data that illuminate the relationship between material living standards and subjective well-being.[7] Easterlin saw three significant patterns in the self-reported satisfaction data. First, he noted that satisfaction levels across individuals within a given country vary directly with income – richer people, on the average, are more satisfied than their poorer countrymen. This relationship is

[5] For surveys of this evidence see Frank (1985*b*, chapter 2) and Clark and Oswald (1996).
[6] Diener and Lucas (1997).
[7] Easterlin (1974).

© Royal Economic Society 1997

1834 THE ECONOMIC JOURNAL [NOVEMBER

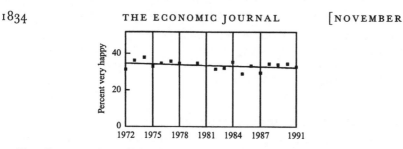

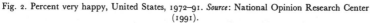

Fig. 2. Percent very happy, United States, 1972–91. *Source*: National Opinion Research Center (1991).

illustrated in Fig. 1, which plots average satisfaction against annual income for a US sample of 4,942 persons surveyed between 1981 and 1984.

Second, Easterlin noted that the average satisfaction levels within a given country tend to be highly stable over time, even in the face of significant economic growth. Fig. 2, for example, plots the percentage of Americans surveyed who respond 'very happy' when asked, 'Taken all together, how would you say things are these days – would you say that you are very happy, pretty happy, or not too happy?' Veenhoven (1993) found mean subjective well-being over time for Japan to be almost completely stable over the period 1958–87, a particularly striking result in view of the fact that *per-capita* income in that country grew more than fivefold during that period.

A third and final pattern noted by Easterlin is that although average reported satisfaction levels exhibit substantial variation across countries, they are not strongly correlated with average levels of national income. Easterlin argued that these patterns are consistent with the hypothesis that relative income is far more important than absolute income as a determinant of individual satisfaction levels. His pessimistic conclusion was that economic growth does not improve the human condition, since no matter how prosperous a society becomes in absolute terms, the frequency with which people experience relative deprivation will not be much affected.

Subsequent work has suggested the need to qualify Easterlin's claims in several ways. For example, most careful studies find a clear time-series relationship between subjective well-being and absolute income at extremely low levels of absolute income. Thus, in a country in which most people lack minimally adequate shelter and nutrition, across-the-board increases in income appear, not surprisingly, to yield significant and lasting improvements in subjective well-being.[8] In the same vein, it now appears that average satisfaction levels are in fact significantly lower in extremely poor countries than in rich ones.[9] Subsequent work has also shown that even within countries, the positive link between income and reported satisfaction is significant primarily at the lowest levels of relative income.[10] For individuals in the middle

[8] Diener and Diener (1995).
[9] *Ibid.*
[10] *Ibid.*

and upper portions of the income distribution within such countries, variations in income explain less than 2% of variations in reported satisfaction levels.[11] But it still does appear that average satisfaction levels within a country are not significantly correlated over time with income.

BEHAVIOURAL EVIDENCE FROM THE ECONOMICS LITERATURE

Unlike psychologists, who often rely on survey evidence, economists prefer behavioural evidence when attempting to make inferences about sources of human satisfaction. The relevant literature is not extensive, but there are several studies that shed light on the strength of concerns about relative consumption. In one recent paper, for example, Neumark and Postlewaite (1996) investigate how individual labour supply decisions depend on the incomes of important reference group members. The difficulty in such efforts has always been that it is hard to know which others a person includes in her reference group. Neumark and Postlewaite solve this problem by examining the behaviour of sisters. Does a woman's decision about whether to work outside the home depend on her sister's economic circumstances? In conventional models it would not, but Neumark and Postlewaite find differently for a sample of women whose sisters are not employed. Specifically, they find that sister A is 16–25% more likely to work outside the home if sister B's husband earns more than sister A's husband.[12]

Sheryl Ball and her co-authors have shown that even simple laboratory manipulations of status can have profound implications for the terms of market exchange.[13] In one experiment, for example, they awarded half of their subjects 'stars' on the basis of their performance on a transparently meaningless quiz. These subjects consistently received better terms when they exchanged goods with subjects who did not receive stars.

In *Choosing the Right Pond*, I described additional behavioural evidence consistent with the view that status concerns have significant weight in economic decisions. There I showed that the wage distributions within firms are typically much more compressed than we would expect if workers did not care about relative income.[14] Likewise, the incidence of piece-rate pay schemes is much lower, and the frequency with which workers go on strike is much higher, than we would expect if relative income did not matter. In addition, the observed structural differences between the compensation packages of unionised firms and non-unionised firms – for example, the fact that unionised workers tend to receive a much larger share of total compensation in the form of non-monetary fringe benefits – are difficult to explain without reference to collective action problems that arise from concerns about status.[15] The fact that the rich save significantly higher proportions of their permanent incomes than

---

[11] *Ibid.*
[12] Their Table 3.
[13] Ball *et al.* (1996).
[14] Frank (1985*b*, chapter 4). See also Frank (1984).
[15] Frank (1985*b*, chapter 8).

1836   THE ECONOMIC JOURNAL   [NOVEMBER

do the poor[16] is inconsistent with traditional economics models,[17] but this pattern is predicted by models in which utility depends on relative consumption.[18]

In a recent paper I have attempted to estimate the significance of occupational status in career choices using earnings and occupation data from a survey of recent graduates of Cornell University.[19] I found a strong negative correlation between annual earnings and the degree to which an employee's occupation was viewed by outsiders as being socially responsible. I found the same pattern by examining the fees paid to expert witnesses who testify on behalf of the tobacco industry and their counterparts who testify for the American Heart Association and other public interest groups; and the same pattern shows up in pay differences between public interest lawyers and those employed in other segments of the legal profession. I also described survey evidence from a sample of graduating seniors who reported that they would require very large premiums before being willing to switch to a less socially responsible employer.

In sum, the claim that satisfaction depends heavily on relative position is supported by considerable evidence from both the psychological literature on subjective well-being and by at least fragmentary evidence from the behavioural economics literature. I am aware of no empirical or theoretical evidence against this claim.

DOES *ANYTHING* MATTER?

Once people escape the physical deprivations associated with abject poverty, do absolute living standards matter at all? It is easy to see how Richard Easterlin could have interpreted patterns in the data on subjective well-being to suggest that they do not. After all, the struggle to get ahead seems to play out with much the same psychological effects in rich societies as in those with more modest levels of wealth. In each case, people who are doing well relative to others, or whose conditions are improving over time, appear more satisfied than those who are doing poorly relative to others or whose conditions are deteriorating over time.

Perhaps the clearest message of the psychological literature is that, beyond some point, across-the-board increases in spending on many types of material goods do not produce any lasting increment in subjective well-being. Imagine people from two societies that are identical in every respect save one: In society *A*, everyone lives in a house with 5,000 square feet of floor space, whereas in society *B* each house has only 3,000 square feet. Provided people from the two societies do not come into frequent contact with one another, psychologists and neuroscientists are unlikely to be able to discern any significant differences in their respective average levels of subjective well-being. Each society will have

[16] Dynan *et al.* (1996).
[17] In particular, it is inconsistent with the permanent income hypothesis (Friedman, 1957) and the life-cycle hypothesis (Modigliani and Brumberg, 1955).
[18] See Duesenberry (1949), Kosicki (1987).
[19] Frank (1996).

its own local norm for what constitutes adequate housing, and people in each society will therefore be equally likely to be satisfied with their houses and other aspects of their lives.

Of course, it takes more real resources to build 5,000 square-foot houses instead of 3,000 square-foot houses. Is there some alternative way of spending these resources that could have produced a lasting increment in subjective well-being? If the answer to this question is no, then policy-makers face an empty agenda. In fact, however, the scientific literature has identified a number of ways in which additional resources can be used to create large and enduring increases in subjective well-being.

Consider the following sequence of thought experiments in which we compare people from two societies with equal wealth levels but different spending patterns. In each case, let us again suppose that residents of one society live in 5,000 square-foot houses while those in the other live in 3,000 square-foot houses. And in each case, let us suppose that the residents of the society with the smaller houses use the resources thus saved to bring about some other change in the conditions of their lives. For example:

Who is more satisfied, residents of Society A, *who have 5,000-square-foot houses and a one-hour automobile commute to work through heavy traffic, or residents of Society* B, *who have 3,000-square foot houses and a 15-minute commute by rapid transit?* The only difference between these societies is that they have allocated their resources differently between housing and transportation. The residents of society *B* have used the same resources they could have employed to build larger housing to transform the nature of their commute to work. The evidence, as noted, suggests that their smaller houses predict no persistent difference in their subjective well-being. Of course, someone who moved from society *B* to society *A* would be pleased at first to experience the additional living space, but in time would adapt and consider the larger house the norm. Someone who moved from society *B* to society *A* would also initially experience stress from the extended commute through heavy traffic. Over time, his consciousness of this stress would diminish. But there is an important distinction: unlike his adaptation to the larger house, which will be essentially complete, his adaptation to his new commuting pattern will be only partial. Even after long periods of adjustment, most people experience the task of navigating through heavy commuter traffic as stressful. In this respect, the effect of exposure to heavy traffic is similar to the effect of exposure to noise and other irritants. For example, even though a large increase in background noise at a constant, steady level is experienced as less intrusive as time passes, prolonged exposure nonetheless produces lasting elevations in blood pressure. If the noise is not only loud but sporadic, people remain conscious of their heightened irritability even after extended periods of adaptation, and their symptoms of central nervous system distress become more pronounced. Commuting through heavy traffic is in many ways more like exposure to loud sporadic noise than to constant background noise. Delays are difficult to predict, and one never quite gets used to being cut off by others who think their time is more valuable than anyone else's.

Neurophysiologists would find higher levels of cortisol, norepinephrine, and other stress hormones in the cerebro-spinal fluid of residents of the society with the lengthy commute. The prolonged experience of such stress is also known to suppress immune function and shorten longevity.[20] Urban bus drivers, for example, experience an unusually high number of stress-related illnesses.[21] Among people who commute to work, the incidence of such illness rises with the length of commute,[22] and is significantly lower among those who commute by bus or rail.[23] No one has done the experiment to discover whether people from Society *A* would report lower levels of life satisfaction than people from Society *B*. But even in the absence of such survey evidence, we may suspect that most people would prefer to see their children live in society *B*.

Who is more satisfied, residents of Society A, *who have 5,000-square-foot houses and no time to exercise each day, or residents of Society* B, *who have 3,000-square-foot houses and exercise for 45 minutes each day?* Again we have two societies that have different bundles from the same menu of opportunities. Residents of society *B* could have built larger houses, but instead they spent less time at work each day and devoted the time saved to exercise. Numerous studies have documented the positive physiological and psychological effects of regular aerobic exercise.[24] Exercisers report more frequent and intense positive feelings and tend to have better functioning immune systems.[25] Exercisers have higher life expectancy and are less likely to suffer from heart disease, stroke, diabetes, hypertension, and a variety of other ailments.[26] Evidence for the causal nature of these relationships is seen in the fact that subjects randomly assigned to exercise programmes experience improved physical and psychological well-being.[27] And although many people report that exercise is an unpleasant experience at first, most adapt to it quickly and come to think of it as pleasurable. Here again, the evidence weighs heavily in favour of the residents of society *B*.

Who is more satisfied, residents of society A, *who have 5,000-square-foot houses and one evening each month to get together with friends, or residents of Society* B, *who have 3,000-square-foot houses and get together with friends four evenings a month?* The question is again whether one use of time produces a larger impact on subjective well-being than another. Because the residents of society *A* work longer hours, they can build larger houses but have less time to socialise with friends. Here again, the evidence suggests that whereas the payoff when all have larger houses is small and fleeting, the pleasures that result from deeper social relationships are both profound and enduring. People with rich networks of active social relationships are much more likely to call themselves happy, and are much more likely to be described as happy by friends.[28] People who lack such

---

[20] DeLongis *et al.* (1988) and Stokols *et al.* (1978).
[21] Evans (1994).
[22] Koslowsky *et al.* (1995).
[23] Taylor and Pocock (1972).
[24] For a survey, see Plante and Rodin (1990).
[25] Fontane (1996).
[26] Blair (1989).
[27] Palmer (1995).
[28] Argyle (1997).

networks tend to be less physically healthy, and confront a higher risk of dying at every age.[29] In this case, too, the neurophysiologists would have no difficulty discerning which people came from society *B*.

IF SPENDING DIFFERENTLY WOULD MAKE US HAPPIER, WHY DON'T WE DO IT?

There are at least two plausible explanations for our failure to allocate available resources in the best possible way. Our spending patterns are in part a result of incomplete information about the extent to which we will adapt to different goods and experiences; and in part they are a result of the fact that many forms of consumption appear much more attractive to individuals than they are to society as a whole. On the first point, consider a person whose wage is such that he could purchase a 30% more expensive car by working an additional Saturday each month, which in his case would mean not spending that Saturday with friends. Standard economic theory suggests that he will work the extra Saturday if the satisfaction afforded by the nicer car outweighs the satisfaction provided by the company of his friends. Since the individual will typically not know how each alternative will alter his subjective well-being, he is forced to construct rough estimates.

Introspection may provide reasonably good estimates of how changes in consumption will affect subjective well-being in the short run. But because adaptation is inherently difficult to anticipate, the long-run effects of such changes will be harder to forecast. In the choice at hand, this may create a strong bias in favour of choosing the more expensive car over the extra day with friends. Thus, if the new car is substantially faster than the individual's current car, its acquisition will provide an initial thrill. Over time, however, he will grow accustomed to the car's capabilities and its capacity to stimulate will decay.

The contribution to subjective well-being of additional time spent with friends will have a markedly different time profile. As relationships continue over time, the satisfaction they provide tends to increase rather than diminish. In the long run, extra time spent with friends might well prove the better choice. Yet the short-run increment in satisfaction might easily be higher with the new car. And to the extent that these short-run effects are the most available source of information to the individual at the moment of decision, they bias choice in favour of the nicer car.

A second, more important, source of bias in our spending patterns would exist even in a world of fully informed consumers. It stems from the fact that when payoffs depend on relative position, the individual payoff from many types of spending is different from the collective payoff. Military arms races provide perhaps the clearest illustration. From each individual nation's point of view, the worst outcome is not to buy armaments while its rivals do. Yet when *all* spend more on weapons, no one is more secure than before. Most

---

[29] Berkman and Syme (1979), House *et al*. (1982).

nations recognise the importance of maintaining military parity, and the result all too often has been a wasteful escalation of expenditures on arms. Nations would spend much less on weapons if they could make their military spending decisions collectively. And with the money thus saved, each side could then spend more on things that promote, rather than threaten, human well-being.

Similar forces affect each family's decision about how much to save. Parents want to save for retirement, but they also have other important goals. For instance, they want to make sure that their children receive an education that qualifies them for the best jobs. For the typical American family, that means buying a home in the best school district it can afford. Most of us thus confront an almost irresistible opportunity to do more for our children: By saving a little less for retirement, we can purchase homes in better school districts.

From the collective vantage point, however, such moves are futile in the same way that military arms races are futile. When each family saves less in order to buy a house in a better school district, the net effect is merely to bid up the prices of those houses. Students end up at the same schools they would have attended if all families had spent less. In the process, an important goal – being able to maintain an adequate living standard in retirement – is sacrificed for essentially no gain. Yet no family, acting alone, can solve this problem, just as no nation can unilaterally stop a military arms race.

Housing is of course not the only expenditure that is driven by forces similar to those that govern military arms races. Spending on cars fits the same pattern, as does spending on clothing, furniture, wine, jewelry, sports equipment, and a host of other goods. The things we feel we 'need' depend on the kinds of things that others have, and our needs thus grow when we find ourselves in the presence of others who have more than we do. Yet when all of us spend more, the new, higher spending level simply becomes the norm.

There is yet another difficulty, one that is independent of the mechanics of the human psychological reward system. It lies in the fact that promotion decisions on the job often depend heavily on the relative number of hours someone works. Thus, an associate in a law firm who goes home at 5 p.m. each day instead of 8 p.m. not only earns less in relative terms, she is also less likely to be promoted to partner. If all the associates left the office a little earlier, of course, no one's promotion prospects would be affected. But each individual has control over only the hours that she herself works. She cannot unilaterally decree that everyone scale back. Landers *et al.* (1996) report that associates in large law firms voice a strong preference for having all work fewer hours, even if that means lower pay, and yet few dare take that step unilaterally.

To the extent that misallocations result from our failure to anticipate different patterns of adaptation in different domains, there is the possibility for unilateral action to improve matters. By becoming better informed and more disciplined, we can make decisions that will better promote our long-term interests. The brisk sales of books urging the adoption of simplified styles of living suggest that many people are at least receptive to this possibility.

To the extent, however, that misallocations are the result of the fact that certain forms of consumption are more attractive to individuals than to society as a whole, the potential for improvement through unilateral action may be sharply limited. Thus, as we have seen, the problem confronting individuals who must decide how to spend their time and money is in many ways like the one confronting nations that must decide how much to spend on armaments. Just as nations end up spending too much on weapons and too little on other things, ordinary people end up spending too much time earning money to buy private goods, and too little time doing other things.

When nations attempt to curtail military arms races, they try to negotiate agreements that specify precisely what kinds and quantities of weapons are permissible. The idea of private citizens conducting similar negotiations about how to allocate their time and money seems wildly impractical. Fortunately, however, the underlying problem can be attacked without trying to micro-manage people's spending decisions at all.

ONE SOLUTION: A PROGRESSIVE CONSUMPTION TAX

If our problem is that certain forms of private consumption currently seem more attractive to individuals than to society as a whole, the simplest solution is to make those forms less attractive by taxing them. Without raising our overall tax bill at all, a progressive consumption tax would change our incentives in precisely the desired ways.

Proposals to tax consumption raise the spectre of forbidding complexity – of citizens having to same receipts for each purchase, of politicians and producers bickering over which products are to be exempt, and so on. Yet a system of progressive consumption taxation could be achieved by a simple one-line amendment to the federal tax code – namely, by making savings exempt from tax. This is so because the amount a family consumes each year is simply the difference between the amount it earns and the amount it saves. Administratively, a progressive consumption tax is thus essentially the same as our current progressive income tax. An example is provided in the appendix.

The progressive consumption tax illustrated in the appendix is different from other consumption taxes like the value added tax or the national sales tax. Those taxes are levied at the same rate no matter how much a family consumes, and have therefore been criticised as regressive on the grounds that wealthy families typically same much higher proportions of their incomes than poor families. But the consumption tax proposed is not a regressive tax. Its escalating marginal tax rates on consumption, coupled with its large standard deduction, assure that total tax as a proportion of income rises steadily with income, even though the assumed savings rate is sharply higher for high-income families.

Consumption taxation has been proposed before.[30] Its proponents have stressed that it will encourage savings, and hence stimulate economic growth. This is indeed an important benefit – more important, by far, than even the proponents of consumption taxation have realised. Yet the most significant gains from progressive consumption taxation lie elsewhere. Properly designed

---

[30] See Hall and Rabushka (1995) for a discussion of the so-called flat tax, a form of consumption tax. The flat tax, value-added tax and national sales tax are discussed extensively in Aaron and Gale (1996).

and implemented, such a tax can eliminate trillions of dollars of waste from the American economy.

The key to understanding how this would work is the observation that when the price of a good rises, we buy less of it. It follows that if consumption were taxed at a progressive rate, we would save more, buy less expensive houses and cars, and feel less pressure to work excessively long hours. And this, on the best available evidence, would improve the quality of our lives.

It might seem natural to worry that a tax that limits consumption might lead to recession and unemployment. This is not a serious concern, however, because money that is not spent on consumption is saved and invested. The result is that some of the people who are now employed to produce consumption goods will instead be employed to produce capital goods – which, in the long run, increase the economy's productive capacity. The government knows how to stimulate the economy when recession threatens. Indeed, a central problem of recent decades has been to contain the inflationary pressures that result when demand grows more rapidly than the economy's capacity to produce goods and services. By stimulating savings and investment, the progressive consumption tax will increase the rate at which the economy's productive capacity grows, and thus reduce the threat of inflation.

The extraordinary beauty of the progressive consumption tax is its ability to generate extra resources almost literally out of thin air. It is a win-win move, even for the people on whom the tax falls most heavily. Transition problems could be minimised by phasing the programme in gradually – with phased increases in the amount of savings a family could exempt and phased increases in the highest marginal tax rates.

EFFECTS ON SAVINGS AND GROWTH

The case for the progressive consumption tax is strong even if we ignore its effects on growth in our national income. But once we take these effects into account, it becomes compelling. Proponents of consumption taxation have long stressed that it will increase savings, and they are right. These same proponents go on to predict that the increase will be small, and that the resulting increase in growth and well-being, though steady, will be small as well.[31] The latter predictions, however, are significantly off the mark.

Switching to a consumption tax from an income tax would affect savings through several channels. Past advocates of consumption taxation have focused on two. First, the tax would put more resources in the hands of those whose savings rates were highest to begin with. (The less someone consumes, the less tax she pays, and hence the more she is able to save.) And second, a consumption tax would increase the monetary reward for saving. But, as past advocates of consumption taxes have realised, both effects are relatively small.[32]

Where past predictions have gone awry is in having ignored the effect of

[31] See Auerbach and Slemrod (1996), Hubbard and Skinner (1996), Poterba *et al.* (1996) and Slemrod (1990).
[32] See especially Engen *et al.* (1996).

community consumption standards on savings rates. This is by far the most important channel through which a progressive consumption tax would stimulate savings. Even though the direct effect of the tax might be to reduce our consumption only slightly, this would initiate a self-reinforcing sequence of indirect effects. Thus, when others consume less, the amount that we consume would decline still further, and our responses would then influence others, and so on. Once these multiplier effects are taken into account, the effect on savings rates turns out to be substantial.

Higher savings rates, in turn, are the surest path to more rapid economic growth. Some might wonder whether achieving higher growth rates would be such a good thing in the end since, after all, people do tend to adjust quickly to changes in material living standards. One might also worry that more consumption means more garbage and more greenhouse gases. On the first point, the evidence suggests that although we adjust rather quickly to any stable standard of living, we seem to derive continuing satisfaction from an ongoing increase in our standard of living.[33] The faster the economy is growing, the more satisfied people seem to be. Opportunities are greater in a rich society than in a poor one. The former Soviet Union generated more pollution than any nation on earth not because of its high rate of economic growth, but because its productivity lagged so far behind that of its rivals. A richer society has more resources for medical research, more resources for rapid transit, more time for family and friends, more time for study and exercise – and more resources for better insulated houses and cleaner, more fuel-efficient cars.

ARE POSITIONAL EXTERNALITIES A LEGITIMATE CONCERN OF TAX POLICY?

Most economists accept the proposition that market allocations may be suboptimal when production is accompanied by the discharge of environmental pollutants. Most tend also to be enthusiastic in their embrace of effluent taxes as a solution to the problem of environmental pollution. The dependence of utility on relative consumption gives rise to what I have elsewhere called positional externalities.[34] Analytically, these externalities are no different from ordinary environmental pollutants. My proposal to tax consumption is thus precisely analogous to an effluent tax.[35] Most economists accept the existence of positional externalities as a purely descriptive matter.[36] Yet many of these same economists may question whether such externalities are proper targets for public policy intervention. On the face of it, this is a curious position for the

---

[33] See Shin (1980) and Frank and Hutchens (1993).

[34] Frank (1992).

[35] Many others have suggested taxes to mitigate the externalities that arise from the dependence of utility on relative income or relative consumption. See, for example, Bagwell and Bernheim (1996), Boskin and Sheshinski (1978), Layard (1980), Ng (1987), Oswald (1983) Kosicki (1987), Ireland (1994, 1997).

[36] There is indeed an extensive literature in which economists have discussed the dependence of satisfaction on relative living standards. In addition to the authors previously cited, see Kapteyn and van Herwaarden (1980), van Praag (1993), Easterlin (1974, 1996), Sen (1983, 1987), Hirsch (1976) and Scitovsky (1976).

profession that has always insisted that 'a taste for poetry is no better than a taste for pushpins'.

Of course, it is one thing to say that a person's tastes are her own business, and quite another to say that A's discomfort from B's consumption constitutes grounds for restricting B's consumption. As parents most of us try to teach our children not to worry about what others consume, and perhaps this is the best posture for the state to assume as well. And yet many forms of consumption cause not only injured feelings in others but also more tangible economic losses.[37] The job seeker gains a leg up on his rivals, for example, by showing up for his interview in a custom-tailored suit. The best response for others may be to show up in custom-tailored suits as well. Yet all job seekers might prefer the alternative in which all spent less on their professional wardrobes. Likewise when A sends his child to an expensive private school, he may not intend to reduce the likelihood that the children of others will be accepted to top universities, but that is a consequence of his action nevertheless, and it may be the best response of others to follow suit. And yet all might find that outcome less attractive than when all send their children to the public schools.

To acknowledge that our utility from consumption depends on context is simply to note an obvious fact of the human condition. Because each individual's consumption affects the frame of reference within which others evaluate their own consumption, this frame of reference becomes, in effect, a public good. The uncoordinated consumption decisions of individuals are not more likely to result in the optimal level of this public good than the uncoordinated actions of individuals are likely to result in an optimal level of military preparedness. The progressive consumption tax is a simple policy measure that can help mould the frame of reference in mutually beneficial ways.

But not even a steeply progressive consumption tax can fully neutralise the externalities that arise from competition for spots atop various local hierarchies. At best, it can reduce some of their costs. Even with such a tax, it will still prove useful to ameliorate consumption externalities through a variety of less formal means – adoption of social norms, choice of personal reference groups, introspection, and so on. As policy interventions go, a consumption tax is not especially intrusive. After all, we have to tax something anyway. And available evidence suggests that across-the-board consumption reductions will not entail significant utility losses for middle- and upper-income citizens, the only people who might experience a heavier tax burden under a progressive consumption tax.

CASH ON THE TABLE

'Cash on the table' is the familiar economist's metaphor for situations in which people seem to be passing up opportunities for gain. Each year, Americans leave literally trillions of dollars on the table as a result of wasteful consumption arms races. This waste can be curbed by a disarmingly simple policy change – in

---

[37] Sen (1987) emphasises this point.

essence, a one-line amendment that exempts savings from the federal income tax. Adoption of a progressive consumption tax would greatly enhance every citizen's opportunity to pursue his or her vision of the good life.

The only intelligible reason for having stuck with our current tax system for so long is that we have not understood clearly how much better the alternative would be. But we now have all the evidence we could reasonably demand on this point. In the face of this evidence, the progressive consumption tax emerges as by far the most exciting economic opportunity of the modern era.

Cornell University

REFERENCES

Aaron, Henry J. and Gale, William G. (1996). *Economic Effects of Fundamental Tax Reform.* Washington, DC: Brookings Institution.

Argyle, Michael (1997). 'Causes and correlates of happiness.' In *Understanding Well-Being: Scientific Perspectives on Enjoyment and Suffering,* (ed. Daniel Kahneman, Ed Diener and Norbert Schwartz) New York: Russell Sage.

Auerbach, Alan and Slemrod, Joel (1997). 'The economic effects of the tax reform act of 1987.' *Journal of Economic Perspectives,* forthcoming.

Bagwell, Laurie Simon and Bernheim, B. Douglas. (1996). 'Veblen effects in a theory of conspicuous consumption.' *American Economic Review,* vol. 86, (June), pp. 349–73.

Ball, Sheryl, Eckel, Catherine, Grossman Philip and Zame, William (1996). 'Status in markets.' Department of Economics Working Paper, Virginia Polytechnic Institute, (January).

Berkman, L. F. and Syme, S. L. (1979). 'Social networks, host resistance, and mortality: a nine-year followup of Alameda county residents.' *American Journal of Epidemiology,* vol. 109, pp. 186–204.

Blair, S. N. (1989). 'Physical fitness and all-cause mortality: a prospective study of healthy men and women.' *Journal of the American Medical Association,* vol. 262, pp. 2396–401.

Boskin, Michael and Sheshinski, E. (1978). 'Optimal redistributive taxation when individual welfare depends on relative income.' *Quarterly Journal of Economics,* vol. 92, pp. 589–601.

Clark, Andrew and Oswald, Andrew (1996). 'Satisfaction and comparison income.' *Journal of Public Economics,* vol. 61, pp. 359–81.

Davidson, Richard J. (1992). 'Emotion and affective style: hemispheric substrates.' *Psychological Science,* vol. 3, pp. 39–43.

DeLongis, Anita, Folkman, Susan and Lazarus, Richard S. (1988). 'The impact of daily stress on health and mood: psychological and social resources as mediators.' *Journal of Personality and Social Psychology,* vol. 54, pp. 486–95.

Diener, Ed and Diener, Carol (1995). 'The wealth of nations revisited: income and the quality of life.' *Social Indicators Research,* vol. 36, pp. 275–86.

Diener, Ed and Lucas, Richard E. (1997). 'Personality and subjective well-being.' In *Understanding Well-Being: Scientific Perspectives on Enjoyment and Suffering* (ed. Daniel Kahneman, Ed Diener and Norbert Schwartz), New York: Russell Sage.

Diener, Ed, Sandvik, Ed, Seidlitz, Larry and Diener, Marissa (1993). 'The relationship between income and subjective well-being: relative or absolute?' *Social Indicators Research,* vol. 28, pp. 195–223.

Duesenberry, James (1949). *Income, Saving, and the Theory of Consumer Behavior.* Cambridge, Mass.: Harvard University Press.

Dynan, Karen E., Skinner, Jonathan and Zeldes, Stephen P. (1996). 'Do the rich save more?' Federal Reserve Board mimeo (November).

Easterlin, Richard (1974). 'Does economic growth improve the human lot?' In *Nations and Households in Economic Growth: Essays in Honor of Moses Abramovitz* (ed. Paul David and Melvin Reder), New York: Academic Press.

Easterlin, Richard (1995). 'Will raising the incomes of all increase the happiness of all?' *Journal of Economic Behavior and Organization,* vol. 27, pp. 35–47.

Engen, Eric, Gale, William and Scholz, John Karl (1996). 'The illusory effects of saving incentives on savings.' *Journal of Economic Perspectives,* vol. 10, pp. 113–38.

Evans, Gary W. (1994), 'Working on the hot seat: urban bus drivers.' *Accident Analysis and Prevention,* vol. 26, pp. 181–93.

Fontane, Patrick E. (1996). 'Exercise, fitness, and feeling well.' *American Behavioral Scientist,* vol. 39, January, pp. 288–305.

Frank, Robert H. (1984). 'Are workers paid their marginal products?' *American Economic Review,* vol. 74, September, pp. 549–71.

Frank, Robert H. (1985*a*). 'The demand for unobservable and other nonpositional goods.' *American Economic Review*, vol. 75, March, pp. 101–16.

Frank, Robert H. (1985*b*). *Choosing the Right Pond*. New York: Oxford University Press.

Frank, Robert H. (1991). 'Positional externalities.' In *Strategy and Choice: Essays in Honor of Thomas C. Schelling* (ed. Richard Zeckhauser), pp. 25–47. Cambridge, MA: MIT Press.

Frank, Robert H. (1996). 'What price the moral high ground?' *Southern Economic Journal*, vol. ?, July, pp. 1–17.

Frank, Robert H. and Hutchens, Robert (1993). 'Wages, seniority, and the demand for rising consumption profiles.' *Journal of Economic Behavior and Organization*, vol. 21, pp. 251–76.

Friedman, Milton (1957). *A Theory of the Consumption Function*. Princeton, NJ: Princeton University Press.

Goleman, Daniel (1996). 'Forget money; nothing can buy happiness, some researchers say.' *New York Times*, 16 July, pp. C1, C3.

Hall, Robert E. and Rabushka, Alvin (1995). *The Flat Tax*, 2nd Ed., Stanford, CA: The Hoover Institution Press.

Hirsch, Fred (1976). *Social Limits to Growth*. Cambridge, MA: Harvard University Press.

House, James S., Robbins, C. and Metzner, H. M. (1982). 'The association of social relationships and activities with mortality: prospective evidence from the Tecumsah community health study.' *American Journal of Epidemiology*, vol. 116, pp. 123–40.

Hubbard, R. Glenn, and Skinner, Jonathan (1996). 'Assessing the effectiveness of savings incentives.' *Journal of Economic Perspectives*, vol. 10, pp. 73–90.

Ireland, Norman (1994). 'On limiting the market for status signals.' *Journal of Public Economics*, vol. 53, pp. 91–110.

Ireland, Norman (1997). 'Status-seeking, income taxation and efficiency.' *Journal of Public Economics* (forthcoming).

Kapteyn, Arie and van Herwaarden, F. G. (1980). 'Interdependent welfare functions and optimal income distribution.' *Journal of Public Economics*, vol. 14, pp. 375–97.

Kosicki, George (1987). 'Savings as a nonpositional good.' *Southern Economic Journal*, vol. 54, October, pp. 422–34.

Koslowsky, Meni, Kluger, Avraham N. and Reich, Mordechai (1995). *Commuting Stress*. New York: Plenum.

Landers, Renee M., Rebitzer, James B. and Taylor, Lowell J. (1996). 'Rate race redux: adverse selection in the determination of work hours in law firms.' *American Economic Review*, vol. 86, June, pp. 329–48.

Layard, Richard (1980). 'Human satisfactions and public policy.' ECONOMIC JOURNAL, vol. 90, pp. 737–50.

Modigliani, Franco and Brumberg, R. (1955). 'Utility analysis and the consumption function: an interpretation of cross-section data.' In *Post-Keynesian Economics* (ed. K. Kurihara). London: Allen and Unwin.

Myers, David G. (1993). *The Pursuit of Happiness: Who is Happy and Why?* New York: Avon.

National Opinion Research Center (1991).

Neumark, David and Postlewaite, Andrew (1996). 'Relative income concerns and the rise in married women's employment,' University of Pennsylvania Department of Economics mimeo.

Ng, Yew-Kwang (1987). 'Diamonds are a government's best friend: burden-free taxes on goods valued for their values.' *American Economic Review*, vol. 77, pp. 186–91.

Oswald, Andrew J. (1983). 'Altruism, jealousy, and the theory of optimal nonlinear income taxation.' *Journal of Public Economics*, vol. 20, pp. 77–87.

Oswald, Andrew J. (1996). 'Happiness and economic performance.' University of Warwick Department of Economics Mimeo (September).

Palmer, Linda K. (1995). 'Effects of a walking program on attributional style, depression, and self-esteem in women.' *Perceptual and Motor Skills*, vol. 81, pp. 891–8.

Plante, Thomas G. and Rodin, Judith (1990). 'Physical fitness and enhanced psychological health.' *Current Psychology: Research and Reviews*, vol. 9, Spring, pp. 3–24.

Poterba, James, Venti, Steven and Wise, David (1996). 'How retirement saving programs increase savings.' *Journal of Economic Perspectives*, vol. 10, Fall, pp. 91–112.

Scitovsky, Tibor (1976). *The Joyless Economy*. New York: Oxford University Press.

Sen, Amartya (1983). 'Poor, relatively speaking.' *Oxford Economics Papers*, vol. 35, July, pp. 153–67.

Sen, Amartya (1987). *The Standard of Living*. Cambridge: Cambridge University Press.

Shin, D. C. (1980). 'Does rapid economic growth improve the human lot?' *Social Indicators Research*, vol. 8, pp. 199–221.

Slemrod, Joel (1990). 'The economic impact of the tax reform act of 1986.' In *Do Taxes Matter? The Impact of the Tax Reform Act of 1986* (ed. Joel Slemrod), pp. 1–12. Cambridge, MA: MIT Press.

Stokols, Daniel, Novaco, Raymond W., Stokols Jeannette and Campbell, Joan (1978). 'Traffic congestion, type A behavior, and stress.' *Journal of Applied Psychology*, vol. 63, pp. 467–80.

Taylor, P. and Pocock, C. (1972). 'Commuter travel and sickness: absence of London office workers.' *British Journal of Preventive and Social Medicine*, vol. 26, pp. 165–72.

van Praag, Bernard, M. S. (1993). 'The relativity of the welfare concept.' In *The Quality of Life* (ed. Martha Nussbaum and Amartya Sen), Oxford: Clarendon, pp. 363–92.
Veenhoven, Ruut (1993). *Happiness in Nations: Subjective Appreciation of Life in 56 Nations.* Rotterdam: Erasmus University.

APPENDIX

The progressive Consumption Tax: An Example

The following example illustrates how a progressive consumption would work for a family of four if the standard deduction were $7,500 per person. With a total standard deduction of $30,000 per year, the family's taxable consumption would be calculated as its income minus $30,000 minus its savings minus its tax. A family whose income was no more than $30,000 plus the amount it saved would thus owe no tax at all under this plan. Suppose the tax rate on families with positive taxable consumption began at 20 % and then gradually escalated as taxable consumption increased, as shown in Table A1.

Table A1
Tax Rates on Taxable Consumption

Taxable consumption($)	Marginal tax rate (%)
0–39,999	20
40,000–49,999	22
50,000–59,999	24
60,000–69,999	26
70,000–79,999	28
80,000–89,999	30
90,000–99,999	32
100,000–129,999	34
130,000–159,999	38
160,000–189,999	42
190,000–219,999	46
220,000–249,999	50

Given this rate schedule, Table A2 shows how much tax families with different income and savings levels would pay.

Table A2
Illustrative Income, Savings, and Tax Values Under a Progressive Consumption Tax ($)

Income	Savings	Taxable consumption	Tax
30,000	1500	0	0
50,000	3000	14,167	2833
100,000	10,000	49,844	10,156
150,000	20,000	81,538	18,462
200,000	40,000	104,265	23,735
500,000	120,000	257,800	92,200
1,000,000	300,000	471,000	199,000

[6]

The Economic Journal, **90** (*December* 1980), 737–750
Printed in Great Britain

HUMAN SATISFACTIONS AND PUBLIC POLICY*

There is much casual evidence that people in the West are not becoming happier, despite economic growth. There is also some systematic evidence.[1] Opinion polls reveal no increase in self-rated happiness in the United States since the War. And, more slippery evidence this, rich countries appear to be no happier than poorer ones – at any rate among the advanced countries.[2] But if growth has not brought happiness, the important question is what policy conclusions follow.

That depends, of course, on why growth has not produced the answer. Why, one might ask, do people seek to be rich if riches do not bring happiness? The answer is that riches do bring happiness, provided you are richer than other people. Thus a basic finding of happiness surveys is that, though richer societies are not happier than poorer ones, within any society happiness and riches go together.[3] I shall therefore assume as my *first* basic proposition that happiness depends, inter alia, on position in some *status ranking*. This explains for example why people are often quite willing to make sacrifices if they are sure everybody else is going to do the same.[4]

However, other factors may also be at work. An obvious problem with high income is that you get used to it, take it for granted and cannot do without it. The same is true of status. So I shall take as my *second* basic fact that happiness also depends on income and status relative to what you *expected* it to be. This explains why people fight much harder against cuts in their income than they fight for increases. It also explains the havoc caused by inflation, which continually reorders people in the status ranking.

Our two psychological facts are well supported by the research on relative deprivation (Runciman, 1966)[5] and must help to explain why happiness has not increased with growth. However, from now on I am simply concerned with the policy implications of these facts, which are only now beginning to become clear.[6] The first fact is particularly relevant to the efficiency branch of government and is discussed in Section I of this paper; and the second is

* I am grateful to D. de Meza, H. Gintis, D. Grubb, J. Margolis, J. Mirrlees, P. Mueser, S. Nickell, M. Reder, S. Streiter and P. Wiles for helpful comments.

[1] For general discussions see Scitovsky (1976), Hirsch (1977), Mishan (1977) and Akerlof (1976). For specific evidence see Easterlin (1972), who cites U.S. time series and provides cross-country comparisons, and Duncan (1975), who reports a time-series for Detroit wives.

[2] The evidence is slippery because the word 'happy' cannot easily be translated and because cultures may differ in their honesty about these questions. Within the United States richer states are not self-reported as happier than poorer ones, but migration between states could be expected to equalise real income anyway.

[3] Easterlin (1972), Duncan (1975), and National Opinion Research Centre surveys.

[4] Keynes had this in mind when he said that real wages could more easily fall through a price rise than through wage cuts, which are likely to affect different people differently. On the role of envy see Schoeck (1966).

[5] The book is an invaluable source on the positive study of relative deprivation, but the concept is surprisingly little used in the normative part of the book.

[6] See in particular Hirsch (1977). Scitovsky (1976) also discusses the facts in an illuminating way but without pursuing the policy implications.

738   THE ECONOMIC JOURNAL   [DECEMBER

particularly relevant to equity questions, and is discussed in Section II. The conclusions are summarised at the end.

I. THE PURSUIT OF STATUS

If status is defined by rank order, the pursuit of status is a zero-sum game – one man's gain in rank is another man's loss. It is not quite the same as Hirsch's example of the situation where everyone stands on tiptoe to see better, and all end up seeing the same but straining to keep on tiptoe. For the status game can lead to changes of view (i.e. of rank order). There might sometimes be an equity case for wanting some of these changes. But, if not, a major task of public policy is to counteract the effects of the desire for status upon human behaviour.[1] For, though individuals are willing to make sacrifices to improve their individual position, the net result of status-motivated action will be no increase in status satisfaction but an increase in sacrifice. So how can the government offset the individual drive for status? As usual, there are three methods – fiscal, institutional and moral.

Taxation

If it could identify the actions that improve status, the government could tax them. For example, if income confers status, it can and should be taxed on efficiency grounds. Thus it may be that the income tax is a lot less inefficient than is sometimes supposed.[2]

The matter is not easy to investigate. The simplest approach is to assume that status depends on income relative to the mean. If in addition we begin with the extreme assumption that net income (y) is not valued for its own sake at all, then

$$u^i = u\left(\frac{y_i}{\bar{y}}, h_i\right) \tag{1}$$

where h_i is work effort. In order to concentrate on efficiency issues, let us assume that all men have the same wage rate. In this case the optimal tax rate is unity.[3]

---

[1] I am ignoring problems of administrative cost, which may be quite severe, especially allowing for the costs of information.

[2] This point was well made by Duesenberry (1949, chapter 6), but lost sight of as alternative theories of consumption developed.

[3] (i) Since $y_i/\bar{y}$ cannot be altered, the social optimum requires h_i be chosen so that $\partial u/\partial h_i = 0$. If w is the gross hourly wage and we tax income at a marginal rate t, the private optimum will be where

$$\frac{\partial u}{\partial(y_i/\bar{y})} \frac{w(1-t)}{\bar{y}} + \frac{\partial u}{\partial h_i} = 0.$$

So we require $t = 1$.

(ii) If $\bar{y}$ includes foreign incomes, the optimal tax would be less than unity, assuming the domestic government does not care about negative externalities affecting foreigners. Provided foreign income is not too large relative to domestic income, an increase in foreign income will increase the socially optimal amount of work in the home country, and thus decrease the optimum tax rate. To see this, suppose for simplicity that $w = 1$ and $u = u[h/(\bar{h}+x), h]$, where x represents foreign income times the weight it assumes in the function. For society $h = \bar{h}$. Now suppose x rises from zero by a small amount. We are worse off and there is a positive return to work which was not there before. If leisure is a normal good we should work more. However, as x rises, the time price of relative income will

However, this assumes that people do not value income at all for its own sake. This does not seem reasonable. All over the world there is net migration towards richer areas. This does not prove that additional income actually makes people happier. For people may move due to misinformation – they may not realise it is the status which income confers rather than its intrinsic worth which leads them to want it. However, many migrants do not return. Here again one could argue that a person who has migrated would be involved in money cost and loss of face if he returned and is not therefore necessarily better off after moving than he would have been had he never moved in the first place. But for the sake of generality I shall from now on assume that income is partly valued for its own sake.[1]

To allow for this we could assume that

$$u^i = u(y_i, \bar{y}, h_i).\tag{2}$$

We now represent the status problem by the negative effect of the average income level upon individual utility ($\partial u / \partial \bar{y} < 0$). In this case the additional tax paid by an individual who does an extra hour of work (wt) should equal the money value of the harm done to others.[2]

$$wt \simeq -n\frac{\partial u}{\partial \bar{y}}\left(\frac{w}{n}\middle/ \frac{\partial u}{\partial y_i}\right),$$

where w is the gross hourly wage and n is population. In other words, the optimum marginal tax rate equals approximately the ratio of the marginal disutility of average income ($\bar{y}$) to the marginal utility of individual income (y_i).

This formulation may begin to catch some elements of the tax problem. But it is probably not very realistic. For the evidence is that people are mainly bothered about the incomes of people close to them in the income distribution and do not suffer greatly from the riches of the rich (or of the poor), unless they happen to be nearly rich (or poor) themselves (Runciman, 1966). Thus

---

eventually rise, and the effect of further rises of x upon optimal hours of work will become ambiguous. If, by contrast, $u = u[(h-x)/h, h]$ the time price of relative income falls continuously, and higher foreign income always implies higher optimal hours of work.

(iii) David Grubb has suggested to me that a better model would have $u^i = u(y_i/\bar{y}, h_i/\bar{h})$, i.e. effort has as much of a social dimension as the income earned. But I doubt whether most peasants would not feel better off if they all worked less for the same income.

[1] If growth has not increased happiness, this must therefore be due to some other offsetting losses.

[2] The social optimum requires h_i be chosen so that

$$\frac{\partial u}{\partial y_i}w + n\frac{\partial u}{\partial \bar{y}}\frac{w}{n} + \frac{\partial u}{\partial h_i} = 0.$$

The private optimum will be where

$$\frac{\partial u}{\partial y_i}w(1-t) + \frac{\partial u}{\partial h_i} \simeq 0, \quad \text{since} \quad \frac{\partial u}{\partial \bar{y}}\frac{w}{n} \quad \text{is small.}$$

Boskin and Sheshinski (1978) pursue much more fully the implications of a utility function like (2) in the context of an optimal income tax model in which wages differ between people. They show how the optimum tax rate rises as the weight attaching to y rises. I became aware of their paper only after writing this one, but as the next paragraph explains, I do not consider this approach fully adequate.

one cannot really assume that status is determined by a person's income relative to mean income. Instead it is more realistic to revert to our basic initial concept that what matters is a person's percentile rank-order (R) in the earnings distribution.

It is expositionally convenient to assume an additive form of utility function so that[1]

$$u_i = aR_i + v_i(h_i).$$

Social utility is now given by a $\Sigma R_i + \Sigma v_i(h_i)$. Since the first term cannot be altered, the social optimum once more requires a tax rate of unity, so that people only work for its own sake.

If, by contrast, people also value income as such, we can, again for simplicity of exposition, write

$$u_i = aR_i + v_i(y_i\,h_i).$$

To produce an optimum we ensure that the additional tax paid by an individual who does an extra hour of work (wt) equals the money value of the harm which others suffer from their consequential loss of rank.[2]

$$wt = -a \sum_{j+i} \frac{\partial R_j}{\partial h_i} \Big/ \frac{\partial v_i}{\partial y_i}.$$

Since the total value which people derive from rank is constant, this tax per hour is also equal to the money value of the benefit to the individual from *his* gain in rank: we tax away all his gains from doing better in the zero-sum game.

There is an apparent worry about the rank-order model that is worth defusing at this point. One might be tempted to argue as follows. If a tax system reduces the money gain from extra work, it will not necessarily affect work choice. For status may depend on gross earnings; or, even if it depends on net earnings, the tax will reduce the money gap between individuals so that the gain in rank order resulting from an extra hour of work may not be reduced by the tax. However, this argument overlooks the fact that the tax does reduce the private return to work via its effect on the enjoyment of income *per se*. Hence (assuming the tax proceeds are distributed) the tax *will* reduce effort and thus offset the tendency towards excessive work induced by status-seeking. Thus, whether we use the relative income model or the rank-order approach, we find a case for government intervention to reduce the private return to work.

As usual in discussions of pollution, there will be people who argue that intervention is also needed to reduce the rate of growth of market output. But,

---

[1] To avoid equity problems, we continue to assume that all men have the same wage rates, and this means that we have to assume they have different utility functions. For, if not, there could be no equilibrium: an infinitesimal increase in hours by one individual would involve him in an infinitesimally small cost and raise his rank from the (tied) median to the top – a non-infinitesimal gain.

[2] The social optimum requires

$$a\frac{\partial R_i}{\partial h_i} + a \sum_{j+i}\frac{\partial R_j}{\partial h_i} + \frac{\partial v_i}{\partial y_i}w + \frac{\partial v_i}{\partial h_i} = 0,$$

where the first two terms sum to zero. The private optimum produces

$$a\frac{\partial R_i}{\partial h_i} + \frac{\partial v_i}{\partial y_i}w(1-t) + \frac{\partial v_i}{\partial h_i} = 0. \quad \text{Hence} \quad wt = -a\sum_{j+i}\frac{\partial R_j}{\partial h_i}\Big/\frac{\partial v_i}{\partial y_i}.$$

as usual, this does not follow, and it is worth a brief digression to prove it. For simplicity we shall assume that intertemporal utility (U^i) equals the sum of the utilities in two periods (o and 1), each of which depends on current individual consumption (y_i) and current average consumption $(\bar{y})$.

$$U^i = u^0(y_i^0, \bar{y}^0) + u^1(y_i^1, \bar{y}^1). \tag{3}$$

The sacrifice of consumption in period o can raise consumption in period 1 (we are for simplicity assuming no capital market). It follows that there will only be too much sacrifice if the marginal disutility of average consumption in period 1 (relative to personal consumption) exceeds the marginal disutility of average consumption in period o (relative to personal consumption).[1]

For there is an external benefit from the lowered consumption in the first period which has to be more than offset by the external disbenefit from the higher consumption in the second period. There is no obvious reason why this should happen and thus in general there does not seem to be any status argument against productive investment.

So far we have assumed that status is conferred only by income. But suppose, for example, that status is conferred directly by effort. This will lead to too much effort.[2] Or, suppose education as such confers status. This leads to over-investment in education. Much has been made of the external benefits of education, and some extraordinary claims made. For example, people have pointed out what fun it will be for the existing graduates to have more other graduates to talk to. I have never seen it pointed out that by the same token the non-graduates will have fewer non-graduates to talk to. In fact there must surely be many perverse incentives encouraging extra education, which all boil down to the reason that other people are getting it.

Likewise, in a poor society a man proves to his wife that he loves her by giving her a rose but in a rich society he must give a dozen roses. A poor family can entertain graciously on beer but a rich one must give champagne. It is not nice to assert that many of the strivings of modern man (to educate himself, to migrate, to entertain well and so on) are in part self-defeating in terms of collective satisfaction, but to pretend otherwise is to ignore the evidence that human satisfaction is not expanding as the economic model without externalities suggests it should be. And many of these externalities can be dealt with by fiscal policy.[3]

---

[1] If r is the physical rate of return on investment plus unity, the social optimum then requires

$$-u_1^0 - nu_2^0\frac{1}{n} + u_1^1 r + nu_2^1\frac{1}{n}r = 0.$$

The private optimum with no taxes will lead to

$$-u_1^0 + u_1^1 r = 0.$$

Hence if $-u_1^0 + u_1^1 r < 0$, a tax is needed on the investment yield, with no tax deductibility for investment cost. Substituting for r gives as an equivalent condition: $-u_2^0/u_1^0 < -u_2^1/u_1^1$.

[2] The simplest way of representing this would be by assuming that status depends on one's own work relative to the mean. So we are back to the model of equation (1) with uniform w: $u^i = u(h_i/\bar{h}, h_i)$.

[3] A major difficulty in fixing the correct tax/subsidy levels for education and migration is that so often these seem to be information problems making for too little of the activity, and these have to be

Institutions

The scope for status competition is also of course affected by institutions. It may be true that human nature is intrinsically competitive (see, for example, Russell, 1949). But the extent to which the competitive motive dominates his behaviour depends upon the number of competitions that are open to him. Every organiser knows this, and when he worries about insufficient motivation among those for whom he is responsible he is tempted to invent a competition. Parents organise races, school teachers publish form orders,[1] Stalin appoints model workers, the Chinese government encourages 'socialist emulation', the Nobel committee offers prizes whose chief value is non-monetary, and the British government offers titles (Sir, Lord). There is no doubt that these devices do motivate.[2] The question is whether they add to or subtract from human welfare.

This is a difficult question. Some competition is enjoyable even for the loser, though most tennis-players choose to play with people they occasionally beat – an option less open to those who have to earn their living. There is also the problem of anomie, if there are insufficient external goals to keep the mind occupied.[3] Competition is also enjoyable to those looking on from outside – as Lucretius said, 'when the sea is tossed with great winds, it is delightful to be on land and watch others sweating it out'. But since the institutions of the world are mainly devised by those who have succeeded in the competitive struggle, one cannot assume that the social cost of competition (to the loser) has been fully taken into account.

To think about the optimum structure of institutions, one can perhaps consider the utility function as follows. There are some rank-orders which are unavoidable and which people will always care about (money, in particular). Call this R^1. But there are other rank-orders which may or may not be made available by the society. For example, the rank-order on an exam (R^2) can only matter to people if a rank-order is published. If there is no rank order in a particular possible dimension, we can proceed as though on that particular variable (t) everyone had $R_i^t = 0.5$ (the median). So, if there are T technically possible rank-orders, we can write the utility function as

$$u_i = \sum_{t=1}^{T} a_t[R_i^t - 0.5] + v_i(y_i, h_i).$$

The question is then what is the optimum degree of differentiation by the non-monetary characteristics 2 up to T.

---

offset against the negative externalities making for too much of the activity. (ii) The liberal argument that equalising taxes would produce a dull uniformity is remarkably at variance with the correct liberal emphasis on the remarkable variety of human nature.

[1] In at least one English public school the place where you pray in chapel has been determined by your exam results, and likewise the place where you sit for your meals and your lessons.

[2] It is of course possible for an incentive to be set at such a high level that the organism seizes up and less productive work is done. But this is not that common. The main problem with incentives is the cost of the effort they bring forth.

[3] As Durckheim (1951) pointed out, humans need an adequate external challenge, but not too great a challenge, in order to enjoy life.

The answer is that we want people to work until the value of their marginal product equals the marginal disutility of work. If we have a competitive (or other) market that pays gross wages equal to the value of the marginal product, and if we need no taxes for other purposes, then we want as little non-monetary differentiation as possible and some taxes to offset the effects of the rank-order differentiation that is inevitable.[1] But if we are prevented (for example by school-teacher unions or Maoist ideology) from paying people for their efforts, then we may need to use other methods of motivation.

Sometimes it is not easy to pay people at the time for their effort – for example, to pay properly the inventors of public goods (such as modern micro-economic theory). In this case any *ex post* money payment almost inevitably brings with it an enormous amount of non-monetary reward.[2] Whether these prizes are a good thing depends on the value of the resulting gains to knowledge compared to the strains induced among the competitors.[3]

An interesting competitive institution that is much hated is the examination system. This has a number of functions. First it provides information to employers, so that good performance leads to higher income. This means that, if the examination can be prepared for, it will motivate study. Moreover, if the examination results are given wide publicity, good performance will also confer status (directly rather than through income) and this further motivates students.

However, students can be over-motivated and, if too much hangs on the results, failure can be very painful. Hence Mao's attack on exams. The Chinese reforms of the late-1960s were designed to remove the anxieties associated with the exam system – and, even wider, with the system by which the individual rather than the bureaucracy takes the initiative in charting his educational and occupational destiny. But the Chinese discovered the inefficiency of the alternative system for mobilising talent, and in 1977/8 restored the system of open examinations for university entry. They thus reinstated just about the most individualistic activity open to man, except perhaps for solo competitive sports and solo writing. This gives us some indication of the productive cost of a system that prevents the individual running in the rat-race.

Yet the rat-race also has its costs. Interestingly the American examination system, which consists of a large number of small hurdles, is probably less costly than the British system, which consists of a small number of 7-footers. The clearest indication of a bad selection system is the extent to which its victims are obsessed by the process of selection. For the costs of education are not just direct costs and earnings foregone, but also the anxieties which

[1] If we allow for differences between people, then we would want to introduce a tax for equity reasons. If this was sufficient of a disincentive to work, the interesting question then arises of whether we should want to restore incentives partially by introducing (disequalising) competitions for non-monetary prizes. The answer seems to be 'yes'.

[2] It may also be appropriate to pay producers of private goods on an *ex post* basis, but this is unlikely to generate large non-monetary rewards.

[3] The question of the optimal reward to invention is of course plagued in addition by two further problems: (i) the fact that the winner takes all and removes all return to the losers' inputs and (ii) problems of uncertainty about when and whether the invention will occur.

students experience. And institutional arrangements like exam systems do affect these anxieties.[1]

Changing Human Nature

Of course the Chinese must be hoping that their new exam system will not have as bad effects as the old one because they have 'changed human nature' in the meantime. At this point we have to distinguish between two forms of moral change. First, there is the argument (stressed by Sen (1973) and Hirsch (1977)) that where there is an externality problem that cannot easily be handled by fiscal policy or regulation it is in the interest of all that all should exercise restraint rather than that none should do so. This does not require a change in people's utility functions – but only in the actions they take in pursuit of utility. Clearly such restraint can happen. Politicians do not always do everything possible to further their cause; they prefer to preserve the political fabric itself. But Hirsch is not at all specific about how private restraint could effectively overcome the externality problem of status competition, if people really do value status. He argues that modern men have been encouraged to think they have a moral duty to do the best for themselves, since this will help out the invisible hand. And he believes that if they were disabused of this fallacy, things would improve. One hopes so. But the problem of status competition is much less clear-cut than the problem of litter, and it is not clear just how a person observing the social contract would know when to stop work.

This brings one to the second possibility: that the utility function could itself be changed by education, so that people got more pleasure from the welfare of others and less from the feeling of being better off than others are.[2] This seems to be a much surer approach. One wants people to work not in order to excel over others (a game against persons) but in order to do the job well (a game against nature). This is not pie in the sky – most people who do crossword puzzles are not competing against other people. But the problem is that every stage of life is littered with institutions that reinforce the competitive value system. To do our work we need to know whose articles are worth reading, who is worth asking for a seminar, and who is worth appointing to a job. If we spend so much time putting people in order, can we really expect ourselves to work for motives unconnected with rank-order? Yet if we cannot, it is not going to be easy to improve human welfare (at any rate once a modicum of physical comfort has been achieved). If personality is largely constructed in the first six years of life, perhaps the best hope lies in a moral

---

[1] I have not mentioned the screening argument, which also implies that the private return to education (Δy_i) exceeds the productive social return ($\Sigma \Delta y_j$), since there is no strong evidence that the screening argument is correct. I disagree with Hirsch here. The main problem is that status competition encourages people to put more effort (and anxiety) into raising income and status via exams than is optimal.

[2] As Weisbrod (1977) has pointed out, it may be possible even in an ordinalist framework to compare economic states A and B in which utility functions are different. For if the outcome in state B is preferred whether we use the utility function of state A or state B, then the utility function of state B can be said to be better.

code which forbids all comparisons between children until they are, say, six.[1]

II. THE ROLE OF EXPECTED INCOME AND EXPECTED STATUS

I now need to bring in another consideration – the role of expectations. Happiness depends not only on status and income (*per se*), but also on what a person expected his income and status to be.

Expected Income

Let us begin with the role of expected income and ignore questions of status for the moment. One obvious reason why higher income has not brought more happiness is that expected income has risen.[2] (By expected income in year t, I mean the income which in some earlier year a person expected to have in year t.)

Even if public policy cannot easily influence expectations, it has to take their existence into account. This means that the ordinary cardinal utility function, $u(y)$, used in public economics is inadequate, and may also be the reason why $u(y)$ has never so far had any impact on practical affairs. A more satisfactory approach would recognise the following:

(*a*) Utility depends negatively on expected income.

(*b*) The marginal utility of a given income depends positively on expected income.

(*c*) Expected income is an increasing function of past income.

(*d*) Marginal utility is much lower for an increase in income than for a fall, if one starts out from the expected level of income.[3]

I suspect that politicians believe many of these propositions, especially (*d*), which explains their unwillingness ever to make anybody worse off. But let us take the propositions in turn and explore their implications.

Suppose social welfare is given by

$$W = \Sigma u^i,$$

where[4]

$$u^i = u(y_i, e_i)$$

and e is expected income. Then the just division of a cake of given size requires

$$\partial u / \partial y_i = u_1(y_i, e_i) = \lambda \quad (\text{all } i).$$

We can compare the implied optimal incomes of people with different expected incomes by totally differentiating:

$$u_{11} \, dy + u_{12} \, de = 0,$$

---

[1] Margaret Mead (1937) and others have shown the wide variations in the degree of competitiveness as between different societies. *Pace* Lynn (1971), these differences are probably socially determined.

[2] Rainwater (1975) has shown how peoples' views of the income needed for an adequate life have risen almost as fast as incomes generally (using answers to Gallup Poll questions).

[3] This is an instance of the 'endowment effect' discussed by Thaler (forthcoming), according to which people have a strong emotional attachment to the *status quo*.

[4] u^i here is not utility but a concave transformation of it.

therefore

$$dy/de = u_{12}/-u_{11}.$$

One would normally assume that $u_{11} < 0$, and our proposition (*b*) says that $u_{12} > 0$. So someone with higher expectations should have higher income. Yesterday's rich should have higher net incomes than if all had the same expectations.[1]

This is clearly a rather conservative outcome. It becomes less so if we allow for the fact that expectations adjust over time towards the level of income actually experienced. Thus there is an optimal time path of the income distribution. If there were no time discounting and a constant cake, the income distribution should eventually become equal.[2] Equality would be approached faster, the faster expectations adjust to actual income experienced.

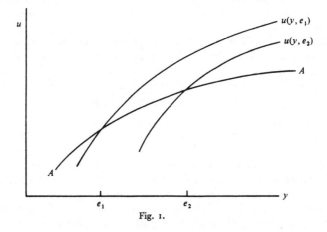

Fig. 1.

The psychological postulates used so far can be summarised graphically in Fig. 1. The utility function for someone with expectations of e_1 is above that for someone with expectations of e_2, but flatter. If, in the long run, expectations tend to actual income, we have a *long run* utility function, $u^*(y)$, shown by the line *AA*. Nothing we have assumed so far requires that *AA* slope up, but it would certainly be odd if it sloped down, so that someone who had got used to a high income was more miserable than someone who had got used to a low income. In fact, there is some not very rigorous evidence that the long-run utility function does slope up.[3]

[1] (i) The exact difference in income that is appropriate depends of course on the form of function. For example, if $u = u(y - \alpha e)$, then $dy/de = \alpha$. The stronger the negative influence of expectations, the bigger the income difference. (ii) If expected income equals current income, redistribution will be from rich to poor if $dy/de < 1$. So $u_{12} < -u_{11}$.

[2] This assumes that the long-run curve *AA* discussed below is concave. In other words, $u_{12} < -(u_{11} + u_{22})/2$, since $d^2u = (u_{11} + u_{12} + u_{21} + u_{22}) dy^2$.

[3] See Van Praag (1978). However, the question that was asked in this survey was not well adjusted to the task of eliciting the utility of income function. A better approach might be to ask questions of the following kind: (*a*) 'Imagine a £100 increase in your income. Having had this increase, how much more would you need to induce an equal further increase in happiness?' And so on up and down the income scale. (*b*) 'How much income would you say you needed to be neither very happy nor unhappy but just happy?'

I now come to assumption (d). People seem to fight against cuts in their living standards much more energetically than they fight for increases.[1] This suggests that the marginal utility of income for decreases in income below what is expected is much greater than the marginal utility for increases in income. In other words, the short-run utility function should be redrawn with a kink as in Fig. 2. This again has rather conservative implications, since the gain to a poorer man from an income transfer can quite easily be less than the loss to a richer man. A feeling that this is so explains the understandable unwillingness of

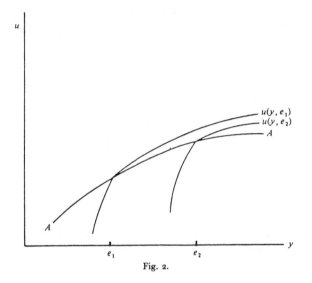

Fig. 2.

politicians to make rationalisations of, for example, social security, in which almost inevitably a few people lose. It also explains their willingness to protect even quite well-off people from the effects of economic change.[2] But if the long-run curve AA is concave, the optimal long-run goal is still equality. In order to achieve this goal it is at first necessary to reduce social welfare by disappointing the expectations of the rich, which then alters appropriately. It is asking a lot of politicians to ask them to embark on this process.

The point I have been making about expectations bears some relation to

[1] Of course one has to distinguish between expressed discontent and actual discontent. For example Runciman (1966, p. 78) reports that in the 1930s there was much more agitation over the proposed standardisation of unemployment benefit in 1934 than there was over unemployment as such. This was because the public believed the government could do nothing about unemployment. But the unemployment benefit reform (though it made most people better off) made some people worse off, and this was not considered inevitable. All the cases of proposed reduction had to be abandoned. Having said this, it may be the case that *actual* discontent in fact depends not only on objective circumstances but also on whether these are thought to be inevitable or due to other peoples' freely chosen actions. For example, I dislike an identical banging at night much less if it is due to the wind than to my neighbours.

[2] I am not implying that politicians are only concerned with maximising an ethical social welfare function, regardless of votes.

Scitovsky's argument about novelty. We need to be surprised, and this is a difficult thing for the individual to contrive for himself. Clearly he will be better off if his income is always running ahead of his expectations. This argues in favour of public policies to encourage low expectations[1] and, perhaps, low juvenile wages. One argument for economic growth is that, at any rate in the 1950s, it surprised people. But people can have expectations of a constant level of income or a constant first derivative, second derivative, or any higher derivative. The trouble with the 1960s may have been that people had become adjusted to expecting constant growth and they got no more than that. This may explain why the Gallup Poll results quoted by Easterlin (1972) suggest an increase in happiness in the United States up to 1965 followed by a decrease.

Expected Status

However, another reason is inflation, which has brought about much more frequent rearrangements of people in the status hierarchy.[2] Once again we may suppose that increases in status above the level expected produce smaller gains in happiness than the loss of happiness caused by a shortfall in status below the level expected. Given this we have a good partial explanation of why inflation reduces social welfare, even when real incomes are rising. For in Britain at least the non-synchronised nature of pay settlements means that, of two groups whose real incomes over a year are equal and rising smoothly, each spend half of the year resenting that the other group is way ahead of them in the ladder of pay.[3]

The importance of expected status is not of course an argument against the redistribution of income. The fact that the poor do not resent the riches of the wealthy does not mean that their happiness could not be increased by a bigger cut. But it does again argue in favour of preserving relative rankings, unless there is some good reason to the contrary.

III. CONCLUSION

Somehow, policy makers need to take into account all the factors we have reviewed, as well as many others. Clearly the job cannot be done perfectly. But if status and expectations are as important determinants of human satisfaction as they seem to be, it will not do for economists to tell policy-makers to ignore them. There is little virtue in tidy solutions that ignore major elements in a situation. However, the arguments in this paper only begin to nibble at the problems.

[1] I do not know quite how to relate this argument to another basic human need – for hope. I have also been deliberately vague about whether by 'expected' income I mean 'forecast' income or income which one 'requires' as a result of habit. If habit is the problem, then no indoctrination about what is going to happen will ease the blow.

[2] Using the General Household Survey, one finds that a male log weekly wage equation that had an R^2 of 0·50 in 1971 had an R^2 of only 0·41 in 1975, although the variance of log earnings had not changed. Apparently, random factors had taken over in part the role of systematic factors in the ranking. For a fuller discussion of the argument in relation to inflation, see Layard (forthcoming).

[3] In addition high price inflation with annual wage settlements means that real wages fall fairly steeply for 364 days a year. If e adjusts up on each settlement day, this provides another explanation of the discontents generated by inflation.

Two features of human nature are considered. The first is the desire for status. Since status depends on rank order, the total amount of status available is given. So if people work partly to improve their status, they will work too hard (assuming no other distortions to exist). This can be corrected by taxing the proceeds of work. It can also be affected by institutional reform. The extent to which people work for status depends on the number of status competitions which are being run. If there are already a number of distortions in an economy discouraging effort, it may be necessary to invent competition to motivate people. But if there are not already large distortions, there may be a presumption against having too many competitions, except perhaps to reward the inventors of public goods. Finally, one can attempt to change human nature. One approach is to accept existing utility functions, but persuade people that the collective interest requires individual restraint in the quest for status. The other, more hopeful, approach is to try to alter utility functions in order to reduce status-consciousness by getting adults to spend less time comparing the performances of young children.

The second feature we investigate is the effect of expected income and expected status on satisfaction. As regards income, this suggests a more conservative approach to income redistribution than follows if the role of expected income is ignored. However, expectations respond to actual income experienced, with a lag. So the case for long-term income redistribution remains, with the speed of equalisation depending on the speed at which expectations adjust. But there is a further problem. In the short-run, the marginal utility for increases in income is much less than for decreases, starting from a given level of expected income. This means that, in the short-run, redistribution may be very unpopular and reduce welfare, even though it may be justified within a long-term context over which expectations adjust. People also have expectations about status. This indicates the importance of avoiding unintended rearrangements in the status hierarchy, such as those often produced by inflation.'

These conclusions are piecemeal and not integrated into an overall model. However, it is important that economists should continue, with other social scientists, to work on these problems, if their advice is to be taken seriously by politicians, who often know a good deal about what makes people tick.

London School of Economics   R. LAYARD

Date of receipt of final typescript: May 1980

REFERENCES

Akerlof, G. (1976). 'The economics of caste and of the rat race and other woeful tales.' *Quarterly Journal of Economics*, vol. 90 (November), pp. 599–618.
Boskin, M. J. and Sheshinski, E. (1978). 'Optimal redistributive taxation when individual welfare depends upon relative income.' *Quarterly Journal of Economics*, vol. 92, no. 4 (November).
Duesenberry, J. S. (1949). *Income, Saving and the Theory of Consumer Behaviour*. Harvard.
Duncan, O. D. (1975). 'Does money buy satisfaction?' *Social Indicators Research*, vol. 2, no. 3 (December), pp. 267–74.

750   THE ECONOMIC JOURNAL   [DECEMBER 1980]

Durckheim, E. (1951). *Suicide*, English edition. Routledge and Kegan Paul.
Easterlin, R. A. (1972). 'Does economic growth improve the human lot?' In P. A. David and
    M. W. Reder (eds.), *Nations and Households in Economic Growth*.
Hirsch, F. (1977). *Social Limits to Growth*. Routledge and Kegan Paul.
Layard, R. (forthcoming). 'Wages policy and the redistribution of income.' In D. Collard and
    R. Lecomber (eds.), *The Limits to Redistribution*. Colston Society.
Lynn, R. (1971). *Personality and National Culture*. Oxford: Pergamon Press.
Mead, M. (1937). *Cooperation and Competition among Primitive Peoples*. New York: McGraw-Hill.
Mishan, E. J. (1977). *The Economic Growth Debate*. Allen and Unwin.
Rainwater, L. (1975). *What Money Buys*.
Runciman, W. G. (1966). *Relative Deprivation and Social Justice*. Now in Penguin.
Russell, B. (1949). *Authority and the Individual*. Allen and Unwin.
Schoeck, H. (1966). *Envy*. London: Secker and Warburg.
Scitovsky, T. (1976). *The Joyless Economy*. Oxford.
Sen, A. K. (1973). 'Behaviour and the concept of preference.' *Economica*, August.
Thaler, R. H. (forthcoming). 'Towards a positive theory of consumer choice.' *Journal of Economic
    Behaviour and Organisation*.
Van Praag, B. (1978). In W. Krelle and A. Shorrocks (eds.). *The Economics of Income Distribution*.
Weisbrod, B. A. (1977). 'Comparing utility functions in efficiency terms or what kind of utility functions
    do we want?' *American Economic Review*, vol. 67 (December).

D
The Leyden Analysis of Income Norms

[7]

The Measurement of Welfare and Well-Being: The Leyden Approach

Bernard M. S. van Praag and Paul Frijters

This chapter focuses on the measurement of individual welfare derived from income, known as the Leyden approach. The approach, initiated by van Praag (1971), is one of the few attempts to measure welfare that has been developed within the economic discipline. The method is based on the Income Evaluation Question, which is intended to get an idea of the individual's norms on income: respondents are asked what they consider to be a "good" income and a "bad" income. The answers to these questions may be used to get an insight into the effects of family size and climate on individual welfare. The influence of past incomes and anticipated incomes on current welfare is also considered. The method is generalized toward the measurement of other norms. We also consider how a social standard may be derived from individual norms. Finally, we address the question of how welfare is related to well-being. By measuring both concepts, it can be shown that they are different. The combination of both measures makes it possible to distinguish between the monetary costs and the nonmonetary benefits of choices, such as having children.

THE UTILITY CONCEPT is a key concept in economics. It is well known that modern economics is a discipline with numerous subfields, but nearly all relevant problems have to do with people and people's choice behavior. Individuals have limited resources and opportunities and therefore must choose between alternatives. An efficient way to describe the choice problem is to attach a *utility value* to these alternatives, for example, U_1, U_2, U_3, . . . , U_i, . . . and to postulate that an individual chooses the alternative that has the highest utility value for him. For example, if there is a choice set {1,2,3, . . . i, . . .}, then the choice behavior is described mathematically by

$$\max_{i\,=\,1,2,3,\,\ldots} U_i$$

The implication of this description is that we could predict the individual's choice behavior by knowing his utility values U_1, U_2, U_3. . . . In empirical reality, it is the other way around. We do not know the values of U, but we can observe the choice process. If an individual consistently chooses alternative 1, economists generally infer that U_1 is larger than U_2, U_3. . . . If we then remove alternative 1 from the choice set and 2 is chosen consistently, we know that $U_1 > U_2$ and that U_2 is larger than other U values. In this way, it is possible to find the preference ordering of the alternatives and also to establish inequality relations between the U values. However, we are unable to say whether U_2 is a *little* smaller than U_1 or if U_2 is *much* smaller than U_1. In short, by observing choices we get an *ordinal* utility ordering.

The choice model may be extended in two ways. First, we can consider a set of alternatives that is infinite. Alternatives can be described by a continuous variable x or by more than one variable, for example, $(x_1, x_2, \ldots x_n) = \mathbf{x}$. Then the utility values are denoted by the ordinal utility function $U(\mathbf{x})$. Second, we may assume that each decision maker z has his own utility ordering. In that case, the ordinal utility function reads $U(\mathbf{x}; z)$ where z may incorporate individually varying parameters such as age, gender, income, social class, and so on. We notice that this ordinal function is of the *decision utility* type in the terminology of Kahneman, Wakker, and Sarin (1997). It is needed to make decisions and is empirically established by observations of choice decisions.[1]

The traditional example of choice behavior in economics is the *purchasing* behavior of consumers. The model starts from a utility function

$$U(x; z)$$

where x stands for quantities of commodities purchased and z for characteristics describing the individual's circumstances (for example, age, gender). The consumer is faced by prices $p_1, \ldots p_n$

for goods x_1 to x_n. If he has income y, his choice set is described by:

$$p_1 x_1 + \ldots + p_n x_n \leq y$$

Any commodity bundle $(x_1, x_2, \ldots x_n)$ violating the constraint is too expensive for him. The behavioral model explains behavior by assuming that individuals maximize $U(.;z)$ with respect to the feasible commodity bundle x subject to the freedom given by the choice set.

Edgeworth (1881) called $U(.)$ the utility function; Pareto (1904) called it the ophelimity function. Edgeworth more or less implicitly assumed that U could be measured in a direct way. Samuelson (1945) therefore stated that "Edgeworth considered utility to be as real as his morning jam" (206). Edgeworth interpreted U as *experienced utility*, that is, a cardinal measure of the joy that the individual derives from the commodity bundle. Pareto became aware of the fact that it could be difficult to establish the individual's utility function over goods. For the description of the consumer choice process, an *experienced utility* function appeared to be unnecessary. Actually, it is a choice between alternatives that can be described by an *ordinal* utility function, as described earlier. If $U(.)$ is an ordinal utility function, any other utility function that assigns the *same ordering* of utility to the alternatives is also a utility function describing that same choice process. For example, if $U_1 > U_2 > U_3 > 0$ describes the choice process between alternatives 1, 2, 3, then $\bar{U}_1 = \sqrt{U_1} > \bar{U}_2 = \sqrt{U_2} > \bar{U}_3 = \sqrt{U_3}$ will describe the same process. Hence, there is a whole equivalence class of *ordinal* utility functions describing the same preference structure.

It is an error to assume that Pareto denied the existence of meaningful cardinal utility measurement or the possibility of measuring it, but he pointed to the fact that utility in the cardinal sense could not be measured by observing consumer behavior, and moreover that it was unnecessary to do so for consumer studies.

Robbins (1932), who had a tremendous influence on economics, was the first to proclaim that utility was immeasurable and that it was more or less a scientific folly to endeavor to measure it. At the very least, it should be left to psychologists.

Other economists, such as Pigou (1948) and the Nobel laureates Tinbergen (1991) and Frisch (1932), have certainly been of a different opinion.

However, the ordinal line has been continued by Arrow (1951) and Debreu (1959), who were able to include decisions over time and/or under

uncertainty in this ordinal framework. They assumed a preference ranking described by a utility function on the dated commodity space. Behavior is subject to a budget constraint where the consumption of goods and the prices of those goods are differentiated according to the date of consumption.

Similarly, they incorporated uncertainty by distinguishing states of nature s varying over S and commodities available only if s prevails. Commodities are then available *contingent* on the status of nature, which is a priori not known to an individual. It can be shown that the model describes consumer choice behavior, but it is also clear that this model leads to a decision problem with an unworkable number of dimensions. Its realism as a positive behavioral model is not significant, and it has never been used, according to our knowledge, in empirical work, except in very simplified versions.

In practice, economists are frequently confronted by problems where more is needed than the ordinal concept (see also Ng 1997).

One such problem concerns decision-making under *uncertainty*, which is the basis for insurance theory, investment and saving behavior. Also, decisions that have to do with different *time* periods, such as saving and investment decisions, need more than the ordinal concept. The objective function in such models is usually simplified to an additive form such as $\Sigma_t w_t U_t$ or $\Sigma p_s U_s$ where U_t stands for *instantaneous* period utilities and w_t for time-discounting weights, and where U_s stands for state-contingent utility and p_s for the (real or perceived) chance that state s occurs. Evidently, time-state mixtures and continuous generalizations are easy to think of.

There are two points of interest in these objective functions. The basic ingredient is a utility function U that is no longer ordinal. We cannot change the individual form at will according to a monotonous transformation. More specifically, maximizing $\Sigma_t w_t \varphi(U_t)$ will yield an optimum that varies with $\varphi(.)$, except if φ is a positive linear transformation (that is, $\varphi(.) = \alpha U + \beta$ with $\alpha > 0$). The utility concept in these kinds of problems is what economists call a *cardinal* utility function. It is a much smaller class that allows only for positive linear transformations.

Most mainstream economists have a very uneasy feeling about cardinal utility functions. This uneasiness seems to be based on the Anglo-American dogmatism against cardinality instilled by Robbins. However, most actual studies conducted by economists start with very general "ordinal formulations" but after a while present a structural specification that nine times out of ten turns out to be of the cardinal type (see also van Praag 1968). These cardinal utility functions are still of the decision utility type. They are instrumental to the description of *decision* processes.

There is a second class of problems for which economists need cardinal utility functions: normative problems. The first example of such problems arises if we try to look for optimal (re)distributions. Notably in income taxation, a progressive tax schedule (richer individuals pay relatively more tax than poorer individuals) is advocated so that the rich man suffers as much as the poor man. Such comparisons are impossible without a cardinal and interpersonally comparable utility function. Obviously, these utility functions are of the *experienced* utility type.

A second example is provided by equity measures: the concepts of a just income distribution and poverty and the evaluation of income inequality. It is evident that nearly all of these measures are based on a cardinal concept of experienced income utility, though this is rarely mentioned explicitly (compare, Atkinson 1970).

A third field where interpersonally comparable and cardinal utility is needed concerns all types of cost-benefit analyses, in which specific measures, such as building a bridge, deregulating markets, establishing a health insurance program, or controlling noise pollution by an airport, have to be evaluated. In these cases, some citizens will profit and others will lose. Those benefits and costs may be partially translated in monetary amounts, but money means different things for different people. For example, when a policy means a loss of $100 to a poor man and a gain of $10,000 to a rich man, it is not at all evident that the policy should be realized. The only way to make a decision is to create a balance in terms of comparable utility gains and losses.

The situation in economics is succinctly and wittily summarized by Wansbeek and Kapteyn (1983):

> Utility seems to be to economists what the Lord is to theologians. Economists talk about utility all the time, but do not seem to have hope of ever observing it this side of heaven. In micro-economic theory, almost every model is built on utility functions of some kind. In empirical work little attempt is made to measure this all-pervasive concept. The concept is considered to be so esoteric as to defy

direct measurement by mortals. Still, in a different role, viz., of non-economists, the same mortals are the sole possessors of utility functions and can do incredible things with it. (249)

By detaching economics from the psychology of "feelings," economists have found it difficult to have anything relevant to say on a whole range of issues. In the next section of this chapter, we review an attempt made by economists to measure utility functions using the evaluations given by individuals themselves. Before we do so, however, we first discuss the approaches taken in general to utility function in the economic literature. We divide the approaches that have been taken concerning the problem of utility functions into five distinct approaches.

GENERAL APPROACHES TO CARDINAL UTILITY TAKEN BY ECONOMISTS

The first approach to cardinal utility, which is by far the most popular in the economic profession, is not to measure utility at all but to simply assume a functional form of the utility function for the theoretical or empirical problem at hand. We ignore this approach in the remainder of this chapter.

Economists who use the second approach, of whom perhaps the best known are Christensen, Jorgenson, and Lau (1975) and Jorgenson and Slesnick (1984), have taken an axiomatic approach to utility functions. They specify the conditions they believe a utility function should satisfy and then derive (a shape of) the utility function that fits these requirements.[2] After inferring the level of utility that individuals enjoy from their observed behavior, they use it to make normative statements. This approach is not elaborated here because utility levels are not directly measured but essentially assumed. Moreover, if this method has validity, it yields a cardinal decision utility.

Economists who take the third approach use subjective and objective indicators of the work and living conditions of individuals to define a measure of utility. This large group is subdivided into three groups: one group is concerned with poor individuals, another with the quality of life of nations, another with the quality of life of individuals.

The empirical literature on poverty centers on the material resources available to individuals (Townsend 1979, 1993; Sen 1987; Ravallion 1994). The standard approach is to define households as poor if their household income falls below a certain cutoff point. This cutoff point can be defined in several ways. For instance, in the "basic needs" approach, the cutoff point is calculated from the expenditures needed to buy a basket of commodities that the researcher considers vital for individuals. In the "relative needs" approach, the cutoff point is defined as a certain percentage of the average or median income in a country. It is clear that neither approach, which together form the bulk of the poverty literature, actually measures utility functions, but that they are based on the *assumption* that the utility of individuals whose income is below the cutoff point is in some sense "low." Callan and Nolan (1991) and Frijters and van Praag (1995) provide a more detailed review of the normative issues involved in poverty measurement.

Other literature examines the "quality of life" of nations. In this literature (Kurian 1984; Maasoumi 1989; Nussbaum and Sen 1992; Sen 1987), economics attempt to rank countries with respect to the quality of life.[3] The quality of life is usually defined as a weighted average of specific country statistics. The statistics used include, for instance, the literacy level of the entire population, the literacy level of women, infant mortality rates, income levels per head, life expectancies of men and women, indicators of political stability, energy consumption per capita, average household size, the number of persons per physician, levels of civil liberties, and so on. It is clear that these variables may be very important for the utility levels of individuals and nations; however, the utility levels themselves are *not* measured by these variables. An obvious problem is then, how should these statistics be weighted? Does the quality of life increase more when the female literacy level increases by 1 percent or when the civil liberty index improves by 1 percent? It is clear that if one does not want to use the evaluations of individuals themselves as a weighting method, the opinions of the researcher become the deciding criterion. The problem of how to weight these different variables into a composite quality-of-life index is, not surprisingly, the main source of dispute in this literature. For an empirical analysis of some of the weighting methods employed, see Hirschberg, Maasoumi, and Slottje (1991).

Some of the works of Clark and Oswald also belong to the third category. In their 1994 paper, Clark and Oswald define "unhappiness" by aggregating the answers to the following twelve questions:

1. Have you been able to concentrate on whatever you are doing?

2. . . . lost much sleep over worry?
3. . . . felt that you are playing a useful part in things?
4. . . . felt capable of making decisions about things?
5. . . . felt constantly under strain?
6. . . . felt you couldn't overcome your difficulties?
7. . . . been able to enjoy your normal day-to-day activities?
8. . . . been able to face your problems?
9. . . . been feeling unhappy and depressed?
10. . . . been losing confidence in yourself?
11. . . . been thinking of yourself as a worthless person?
12. . . . been feeling reasonably happy, all things considered?

The variable "unhappiness" ranges from 0 to 12, with 12 denoting the maximum level of unhappiness and 0 a complete lack of unhappiness. Although some of these questions could arguably be seen as a measure of utility, such as questions 9 and 12, the simple aggregate of all twelve questions cannot be seen as a direct measurement of utility: utility is an evaluation of an individual of his circumstances. Although "losing a lot of sleep" or "being under strain" may either affect utility or be affected *by* utility, these factors do not directly measure a utility level for they are not an evaluation of "losing sleep" or "being under strain." This measure of happiness may correlate perfectly with the experienced utility of individuals and may hence be as useful as any other measure of experienced utility. Nevertheless, it remains an *indirect* measure of experienced utility that is useful only if "losing sleep" and "being under strain" correlate with experienced utility (which seems very likely). Hence, it is a measure of the quality of life entirely on its own. Clark and Oswald (1994) seem to acknowledge this by arguing that the individual scores are "more accurately" described as "mental stress" scores. Other individual measures of an individual's quality of life that are based on aggregations of individual circumstances also fall into this category.

A fourth approach is to estimate decision utility functions by performing probability-choice experiments on individuals: When individuals must choose between either a certain outcome Y or a lottery in which fate decides whether they will receive an outcome less than Y or an outcome greater than Y, individuals will reveal the relative attractiveness of the sure Y versus the proposed lottery. The main problem is this line of research has been that individuals are not good at using probabilities: they overestimate small probabilities and underestimate large probabilities, as was first demonstrated by the Allais paradox (see Allais and

FIGURE 21.1   A Value Function of Income

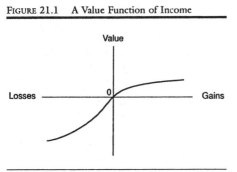

Hagen 1979). This means that an individual's choice of a lottery is the result of a combination of the individual's valuation of the outcomes and his or her perception of the probability of the outcomes. Following the theoretical advances by Kahneman and Tversky (1979) and Wakker and Tversky (1993), Kahneman, Knetsch, and Thaler (1991) have managed to isolate the effect of gains and losses on the individual's evaluation of outcomes. We will ignore the results on probabilities and focus on the value function they find. The shape of the value function suggested by the choice experiments of Kahneman and his colleagues (1991) is sketched in figure 21.1.

The main feature of this function is that losses are found to have a greater impact than gains. A second characteristic of this value function, leveling off at either end of the loss or gain scale, implies decreasing marginal value of losses and gains, as well as a convex-concave shape (also suggested by Markowitz [1952] and van Praag [1968]).

Finally, the fifth approach, initiated by the Leyden group, is to assume that individuals are able to describe their utility level by means of *verbal* qualifications. The rest of this chapter will be devoted to discussing the efforts of economists who belong to this group. There are other economists, of course, who use verbal qualifiers as measures of experienced utility (for example, Clark 1996; Clark and Oswald 1996; Dow and Juster 1985; Easterlin 1974; Heywood, Siebert, and Wei 1997; Levy-Garboua and Montmarquette 1997; and Gershuny and Halpin 1995).

UTILITY MEASUREMENT BASED ON VERBAL QUALIFIERS: THE LEYDEN APPROACH

In this section, we discuss an economic line of research that tries to operationalize the concept of

experienced utility. It originated at Leyden University in the Netherlands in the early 1970s. Its main contributors are Bernard van Praag, Ari Kapteyn, Paul Wansbeek, Aldi Hagenaars, Edwin Van der Sar, Erik Plug, and Paul Frijters. It is known in the literature as the Leyden approach (or school). For psychologists, the ideas in this approach may not appear alien, but for most economists they were and still are. Most economists still believe that cardinal experienced utility is unmeasurable and that any measurement should be based on observed decision behavior. Consequently, the Leyden approach has met with stiff opposition, disbelief, and outright hostility. The most outspoken example of this attitude is found in an article by Seidl (1994) in the *European Economic Review* in which he criticizes van Praag (1968).[4]

Although van Praag (1968) served as a theoretical basis, the ensuing literature on the Leyden approach started with van Praag (1971) and is mainly empirical and data-oriented. The Leyden approach focuses primarily on the evaluation of *income*, although in later work the focus was extended. We also speak of utility of income, income satisfaction, or, in other words, economic *welfare*. We drop the adjective "economic" from now on, but when we use the term "welfare," we have welfare derived from income in mind. This concept is narrower than the concept of well-being that includes feelings associated with factors unconnected to income or purchasing power. Later we shall consider well-being and its relationship with welfare in greater detail.

The Leyden approach is based on two assumptions. The first is that individuals are able to evaluate income levels in general, and their own income in particular, in terms of "good," "bad," sufficient," and so on. We call these terms *verbal qualifiers*. The second assumption is that verbal labels can be translated in a meaningful way into a numerical evaluation on a bounded scale, for example [0,1]. We shall consider both steps of the measurement procedure in detail.

If we are interested in how a specific income level is evaluated, there are two ways to gather information. The first and most natural way is to propose a sequence of income levels and to ask for their verbal qualifications. An example of this type of question follows:

> Here is a list of income levels per month, after tax: please evaluate these amounts using verbal qualifications, such as "very bad," "bad," "insufficient," "sufficient," "good," "very good":

$2,000
$4,000
$6,000
$8,000
$10,000

It is obvious that someone who earns $20,000 a month would be unable to make a distinction between most of these levels. All the incomes are insufficient or worse for him. Therefore, instead of staring with income levels, we can also supply the verbal qualifications as *stimuli* and ask the respondent which income level corresponds with the verbal label. This leads to the so-called Income Evaluation Question (IEQ):

While keeping prices constant, what after-tax total monthly income would you consider for your family to be:

very bad _____ $_____
bad _____ $_____
sufficient _____ $_____
insufficient _____ $_____
good _____ $_____
very good _____ $_____

This question appears to have been successful in anonymous mail-questionnaires, although it has also been posed orally with success. Theoretically, finding a continuous relationship between income and utility would require an infinite number of levels, but in practice between four and nine levels have been and can be used. We discuss here the format used most often, the six-level format.

The question is now, how do we derive a welfare function from the answers to this question? Or more precisely, how do we translate the verbal labels into numbers on a [0,1] scale? Following van Praag (1971), we make an assumption about the way individuals answer the question. We assume that respondents try to provide information to the interviewer about the shape of their welfare function. The most accurate way for individuals to provide information then depends on the accuracy criterion. Van Praag (1971) and Kapteyn (1977) show that, for a broad class of intuitively plausible criterion functions, the best way for a respondent to provide information is to choose the answers in such a way that each of the six levels corresponds to a jump of 1/6. This is the so-called Equal Quantile Assumption (EQA). It implies that

$$U \text{ (very bad)} = U \text{ (first interval)} = 1/12$$
$$U \text{ (bad)} = U \text{ (second interval)} = 3/12$$

. . .
. . .
$$U \text{ (very good)} = U \text{ (last interval)} = 11/12$$

It may be surmised that, even if the verbal descriptions are somewhat vague, the respondent will tend to interpret the question as if it were an equal partition. Only if the verbal labels are ambiguous, are practically equal, or strongly suggest an unequal partition should we no longer expect this effect.

If the number of verbal labels is k, the general formula for the welfare corresponding to the ith verbal label is obviously $\frac{2i-1}{2k}$. This reasoning and the EQA assumption are very similar to the thesis developed by Parducci (see, for example, Parducci 1995). It is obvious that this translation of verbal labels into numbers is a linch pin in this measurement procedure. Although it has been subject to criticism by some economists, experimental psychologists do not find much to criticize: it is a type of Thurstonian measurement. If we do not accept this or any translation into figures, it is obvious that a meaningful analysis of the response is severely hampered, although not impossible (see later discussion).

In van Praag (1991), an experiment is described in which five labels were supplied and 364 respondents were asked to "translate" these verbal labels into a [0,100]-scale. Similarly, the same labels had to be linked with line segments. Both the numbers between [0,100] and the lengths of the line segments were re-scaled onto a [0,1] mapping. We present the average results for 364 respondents in table 21.1.

TABLE 21.1   Translation into Numbers and Line Segments

Numbers		Empirical Mean	Standard Deviation	Theoretical Prediction
Very bad	$\bar{v}_1 = 0.0892$		0.0927	0.1
Bad	$\bar{v}_2 = 0.2013$		0.1234	0.3
Not bad, not good	$\bar{v}_3 = 0.4719$		0.1117	0.5
Good	$\bar{v}_4 = 0.6682$		0.1169	0.7
Very good	$\bar{v}_5 = 0.8655$		0.0941	0.9
Line segments				
Very bad	$\bar{w}_1 = 0.0734$		0.0556	0.1
Bad	$\bar{w}_2 = 0.1799$		0.0934	0.3
Not good, not bad	$\bar{w}_3 = 0.4008$		0.1056	0.5
Good	$\bar{w}_4 = 0.5980$		0.1158	0.7
Very Good	$\bar{w}_5 = 0.8230$		0.1195	0.9

Source: van Praag (1991).

For the "numbers" case, one can see that all averages fall within a one σ–interval of their theoretical prediction. This also holds for all levels for the line segments, except one. It is intriguing that the averages are all *below* their theoretical prediction. Perhaps this is due to the order in which the verbal labels were supplied. We think, but do not know, that the bias would have been the other way around if the order in which the verbal labels were supplied was reversed. When we regress the translation of the verbal labels into numbers by individual i, say, $v_{i,n}$ onto the translation of the verbal label into a line segment, say, $w_{i,n}$, we find

$$v_{i,n} = 0.056 + 0.974 w_{i,n}$$
$$\phantom{v_{i,n} =} (0.005) \ (0.010)$$

$$R^2 = 0.848$$

for 364*5 observations, where we did not account for the fact that the five level disturbances per individual will be strongly correlated. The fit is, however, remarkably good. From table 21.1 and this regression, we can draw some tentative conclusions:

1. A verbal label sequence seems to be understood in a similar way by different respondents, irrespective of the context of the individual respondent.
2. A verbal label sequence may be translated on a numerical scale or on a line scale: in both cases the translations are uniform over individuals.
3. Translations via various translation mechanisms (lines and figures) are consistent with each other. That is, we seem to be measuring the same thing whether we use line segments or numbers.
4. The verbal labels are translated on a bounded scale roughly in accordance with the Equal Quantile Assumption.

An interesting point is that these results were found in a context-free setting, that is, the respondents did not know which concept they were evaluating.

A final point of critique is whether the verbal labels "good," "bad," and so on, convey the same feeling to every respondent. If not, we falsely assume that individuals derive the same degree of joy from their income when describing the same verbal label. Actually, this is a question of psycholinguistics. Generally, the basic idea of language is that frequently used words will have the same meaning and emotional connotation for the members of a language community. It is the main tool of communication between people. Hence, we must assume that verbal labels like "good," "bad,"

and so on, mean approximately the same thing to all respondents sharing the same language.

The Shape of the Welfare Function

For each respondent we now have six income levels connected to six utility levels. The shape of the function can be inferred from these six combinations. Many functions can be fitted using these six points. In van Praag (1968), it was argued on theoretical grounds that it would be a lognormal distribution function. We use a distribution function because we assume boundedness of the utility function: there is a worst and a best position in terms of welfare (satisfaction). It is also known that the Von Neumann–Morgenstern model requires a bounded utility function (see Savage 1954).

Van Herwaarden and Kapteyn (1981) showed that the points of the welfare function, which were found empirically, best fitted a lognormal curve within the class of distribution functions. The logarithmic function did slightly better, but it is not bounded. Also, the logarithmic function is not borne out by the choice experiments of Kahneman, Knetsch, and Thaler (1991) and others: the marginal effect of greater losses is found to decrease, whereas the logarithmic function would imply that they should increase.

The lognormal function is defined as

$$\Lambda\,(y;\,\mu,\,\sigma) = N\,(\ln y,\,\mu,\,\sigma)$$

$$= N\,(\frac{\ln y - \mu}{\sigma};\,0,\,1)$$

where $N\,(.;0,1)$ stands for the standard lognormal distribution function. The lognormal function is sketched in figure 21.2. Notice the resemblance to the shape suggested by the experiments of Kahne-

FIGURE 21.2 The Welfare Function of Income

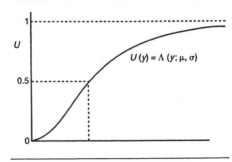

$$U(y) = \Lambda\,(y;\,\mu,\,\sigma)$$

man, Knetsch, and Thaler (1991): in both cases the function is S-shaped. Also, it is generally the case that losses to an individual have a greater effect than gains.[5]

The parameter μ is interpreted by realizing that $\Lambda\ (e^\mu; \mu, \sigma) = 0.5$. Hence, the income level e^μ is halfway between the worst and the best situation.

There are two interesting aspects of this function. First, the function is not concave for all income levels, but convex for low incomes. This runs counter to mainstream economic assumptions. In economics, it is conventional wisdom that the utility function of income is always concave. This is known as the so-called Law of Decreasing Marginal Utility, also known as Gossen's first law. It has always been based on introspection. Concavity implies that individuals are risk-averse, but scientific experiments with insurance and gambling behavior show that this is not always true; it therefore follows that a utility function may be convex in certain regions.[6]

The second point of interest about the lognormal utility function consists of the two parameters μ and σ, which may *vary individually*. Two functions with different μ and equal σ are sketched in figure 21.3. In figure 21.4, two functions are sketched with different σ and equal μ.

One can see that as μ increases, the individual needs more income to reach the same welfare level. For instance, in order to reach the welfare level 0.5, person A with $\mu_A = \ln(4,000)$ needs $4,000 per month, while B needs $6,000 per month to reach the same welfare level. If the welfare levels of individuals A and B are to be equal for other welfare levels (if σ is equal for both persons), it should hold that

$$\ln y_A - \mu_A = \ln y_B - \mu_B$$

FIGURE 21.3   Welfare Function of Income with Different μ_A μ_B (σ Constant)

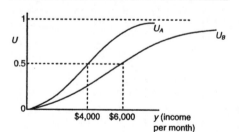

FIGURE 21.4   Welfare Function of Income with Different σ_A σ_B (μ Constant)

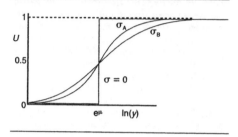

Hence, for any welfare level, income levels are equivalent to A and B if

$$\ln \frac{y_A}{y_B} = \mu_A - \mu_B$$

and therefore

$$\frac{y_A}{y_B} = e^{\mu_A - \mu_B} = \frac{4,000}{6,000}$$

Hence, a change in μ implies a proportional shift of the welfare function. One of our main preoccupations in the remaining section is to discover why individual's μ−values differ.

The parameter σ defines the slope of the welfare function.

In figure 21.4, two functions are sketched with $\sigma_A < \sigma_B$. If $\sigma = 0$, we get the limiting case where individuals are completely unsatisfied with any income until their income reaches e^μ, and where they are completely satisfied if income exceeds e^μ. It is the welfare function of a hermit. The parameter σ is called the *welfare sensitivity* of the individual.

The parameters μ and σ are estimated for each individual by

$$\hat\mu = \frac{1}{6} \Sigma \ln c_j \text{ and } \hat\sigma = \frac{1}{5} \Sigma (\ln c_j - \mu)^2$$

where $c_1, \ldots c_6$ stand for the six income levels reported in the IEQ.

The Definition of Income

In the usual IEQ version, the income concept is after-tax *monthly* household income. In some versions income *per year* has also been used and/or *before-tax* income (see Dubnoff, Vaughan, and Lancaster 1981). The choice of the definition should be adapted to what is well known to the individual. Hence, an entrepreneur who knows his annual income better than his monthly income should be questioned in terms of his annual income, while a civil servant who is paid monthly should be approached in terms of his monthly income.

THE EXPLANATION OF THE WELFARE FUNCTION

In mainstream literature, it is always assumed that the utility function of income is the same for all individuals. A major finding of our empirical research, although intuitively completely plausible, is that individual welfare functions differ between individuals. When differences are found, the imminent question is whether such differences are structural and can be correlated with observable variables. In our case, this means that we try to "explain" the variable μ by other factors, varying by individual and/or environment. In the studies, it appeared that μ could be explained to a large extent.[7] The parameter σ posed much more of a problem. We shall therefore concentrate on the explanation of μ and assume that σ is constant.

We recall that μ determines the position of $U(y)$. If μ increases, the individual becomes less satisfied with the same amount of income. In other words $U(y;\mu)$ is decreasing in μ. The first determinant that naturally comes to mind is the size of the family to be supported from the income. Income needs are probably also determined by the actual circumstances of the individual, for instance, as reflected by the individual's current income y_c. We therefore expect that needs will increase with family size (denoted by fs) and with current income y_c. Hence, fs and y_c are parameters in the individual welfare function. In van Praag (1971) and van Praag and Kapteyn (1973), the following simple relation has been found

$$\mu_i = \text{constant} + \beta_1 \ln fs_i + \beta_2 \ln y_{i,c}$$

In van Praag and Kapteyn (1973), the following (approximate values) were found: $\beta_1 = 0.1$ and $\beta_2 = 0.6$, $R^2 = 0.6$, where fs_i denotes the number of individuals living in the household of respondent i, and $y_{i,c}$ denotes the current household income of i.

Since then, the IEQ has been posed in many countries, and similar results have been found. We give an example drawn from a study on poverty by van Praag, Hagenaars, and Van Weeren (1982), based on a 1979 EUROSTAT survey of eight European countries. Moreover, we add values for

Russia estimated by Frijters and van Praag (1995). In table 21.2, we present the regression estimates for the nine countries using the equation

$$\mu_i = \beta_0 + \beta_1 \ln fs_i + \beta_2 \ln y_{i,c} + f(X_i) + u_i$$

where X denotes a number of variables used in the regression that we do not show (including age, education, employment levels, and gender), and u_i denotes the normally distributed error term. All coefficients are highly significant.

The variables vary over the nine countries, but not dramatically. The value of β_1, of course, depends on the national family allowance system. If the family allowance is high and compensates for the additional child costs, we may expect a β_1 of about zero. On the other hand, in poor countries with a less liberal system, β_1 may be rather high. This is indeed what we observe: the highest coefficient of β_1 is for Russia (in 1995), where family allowances and child support are virtually nonexistent.

It is not surprising that the satisfaction derived from a specific income level depends on the size of the household. Somewhat more surprising, especially for most economists, is that income satisfaction for any income level, not only for an individual's own current income, depends on an individual's own current income. It implies that two individuals A and B with current incomes $y_{A,c}$ and $y_{B,c}$ will evaluate any income differently. More precisely, the following is usually true:

$$U(y_B; fs, y_B) \neq U(y_B; fs, y_A)$$

That is, B evaluates his own income differently than A would evaluate the income of B. It is obvious that this fact is very relevant for the evaluation of social inequality, for the theory of a fair income distribution, and for the evaluation of social welfare. The outcomes of such normative eval-

TABLE 21.2 Estimates of Welfare Parameters for Nine Countries

	β_1	β_2^*	N	R^2
Belgium	0.097	0.433	1272	0.695
Denmark	0.075	0.631	1972	0.829
France	0.059	0.505	2052	0.676
West Germany	0.112	0.583	1574	0.693
Great Britain	0.115	0.364	1183	0.575
Ireland	0.169	0.455	1733	0.636
Italy	0.156	0.381	1911	0.510
The Netherlands	0.100	0.537	1933	0.664
Russia (1995)	0.250	0.501	1444	0.501

Source: van Praag, Hagenaars, and Van Weeren (1982).

uations depend on the income norm of the evalua-tions. Actually, U_A $(y, f_A, y_{A,c})$ describes the norms of A with respect to what equals a "bad"/"good" income and all levels in between.

A person's income may increase, for example, from $y_c^{(1)}$ to $y_c^{(2)}$. The evaluation of this change will be evaluated *differently* before the change and af-ter the change, or, as economists say, *ex ante* and *ex post*. The ex ante evaluation of future income is U_A $(y_c^{(2)}; f_s, y_c^{(1)})$, while the ex post evaluation is U_A $(y_c^{(2)}; f_s, y_c^{(2)})$. We sketch the difference between the ex ante and ex post welfare function in figure 21.5.

Due to the fact that μ increases with the income change, the welfare function shifts to the right. The effect of this is that the ex post evaluation of both $y_c^{(1)}$ and $y_c^{(2)}$ falls compared to the corre-sponding ex ante evaluations. It can be seen, and also shown, that the ex ante welfare gain is larger than the ex post gain. As a consequence, the ex ante evaluation is exaggerated when reconsidered later on, or to put it differently, the income in-crease will be a disappointment in retrospect. The value of the coefficient β_2 is crucial in this context. If $\beta_2 = 0$, the curve will not shift to the right and the whole income increase will be translated as a welfare increase. In that case, ex ante and ex post evaluations are equal.

On the other hand, if $\beta_2 = 1$, perceived welfare will not increase at all. This can be seen by exam-ining

$$\ln y_c - \mu = \ln y_c - \beta_0 - \beta_1 \ln f_s - 1.00$$
$$\ln y_c = -\beta_0 - \beta_1 \ln f_s$$

In this case, the subjective ex post welfare eval-uation does not depend on actual income. Evi-dently, this is a pathological case that has not been found in reality. The anticipated welfare increase would end with a complete deception.

The phenomenon of a shifting welfare function arising from a partial adaptation of income norms

to changing current incomes is what Brickman and Campbell (1971) called the hedonic "tread-mill." Van Praag (1971) introduced the term "preference drift" for the same phenomenon.

If all individuals have their own norms with re-gard to income levels, which depend on their own circumstances, it is justified to ask whether it is possible to construct *social standards* with respect to what is a "good" income, a "bad" income, and so on. This is possible in a certain sense. We define a social standard for a "good" income, say $\bar{y}_{good}$, as that level of income that is evaluated to be "good" by an individual with that current income. If "good" income corresponds with a welfare value of 0.7 on a [0,1] scale, it implies that $\bar{y}_{good}$ is the solution to the equation

$$U(\bar{y}_{good}; f_s, \bar{y}_{good}) = 0.7$$

Using lognormality and our estimate of μ, it is possible to show that

$$U(\bar{y}_{good}; f_s, \bar{y}_{good}) = \Lambda \bar{y}_{good};$$
$$\frac{\beta_0 + \beta_1 \ln f_s}{1 - \beta_2}, \frac{\sigma}{1 - \beta_2})$$

Similarly, we can obtain a social standard income for each possible welfare level, sketched in figure 21.6.

We call the ensuing welfare function of the so-cial standard income levels, which is also lognor-mal, a *social standard function*. We know that someone with $\bar{y}_{0.4}^*$ current income will evaluate his own income by 0.4. This analysis is frequently used to define a *subjective poverty* line as $\bar{y}_{0.4}^*$ for poverty and $\bar{y}_{0.5}^*$ as near-poverty. Notice that this line varies as a function of family size. Hence, there is a two-person household poverty line, a

FIGURE 21.6   The Social Standard Welfare Function

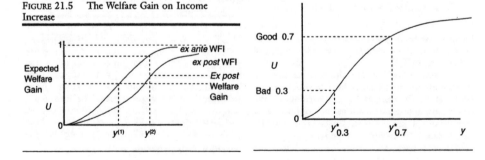

FIGURE 21.5   The Welfare Gain on Income Increase

three-person poverty line, and so on. The social standard function is an obvious tool for social policy and the evaluation of income redistribution and tax policy.

From a social-psychological viewpoint, it is very interesting to compare the welfare sensitivity of the *individual* welfare function σ with the corresponding slope parameter of the social standard function $\frac{\sigma}{1-\beta_2}$. If $0 < \beta_2 < 1$, the latter function is less steep than its individual counterpart. In other words, the larger the preference drift β_2, or in psychological terms, the stronger the working of the hedonic treadmill, the flatter the social standard curve will be compared to the individual welfare function.

Obviously, the difference between the two functions explains why a person with moderate income, for instance, $40,000 a year, thinks that someone with $100,000 is rich, while the rich person himself with $100,000 does not perceive himself to be rich. In the same way, people with $20,000 do not feel as poor as the observer earning $40,000 thinks they would.

The explanation of μ by individual variables and the stability of these explanations over samples (see also van Praag and Van der Sar 1988) may be seen as indirect evidence for the validity of the Welfare Function of Income (WFI). The measured concept may be explained to a certain extent by individual circumstances in a plausible way. One of the more recent additions is a quadratic part in age. It is seen that financial needs are greatest at the age of about forty.

However, the explanation of μ may be useful for *policy* purposes as well. If we find that the welfare derived from income depends on family size, this gives a natural clue to the question what *family allowance* would keep the family at the same household level if family size is increased from two to three by having a child. The welfare a household derives from income is

$$U_{ind} = \Lambda \; (y_{i,c}; \text{constant} + 0.1 \ln fs_i + 0.6 \ln y_{i,c}, \sigma)$$

In order to keep welfare constant if fs increases from 2 to 3, we should add $0.1 \ln (\frac{3}{2})$ to $\ln y_{i,c}$ or multiply $y_{i,c}$ by $(\frac{3}{2})^{0.1}$.

However, in the long run, this increase will not be enough to compensate the family for an increase in family size, as current income $y_{i,c}$ increases and hence μ. Therefore, we need a second increase of $0.1 \ln (\frac{3}{2}) * 0.6$, and so forth. The total increase necessary to compensate the household equals

$$0.1 \ln \left(\frac{3}{2}\right) [1 + 0.6 + 0.6^2 + \ldots]$$

$$= \frac{0.1 \ln (\frac{3}{2})}{1 - 0.6}$$

and this is precisely what the social standard welfare function would prescribe. Here we encounter a dynamic aspect, viz., that the individual welfare function is **anchored** on the individual's own current income. That is the meaning of preference drift. People adapt their norms to the present situation.

Parts of this analysis are also possible on the separate c_i levels without any reference to a cardinal utility function (see van Praag and Van der Sar 1988).

DYNAMICS

In the previous section, we described how the need parameter μ could be explained by variables such as family size and current income y_c. The latter effect is now refined by supposing that μ depends not only on *present* income but also on income in the past and income that is anticipated in the future. It follows that in the μ-equation we replace y_c by $\ldots y_{-2}, y_{-1}, y_0, \hat{y}_1, \hat{y}_2, \ldots$ whereby y_0 denotes current income, y_{-2}, y_{-1} denotes incomes one or two years in the past, and $\hat{y}_1$ stands for anticipated future income in one year's time. All experienced and anticipated incomes contribute to the formation of our present norm on incomes. In its simplest form, the μ-equation looks like

$$\mu_i = \beta_0 + \beta_1 \ln fs_i + \beta_2 \left(\sum_{t=-\infty}^{+\infty} w_t \ln y_{i,t} \right)$$

where i refers to respondent i.

The coefficients $\ldots w_{-2}, w_{-1}, w_0, w_1, w_2 \ldots$ are weights that add up to one, whereby weight w_0 denotes the weight of the present income, and $w_p = \Sigma_{t=-\infty}^{-1} w_t$ and $w_f = \Sigma_{t=1}^{\infty} w_t$ denote the weight of all past incomes and anticipated future incomes, respectively. Van Praag and Van Weeren (1983, 1988) estimated the parameters of this model on Dutch panel data. The main question concerns how the distribution of time weights will look. They regressed θ_i on the incomes of the three years in which the panel was held. For the second wave they found

$$\mu_i = 3.04 + 0.10 \ln f_{i} + 0.68(0.16 \ln y_{i,t-1}$$
$$+ 0.75 \ln y_{i,t} + 0.09 \ln y_{i,t+1})$$
$$\bar{R}^2 = 0.69$$
$$N = 645$$

where all coefficients are significant. The results tell us that current income has the greatest time weight, which implies that the time-weight distribution peaks near the present. Also, incomes in the past carry more time weight than incomes in the future, which suggests that on aggregate the time-weight distribution peaks just before the present. Of course, this is an aggregate relationship that will differ for individuals of different ages and education profiles. For a more complete analysis, more incomes than the three available were needed. Therefore, van Praag and Van Weeren (1988) used econometric techniques to *estimate* the incomes that were further back than one year (. . . y_{-3}, y_{-2}). They also estimated incomes further than one year in the future (y_2, y_3 . . .). With the use of this complete income stream, they looked somewhat further at the shape of the time-weight distribution.[8] In general, they found the time-weight distribution to have the shape of a normal curve. More specifically, the time-weight distribution may be characterized by a mode parameter, μ_τ, and a dispersion parameter, σ_τ. The empirically estimated shapes of the time-weight distribution are presented in figure 21.7 for three age brackets: thirty, fifty, and seventy.

The most interesting points are that:

- The time-weight distribution varies for different ages.
- The distribution is not symmetric around the present.
- The time weights of the past are greatest for young and old people.
- The middle-aged bracket derives its norm mostly from the present and the anticipated future.

FIGURE 21.7　Time-Discounting Density Functions for Various Ages

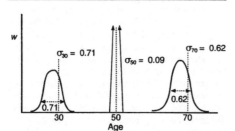

- The dispersion of the distribution varies considerably over different ages. In midlife, the time weights are extremely concentrated.

The mode and symmetry point of the time-weight distribution is at μ_τ. We call it the *time focus* of the individual. It shifts from more than one year in the past (-1.3), at twenty, to almost half a year in the future (0.45), at fifty, while it shifts back to the past (-0.43) for the age of seventy.

The change of σ_τ is also interesting. We call σ_τ the *time span* of the individual. It is rather long for young individuals and shortens when people approach midlife. The time span is intimately related to the *velocity of time* as it is perceived by the individual. The midlife has a narrow time horizon, which implies that the individual lives "day by day." The velocity of middle-aged time is high. For young and old people, the time horizon is wider, and hence the velocity of time is lower. We call the reciprocal of σ_τ, that is, $\frac{1}{\sigma_\tau}$, the *subjective velocity of time*.

In table 21.3, we present the relevant figures for several age classes. It is seen that the subjective velocity of time $\frac{1}{\sigma_\tau}$ increases by a factor $\frac{1.44}{0.09} \approx 15$ up to midlife, and then falls by a factor 6 at age seventy, and still more at later ages.

The time-weight distribution is clearly important for individuals because it determines the speed of adaptation of the income norms of the individual when faced with changing circumstances. This may be the case for individuals who become jobless and then become dependent on social benefits. The adaptation process may be a reason to smooth the path of the income reduction over time, in order to smooth the decline in welfare.

Another potential application is to evaluate the impact of inflation and accelerating inflation on the income norms and the satisfaction level derived from income. These applications are discussed in greater detail in van Praag and Van Weeren (1988).

TABLE 21.3　Values of μ_τ, σ_τ, w_P, w_O, w_F

Age	μ_τ	σ_τ	w_P	w_O	w_F
20	−1.32	1.44	0.72	0.18	0.10
30	−0.32	0.71	0.40	0.48	0.12
40	0.27	0.26	0.00	0.81	0.19
50	0.45	0.09	0.00	0.70	0.30
60	0.22	0.21	0.00	0.91	0.09
70	−0.43	0.62	0.46	0.48	0.07

The research on the time-weight distribution has not been repeated since 1988. Therefore, this must be seen as a first attempt and the results have to be considered with care. It may be that other models would yield other results. This method of obtaining time weights is based on a simple household survey and is very cheap compared to experimental laboratory experiments.

The estimates of time weights are exclusively based on the analysis of income norms. The memory and anticipation weights from norms on other subjects—for instance, on fashion, housing, or ethics—may be determined by other variables and have different time-weight distributions. There is a great need for more research in this area and for cooperation with psychologists.

METHODOLOGICAL DISCUSSION

The approach outlined above for measuring individual norms on income has been expanded to other aspects such as age and education by van Praag, Dubnoff, and Van der Sar (1988). More specifically, individuals were asked to connect age levels to subjective labels in the following Age Evaluation Question (AEQ):

When I think of other adults, I consider people to be

. . . *young,* if they are younger than ____ years old
. . . *somewhat young,* if they are about ____ years old
. . . *middle aged,* if they are about ____ years old
. . . *somewhat old,* if they are about ____ years old
. . . *old,* if they are older than ____ years old

Similar to the analysis of the IEQ, it is possible to analyze the age norms of respondents, for ex-

ample, by explaining the answers by means of regression analysis. In van Praag, Dubnoff, and Van der Sar (1988), this is done level by level for the Boston data set. Letting a_i $(i = 1 \ldots 5)$ be the respondents' age levels, they consider the equation

$$\ln a_i = \alpha_{0,i} + \alpha_{1,i} \ln age + \alpha_{2,i} \ln schooling + \alpha_{3,i} \ln fs + \alpha_{4,i} D_{gender}$$

where they assume that what is considered "young" or "old" depends on the age of the respondent, the number of years of schooling, the size of the family, and the gender of the respondent. The results of the regressions are presented in table 21.4.

From a statistical point of view, most coefficients are significant and follow a definite pattern. Our evaluation is that there is a strong systematic pattern that indicates that there is no confusion in connotation. The fraction of the variance explained, as measured by R^2, is poor in comparison to that of the IEQ but is certainly not below standard for samples of microdata of this size (≈ 500). However, it implies that there are more individual factors that were not covered in the survey than in the case of income standards, and they must be added to the systematic structure.

With respect to the interpretation of the coefficients, we make the following observations. The older the respondent is, the higher his age standards. It follows that if A is 10 percent older than B, he will have an age standard for "younger" that is about 3 percent higher (0.319*10 percent). Or in other words, if someone aged twenty finds himself "somewhat young," an older person will find him still "young." For the age standards of "old," there is much less divergence between respondents of different ages.

We see that schooling has a strong impact on the definition of "young"; people tend to stay

TABLE 21.4   Regression Equations for the Age Standards ($N = 538$)

	Constant	Age	Education	Family Size	Gender	R^2
Young	1.414	0.319	0.180	0.069	0.027	0.091
	(0.270)*	(0.043)	(0.067)	(0.026)	(0.030)	
Somewhat young	2.329	0.266	0.045	0.056	0.019	0.135
	(0.183)	(0.029)	(0.045)	(0.018)	(0.020)	
Middle-aged	3.160	0.177	0.014	0.016	0.048	0.163
	(0.115)	(0.018)	(0.028)	(0.011)	(0.013)	
Somewhat old	3.740	0.117	0.018	0.003	0.047	0.132
	(0.095)	(0.015)	(0.023)	(0.009)	(0.011)	
Old	4.243	0.058	0.067	0.003	0.048	0.071
	(0.099)	(0.016)	(0.025)	(0.010)	(0.011)	

Source: van Praag, Dubnoff, and Van der Sar (1988).
*Standard deviations in parentheses.

"young" longer. The impact of a large family on age standards is also evident. In such families, youngsters are considered to be children longer.

The social implications of these tendencies are not imminent. However, culturally it might be of interest that, in Western countries, where the level of education has been increasing for decades, the concept of adulthood has become identified with an increase in age. Finally, the gender of the respondent also plays a role. If the respondent is female, the age standards are somewhat higher than for males, which implies that females tend to diminish the impact of age slightly. Except for the female tendency to stay and look young as long as possible, the gender difference also conforms to the longevity of women compared to men.

Again we see that "young" does not mean the same thing to young people as to old people. We can derive a general age a_i^* standard by setting a_i^* = age, yielding

$$\ln a_i^* = \frac{1}{1 - \alpha_{1,i}}$$
$$[\alpha_{0,i} + \alpha_{2,i} \ln schooling + \alpha_{3,i} \ln fs + \alpha_{4,i} D_{gender}]$$

The resulting age standards are tabulated in table 21.5.

Similarly to the Age Evaluation Question, individuals were asked which education level they thought was "very educated," "uneducated," and so on. By explaining the answers to this Education Evaluation Question (EEQ), Van der Sar (1991) was able to measure an individual norm on education as well. The interested reader is referred to Van der Sar (1991) for a full discussion of the AEQ, EEQ, and related questions.

Individual Norms and General Standards

The evidence described earlier suggests that people have *subjective norms* concerning various

concepts. These norms will differ among individuals. They are measured by questions such as the IEQ, AEQ, and EEQ, which supply us with numerical levels related to verbal labels or other symbols.

These questions may be posed theoretically in two ways: one may supply the label as stimulus and ask for an amount as a reply, or one may supply an amount as stimulus and ask for a label as a reply. The first way has been selected as the most practical when there are many different respondents with differing norms. It is also somewhat more informative, as people can space their answers.

In addition, we have *evaluations* by individuals of their *own situation*. This is done by fitting their own situation on their own norm. For instance, an individual i with current income y_c evaluates his own income by $U_i(y_c; y_c, fs)$.

A final point is whether we may in some sense speak of general or social objective standards in contrast to individual subjective norms. Each individual may have an idea about what he thinks is a "bad" or a "good" income, but is there also a way to give content to a social norm with respect to what is a "good" income and what is a "bad" income? This question is especially pertinent when we think of a socially acceptable definition of poverty, or eligibility for social assistance. A second example is the general standard for being "old," which is relevant for fixing the retirement age. A general standard may be derived from the individual standards by calculating the income level, age, education, and so on, where people evaluate their *own* income, age, and so on, as "bad," "good," or "young," "old."

Political applications of the IEQ are not extensively dealt with in this chapter, but we mention applications to poverty measurement (Goedhart et al. 1977; van Praag, Hagenaars, and Van Weeren 1982; Hagenaars 1986; Plug et al. 1996; van Praag and Flik 1992; Frijters and van Praag 1995; Colasanto, Kapteyn, and Van der Gaag 1983; Stanovnik 1992). Further applications concern income inequality (van Praag 1977), household equivalence scales (Kapteyn and van Praag 1976; Kapteyn 1994; van Praag and Warnaar 1997), and climate equivalence scales (Frijters and van Praag 1998; van Praag 1988).

In this method, there is a strong anchor effect. The answer of the respondent depends very strongly on his own situation. One may attempt to avoid this, for example, by asking "Thinking about an *average* family with two children, what does it

TABLE 21.5   General Age Standards

| | General Standards | |
	Male Respondents	Female Respondents
Young	17.69	18.41
Somewhat young	30.16	30.95
Middle-aged	49.54	52.50
Somewhat old	65.73	69.31
Old	75.06	78.91

Source: van Praag, Dubnoff, and Van der Sar (1988).

need per month for an adequate living?" (compare, Rainwater 1971). While avoiding the anchor effect of one's own situation, this question introduces a new problem: what is regarded as an average family will depend on the reference weighting system of the respondent. We can at least deal with the anchor effect of the individual's situation, as we know the respondent's own situation, but we do not know what the respondent considers to be an average family. The usefulness of this question thus depends on whether it is reasonable to assume that there is common agreement about what constitutes an average family. In heterogeneous populations, such agreement will be absent.

Obviously, the method works only to evaluate one-dimensional situations where numbers may be assigned and where a natural ordering is manifest.

The described IEQ method breaks down when the society is only partly monetized. In that case, welfare cannot be characterized on the one-dimensional income scale. An ingenious way out of this problem has been suggested by Pradhan and Ravallion (1998). Their approach is to ask for evaluations of consumption levels instead of evaluations of income levels.

At present, welfare functions have been measured in nearly all EC countries, the United States, Hungary, Slovenia, Poland, and Russia. In almost all cases, except in the United States, the samples were fairly large-scale, ranging from one thousand respondents to over twenty thousand. Panel data are scarce; the Dutch Socio-Economic Panel carried the question for a number of years, while at present a Russian large-scale household panel includes the question as well (see Frijters and van Praag 1995).

FUTURE DIRECTIONS: WELL-BEING *AND* WELFARE

Traditionally, economists identify welfare (or even happiness) with income. However, it is well known and also fully recognized by other disciplines that there is more between heaven and earth than income and everything that can be bought with income.

This calls for an operational distinction between economic *welfare* and *well-being*. Welfare is the evaluation assigned by the individual to income or, more generally, to the contribution to his well-being from those goods and services that he can buy with money.

Next to material resources, other aspects determine the quality of our life. We can think of our health, the relationship with our partner and family and friends, the quality of our work (job satisfaction), our political freedom, our physical environment, and so on. We shall call this comprehensive concept *well-being* or quality of life (see Nussbaum and Sen [1992] for philosophical discussions about this concept).

It is empirically possible for most individuals to evaluate their life as a whole. A well-known example is the following question devised by Cantril (1965): "Here is a ladder with ten steps which denote the 'ladder of life.' The bottom step stands for the worst possible life. If you climb up and arrive at the tenth step, you arrive at the best possible life. Can you indicate where you are at the moment?" Other questions that are very similar to Cantril's question ask individuals to denote how *satisfied* or how *happy* they are with their life as a whole. The concept of well-being is thus very similar to that of life satisfaction or happiness, and we will not discuss the differences.

These questions are a standard module in many psychosociological surveys, and respondents have no difficulty responding. See Veenhoven (1996) and Diener and Suh (1997) for reviews of the psychological literature on well-being. It is also obvious that responding to these questions is tantamount to evaluating one's life situation on a bounded numerical scale between 0 and 10.

In fact, we have here a measurement method that *defines* the well-being concept in an operational way. We notice that what we measure is an evaluation of the individual's actual situation. Hence, it is not an "individual norm," as measured by the IEQ, where six qualitative labels are linked to income levels, yielding an "income norm." The Cantril question provides us with a *social standard* on well-being.

We assume again, as is always done implicitly, that the respondents' answers are comparable, in the sense that individuals evaluating their lives with the same grade, such as a 5 or an 8, are equally unhappy or happy. The main questions are:

• What determines well-being?
• What are the differences between welfare and well-being?

Plug and van Praag (1995) and Plug (1997), analyzed these two questions on a large sample (1991) of about six thousand Dutch married couples, with the husband younger than sixty-five years of age. They hypothesized that well-being, to be denoted by W, depends on various contributing factors and determinants. Some of these factors are objective ones, like family size, income, age, and religion. Other variables are called "problem intensities." They relate to the intensity with which an individual "has problems" with his health, job, marriage, physical environment, and so on.[9] Formally we write

$$W = W(P, z)$$

where P stands for a vector of problem areas, and z for a number of objective variables. Problem intensities, such as P_{health}, P_{job} . . . , are operationalized by asking individuals "many/few/no problem" questions. An example of such a question is: "Have you had problems in the last three months with your health?" (no/a little/some/serious?). The outcomes are on a numerical scale.[10] Plug and van Praag (1995) found the estimates presented in table 21.6.

The first column refers to the explanation of well-being, while the second column refers to the explanation of μ by the *same* variables. The first nine variables stand for problems with health, with partner, with job, with sleep, with alcohol and drugs, with family, sexual problems, problems with parents, and the evaluation of the neighborhood. These variables reach their highest value when there are no problems. "Religion" stands for the intensity of religious feelings where the highest value corresponds to "nonreligious." The IEQ measures welfare, while the Cantril question measures the broader concept of life satisfaction or well-being.

The main difference between welfare and well-being is that "problem" variables hardly affect the evaluation of income but do, however, affect well-being.

The second question is also answered at the same time. Welfare and well-being are different concepts, where welfare is dependent only on a small subset of the set of variables that influence well-being. The size and sign of the effect is also different.

To illustrate the relevance of the results, Plug and van Praag (1995) estimated the optimum number of children, as family size appears quad-

TABLE 21.6 Estimation Results of w and μ

	w	μ
Health	0.08	−0.00
	(11.43)	(−1.11)
Partner	0.04	−0.01
	(3.62)	(−1.13)
Job	0.07	−0.01
	(9.57)	(−1.67)
Sleep	0.07	0.00
	(8.90)	(0.55)
Alcohol/drugs	0.04	−0.01
	(4.27)	(−1.22)
Family	0.07	−0.01
	(7.92)	(−2.61)
Sexuality	0.03	0.00
	(3.50)	(0.86)
Parents	0.05	−0.01
	(6.53)	(−2.16)
Neighborhood	0.08	0.00
	(13.61)	(0.26)
Religion	0.02	−0.01
	(4.00)	(−3.54)
ln y	0.12	0.55
	(5.13)	(41.49)
ln fs	−0.81	−0.34
	(−3.60)	(−2.66)
ln y ln fs	0.09	0.03
	(4.13)	(2.44)
$\ln^2 fs$	−0.06	0.03
	(−3.36)	(2.49)
ln age	−2.14	1.10
	(−5.88)	(5.27)
$\ln^2 age$	0.30	−0.14
	(4.13)	(−4.82)
Dummy-job	−0.10	0.01
	(−5.07)	(−0.57)
Constant	3.10	2.24
	(4.72)	(5.93)
R^2	0.24	0.61

Source: van Praag and Plug (1995).

ratically in W. This optimum number of children depends on such factors as income. Table 21.7 was derived for the Netherlands. It shows that the optimum number of children is zero for a family with an annual after-tax income of NLG20,418. For a family with an annual income of NLG51,451, two children are the optimum family size.

TABLE 21.7 The Optimum Family Size for Specific Income Levels

$fs = 1$	$fs = 2$	$fs = 3$	$fs = 4$	$fs = 5$	$fs = 6$
8,103	20,418	35,060	51,451	69,280	88,346

Note: Family income is measured in Dutch guilders (NLG2 is about $1.00).

An especially promising path is the *combination* of more than one satisfaction measure. We will explain this idea with a specific example from van Praag and Plug (1995).

We consider again the social standard function of income as derived earlier, which we denote by $\bar{U}(y;fs)$ and where we ignore other variables. We know already that $\bar{U}$ decreases with the number of children. More specifically, it is possible to assess the monetary value of the "welfare cost of additional children." Assuming that a representative couple has two children and an annual income of $50,000, their welfare will be $\bar{U}(50;4)$. Assume now that the couple has another child, which causes $\bar{U}$ to change to $\bar{U}(50;5)$. The welfare decline may be compensated by an income increase Δ^U_y such that

$$\bar{U}(50 + \Delta^U_y; 5) = \bar{U}(50; 4)$$

We call Δ^U_y the *shadow price* of the additional child, which is the monetary amount needed to keep a household on the same welfare level.[11] Notice that this depends on the rank order of the child and that the shadow price will depend on income.

On the other hand, we have the well-being measure *W*, based on the Cantril question, yielding a well-being function

$$W(y, fs)$$

again ignoring all other variables. Given our estimates of the previous table, *W* is strongly quadratic in *fs*, implying that well-being initially increases with family size up to a certain point, thereafter falling with increasing family size. This *nonmonotonic* behavior points to the fact that an extra child may be wanted for its non-economic contribution. It is a gain for well-being while at the same time a loss in terms of welfare. Hence, there are *nonmonetary* benefits of having children and monetary costs. The *W* function captures both and increases with family size if the benefits outweigh the costs, and decreases if the costs outweigh the benefits. There is equality at the optimum family size.

Considering $W(y,fs)$, we may calculate the *shadow well-being* price of an additional child $\Delta^W y$, by solving

$$W(y, fs) = W(y + \Delta^W y, fs + \Delta fs)$$

Here $\Delta^W y$ is the monetary counter value of this difference:

$$\Delta^W y = Benefits - Costs$$

We call it the shadow price with respect to well-being. It is positive if we welcome a child and neg-

ative if the opposite holds. From the calculation on *U*, we obtained an estimate of the cost

$$\Delta^U y = Costs$$

Adding $\Delta^W y$ and $\Delta^U y$ yields the monetary value of benefits.

The benefits may be considerable, as witnessed by the fact that childless couples try to adopt children or are willing to undergo expensive medical treatment. The benefits of children as calculated for Dutch families in 1991 are shown in table 21.8

We see that the value of the (nonmonetary) benefits of the first child is negative at a low income level. The benefit of the first child becomes positive for incomes above NLG20,000. For the second child, the benefits remain negative until an income of about NLG40,000. For the third and fourth children, the benefits remain negative for even longer. With respect to costs, there is no ambiguity: costs are always positive. However, the cost of each additional child decreases. As we can see, these nonmonetary benefits are substantial and increase strongly with income.

At this stage, we warn that the study is in the beginning stage and that not too much value should be assigned to this or other results without replication. However, the path seems promising. A future step is to estimate the substitution and trade-off between variables and the calculation of

TABLE 21.8 Money Value of Nonmonetary Child Benefits

	One Breadwinner			
Income*	First Child	Second Child	Third Child	Fourth Child
20,000	−262	−838	−1,005	−1,039
30,000	1,114	−236	−748	−959
40,000	2,911	651	−279	−713
50,000	5,023	1,749	348	−341
60,000	7,383	3,018	1,100	130

	Two Breadwinners			
Income	First Child	Second Child	Third Child	Fourth Child
20,000	−726	−1,153	−1,240	−1,223
30,000	419	−708	−1,100	−1,236
40,000	1,983	22	−747	−1,082
50,000	3,871	964	−237	−802
60,000	5,990	2,074	399	−423

Source: van Praag and Plug (1995)
*Family income is measured in Dutch guilders (NLG2 is about $1.00).

430   *Well-Being*

monetary values of health increases, family increases, education, marriage quality, and so on.

See Frijters (1998) for other applications and extensions of Leyden methodology on welfare and satisfaction.

CONCLUSIONS

The work originating from Leyden School has tried to operationalize the concepts of welfare, well-being, and so on, which are considered immeasurable and esoteric by most of the economic profession. With rather simple and inexpensive questions in large-scale surveys, considerable information has been found on feelings. At least the feelings of welfare and well-being may be "explained" by objectively measurable variables and by partial satisfaction measures with respect to aspects of life. The information is helpful for quantifying memory and anticipation weights.[12] The potential policy applications are plentiful. We briefly described its use to calculate family equivalence scales. A rather recent development is the combination of the welfare and well-being measurements, which makes it possible to identify the costs and benefits of various choices. We demonstrated this for the option of choosing to have children.

The apparatus developed thus far is not typically restricted to economic problems but can also be used by psychologists, sociologists, and political scientists. Its use in health economics seems straightforward.

The story, we hope, is not finished but only in the early stages. The main empirical restriction is that the data sets are scattered and almost never contain the IEQ, sound economic information (consumption, income, job characteristics), and "soft" information on feelings on several aspects of life, such as the Cantril question. In this respect, the United States, where so much effort is given to research, is conspicuously absent.

NOTES

1. Decision utility as defined by Kahneman, Wakker, and Sarin (1997) may be ordinal or cardinal.
2. See also van Praag (1968) for an attempt to find a functional form of the utility function with the use of axioms and secondary assumptions.
3. The "quality-of-life" concept is very broad and interpreted by some to mean the same thing as happiness (Veenhoven 1996) or average satisfaction (Dow and

Juster 1985). We discuss here the interpretation we believe most *economists* in this field use.
4. A reply was given by van Praag and Kapteyn (1994).
5. One particular feature of the value function found by Kahneman, Knetsch, and Thaler (1991) cannot be replicated: they find a value function that changes direction abruptly at the reference position. The number of levels used in our measure is simply too small to find such a jump in direction.
6. A variable of much economic interest, Pratt's (1964) measure of relative risk aversion (or Frisch flexibility), can be directly calculated as

$$\frac{\partial \ln u}{\partial \ln y} = -\frac{1}{2\sigma^2}(\ln y - \mu) - 1$$

It varies from highly positive for small y to very negative for large y.
7. An explanation does not necessarily mean a one-way causal relationship.
8. The likely result of using estimates for some incomes is that the effect of income different from the present income will be underestimated. The qualitative results should, however, remain the same.
9. Plug and van Praag (1995) name the extent to which individuals are free of a problem, a "partial satisfaction." However, given that this term may be confusing, we use here the term "problem intensities."
10. For estimation purposes, they prefer to transform W and P from their bounded scale into $(-\infty, +\infty)$. It might be feared that people will center in the middle and that extreme answers will be rare. To solve both problems, the *empirical* distribution functions $\hat{F}$ of the W and P values are calculated, and the value $\hat{F}$ is assigned to the various levels instead of the original ones. Then they transform $\hat{F}$ again by taking the inverse standard normal, which means that instead of W and P, $\tilde{W} = N^{-1}(\hat{F}_w(W); 0, 1)$ and $\tilde{P} = N^{-1}(\hat{F}_p(P); 0, 1)$ are utilized. The transformations do no intrinsic harm, but they are used only to get more response differentiation and a stretching on $(-\infty, +\infty)$. From now on, we will drop the tildes.
11. The "cost of children" will at least include the expenditures on an additional child. Future research looks at whether it also includes the monetary shadow value of time spent on a child.
12. In van Praag (1981), Kapteyn (1977), Van der Sar (1991), Van de Stadt, Kapteyn, and Van de Geer (1985), Kapteyn, van Praag, and van Heerwaarden (1976), and van Praag, Kapteyn, and van Heerwaarden (1979) the IEQ was also used for the extraction of information on the social reference mechanism, as the answers to the IEQ are influenced by social reference groups. This application was not dealt with in this chapter.

REFERENCES

Allais, M., and Hagen, O. (1979). *Expected utility hypothesis and the Allais paradox.* Dordrecht: Reidel.

Arrow, K. (1951). *Social choice and individual values.* New York: Wiley.

Atkinson, A. B. (1970). On the measurement of inequality. *Journal of Economic Theory, 2,* 244–63.

Brickman, P., and Campbell, D. T. (1971). Hedonic relativism and planning the good society. In M. H. Appley (Ed.), *Adaptation-level theory: A Symposium* (pp. 287–304). New York: Academic Press.

Callan, T., and Nolan, B. (1991). Concepts of poverty and the poverty line. *Journal of Economic Surveys, 5,* 243–61.

Cantril, H. (1965). *The pattern of human concerns.* New Brunwick, N.J.: Rutgers University Press.

Christensen, L. R., Jorgenson, D. W., and Lau, L. J. (1975). Transcendental logarithmic utility functions. *American Economic Review, 65,* 367–83.

Clark, A. E. (1996). Job satisfaction in Britain. *British Journal of Industrial Relations, 34,* 189–217.

Clark, A. E., and Oswald, A. J. (1994). Unhappiness and unemployment. *Economic Journal, 104,* 648–59.

———. (1996). Satisfaction and comparison income. *Journal of Public Economics, 61,* 359–81.

Colosanto, D., Kapteyn, A., and Van der Gaag, J. (1983). Two subjective definitions of poverty: Results from the Wisconsin basic needs study. *Journal of Human Resources, 28,* 127–38.

Debreu, G. (1959). *Theory of value.* New Haven, Conn.: Yale University Press.

Diener, E., and Suh, E. (1997). Measuring quality of life: Economic, social, and subjective indicators. *Social Indicators Research, 40,* 189–216.

Dow, G. K., and Juster, F. T. (1985). Goods, time, and well-being: The joint dependency problem. In F. T. Juster and F. P. Stafford (Eds.), *Time, goods, and well-being.* Ann Arbor, Mich.: Institute of Social Research.

Dubnoff, D., Vaughan, D., and Lancaster, C. (1981). Income satisfaction measures in equivalence scale applications. *Proceedings of the Social Statistics Section, American Statistical Association,* 348–52.

Easterlin, R. (1974). Does economic growth improve the human lot? Some empirical evidence. In P. David and R. Reder (Eds.), *Nations and households in economic growth: Essays in honor of Moses Abramovitz* (pp. 89–125). New York: Academic Press.

———. (1995). Will raising the incomes of all increase the happiness of all? *Journal of Economic Behavior and Organization, 27,* 35–47.

Edgeworth, F. Y. (1881). *Mathematical psychics.* London: Kegan Paul.

Frijters, P. (1998). Explorations of welfare and satisfaction. Ph.D. diss. University of Amsterdam.

Frijters, P., and van Praag, B. M. S. (1995). Estimates of poverty ratios and equivalence scales for Russia and parts of the former USSR. *Tinbergen Discussion Papers,* 95–149.

———. (1998). Climate equivalence scales and the effect of climate change on Russian welfare and well-being. *Climate Change, 39,* 61–81.

Frisch, R. (1932). *New methods of measuring marginal utility.* Tübingen: Mohr.

Gershuny J., and Halpin, B. (1995). Time use, quality of life, and process benefit. In A. Offer (Ed.), *In pur-suit of the quality of life* (pp. 188–210). Oxford: Clarendon Press.

Goedhart, T., Halberstadt, V., Kapteyn, A., and van Praag, B. M. S. (1977). The poverty line: Concepts and measurement. *Journal of Human Resources, 12,* 503–20.

Hagenaars, A. J. M. (1986). *The perception of poverty.* Amsterdam: North-Holland.

Heywood, J. S., Siebert, W. S., and Wei, X. (1997). Are union jobs worse? Are government jobs better? University of Birmingham. Unpublished paper.

Hirschberg, J. G., Maasoumi, E., and Slottje, D. J. (1991). Cluster analysis for measuring welfare and quality of life across countries. *Journal of Econometrics, 50,* 131–50.

Jorgenson, D. W., and Slesnick, D. T. (1984). Aggregate consumer behavior and the measurement of inequality. *Review of Economic Studies, 166,* 369–92.

Kahneman, D., Knetsch, J., and Thaler, R. (1991). The endowment effect, loss aversion, and status quo bias. *Journal of Economic Perspectives, 5,* 193–206.

Kahneman, D., and Tversky, A. (1979). Prospect theory: An analysis of decision under risk. *Econometrica, 47,* 263–91.

Kahneman, D., Wakker, P. P., and Sarin, R. (1997). Back to Bentham? Explorations of experienced utility. *Quarterly Journal of Economics* (May) 375–405.

Kapteyn, A. (1977). A theory of preference formation. Ph.D. diss., Leyden University.

———. (1994). The measurement of household cost functions: Revealed preference versus subjective measures. *Journal of Population Economics, 7,* 333–50.

Kapteyn, A., and van Praag, B. M. S. (1976). A new approach to the construction of equivalence scales. *European Economic Review, 7,* 313–35.

Kapteyn, A., van Praag, B. M. S., and Van Heerwaarden, F. G. (1976). Individual welfare functions and social reference spaces. Report 76.01. Economic Institute, Leyden University.

Kurian, G. T. (1984). *The new book of world rankings,* London: Macmillan.

Levy-Garboua, L., and Montmarquette, L. C. (1997). Reported job satisfaction: What does it mean? Cahier de Recherche 1. University of Paris.

Maasoumi, E. (1989). Composite indices of income and other developmental indicators: A general approach. *Research on Economic Inequality, 1,* 269–86.

Markowitz, H. M. (1952). The utility of wealth. *Journal of Political Economy, 60,* 51–58.

Ng, Y. K. (1997). A case for happiness, cardinalism, and interpersonal comparability. *Economic Journal, 107,* 1848–58.

Nussbaum, M., and Sen, A. K. (Eds.). (1992). *The quality of life.* Oxford: Clarendon Press.

Parducci, A. (1995). *Happiness, pleasure, and judgment: The contextual theory and its applications.* Mahwah, N.J.: Erlbaum.

Pareto, V. (1904). *Manuel d'economie politique.* Paris: Girard.

432 *Well-Being*

Pigou, A. C. (1948). *The economics of welfare*. 4th ed. London: Macmillan.

Plug, E. J. S. (1997). Leyden welfare and beyond. Ph.D. diss. University of Amsterdam.

Plug, E. J. S., Krausse, P., van Praag, B. M. S., and Wagner, G. G. (1996). The measurement of poverty: Exemplified by the German case. In N. Ott and G. G. Wagner (Eds.), *Income inequality and poverty in Eastern and Western Europe* (pp. 69–90). Heidelberg: Springer.

Plug, E. J. S., and van Praag, B. M. S. (1995). Family equivalence scales within a narrow and broad welfare context. *Journal of Income Distribution*, 4, 171–86.

Pradhan, M., and Ravallion, M. (1998). Measuring poverty using qualitative perceptions of welfare. *World Bank Policy Research Working Paper, NR 20-11*.

Pratt, J. W. (1964). Risk aversion in the small and in the large. *Econometrica*, 32, 122–26.

Rainwater, L. (1971). Interim report on explorations of social status, living standards, and family life styles. Cambridge Mass.: Joint Center for Urban Studies of the Massachusetts Institute of Technology and Harvard University. Unpublished paper.

Ravallion, M. (1994). *Poverty comparisons*. Fundamentals in Pure and Applied Economics 56. Chur, Switzerland: Harwood Academic Press.

Robbins, K. (1932). *An essay on the nature and significance of economic science*. London: Macmillan.

Samuelson, P. A. (1945). *Foundations of economic science*. Cambridge Mass.: Harvard University Press.

Savage, L. J. (1954). *The foundations of statistics*. New York: Wiley.

Seidl, C. (1994). How sensible is the Leyden individual welfare function of income? *European Economic Review*, 38, 1633–59.

Sen, A. K. (1987). *The standard of living*. Tanner Lectures. Cambridge: Cambridge University Press.

Stanovnik, T. (1992). Perception of poverty and income satisfaction. *Journal of Economic Psychology*, 13, 57–69.

Tinbergen, J. (1991). On the measurement of welfare. *Journal of Econometrics*, 50, 7–13.

Townsend, P. (1979). *Poverty in the United Kingdom*. Harmondsworth: Penguin.

————. (1993). *The analysis of poverty*. London: Harvester/Wheatsheaf.

Van der Sar, N. L. (1991). Applied utility analysis. Ph.D. diss. Erasmus University, Rotterdam, Haveka (Alblasserdam).

Van de Stadt, H., Kapteyn, A., and Van de Geer, S. (1985). The relativity of utility: Evidence from panel data. *Review of Economics and Statistics*, 67, 179–87.

van Herwaarden, F. G., and Kapteyn, A. (1981). Empirical comparison of the shape of welfare functions. *European Economic Review*, 15, 261–86.

van Praag, B. M. S. (1968). Individual welfare functions and consumer behavior: A theory of rational irrationality. Ph.D. diss. University of Amsterdam.

————. (1971). The welfare function of income in Belgium: An empirical investigation. *European Economic Review*, 2, 337–69.

————. (1977). The perception of welfare inequality. *European Economic Review*, 10, 189–207.

————. (1981). Reflections on the theory of individual welfare functions. Report 81.14. Center for Research in Public Economics, Leyden University. *Proceedings of the American Statistical Association*.

————. (1988). Climate equivalence scales: An application of a general method. *European Economic Review*, 32(4), 1019–24.

————. (1991). Ordinal and cardinal utility: An integration of the two dimensions of the welfare concept. *Journal of Econometrics*, 50, 69–89.

van Praag, B. M. S., Dubnoff, S., and Van der Sar, N. L. (1988). On the measurement and explanation of standards with respect to income, age, and education. *Journal of Economic Psychology*, 9, 481–98.

van Praag, B. M. S., and Flik, R. J. (1992). Poverty lines and equivalence scales: A theoretical and empirical investigation. Poverty Measurement for Economies in Transition in Eastern Europe, International Scientific Conference, Warsaw, October 7–9. Polish Statistical Association, Central Statistical Office.

van Praag, B. M. S., Hagenaars, A., and Van Weeren, J. (1982). Poverty in Europe. *Review of Income and Wealth*, 28, 345–59.

van Praag, B. M. S., and Kapteyn, A. (1973). Further evidence on the individual welfare function of income: An empirical investigation in the Netherlands. *European Economic Review*, 4, 33–62.

————. (1994). How sensible is the Leyden individual welfare function of income? A reply. *European Economic Review*, 38, 1817–25.

van Praag, B. M. S., Kapteyn, A., and Van Herwaarden, F. G. (1979). The definition and measurement of social reference spaces. *Netherlands Journal of Sociology*, 15, 13–25.

van Praag, B. M. S., and Plug, E. J. S. (1995). New developments in the measurement of welfare and well-being. Tinbergen Discussion Paper 95–60. University of Amsterdam.

van Praag, B. M. S., and Van der Sar, N. L. (1988). Household cost functions and equivalence scales. *Journal of Human Resources*, 23, 193–210.

van Praag, B. M. S., and Van Weeren, J. (1983). Some panel-data evidence on the time-discounting mechanism in the formation of value judgments on income with applications to social security and income policy. Report 83.22. Center for Research in Public Economics, Leyden University.

————. (1988). Memory and anticipation processes and their significance for social security and income inequality. In S. Maital (Ed.), *Applied behavioral economics* (pp. 731–51). Brighton: Wheatsheaf Books.

van Praag, B. M. S., and Warnaar, M. (1997). The cost

of children and the effect of demographic variables on consumer demand. In M. R. Rosenzweig and O. Stark (Eds.), *The handbook of population and family economics* (pp. 241–72). Amsterdam: North Holland.

Veenhoven, R. (1996). Happy life expectancy: A comprehensive measure of quality of life in nations. *Social Indicators Research, 39,* 1–58.

Wakker, P. P., and Tversky, A. (1993). An axiomatization of cumulative prospect theory. *Journal of Risk and Uncertainty, 7,* 147–76.

Wansbeek, T., and Kapteyn, A. (1983). Tackling hard questions by means of soft methods: The use of individual welfare functions in socioeconomic policy. *Kyklos, 36,* 249–69.

[8]

The Review *of* Economics *and* Statistics

VOL. LXVII   MAY 1985   NUMBER 2

THE RELATIVITY OF UTILITY: EVIDENCE FROM PANEL DATA

Huib van de Stadt, Arie Kapteyn, and Sara van de Geer*

Abstract—The paper addresses the question whether utility may be viewed as a completely relative concept. In a dynamic setting this means that one has to model both habit formation and utility interdependence. The resulting model contains unobservable variables and requires panel data to be estimated. Using the first two waves of an annual panel in The Netherlands, different specifications of the model are estimated, involving alternative sets of identifying restrictions. It turns out that the data are compatible with the hypothesis that utility is completely relative, but we cannot exclude the possibility that utility is partly relative and partly absolute.

I. Introduction

MOST economic models of human behavior assume that individual utility functions are constant, i.e., not influenced by the behavior of others or by own past behavior. This does not imply that economists building these models necessarily believe in the invariance of utility functions. In fact, papers explicitly defending the invariance of utility are rather scarce, Stigler and Becker (1977) being a notable exception. For most others, constant utility functions may serve primarily as a first approximation or a convenient starting point. Whatever the exact motivation may be, endogenous preferences have not gained a strong foothold in economics, despite a long history of economists acknowledging that preferences are not constant and can be influenced by a variety of variables.[1] In contrast, major parts of psy-

chology and sociology assume the variability of preferences (and opinions, values, norms, etc.) and construct models to explain the variation. These theories come under headings such as relative deprivation theory (e.g., Davis (1959), Runciman (1966)), adaptation level theory (e.g., Helson (1964, 1971)), reference group theory (Hyman and Singer (1968)), etc.

There is a small group of economists who maintain that utility is a completely relative concept, that is, an individual evaluates a bundle of consumption goods by comparing it to the consumption bundles of others, or perhaps to the bundles the individual has consumed in the past. Duesenberry's relative income hypothesis is probably the best known example of a theory that rests on a relative utility concept (Duesenberry (1949)). Before Duesenberry, the Dutch economist Van der Wijk (1939) already hypothesized: "Within a very wide range of incomes, every group in society feels equally poor" (p. 57). In turn, he quotes Marx (1930) as one of the proponents of similar ideas. In more recent times, Easterlin (1974) has provided evidence that the level of income contributes little to one's subjective feeling of well-being, whereas one's *ranking* in the income distribution of a country has a significant effect. At about the same time, Duncan (1975), a sociologist, came to similar conclusions.

One of us (Kapteyn (1977)) has formalized the notion of relative utility into a theory of preference formation. Empirical studies have turned up evidence in favor of the theory (e.g., Van Herwaarden et al. (1977), Kapteyn (1977), Kapteyn et al. (1980), Kapteyn and Wansbeek (1982)). The theory is essentially dynamic, but hitherto only cross-sectional data have been available to test it. In this paper, longitudinal (panel) data are used to investigate the empirical validity of the theory.

The utility concept used in the empirical analysis is the individual welfare function of income due to Van Praag (1968, 1971). It is briefly described in

Received for publication October 27, 1983. Revision accepted for publication August 28, 1984.

*The Netherlands Central Bureau of Statistics, Tilburg University, and Tilburg University, respectively.

While working on the paper, Van de Stadt spent most of his time at the Center for Research in Public Economics of Leyden University, where the computations were carried out by Eitel Homan. The study is part of the Leyden Income Evaluation Project. Financial support from the Netherlands Organization for the Advancement of Pure Research and comments by the referees are gratefully acknowledged. The views expressed in this paper are those of the authors and do not necessarily reflect those of the Netherlands Central Bureau of Statistics.

[1] A fairly extensive discussion of the economic literature on variable preferences is given by Pollak (1978) and Kapteyn et al. (1980). Additional references are Pigou (1903), Becker (1974), Layard (1980), Rader (1980), and Frank (1982). For reasons of space, no literature overview is attempted here.

section II. The relativity theory, which explains differences in utility functions between different individuals, is presented next (section III). Since the ideas investigated here have been motivated and explained at various places (see the references above), the theory is not presented in its greatest generality, but in a form that corresponds to the data at hand. In section IV the estimating equation is derived. The empirical results are presented and discussed in section V.

II. The Utility Concept

Consider an indirect utility function defined on prices and income.[2] Within a community where individuals can be assumed to face the same prices, the indirect utility function can be taken to be exclusively a function of income. Suppose we are able to observe this indirect utility function for each individual in the community. Partly due to the lack of price variation across individuals, it will generally be impossible to retrieve the corresponding direct utility functions solely on the basis of this information. However, for tests of a relative theory of utility we do not need to know the complete direct utility function per individual. Implications of the theory for differences in direct utility functions between individuals carry over to implications regarding indirect utility functions. If we are thus able to measure indirect utility functions per individual, we may expect to be able to perform at least some tests of a relative utility theory.

In this study we use individually measured utility functions of income, whose theoretical basis is similar, though not identical, to that of an indirect utility function. The concept used is the *individual welfare function of income* (WFI), introduced by Van Praag (1968, 1971). Van Praag assumes that individuals are able to rate income levels on a bounded ratio scale. More specifically, his theory implies that an individual n will evaluate any income y according to his WFI $U_n(y)$, which has approximately the following functional form:

$$U_n(y) \approx \Lambda(y; \mu_n, \sigma_n) \equiv N(\ln y; \mu_n, \sigma_n), \quad (1)$$

where $\Lambda(\cdot; \mu_n, \sigma_n)$ is the lognormal distribution function with median $\exp(\mu_n)$ and log-variance σ_n^2, and $N(\cdot; \mu_n, \sigma_n)$ is the normal distribution function with mean μ_n and variance σ_n^2. The

[2] "Income" always means "after-tax family income."

lognormal distribution function serves here as a purely mathematical description of $U_n(y)$. It does not entail any probabilistic connotation. Yet, its isomorphism with a probability distribution function will be exploited extensively in the sequel. For lack of space we refer to Van Herwaarden and Kapteyn (1981) and Buyze (1982) for details of measurement and tests of Van Praag's hypothesis.

III. Relative Utility

In line with the various theories mentioned in the introduction, Kapteyn (1977) has formulated a theory which assumes that utility is completely relative. For expositions of his so-called theory of preference formation we refer to Kapteyn (1977, 1980) or Kapteyn et al. (1980). Here we shall present only a simplified version which can be tested against the data at hand.

The basic idea is that an individual's WFI is nothing else than a perceived income distribution. That is, an individual evaluates any income level by its ranking in the income distribution that he perceives. To operationalize this idea, we have to explain what is meant by a perceived income distribution. To that end some notation is introduced.

Let there be N individuals in society. Time is measured in years, $t = -\infty, \ldots, 0$, where $t = 0$ represents the present. At each moment of time an individual n ($n = 1, \ldots, N$) is assumed to assign non-negative *reference weights* $w_{nk}(t)$ to any individual k in society ($k = 1, \ldots, N$), $\sum_{k=1}^{N} w_{nk}(t) = 1$. The reference weights indicate the importance individual n attaches to the income of individual k at time t. Obviously, quite a few of the $w_{nk}(t)$ will be zero. On the other hand, $w_{nn}(t)$, i.e., the weight that individual n attaches to his own income at time t, may be substantial. The vector $(w_{n1}(t), \ldots, w_{n,n-1}(t), \ w_{n,n+1}(t), \ldots, w_{nN}(t))$ will sometimes be referred to as n's *social reference group* at time t.[3]

Furthermore, let $y_k(t)$ be the income of individual k at time t. The reference weights now allow for the definition of a *perceived income distribution at time t*. Denote this function by $F_n(y|t)$, then its

[3] The term "reference group" is due to Hyman (1942). The term can have different meanings. Here we use it in the sense of a *comparative* reference group, i.e., the reference group serves as "a standard or comparison point against which the individual can evaluate himself and others" (Kelley, 1947).

definition is

$$F_n(y|t) \equiv \sum_{\{k;\, y_k(t) \leq y\}} w_{nk}(t). \qquad (2)$$

The $F_n(y|t)$ for any t can be aggregated to one *presently perceived income distribution*, $F_n(y)$. To that end a non-negative *memory function* $a_n(t)$ is introduced, which describes individual n's weighting of perceived incomes over time,

$$\sum_{t=-\infty}^{0} a_n(t) = 1, \qquad n = 1, \dots, N. \qquad (3)$$

The presently perceived distribution function $F_n(y)$ can now be defined as

$$F_n(y) \equiv \sum_{t=-\infty}^{0} a_n(t) F_n(y|t). \qquad (4)$$

As indicated above, the preference formation theory claims that this perceived income distribution equals the utility function $U_n(y)$ of the individual. It is this claim that we want to shed some light on in this paper.

The development of the argument so far has been in terms of individual incomes, whereas our data refer to family income (cf. the wording of the survey question above). Hence, we reformulate the preference formation theory in terms of incomes per *equivalent adult*. Let $f_k(t)$ be the number of equivalent adults in family k at time t. The income per equivalent adult in this family at time t is denoted by

$$\tilde{y}_k(t) \equiv y_k(t)/f_k(t). \qquad (5)$$

The reformulation of $U_n(y)$ in terms of incomes per equivalent adult amounts to a transformation of the income scale: y is replaced by $\tilde{y} \equiv y/f_n$ and e^{μ_n} by e^{μ_n}/f_n.[4] Consequently,

$$U_n(y) = N(\ln y; \mu_n, \sigma_n)$$
$$= N\left(\ln\left(\frac{y}{f_n}\right); \mu_n - \ln f_n, \sigma_n\right)$$
$$= N(\ln \tilde{y}; \tilde{\mu}_n, \sigma_n) = \tilde{U}_n(\tilde{y}). \qquad (6)$$

Replacing $y_k(t)$ and y in (2) and (4) by $\tilde{y}_k(t)$ and $\tilde{y}$, we obtain the perceived distribution of incomes per equivalent adult $\tilde{F}_n(\tilde{y})$.

The theory of preference formation now states

$$\tilde{U}_n(\tilde{y}) = \tilde{F}_n(\tilde{y}); \qquad n = 1, \dots, N; \quad \tilde{y} \in (0, \infty). \qquad (7)$$

---

[4] For convenience, we generally omit arguments equal to zero, so $f_n \equiv f_n(0)$, etc.

To investigate the empirical validity of the theory, we derive from (7) implications for variations in μ and σ over individuals, which can be confronted with the data at hand. Denote the first log-moment of $\tilde{F}_n(\tilde{y})$ by $\tilde{m}_n$:

$$\tilde{m}_n = \int_0^{\infty} \ln \tilde{y}\, d\tilde{F}_n(\tilde{y})$$
$$= \sum_{t=-\infty}^{0} a_n(t) \sum_{k=1}^{N} w_{nk}(t) \ln \tilde{y}_k(t). \qquad (8)$$

The equality of the two distribution functions $\tilde{U}_n$ and $\tilde{F}_n$ implies the equality of the first two log-moments:

$$\mu_n = \ln f_n + \tilde{m}_n + \epsilon_n$$
$$= \ln f_n + \sum_{t=-\infty}^{0} a_n(t) \sum_{k=1}^{N} w_{nk}(t)$$
$$\times \ln \tilde{y}_k(t) + \epsilon_n, \qquad (9)$$
$$\sigma_n^2 = \sum_{t=-\infty}^{0} a_n(t) \sum_{k=1}^{N} w_{nk}(t)$$
$$\times \left[\ln \tilde{y}_k(t) - \tilde{m}_n\right]^2 + \delta_n, \qquad (10)$$

where measurement errors in μ_n and σ_n^2 and errors in the equations are taken into account by means of the identically and independently distributed (i.i.d.) disturbance terms ϵ_n and δ_n, with zero means and variances σ_ϵ^2 and σ_δ^2.

To facilitate estimation of (9) and (10), a few more assumptions and definitions are needed. We assume that $w_{nn}(t)$ is the same for all individuals and constant over time, i.e., all individuals give themselves the same constant weight. We write $\beta_2 \equiv w_{nn}(t)$ and $\beta_3 \equiv \sum_{k \neq n} w_{nk}(t) = 1 - \beta_2$. The function $\ln f_k(t)$ is specified as $\beta_0 + \beta_1 \ln fs_k(t)$ where $fs_k(t)$ is the number of members of family k at time t. The memory function $a_n(t)$ is assumed to be the same for everyone and is specified as $a_n(t) = (1 - a)a^{-t}$. Furthermore, we define

$$q_{nk}(t) \equiv w_{nk}(t)/\beta_3, \qquad k \neq n$$
$$\equiv 0, \qquad k = n \qquad (11)$$
$$\tilde{m}_n(t) \equiv \sum_k q_{nk}(t) \ln y_k(t), \qquad (12)$$
$$\tilde{h}_n(t) \equiv \sum_k q_{nk}(t) \ln f_k(t)$$
$$= \beta_0 + \beta_1\left\{\sum_k q_{nk}(t) \ln fs_k(t)\right\}$$
$$\equiv \beta_0 + \beta_1 \overline{hs}_n(t), \qquad (13)$$

where $\overline{hs}_n(t)$ is defined implicitly. So, $\overline{m}_n(t)$ and $\overline{hs}_n(t)$ are the log-means of incomes and family sizes in family n's social reference group at time t.

All this makes it possible to rewrite (9) as

$$\mu_n = \ln f_n + (1-a)$$
$$\times \sum_{t=-\infty}^{0} a^{-t} \big[\beta_2 \{\ln y_n(t) - \ln f_n(t)\}$$
$$+ \beta_3 \{\overline{m}_n(t) - \overline{h}_n(t)\} \big] + \epsilon_n. \tag{14}$$

Using the expression for $\ln f_n$ and applying a Koyck transformation, (14) can be written as

$$\mu_n = \big[1 - \beta_2(1-a)\big] \beta_1 \ln fs_n$$
$$- a\beta_1 \ln fs_n(-1) + \beta_2(1-a)\ln y_n$$
$$+ \beta_3(1-a)\overline{m}_n - \beta_3(1-a)\beta_1 \overline{hs}_n$$
$$+ a\mu_n(-1) + \epsilon_n - a\epsilon_n(-1). \tag{15}$$

We observe that (15) has no constant term (the terms in β_0 cancel out). If we allow for the fact that incomes in previous years have to be deflated by a price index it is easy to show that this does not influence the coefficients in (15), but only gives rise to a constant term. In the empirical application (15) has been estimated with a constant term included.

It is rather straightforward to use (10) and derive an expression for σ_n^2 similar to (15). However, that expression is non-linear in both parameters and variables. It will be seen in the next section that estimation of (15), which is non-linear in parameters but linear in variables, is already complicated. Estimation of a similar relation for σ_n^2 would involve problems of measurement errors in a non-linear model. Since we have not yet solved the estimation problems posed by such a model satisfactorily, only (15) will be confronted with the data.

IV. Estimation of the μ_n-equation

The data consist of the first two waves of a panel of 775 households in The Netherlands. The panel survey is conducted by the Netherlands Central Bureau of Statistics. The main bread-winner of each household was interviewed in March 1980 and in March 1981. The items in the questionnaire included questions to measure the respondent's WFI, the after-tax family income, family composition, and a number of demographic and socio-economic characteristics. On the basis of this information (15) is estimated.

The main problem with the estimation of (15) is that $\overline{m}_n$ and $\overline{hs}_n$ are unobservable. To solve this problem we model the reference weights w_{nk} as realizations of a stochastic process. Two assumptions are made about this stochastic process.

The first assumption is that society can be partitioned in *social groups* $G_1, \ldots, G_i, \ldots, G_I$, such that there exist constants P_i satisfying

$$q_{nk} = \begin{cases} P_i/(N_i - 1) + \delta_{nk} & \text{if } n \in G_i, \\ & k \in G_i, \\ (1 - P_i)/(N - N_i) + \delta_{nk} & \text{if } n \in G_i, \\ & k \notin G_i, \end{cases} \tag{16}$$

where N_i is the number of individuals in group i and where δ_{nk} is an error term with zero mean, distributed independently of all P_i, all incomes and all family sizes in society. Note that

$$E \sum_{k \in G_i} q_{nk} = P_i \quad \text{if } n \in G_i, \ i = 1, \ldots, I. \tag{17}$$

Thus, P_i is the total reference weight that an individual n in G_i assigns, on average, to the other individuals $k \in G_i$. Assumption (16) therefore states that, on average, individuals within a group G_i give a total weight P_i to others in the same group and a total weight $(1 - P_i)$ to individuals outside their own group.

The second assumption is that the P_i themselves are (realizations of) random variables which are generated according to

$$\frac{1 - P_i}{N - N_i} = \tilde{q} + \Delta_i, \quad i = 1, \ldots, I, \tag{18}$$

where Δ_i is an i.i.d. random variable with mean zero and variance σ_Δ^2. Since $(1 - P_i)$ is the total weight given to individuals outside group i and $N - N_i$ is the number of individuals outside group i, the interpretation of $\tilde{q}$ is that it is the mean reference weight assigned by individuals to others *outside* their own group.

The first assumption makes it possible to rewrite $\overline{m}_n$ as follows:

$$\overline{m}_n = \sum_k q_{nk} \ln y_k$$
$$= P_i y_n^* + (1 - P_i)\tilde{y}_n^* + \sum_k \delta_{nk}\ln y_k,$$
$$\text{for } n \in G_i, \tag{19}$$

where y_n^* is the mean log-income of individuals in group i, other than n; $\tilde{y}_n^*$ is the mean log-income

THE RELATIVITY OF UTILITY   183

of individuals outside G_i. Let $\bar{Y}$ be the mean log-income in society, then

$$\bar{Y} = y_n^*(N_i - 1)/N + \tilde{y}_n^*(N - N_i)/N + \frac{1}{N}\ln y_n$$

$$\text{for } n \in G_i. \quad (20)$$

Next define $\kappa \equiv (N - 1)\tilde{q}$. It is straightforward to show that (18)–(20) imply

$$\bar{m}_n = (1 - \kappa)y_n^* + \kappa \cdot \bar{Y} + \tilde{q}(\bar{Y} - \ln y_n)$$
$$+ \Delta_i\left[N \cdot \bar{Y} - (N - 1)y_n^* - \ln y_n\right]$$
$$+ \sum_k \delta_{nk}\ln y_k. \quad (21)$$

According to (18) $\tilde{q}$ is of the order of magnitude of $1/(N - N_i)$, so that $\tilde{q}(\bar{Y} - \ln y_n)$ can be neglected without losing much precision, provided that groups are defined in such a way that $N - N_i$ is large.[5]

Defining

$$u_n \equiv \sum_k \delta_{nk}\ln y_k$$
$$+ \Delta_i\left[N \cdot \bar{Y} - (N - 1)y_n^* - \ln y_n\right],$$

(21) can then be written as

$$\bar{m}_n = (1 - \kappa)y_n^* + \kappa \cdot \bar{Y} + u_n. \quad (22)$$

We can derive a similar expression for $\overline{hs}_n$:

$$\overline{hs}_n = (1 - \kappa)f_n^* + \kappa \cdot \bar{F} + v_n, \quad (23)$$

where f_n^* is the mean log-family size of families in the group individual n belongs to, excluding his own family, and $\bar{F}$ is mean log-family size in society; a term $\tilde{q}(\bar{F} - \ln fs_n)$ has been neglected.

The assumptions (16) and (18) have thus allowed for very simple operationalizations of $\bar{m}_n$ and $\overline{hs}_n$ by means of (22) and (23). Both $\bar{m}_n$ and $\overline{hs}_n$ are written as convex combinations of a social group mean (y_n^* and f_n^*) and a society mean ($\bar{Y}$ and $\bar{F}$). Whether the operationalization is successful in practice depends on κ. If we are able to find a partitioning into social groups G_i such that κ is close to zero, then reference groups hardly cross the boundaries of the social groups (if $\kappa \approx 0$, $N \cdot \tilde{q} \approx 0$ so $P_i \approx 1$, cf. (18)). In that case, social groups are informative about reference groups. If, on the other hand, for a partitioning into social groups we find that $\kappa \approx 1$, the social groups give no information on reference groups (if $\kappa \approx 1$, $N \cdot$

$\tilde{q} \approx 1$, so $(1 - P_i)/(N - N_i) \approx 1/N$. Hence $P_i \approx N_i/N$, i.e., weights are assigned to social groups roughly in proportion to their share of the population).

In the present application we have partitioned the sample in groups of respondents who have the same education level, the same employment status and who are of about the same age.[6] For these groups we have calculated the sample counterparts of y_n^* and f_n^* for each individual (i.e., within a group the mean log-income and log-family size varies slightly per respondent because the respondent's own income and family size are not part of the definition of y_n^* and f_n^*).[7] The definition of the social groups is partly dictated by the available data, but there is also some evidence in the literature that age, employment and education are important determinants of reference groups.[8]

Inserting (22) and (23) into (15) yields the following estimating equation:

$$\mu_n = \left[1 - \beta_2(1 - a)\right]\beta_1\ln fs_n$$
$$- a\beta_1\ln fs_n(-1) + \beta_2(1 - a)\ln y_n$$
$$+ \beta_3(1 - a)(1 - \kappa)y_n^*$$
$$- \beta_3(1 - a)(1 - \kappa)\beta_1 f_n^*$$
$$+ a\mu_n(-1) + \gamma_0 + \zeta_n$$
$$\equiv (1 - \gamma_2)\beta_1\ln fs_n - a\beta_1\ln fs_n(-1)$$
$$+ \gamma_2\ln y_n + \gamma_3 y_n^* - \gamma_3\beta_1 f_n^*$$
$$+ a\mu_n(-1) + \gamma_0 + \zeta_n \quad (24)$$

---

[5] Given that N is the number of families in society, $N - N_i$ will be large as long as the different groups are of comparable size.

[6] Five education levels are distinguished, three employment situations (self-employed, employee, not employed) and five age brackets (less than 30, 30–39, 40–49, 50–65, over 65). This leads to 51 social groups in the sample.

[7] Moreover, $\ln y_n$ and fs_n are explanatory variables in (15), so also including them in the computation of the sample counterparts of y_n^* and f_n^* would introduce unnecessary multicollinearity.

[8] It follows from Festinger's theory of social comparison processes (Festinger, 1954) that people will compare primarily to others who are similar, and a large amount of empirical evidence supports this contention to varying degrees. Borrowing from attribution theory, Goethals and Darley (1977) are able to be more specific about how "similar others" have to be defined. If an individual wants to evaluate a particular ability, he will seek comparison with others who are comparable with respect to attributes related to that ability. For example, a runner will compare her or his performance to the performance of others who are of the same sex, who are of approximately the same age, practice a similar number of hours per week and run in similar circumstances. Translating this to the evaluation of income, people will compare themselves to others whose income generating attributes are similar: employment situation, education and age are then highly relevant attributes (witness the fact that education and age are almost invariably used by economists as predictors in wage equations).

where

$$\gamma_0 \equiv \beta_3(1-a)\kappa(\bar{Y} - \beta_1\bar{F});$$

$$\zeta_n = \epsilon_n - a\epsilon_n(-1)$$

$$+ \beta_3(1-a)u_n - \beta_3(1-a)\beta_1 v_n. \quad (25)$$

The reparameterization in the last member of (24) is given to facilitate the presentation of the results in the next section.

Given the stochastic assumptions introduced so far, the error term ζ_n is uncorrelated with all explanatory variables on the right hand side of (24), except $\mu_n(-1)$. The covariance between $\mu_n(-1)$ and ζ_n is unrestricted and will be estimated.

As a second observation on the stochastic specification of (24), note that replacing y_n^* and f_n^* in (24) by their sample counterparts induces measurement error. Since y_n^* and f_n^* are simply estimated as sample means, the variance-covariance matrix of their measurement errors can be obtained in the usual way. In principle, this covariance matrix is different for different social groups. For simplicity, we have averaged all these matrices and used the result as our estimate of the error variance-covariance matrix for all observations.

Assuming that the random variables involved all follow approximately a normal distribution, (24) can be estimated by means of maximum likelihood. To that end, the LISREL computer program (version IV) has been used.[9]

V.   Results and Discussion

We have estimated thirteen different specifications of (24) to bring out the sensitivity of the results to the assumptions made. This follows suggestions by Leamer (1983).

As a bench-mark we present ordinary least squares (OLS) results of a regression of μ_n on the right hand side variables in (24):

$$\mu_n = \underset{(0.031)}{0.066} \ \ln fs_n - \underset{(0.032)}{0.013} \ \ln fs_n(-1)$$

$$+ \underset{(0.023)}{0.298} \ \ln y_n + \underset{(0.029)}{0.072} \ y_n^*$$

$$- \underset{(0.025)}{0.032} \ fs_n^* + \underset{(0.026)}{0.509} \ \mu_n(-1) \quad (26)$$

number of observations: 775, $R^2 = 0.808$.

[9] The LISREL-specification and the variance-covariance matrix of the data are available from the authors on request. Write to Arie Kapteyn, Department of Econometrics, Tilburg University, P.O. Box 90153, 5000 LE Tilburg, The Netherlands.

All coefficients have the predicted sign. Both habit formation and preference interdependence (represented by the coefficients of $\ln y_n$, y_n^* and $\mu_n(-1)$) contribute significantly to the explanation of μ_n. The coefficient of determination is quite satisfactory, although the main contribution comes from the lagged dependent variable $\mu_n(-1)$.

The remaining twelve specifications can be grouped in two sets. In the first set we treat the measurement errors in y_n^* and f_n^* in the way indicated in the previous section. In the second set of specifications measurement errors in y_n^* and f_n^* are assumed to be absent. For the rest, the six specifications in both sets are pairwise identical. Table 1 presents the results.

Columns A1 and B1 contain the results based on the statistical assumptions spelled out in the previous section. The differences between both columns are generally small. The χ^2-values indicate a satisfactory fit.[10] The parameter estimate most affected by the assumption on the errors in y_n^* and f_n^* is that of κ. Given the high standard errors we can neither exclude the possibility that $\kappa = 0$ nor that $\kappa = 1$. The latter possibility suggests that our definition of social groups may have been a poor one (cf. the previous section).

This is further illustrated by columns A2 and B2, where estimation results are given after imposing $\gamma_3 = 0$, i.e., no effect of y_n^* on μ_n is allowed. Since $\gamma_3 = \beta_3(1-a)(1-\kappa)$, cf. (24), $\gamma_3 = 0$ can be the result of either $\beta_3 = 0$ or $\kappa = 1$ (according to the first row, $a \neq 1$). The values of β_3 and κ in columns A2 and B2 (and A3 and B3) have been computed by assuming $\kappa = 1$ and using $\beta_2 + \beta_3 = 1$. The restriction $\beta_2 + \beta_3 = 1$ is necessary for the identification of β_3. Dropping the restriction, we could equally well assume $\beta_3 = 0$ and leave κ unrestricted. Empirically, both sets of assumptions are equivalent. The restriction $\beta_2 + \beta_3 = 1$ can only be tested if we are willing to impose further restrictions (see below).

The restriction $\gamma_3 = 0$ does not worsen the fit of the model significantly,[11] as could already be ex-

[10] Each specification considered imposes restrictions on the variance-covariance matrix of the observable variables. The χ^2-value for a given specification is minus two times the log-likelihood ratio which tests this specification (the null hypothesis) against the alternative hypothesis that the variance-covariance matrix of the observables is unrestricted.
[11] The difference in χ^2-values between columns 1 and 2 provides the likelihood ratio test statistic (with one degree of freedom) to test the null hypothesis that $\gamma_3 = 0$ against the specification in column 1.

TABLE 1.—ESTIMATION RESULTS

Restriction	Measurement Error[a]					
$\beta_2 + \beta_3 = 1$	yes	yes	yes	—	no	yes
$\gamma_3 = 0$	no	yes	yes	yes	no	no
$\zeta_n = \epsilon_n - a\epsilon_n(-1)$	no	no	yes	yes	no	no
$\gamma_2 = 0$	no	no	no	yes	no	no
$\kappa = 0$	no	no	no	—	yes	yes
Parameter	A1	A2	A3	A4	A5	A6
a	0.833	0.919	0.813	0.972	0.833	0.902
	(0.147)[b]	(0.132)	(0.039)	(0.022)	(0.147)	(0.081)
γ_2	0.109	0.067	0.136	0[c]	0.109	0.068
	(0.088)	(0.087)	(0.029)		(0.088)	(0.051)
γ_3	0.033	0[c]	0[c]	0[c]	0.033	0.028
	(0.039)				(0.039)	(0.043)
β_2	0.657	0.833	0.730	—	0.657	0.703
	(0.140)	(0.302)	(0.083)		(0.140)	(0.240)
β_3	0.343	0.167	0.270	—	0.200	0.297
	(0.140)	(0.302)	(0.083)		(0.196)	(0.240)
κ	0.421	1[c]	1[c]	—	0[c]	0[c]
	(0.502)					
β_1	0.114	0.121	0.112	0.127	0.114	0.120
	(0.039)	(0.039)	(0.038)	(0.037)	(0.039)	(0.038)
σ_ϵ^2	—	—	0.017	0.018	—	—
			(0.001)	(0.001)		
σ_ζ^2	0.029	0.032	—	—	0.029	0.031
	(0.055)	(0.005)			(0.005)	(0.003)
$\text{cov}(\mu(-1),\zeta)$	-0.015	-0.019	—	—	-0.015	-0.019
	(0.007)	(0.006)			(0.007)	(0.004)
χ^2	0.72	1.37	2.18	20.25	0.72	0.96
df	1	2	3	4	1	2
Restriction	No Measurement Error					
$\beta_2 + \beta_3 = 1$	yes	yes	yes	—	no	yes
$\gamma_3 = 0$	no	yes	yes	yes	no	no
$\zeta_n = \epsilon_n - a\epsilon_n(-1)$	no	no	yes	yes	no	no
$\gamma_2 = 0$	no	no	no	yes	no	no
$\kappa = 0$	no	no	no	—	yes	yes
Parameter	B1	B2	B3	B4	B5	B6
a	0.828	0.904	0.812	0.972	0.828	0.908
	(0.144)	(0.132)	(0.039)	(0.022)	(0.144)	(0.076)
γ_2	0.114	0.077	0.137	0[c]	0.114	0.066
	(0.088)	(0.087)	(0.029)		(0.088)	(0.050)
γ_3	0.029	0[c]	0[c]	0[c]	0.029	0.024
	(0.035)				(0.035)	(0.036)
β_2	0.663	0.805	0.729	—	0.663	0.730
	(0.128)	(0.268)	(0.077)		(0.128)	(0.220)
β_3	0.337	0.195	0.271	—	0.170	0.270
	(0.128)	(0.268)	(0.077)		(0.173)	(0.220)
κ	0.500	1[c]	1[c]	—	0[c]	0[c]
	(0.462)					
β_1	0.114	0.120	0.117	0.127	0.114	0.120
	(0.039)	(0.039)	(0.039)	(0.037)	(0.039)	(0.039)
σ_ϵ^2	—	—	0.017	0.018	—	—
			(0.001)	(0.001)		
σ_ζ^2	0.029	0.031	—	—	0.029	0.032
	(0.005)	(0.005)			(0.005)	(0.003)
$\text{cov}(\mu(-1),\zeta)$	-0.15	-0.018	—	—	-0.015	-0.019
	(0.007)	(0.006)			(0.007)	(0.004)
χ^2	0.50	1.14	1.73	19.89	0.50	0.83
df	1	2	3	4	1	2

[a] Variance of error in $v_n^* = .0066$, variance of error in $f_n^* = .0095$, covariance of errors in $v_n^*, f_n^* = .0016$. See the end of section V for an explanation.
[b] Asymptotic standard errors are in parentheses.
[c] Restricted.

pected on the basis of columns A1 and B1. Thus we cannot reject the possibility that y_n^* has no influence on μ_n. Under the assumption that $\beta_2 + \beta_3 = 1$, columns A1 and B1 would suggest that this is primarily due to a poor choice of social groups, because β_3 differs significantly from zero but κ is not significantly different from one.

In columns A3 and B3 the further restriction is imposed that $\zeta_n = \epsilon_n - a\epsilon_n(-1)$, i.e., in (25) u_n and v_n are zero. Also this restriction is not rejected by the data. Notice that as a result it is possible to estimate σ_ϵ^2. Referring to model (14), $1 - \sigma_\epsilon^2/\text{var}(\mu_n)$ is the proportion of variance in μ_n explained by the theoretical model. We find that $1 - 0.017/0.125 = 0.864$.

In columns A4 and B4 the additional restriction $\gamma_2 = 0$ is imposed. So model (14) can be written as

$$\xi_n(\tau) = a\xi_n(\tau - 1) \qquad (27)$$
$$\mu_n(\tau) = \beta_0 + \beta_1 \ln fs_n(\tau) + \xi_n(\tau) + \epsilon_n(\tau),$$
$$\tau = -\infty, \ldots, 0 \qquad (28)$$

where $\xi_n(\tau)$ is an individual specific effect. So $\mu_n(\tau)$ is only influenced by family size and random shocks. For the rest $\mu_n(\tau)$ evolves over time autonomously as described by (27).

If $a = 1$, this model reduces to

$$\mu_n(\tau) = \beta_0 + \beta_1 \ln fs_n(\tau) + \xi_n + \epsilon_n(\tau), \qquad (29)$$

i.e., there is no habit formation or preference interdependence. Apart from a correction for family size, the observed value $\mu_n(\tau)$ then fluctuates randomly around the true and constant ξ_n. The possibility that $a = 1$ cannot be rejected within this specification, but the "absolute" specification itself is decisively rejected by the data.

Columns A5 and B5 are just reparameterizations of columns A1 and B1. In A1 and B1, $\beta_2 + \beta_3 = 1$ is a maintained hypothesis. This hypothesis is testable only if we are willing to make additional assumptions; $\kappa = 0$ (no reference weights assigned to people outside one's social group) is one such assumption. Notice that, for $\kappa = 0$, $\beta_2 + \beta_3 = 1$ is equivalent to $\gamma_2 + \gamma_3 + a = 1$. We find that $\gamma_2 + \gamma_3 + a = .976(.045)$ in column A1 and $\gamma_2 + \gamma_3 + a = .972(.046)$ in B1. These numbers do not differ significantly from one. This is confirmed by columns A6 and B6 where the restrictions $\kappa = 0$ and $\beta_2 + \beta_3 = 1$ are imposed simultaneously. The fit does not worsen signifi-

cantly, so given $\kappa = 0$ we cannot reject $\beta_2 + \beta_3 = 1$, i.e., that utility is completely relative.

In sum, the empirical evidence presented is compatible with a theory implying that utility is completely relative, whereas an absolute utility concept appears to be incompatible with the data. Of course, the data also allow for specifications that make utility partly relative.

To conclude this section, we take the relativity model for granted and discuss the meaning of the parameter estimates. First of all, the estimates of β_2 and β_3 suggest that the total weight which an individual assigns to the incomes of all other people is about half the weight which he gives to his own income (in present and past). This contrasts with earlier results obtained by Kapteyn et al. (1980) who found β_3 to be approximately twice as large as β_2. Apart from data differences, this can be explained by noting that their analysis pertains to holiday expenditures rather than income. The more conspicuous a good, the higher β_3 probably is. Since holidays are among the most conspicuous consumption items, the corresponding β_3 should be substantially higher than for income, which is an aggregate of all consumption possibilities, both conspicuous and unconspicuous ones.

The parameter β_1 measures the increase in a family's cost of living due to an increase in family size. If the size of the family increases by 1% then the cost of living of the family increases by β_1%. The low values of β_1 suggest substantial economies of scale in the operation of a family. In itself it is of interest to see how a purely subjective model provides estimates of seemingly "objective" quantities like cost of living. It has been argued elsewhere (e.g., Kapteyn and Van Praag (1980)) that the methodological basis of the present measurement method is identical to the one underlying conventional demand systems approaches to the measurement of differences in cost of living. Although the specification of $\ln f_n$ by $\beta_0 + \beta_1 \ln fs_n$ is very primitive, it is noteworthy that never before in cost of living studies was account taken of both preference interdependence and habit formation.

The estimate of a (approximately 0.83) suggests a fairly strong influence of past income distributions. For instance, weights given to years 0, -1, -2, etc. are 0.17, 0.14, 0.12, 0.10, 0.08, 0.07, 0.06, 0.05, 0.04, 0.03, etc. So the present year receives a weight which is about six times as high as the weight given to an income ten years ago, but all past years combined get a total weight equal to 0.83 as compared to 0.17 for the present year. According to these results, a discussion of the relativity of utility framed exclusively in cross-sectional terms would be highly incomplete.

VI. Conclusion

To the extent that the utility concept used in this paper (the WFI) is a sufficiently close approximation to the indirect utility function defined in economic theory, it seems rather clear that utility functions are subject to preference formation (although, of course, we have in no way "proved" that utility is *completely* relative). This has far reaching consequences for both positive and normative economics. It may be held, of course, that direct questions about satisfaction measure something entirely different from the economic utility concept. Although, on intuitive grounds, we find this hard to accept, further research into the relation between verbal statements about satisfaction and economic behavior is evidently needed.

REFERENCES

Becker, Gary S., "A Theory of Social Interactions," *Journal of Political Economy* 82 (1974), 1063–1091.

Buyze, Jeanine, "The Estimation of Welfare Levels of a Cardinal Utility Function," *European Economic Review* 17 (1982), 325–332.

Davis, James A., "A Formal Interpretation of the Theory of Relative Deprivation," *Sociometry* 22 (1959), 280–296.

Duesenberry, James S., *Income, Saving and the Theory of Consumer Behavior* (Cambridge: Harvard University Press, 1949).

Duncan, Otis D., "Does Money Buy Satisfaction?" *Social Indicators Research* 2 (1975), 267–274.

Easterlin, R. A., "Does Economic Growth Improve the Human Lot? Some Empirical Evidence," in P. A. David and M. W. Reder (eds.), *Nations and Households in Economic Growth. Essays in Honor of Moses Abramowitz* (New York: Academic Press, 1974).

Festinger, Leon, "A Theory of Social Comparison Processes," *Human Relations* 7 (1954), 117–140.

Frank, Robert H., "How Interdependent Preferences Affect Demands for Unobservable and Contingent Goods," Cornell University, mimeo (1982).

Goethals, G. R., and J. M. Darley, "Social Comparison Theory. An Attributional Approach," in J. M. Suls and R. L. Miller (eds.), *Social Comparison Processes* (New York: Hemisphere Publishing Corporation, 1977).

Helson, H., *Adaptation-Level Theory: An Experimental and Systematic Approach to Behavior* (New York: Harper, 1964).

———, "Adaptation-Level Theory: 1970—And After," in M. H. Appley (ed.), *Adaptation-Level Theory: A Symposium* (New York: Academic Press, 1971).

Hyman, H. H., "The Psychology of Status," *Archives of Psychology* 269 (1942), 5–38, 80–86. Reprinted in part in Hyman and Singer (1968), 147–165.

Hyman, H. H., and E. Singer (eds.), *Readings in Reference Group, Group Theory and Research* (New York: The Free Press, 1968).

Kapteyn, Arie, "A Theory of Preference Formation," unpublished Ph.D. Thesis, Leyden University (1977).

———, "A Theory of Preference Formation," MRG Working Paper 7933, University of Southern California (1980).

Kapteyn, Arie, and Bernard M. S. van Praag, "Family Composition and Family Welfare," in J. L. Simon and J. DaVanzo (eds.), *Research in Population Economics* II (Greenwich, CT: JAI Press, 1980), 77–97.

Kapteyn, Arie, and Tom J. Wansbeek, "Empirical Evidence on Preference Formation," *Journal of Economic Psychology* 2 (1982), 137–154.

Kapteyn, Arie, Tom J. Wansbeek, and J. Buyze, "The Dynamics of Preference Formation," *Journal of Economic Behavior and Organization* 1 (1980), 123–157.

Kelley, H. H., "Two Functions of Reference Groups," in G. E. Swanson, T. M. Newcomb and E. L. Hartley (eds.), *Readings in Social Psychology* (1947). Reprinted in Hyman and Singer (1968), 77–83.

Layard, Richard, "Human Satisfactions and Public Policy," *The Economic Journal* 90 (1980), 737–750.

Leamer, Edward E., "Let's Take the Con Out of Econometrics," *American Economic Review* 73 (1983), 31–43.

Marx, Karl, *Lohnarbeit und Kapital* (Berlin: Karl Kautsky, 1930).

Pigou, A. C., "Some Remarks on Utility," *The Economic Journal* 13 (1903), 58–68.

Pollak, Robert A., "Endogenous Tastes in Demand and Welfare Analysis," *The American Economic Review* 68 (1978), 374–379.

Rader, Trout, "The Second Theorem of Welfare Economics When Utilities Are Interdependent," *Journal of Economic Theory* 23 (1980), 420–424.

Runciman, W. G., *Relative Deprivation and Social Justice* (London: Routledge and Kegan Paul, 1966).

Stigler, George J., and Gary S. Becker, "De Gustibus non est Disputandum," *The American Economic Review* 67 (1977), 76–90.

Van der Wijk, J., *Inkomens- en Vermogensverdeling* (Haarlem: De Erven F. Bohn N. V., 1939).

Van Herwaarden, Floor G., Arie Kapteyn and Bernard M. S. van Praag, "Twelve Thousand Individual Welfare Functions of Income," *European Economic Review* 9 (1977), 283–300.

Van Herwaarden, Floor G., and Arie Kapteyn, "Empirical Comparison of the Shape of Welfare Functions," *European Economic Review* 15 (1981), 261–286.

Van Praag, Bernard M. S., *Individual Welfare Functions and Consumer Behavior* (Amsterdam: North-Holland Publishing Company, 1968).

———, "The Welfare Function of Income in Belgium: An Empirical Investigation," *European Economic Review* 2 (1971), 337–369.

[9]

Relative Utility and Income Growth: An Example

Arie Kapteyn[1]

An implication of the preceding article is that an increase in the incomes of everyone does not increase subjective well-being. The purpose of this chapter is to demonstrate this point and the underlying causal mechanisms.

Take equation (15) in the preceding chapter as a starting point. For simplicity we ignore family size and the error terms. We also omit the subscript n. So we consider:

$$\mu = \beta_2 (1-a) \ln y + \beta_3 (1-a) \bar{m} + a\mu(-1) \tag{1}$$

Let's start from an equilibrium situation, i.e. where $\mu = \mu(-1)$. Inserting this in (1) yields as an equilibrium value for μ:

$$\mu^* = \beta_2 \ln y + \beta_3 \bar{m} \tag{2}$$

In others words, in equilibrium μ (the log of the consumption standard to which income is compared) is a weighted average of log-income and the mean of log-incomes in one's reference group. Since welfare (that is, self-reported satisfaction with income) is determined by $\ln y - \mu$, we observe that

$$\ln y - \mu^* = \beta_3 (\ln y - \bar{m}) \tag{3}$$

Thus, in equilibrium one's welfare is determined by the value of own income compared to mean income in the reference group.[2]

Let us now consider deviations from the equilibrium. First consider an individual income increase by a factor $(1 + \eta)$, keeping all other incomes constant. In other words, $\ln y$ increases to $\ln y + \ln(1 + \eta)$. We can now trace the effect of this change on μ by using (1). In successive periods we get:

$$
\begin{aligned}
\mu(+1) &= \mu^* + \beta_2(1-a)\ln(1+\eta) \\
\mu(+2) &= \mu^* + (1+a)\beta_2(1-a)\ln(1+\eta) \\
\mu(+3) &= \mu^* + (1+a+a^2)\beta_2(1-a)\ln(1+\eta) \\
&\;\;\vdots \\
\mu(+t) &= \mu^* + (1+a+a^2+\ldots+a^{t-1})\beta_2(1-a)\ln(1+\eta)
\end{aligned}
\tag{4}
$$

For $t \to \infty$ we obtain

$$\mu\left(\infty\right) = \mu^* + \beta_2 \ln\left(1 + \eta\right) \tag{5}$$

And for $\ln y - \mu$ we obtain:

$$\ln y + \ln\left(1 + \eta\right) - \mu\left(\infty\right) = \ln y - \mu^* + \left(1 - \beta_2\right) \ln\left(1 + \eta\right) \tag{6}$$

In other words, compared to (3) the welfare indicator $\ln y - \mu$ increases in the long run by $\left(1 - \beta_2\right) \ln\left(1 + \eta\right)$. Of the initial income gain $\ln\left(1 + \eta\right)$ an amount $\beta_2 \ln\left(1 + \eta\right)$ has "leaked away". The size of the leak is determined by β_2, the preference drift due to habit formation.

In Table 1 (columns 1 and 2), I present the time path of both μ and $(\ln y - \mu)$ using the parameter values that were estimated in the 1985 article. I have normalized μ^* to be equal to zero, and I have chosen $\eta = .1$, that is, I consider a one-time income increase by 10 per cent. The column "μ" gives the increase of μ in consecutive years. The last number in the column is the new equilibrium value ("∞"). We observe that after ten years most of the adjustment has taken place, and μ is close to its new equilibrium. The evolution of $\ln y - \mu$ is the mirror image of this. The increase in welfare measured by $\ln y - \mu$ is initially equal to $\ln\left(1 + \eta\right) = \ln\left(1.1\right) = 0.09531$. Due to the increase in μ, $\ln y - \mu$ gradually falls to an equilibrium value of 0.03269 $\left(= \left(1 - \beta_2\right) \ln\left(1.1\right)\right)$.

Now consider the generic case of economic growth, that is, where both own income and the incomes of others grow at the same rate. According to (1) the effect on μ in subsequent periods is equal to

$$\mu\left(+1\right) = \mu^* + \left(1 - a\right) \ln\left(1 + \eta\right)$$
$$\mu\left(+2\right) = \mu^* + \left(1 + a\right)\left(1 - a\right) \ln\left(1 + \eta\right)$$
$$\mu\left(+3\right) = \mu^* + \left(1 + a + a^2\right)\left(1 - a\right) \ln\left(1 + \eta\right)$$
$$\vdots$$
$$\mu\left(+t\right) = \mu^* + \left(1 + a + a^2 + \ldots + a^{t-1}\right)\left(1 - a\right) \ln\left(1 + \eta\right) \tag{7}$$

For $t \to \infty$ we obtain

$$\mu\left(\infty\right) = \mu^* + \ln\left(1 + \eta\right) . \tag{8}$$

And for $\ln y - \mu$ we obtain:

$$\ln y + \ln\left(1 + \eta\right) - \mu\left(\infty\right) = \ln y - \mu^* \tag{9}$$

Since the incomes of others in one's reference group also increase by the same amount, the ultimate effect of an income increase on welfare is zero. A part β_2 leaks away through the preference drift, due to habit formation, that is, one gets used to the higher income after a while; another part β_3 leaks away through preference drift due to interpersonal comparison, that is, one compares one's own consumption to that of others.

In Table 1 (columns 3 and 4) I have also given the time path of μ and $(\ln y - \mu)$ for the case where all incomes exhibit a one-time increase by a factor $\left(1 + \eta\right)$. The column "μ" for this case shows that μ gradually increases until it reaches the equilibrium value $\ln(1+\eta) = \ln(1.1) =$ 0.09531. $\ln y - \mu$ starts at 0.09531 and gradually falls to zero. Thus, when all incomes grow, the net effect on welfare is nil.

Table 1   *Time paths of μ (the consumption standard) and $\ln y - \mu$ (welfare) for different income scenarios*

| period | One time increase of own income by 10% | | One time increase of all incomes by 10% | |
	(1)	(2)	(3)	(4)
	μ	$\ln y - \mu$	μ	$\ln y - \mu$
0	0	0.0953	0	0.0953
1	0.0105	0.0849	0.0159	0.0794
2	0.0192	0.0761	0.0292	0.0661
3	0.0284	0.0689	0.0402	0.0551
4	0.0325	0.0628	0.0494	0.0459
5	0.0375	0.0578	0.0571	0.0382
6	0.0417	0.0536	0.0635	0.0318
7	0.0452	0.0501	0.0688	0.0265
8	0.0481	0.0472	0.0732	0.0221
9	0.0505	0.0448	0.0769	0.0184
10	0.0525	0.0428	0.0800	0.0153
∞	*0.0626*	*0.0327*	*0.0953*	*0*

Notes:
Assumed parameter values: $\eta = 0.1$; $\beta_2 = 0.657$; $\beta_3 = 0.343$, $a = 0.833$
I normalize all incomes so that logs are zero in period 0

Notes
1. RAND corporation.
2. Since the expression is in logs, a somewhat more exact formulation is that one's welfare is determined by the ratio of one's own income and the geometric mean of incomes in the reference group.

Part II
Recent Contributions: The
Determinants of Happiness

[10]

The Economic Journal, **107** (*November*), 1815–1831. © Royal Economic Society 1997. Published by Blackwell Publishers, 108 Cowley Road, Oxford OX4 1JF, UK and 350 Main Street, Malden, MA 02148, USA.

HAPPINESS AND ECONOMIC PERFORMANCE*

Andrew J. Oswald

Those who say that money can't buy happiness don't know where to shop.
Anon.

Do you think your children's lives will be better than your own? Probably not; nobody does these days... In all countries there is doom and gloom, a universal sense of decay.
Norman Stone, historian.

What we call happiness in the strictest sense of the word comes from the (preferably sudden) satisfaction of needs which have been dammed up to a high degree.
Sigmund Freud, psychologist.

Happiness is the sublime moment when you get out of your corsets at night.
Joyce Grenfell, actress.

Economic performance is not intrinsically interesting. No-one is concerned in a genuine sense about the level of gross national product last year or about next year's exchange rate. People have no innate interest in the money supply, inflation, growth, inequality, unemployment, and the rest. The stolid greyness of the business pages of our newspapers seems to mirror the fact that economic numbers matter only indirectly.

The relevance of economic performance is that it may be a means to an end. That end is not the consumption of beefburgers, nor the accumulation of television sets, nor the vanquishing of some high level of interest rates, but rather the enrichment of mankind's feeling of well-being. Economic things matter only in so far as they make people happier.

This paper is concerned with the economics of happiness. Unlike gross domestic product and inflation, happiness is not something that governments try to record from year to year. This essay will show that they could and, for the issues of *Economic Trends* in the next century, possibly should.[1]

* For helpful advice, and for allowing me to draw upon joint research, I am grateful to Kamal Birdi, Danny Blanchflower, Andrew Clark, Rafael Di Tella, Robert MacCulloch, and Peter Warr. For research assistance, I thank Ed Butchart, Antonia Sachtleben and Francesca Silverton. For valuable discussions, I thank Michael Argyle, Nick Crafts, Mark Harrison, Daniel Kahneman, Mozaffar Qizilbash, Richard Layard, and Robert Skidelsky. Helpful comments were also received during presentations at Durham University and the London School of Economics. This work was financed by the Economic and Social Research Council (UK) and the Leverhulme Trust.

[1] Should economists study happiness, one might ask? There are some natural answers. First, presumably this subject really matters. Second, psychologists have for many years worked with data on self-reported happiness. They ought to know more about human psychology than we do. Third, there are grounds – laid out later – to believe that subjective well-being can be studied in a systematic way. Well-being regression equations have the same structure all over the world. Fourth, subjective wellbeing measures are correlated with observable phenomena. For example, people who report high happiness scores tend to laugh and smile more, and to be rated by others as happier (Pavot, 1991; Diener, 1984; Watson and Clark, 1991). Fifth, we might be able to use happiness data to test old ideas in new ways. For example, if one wished to know whether inflation is bad, one might ask whether, in inflationary periods, people *en masse* unknowingly tick lower down their happiness score sheets (Di Tella *et al*, 1996).

Most politicians who pronounce about the economic matters of the day do so under a set of assumptions about human enjoyment that are usually not articulated to the listener. The chief of these, perhaps, is the belief that by raising its output and productivity a society truly betters itself. Real income has been rising in the Western countries for a long time. Like most other industrialized nations, Britain is approximately twice as rich as it was as recently as 1960, and almost three times richer than after the War. Has this new real income – an enormous improvement by the standards of the last few centuries – bought extra happiness? If so, how much, and what should governments now be trying to do? If not, why not, and what should governments now be trying to do?

Deciding how much authentic well-being is bought by economic progress is a difficult task. It seems logically necessary, however, if economic and social policy is to be designed in a rational way. If taxpayers' pound notes can be thought of as seed-corn, they could be scattered upon ground devoted to raising innovation and economic growth, or, for example, upon that aimed at combating social problems, or upon something different. Society has to pick those places to throw the seed-corn especially thickly. It is not easy to know how such choices can be made in a systematic way. However, a social scientist might help those who mould policy if he or she could point to unnoticed patterns in data on happiness and satisfaction. This paper takes a small step along that path.

I. HAPPINESS AND REAL INCOME IN THE UNITED STATES

Later pages use the answers that people give when asked questions about how happy they fell with life or how satisfied they feel with their job and work. There are limitations to such statistics, but, if the aim is to learn about what makes people tick, listening to what they say seems likely to be a natural first step. Sources of information exist that have for many years recorded individuals' survey responses to questions about subjective well-being. These responses have been studied intensively by psychologists,[2] studied a little by sociologists, and ignored by economists.[3] Some economists may wish to defend this neglect by emphasising the unreliability of such data. Most, however, are probably unaware that data of this sort are available, and have not thought of how such empirical measures might be used in their discipline.

Richard Easterlin (1974, 1995) was one of the first economists to study statistics over time on the reported level of happiness. His data came from the United States. Easterlin's 1974 paper's main objectives were, first, to suggest that individual happiness appears to be the same across poor countries and rich countries, and, second, to argue that economic growth does not raise well-being. Easterlin suggested that we should think of people as getting utility from a comparison of themselves with others close to them: happiness is relative. The

[2] Recent work includes Argyle (1989), Douthitt *et al.* (1992), Fox and Kahneman (1992), Larsen *et al.* (1984) and Mullis (1992). Comparatively little research seems to have addressed the issue of how well-being changes through the years.
[3] Andrew Clark's recent work (for example, 1992, 1996*a*, *b*) is an exception.

modern stress on the benefits of higher total national income is then misplaced, because individuals all move up together. A similar theme is taken up in Hirsch (1976) and Scitvosky (1976), and still more recently in Frank (1985).[4]

Easterlin (1974) suggested a test for whether greater riches had made Americans happier. He looked at whether reported happiness rose as national income did. His paper concludes: '...in the one time series studied, that for the United States since 1946, higher income was not systematically accompanied by greater happiness' (p. 118). This result would mean that economic growth does not buy well-being.

Unfortunately, it is not obvious that Easterlin's data entirely support his conclusion. For example, his longest *consistent* set of happiness levels show the following for the percentages of Americans saying they were 'very happy' and 'not very happy' (the highest and lowest of three bands into which they could place themselves):

Happiness in the United States 1940s–1950s

Date	% Very happy	% Not very happy	N
1946	39	10	3,151
1947	42	10	1,434
1948	43	11	1,596
1952	47	9	3,003
1956	53	5	1,979
1957	53	3	1,627

Source: Table 8 of Easterlin (1974) using US AIPO poll data.

Other data – using statistics with breaks and changes in definitions – given by Easterlin differ. But the above is the longest consistent series and might be thought to command the most weight. According to these data, well-being did rise through time in the United States.[5]

A more modern calculation can be done with the General Social Surveys of the United States, which have for many years been interviewing people annually about their levels of happiness. These surveys are of randomly selected samples of Americans, so the information they provide can be treated as representative of the nation as a whole. GSS data are available for almost all of the years from 1972 to the 1990s (there are no data for 1979 or 1981). The size of sample averages approximately fifteen hundred individuals per annum. Different people are interviewed each year: the GSS does not follow the same individuals.

Is America getting happier as it gets richer? Table 1 tabulates for three years the raw answers to the question:

Taken all together, how would you say things are these days – would you

[4] The late Fred Hirsch was a Warwick professor in the 1970s.
[5] The new paper by Easterlin (1995) presents modern US data showing that the % of people 'very happy' did not rise between 1972 and 1991. This appears a touch misleading, because the % unhappy fell quite markedly.

Table 1

Happiness in the United States: 1972–90

	1972	1980	1990
Very happy %	30·3	33·9	33·4
Pretty happy %	53·2	52·7	57·6
Not too happy %	16·5	13·3	9·0
Number in sample	1,606	1,462	1,361

Source: Blanchflower *et al.* (1993) from US General Social Surveys. That paper gives data for each year. Weighted to control for oversampling of blacks in certain years.

say that you are very happy, pretty happy, or not too happy? (GSS Ques. 154–6)

The first thing that is noticeable is that 'pretty happy' is the typical answer, and that 'not too happy', which is the lowest score people can assign themselves, is given by slightly more than a tenth of the population.

First indications from Table 1 are not encouraging to the idea that growth leads to more well-being. There is little sign of a time trend in the answer 'very happy'. The proportion of American respondents saying this was around one third both early in the 1970s and late in the 1980s. Over the period, however, a declining number of people seem to say that they are not too happy, and more state that they are pretty happy.

The raw data are consistent with the view that the category 'pretty happy' is expanding while 'not too happy' is shrinking. Nevertheless, the effect is not dramatic, and these are only raw data that may be being moulded predominantly by a population that is changing its composition. Blanchflower *et al.* (1993) explore the matter more systematically. They examine whether there is an upward trend in well-being after controlling for demographic and other compositional changes in the American economy. Their conclusion is that there is a positive time trend, but that it is very slight. Intriguingly, there seems to be evidence of a cycle in happiness (especially for men). Blanchflower *et al.* show that the rise in happiness has not been spread evenly. It seems that American men have got happier while American women have experienced little growth in subjective well-being. Blanchflower and Oswald (1996) find some evidence that the young are growing relatively happier.

These results are not consistent with the conclusion of Easterlin (1974) that, perhaps because of ever-increasing aspirations and concern for relativities, the human lot does not improve over time. They are more like the arguments of Andrews (1991) and Veenhoven (1991). Nevertheless, Easterlin was on the right track. It may be correct to suggest that little national happiness is bought by rising national income.

FINDING 1. *Happiness with life appears to be increasing in the United States. The rise is so small, however, that it seems extra income is not contributing dramatically to the quality of people's lives.*

II. SATISFACTION WITH LIFE: EUROPE SINCE 1973

There is similar information for European countries. Although few economists seem to have used the data, the Eurobarometer Survey Series asks:

> On the whole, are you very satisfied, fairly satisfied, not very satisfied, or not at all satisfied with the life you lead?

Answers are available for random samples, from 1973 to the present, of approximately 1,000 people per year per country. The nations are Belgium, Denmark, West Germany, Greece, Spain, France, Ireland, Italy, Luxembourg, The Netherlands, Portugal and Great Britain. Surveys have been held twice a year in each European Community country. Because of their late entry to the EC, there is no full run of data for Spain, Portugal and Greece. A valuable source of information about the Eurobarometer surveys is the comprehensive study by Inglehart (1990), who uses them to study changing cultural values.

Table 2 reports some of the data on life satisfaction for these countries. The first thing that is obvious is the large differences across nations. In Denmark, for example, more than half the population say they are 'very satisfied', while in Italy the figure is around one in ten. These divergent numbers are likely to reflect cultural and linguistic differences. This is partly the difficulty of translation (words like happiness, contentment and satisfaction have subtle distinctions in English, and in other languages). But it is not all variation in language. As Inglehart (1990) points out, Switzerland makes an ideal laboratory to test this. German-speaking Swiss, French-speaking Swiss, and Italian-speaking Swiss all express higher satisfaction levels than do native Germans, French and Italians.

Table 2

Life Satisfaction in Nine European Countries from One Decade to the Next

Country	Average % 1973–81	Average % 1982–90	Well-being increased?
Proportion of the sample who reported themselves as 'very satisfied' with their lives			
Belgium	39·5	24·7	No
Denmark	51·7	62·8	Yes
France	12·4	13·7	Yes
West Germany	18·8	23·4	Yes
Ireland	38·8	31·1	No
Italy	9·0	13·2	Yes
Luxembourg	34·6	39·1	Yes
Netherlands	41·3	41·8	Yes
UK	31·7	30·9	No

Source: Own calculations using Eurobarometer Survey numbers provided by Ronald Inglehart of the University of Michigan. Sample size is approximately 1,000 people per year per country.

The second thing that is noticeable is that well-being is not moving uniformly upwards. Table 2 calculates from country to country the mean level, for each of the two halves of the period, of those answering 'very satisfied'. This smooths out some of the (fairly large) fluctuations in people's year-to-year

1820   THE ECONOMIC JOURNAL   [NOVEMBER

answers. Thus in the period 1973–81 in Belgium, for example, on average
39·5 % of the people interviewed said that they were very satisfied with their
lives. Over the ensuing decade, this figure dropped dramatically. For 1982–90,
the proportion of respondents saying very satisfied was 24·7 %. This evidence
shows no gain over time of the sort to be expected if real income growth raises
well-being. However, as the rest of Table 2 reveals, Belgium is not typical.
Denmark, France, West Germany, Italy, Luxembourg and Netherlands all
record increases in the numbers of individuals saying they feel very satisfied
with life. Ireland posts a large drop. The United Kingdom experiences a small
fall.

   There is only slight evidence here that greater economic prosperity leads to
more well-being in a nation:

   FINDING 2. *Since the early 1970s, reported levels of satisfaction with life in the European
countries have on average risen very slightly.*

There is another way to measure well-being, and that is to study psychiatric
measures of mental distress. The new British Household Panel Study gives
mental well-being scores from a form of psychiatric evaluation known as the
General Health Questionnaire. The first sweep of the British Household Panel
Study provides information, for the year 1991, about a random sample of
approximately six thousand working Britons. One way to assess these people's
feelings of subjective well-being is to use their scores from the General Health
Questionnaire (GHQ) section of the survey. Argyle (1989) argues that a GHQ
assessment is one of the most reliable indicators of psychological distress or
'disutility'. In its simplest form this assessment weights the answers to the
following set of questions.

   Have you recently:
      *1. been able to concentrate on whatever you are doing?
       2. lost much sleep over worry?
      *3. felt that you are playing a useful part in things?
      *4. felt capable of making decisions about things?
       5. felt constantly under strain?
       6. felt you couldn't overcome your difficulties?
      *7. been able to enjoy your normal day-to-day activities?
      *8. been able to face up to your problems?
       9. been feeling unhappy and depressed?
      10. been losing confidence in yourself?
      11. been thinking of yourself as a worthless person?
      *12. been feeling reasonably happy all things considered?

People's answers to these questions are coded on a four-point scale running
from 'disagree strongly' to 'agree strongly'. Starred items are coded in reverse,
so that, for example, zero then corresponds to 'agree strongly'. These twelve
are then combined into a total GHQ level of mental distress in which high
numbers correspond to low feelings of well-being. The data provide a mental
stress or, much less accurately, unhappiness level for each individual in the
sample.

There are various ways to work with GHQ responses. One is to calculate so-called Caseness scores. These are produced by taking people's answers to the twelve questions that are listed above and summing the number of times the person places himself or herself in either the fairly stressed or highly stressed category. With this method, the lowest possible level of well-being corresponds to a caseness level of 12 (meaning that the individual felt stressed on every one of the twelve questions). The highest level of well-being corresponds to 0 (meaning that the individual felt stressed on none of the twelve questions). Individuals with high caseness levels are viewed by psychologists as people who would benefit from psychiatric treatment.

The British Household Panel Survey data show that income has no strong role to play, but that joblessness does. Clark and Oswald (1994) fail to find any statistically significant effect from income. The sharp impact of unemployment, however, is illustrated by Tables 3 and 4. These use data on 6,000 British

Table 3

Measuring the Distress Levels of People in the Labour Force in Britain in 1991

Labour market status	Number in sample	Average mental distress*
Unemployed	522	2·98
Employee	4,893	1·45
Self-employed	736	1·54

* These numbers are on a scale where the minimum is 0 and the maximum is 12. Calculating means in this way imposes an implicit assumption of cardinality.

Table 4

Distress Levels in Britain by Educational Attainment

	Number in sample	Mental distress
High education (HNC up to degree)		
In work	1,612	1·48
Unemployed	86	3·44
Medium education (GCSE up to A level)		
In work	2,157	1·43
Unemployed	161	3·15
Low education (less or no qualifications)		
In work	1,848	1·43
Unemployed	273	2·70

Source for both Tables: Clark and Oswald (1994) using BHPS data on GHQ scores.

workers in 1991. Mental distress is twice as high among the unemployed as among those who have work.

Interestingly, research suggests that the worst thing about losing one's job is not the drop in take-home income. It is the non-pecuniary distress. To put this differently, most regression results imply that an enormous amount of extra income would be required to compensate people for having no work.

Table 5

The Microeconomics of Happiness in Europe: 1975–86

	All	Unemployed
Very happy (%)	23·4	15·9
Pretty happy (%)	57·9	51·1
Not too happy (%)	18·6	33·0
	Lowest-income quartile people	Highest-income quartile people
Very happy (%)	18·8	28·4
Pretty happy (%)	54·5	58·5
Not too happy (%)	26·7	13·1

Source: Di Tella *et al.* (1996) using Eurobarometer data. Total sample 108,802 observations.

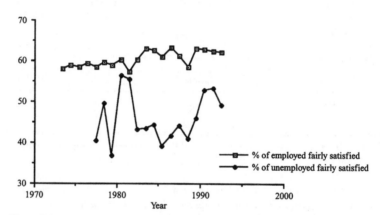

Fig. 1. Life-satisfaction levels of the employed and the unemployed: the European countries 1970s–1990s. *Notes.* The vertical axis measures the proportion of people saying they were 'fairly satisfied with life' as a whole. The data source is the Eurobarometer Surveys, which provide a random sample here of approximately 120,000 European men. Running a trend line through each series produces almost exactly the same gradient, namely, just over 0·2.

Eurobarometer data, in Table 5 and Fig. 1, also show that the unemployed feel much less satisfied with life,[6] and indicate that the relative distress from unemployment does not appear to be trending downwards through the years (the 'unhappiness gap' is not secularly shrinking). In passing, this might be thought to raise doubts about the oft-expressed view that an increasingly generous welfare state is somehow at the root of Europe's economic problems. A review of psychologists' earlier work is available in Warr *et al.* (1988).[7] The upshot of all this evidence is:

FINDING 3. *Unemployed people are very unhappy.*

[6] Longitudinal studies by psychologists have demonstrated that this is not merely because unhappy people have trouble finding jobs.
[7] New work by Kammerling and O'Connor (1993) shows that around Bristol the local area unemployment rates are strong predictors of the rate of psychiatric admission by area.

More generally, it is now well known that there are systematic patterns in micro data on people's subjective well-being. In other words, if one takes a random sample of people, and estimates a well-being regression equation of form 'reported well-being = *f*(personal characteristics)', the results tend to be the same across different periods, different countries, and even different measures of well-being. Summarising:

FINDING 4. *Reported happiness is high among those who are married, on high income, women, whites, the well-educated, the self-employed, the retired, and those looking after the home. Happiness is apparently U-shaped in age (minimising around the 30s).*

These stem from coefficients in cross-section equations, but some have been verified in panel data.

III. EXTREME UNHAPPINESS: SUICIDE AND ATTEMPTED SUICIDE

Getting information on high levels of happiness is likely to be difficult, because there is no need for such statistics to be recorded. There is, however, a method of studying the other extreme.

Suicide is a significant cause of death across the world. In Denmark it accounts for approximately 1 in every 3,000 deaths; in Britain the figure is approximately 1 in every 12,000 deaths; in the United States of America around 1 in every 7,000 deaths are the result of suicide. Large numbers of people, therefore, take the decision that life is not worth living. Moreover, the numbers just given understate what is really happening. First, most writings on the subject express the view that, for understandable reasons, suicide statistics are probably under-reported versions of the truth. Second, the number of individuals attempting suicide is much larger than of those who do kill themselves.

The medical term for attempted suicide is para-suicide. Data in Smith (1985) record the probably little-appreciated fact that in Britain a fifth of all emergency admissions to hospital are due to para-suicide. Dooley *et al.* (1989) report that para-suicide is between 8 and 20 times more common than successful suicide. Five million Americans, they estimate, have attempted suicide at some time in their lives. The data that Platt and Kreitman (1985) gather on Edinburgh males suggest that, among unemployed men in the lowest social class (Class V), one in twenty try to kill themselves in a given year.

Is this topic best left to doctors? Although analysis has a long history (Durkheim, 1897, being a landmark), most social scientists are not used to working with suicide statistics. Economists, especially, are likely to see this area as far from their usual concerns, and of little relevance to them.

This attitude may not be the right one. As writer Wilfred Sheen remarked: suicide is about life, being in fact the sincerest criticism that life gets. If the aim is to understand human well-being and the value of life, suicide data offer rich – though upsetting – information that would be impossible to glean in any other way. The reason is that suicides represent choices in response to (un)happiness that are intrinsically more compelling than replies made to

1824 THE ECONOMIC JOURNAL [NOVEMBER

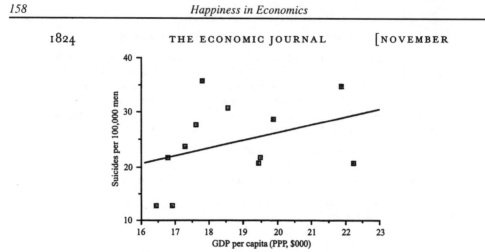

Fig. 2. Suicides and GDP in the rich industrial nations. *Notes.* This figure depicts the suicide rates and purchasing power parity GDP per capita figures of the dozen nations with the highest HDI (human development index) scores as calculated by the UN. The twelve countries are Canada, Switzerland, Japan, Sweden, Norway, France, Australia, United States, Netherlands, UK, Germany, and Austria. The data are for the early 1990s. Source of the data: Tables 28 and 30 of *Human Development Report*. United Nations, Oxford University Press, 1994.

happiness survey questions, and data that, by their nature, cannot be generated in a laboratory experiment. It might, of course, be argued by a social scientist that suicide decisions are not rational. Perhaps they are simply a sign of mental illness, and therefore do not contain reliable information. Medical opinion has debated this view and not accepted it in a wholehearted way. There is evidence that suicides occur more frequently both among those who in an objective sense have the least to live for, and after unpleasant events in a person's life. The latter include unpleasant economic events. Humphry (1992) and Richman (1992) discuss the notion of, and evidence for, rational suicide.

For the post-war period, suicide is dropping through time. By such a benchmark, life looks like it is improving. There is little reason to impute causality, but the data do not contradict the natural idea that greater real income might make fewer people so miserable that they want to kill themselves. Data for the whole century, in so far as they are reliable, suggest the same. In 1911, 2,600 men committed suicide in England and Wales. In 1990, 2,800 did so. The population over that period nearly doubled. In this sense, extreme unhappiness might be said to be dropping. Historical statistics also reveal that total suicide deaths reached their maximum in the Great Depression, which is consistent with the idea that economics may have some role to play in this area.

Figure 2 provides data on a dozen rich countries. Although it would probably be unwise to read too much into the plot, high real income is positively, not negatively, correlated with the suicide rate.

To explore the idea that money buys happiness, it might be natural to look at data on suicide and low income. This can be done in an indirect way. Charlton *et al.* (1992) show that the suicide death rate is largely independent of social class. Thus, roughly speaking, economically prosperous people do not take their own lives less than the poor. There is one type of exception to this: those men unemployed and seeking work at census were at 2–3-fold greater risk of suicide death than the average, Charlton *et al.* (1992). The study by Platt and Kreitman (1985) produces Table 6, on para-suicide by length of jobless-

Table 6

Parasuicide Rates by Duration of Unemployment: Edinburgh City Males, 1982

Duration of unemployment	Para-suicide rate/100,000	Relative risk
Less than 4 weeks	1,012	8·8
5–26 weeks	615	5·4
27–52 weeks	1,193	10·4
Over 52 Weeks	2,164	18·9
All unemployed	1,345	11·8
All employed	114	1·0

Source: Platt and Kreitman (1985).

ness. It shows that being without work is associated with a twelve times greater-than-average chance of attempted suicide, and that the long-term unemployed are especially at risk.

There is a little evidence that time-series movements in unemployment are accompanied by movements in suicide. *Population Trends* of Spring 1994 recorded the fact that, among men, suicide has been rising in almost all Western countries since the early 1970s. This period coincides with the mushrooming of unemployment.

Divorce and being single are apparently also significant triggers of suicidal behaviour. In the words of Charlton *et al*, there may be a protective effect from marriage. Married men commit suicide – holding age constant – only one third as often as others.

FINDING 5. *Consistent with the patterns in happiness data, suicidal behaviour is more prevalent among men, the unemployed, and those with marital problems. Over the long run, as Britain has got richer, the suicide rate has declined (though this is not true for men since the 1970s). Rich countries apparently have more suicides.*

FINDING 6. *High unemployment may swell the number of people taking their own lives. Suicide data suggest that joblessness is a major source of distress.*

IV. JOB SATISFACTION IN BRITAIN AND THE UNITED STATES

On the grounds that work is a big part of life, this section examines information about job satisfaction. Following Blanchflower *et al.* (1993), data are available for Great Britain and the United States. The *General Social Surveys* of 1972–90 are again the source of US information. The relevant question, asked of approximately 13,000 workers, is:

1826   THE ECONOMIC JOURNAL   [NOVEMBER

Table 7

Job Satisfaction in the United States: 1972–90

	1972	1980	1990
Very satisfied %	46·2	44·4	46·0
Moderately satisfied %	38·0	37·7	40·1
A little dissatisfied %	12·2	13·8	9·9
Very dissatisfied %	3·6	4·2	4·0
Number in sample	777	698	734

Source: Blanchflower *et al.* (1993) from US *General Social Surveys*. That paper gives data for each year. Weighted to control for oversampling of blacks in certain years.

Table 8

Job Satisfaction in the United Kingdom: 1973–83

	1973	1978	1983
Very satisfied %	42·7	44·5	39·3
Fairly satisfied %	42·8	39·4	43·5
Neither sat. nor dissat.	7·7	4·6	5·3
Rather dissatisfied %	4·4	7·9	8·0
Very dissatisfied %	2·4	3·5	4·3
Number in sample	13,845	11,814	8,417

Source: Blanchflower *et al.* (1993) from the *General Household Surveys*.

On the whole, how satisfied or dissatisfied are you with the work you do – would you say you are very satisfied, moderately satisfied, a little dissatisfied, or very dissatisfied? (GSS Ques.)

For Britain, the *General Household Surveys* of 1973–83 can be used. These offer a sample of approximately 126,000 employed individuals. The question asked is:

How satisfied are you with your job as a whole – very satisfied, fairly satisfied, neither satisfied nor dissatisfied, rather dissatisfied, or very dissatisfied? (GHS Ques.)

The wordings thus differ slightly between countries, but seem sufficiently similar to allow rough comparison. In both countries the samples for the paper's analysis are restricted to current employees. Although an interesting special case, the self-employed are omitted. There is a small literature suggesting that they have intrinsically greater job satisfaction than employees.

Tables 7 and 8 give the raw numbers on job satisfaction for each country. Table 7 reports the statistics for the overall US sample. The raw numbers reveal fairly large fluctuations – the number jumped to almost 56% in 1975 and was as low as 43% in 1987 – so it is especially difficult to find a time trend in the statistics.

British data are given in Table 8. The proportion stating 'very satisfied' with their job is on average 43% over the period, which is similar to the numbers for the United States. In 1973, the proportion of British adults calling themselves very satisfied at work was 42·7%. In 1983, at the end of the period for which GHS data are available, the number was 39·3%. There is thus if anything some sign of a slight fall in the level of job satisfaction in Britain.

This finding of fairly flat job satisfaction levels through time mirrors Weaver (1980) on earlier US data. One interpretation, supported by the evidence in Clark and Oswald (1994), is that satisfaction is somehow inherently relativistic, and based on comparisons with others.

FINDING 7. *In Britain and America the level of job satisfaction is not rising over time.*

V. CONCLUSIONS

Every day, in every industrialised country of the world, journalists and politicians give out a conscious and unconscious message. It is that better economic performance means more happiness for a nation. This idea is rarely questioned. We feel we would be more cheery if our boss raised our pay, and assume that countries must be roughly the same.

The results in this paper suggest that, in a developed nation, economic progress buys only a small amount of extra happiness. Four main pieces of evidence have been offered for this claim.

1. Reported happiness in the United States has gone up only fractionally over the post-war period.

2. Reported levels of 'satisfaction with life' in Europe are only slightly higher than they were twenty years ago. Some countries show falls.

3. Although the rate of suicide in Britain has fallen by approximately one third over the last hundred years, the number for men has risen, in almost all Western nations, from the 1970s to the present. Rich countries seem to have high suicide rates.

4. Job satisfaction has not increased, over those parts of the last quarter of a century for which data are available, in the United States and the United Kingdom.

These gains in national well-being appear to be so slight that a case could be made, as by Richard Easterlin (1974), that economic growth is worthless. This paper argues that Easterlin is wrong – but only just.

Because the task of measuring well-being is a difficult and relatively unconventional one, the paper's results cannot be accepted uncritically. First, it might be argued that interview responses to happiness and satisfaction questions do not mean anything reliable. Second, it might be argued that the use of suicide data as an indicator of a society's happiness is too strange to be taken seriously, or that such data are unhelpful because they are a reflection of mental illness and not of any objectively low quality of life. There is no wholly convincing way to dispose of such objections. As in any area of social science, it is prudent to view the paper's punchlines cautiously. Nevertheless, a simple reply to critics is that these kinds of statistics are probably the only ones available to us if we wish to measure well-being, and that, at the very least, they raise doubts about routine beliefs. Moreover, counter-arguments to the methodological criticisms have been produced many times. It is known in the psychological and medical literatures that objective economic events are correlated with happiness scores and with suicide (and para-suicide).

Another possible line of attack on the paper's conclusions is to appeal to common-sense observation. How can it be, one might ask, that money buys little well-being and yet we see individuals around us constantly striving to make more of it? The answer may be that what matters to someone who lives in a rich country is his or her relative income. A spectator who leaps up at a football match gets at first a much better view of the game; by the time his neighbours are up it is no better than before. If there is something to this, it would explain why intuition is capable of misleading us about the national benefits of economic performance. Such intuition has been built up by observing how each of us feels as our income rises. Yet, implicitly, that holds others' incomes constant. Hence common-sense may not be a good guide to what happens when a whole society gets richer.

The conclusions of the paper do not mean that economic forces have little impact on people's lives. A consistent theme through the paper's different forms of evidence has been the vulnerability of human beings to joblessness. Unemployment appears to be the primary economic source of unhappiness. If so, economic growth should not be a government's primary concern.

University of Warwick

BACKGROUND NOTES

The main sources of information used in the paper are the *Eurobarometer Surveys* of 1973 onwards, the British *General Household Surveys* of 1973 onwards, the first 1991 sweep of the *British Household Panel Study*, and the US *General Social Surveys* of 1972 onwards. These are face-to-face surveys of randomly sampled individuals. Suicide data come from the Office of Population Censuses and Surveys. All the paper's sources of data are publicly available. This paper has not attempted to document its literature sources in the way a normal academic paper would. The paper's general conclusions in some cases agree or overlap with those in Andrews (1991), Smith (1979), Shin (1980), Thomas and Hughes (1986), Veenhoven (1991, 1993) and Weaver (1980). Although little-read by economists, the pioneering work on the statistical study of well-being includes Andrews and Withey (1976), Andrews and Inglehart (1978), Campbell *et al.* (1976), Campbell (1981), Cantril (1965), Diener (1984), and Larsen *et al.* (1984). A good introduction is Argyle (1989). Economists interested in dipping into a huge recent literature might also look at Andrews (1991), Warr (1987, 1990*a*, *b*) and Ng (1996). Blanchflower and Oswald (1996) conclude that the young are getting systematically happier. Birdi *et al.* (1995), Clark *et al.* (1996) and Warr (1992) argue that job satisfaction is U-shaped in age, and give other results. Blanchflower and Oswald (1997) find the self-employed are happier.

Hirsch (1976) is a well-known critique of the value of increased real national income. Scitovsky (1976) makes similar arguments. My attention has been drawn to an early happiness study in this JOURNAL, Morawetz *et al.* (1977). Many of the British results on the distress caused by unemployment are due to Jahoda (1982), Warr (1978 onwards) and Jackson *et al.* (1983). New work includes Whelan (1992) and Gallie and Russell (1995). The unemployment findings are now conventional in the psychology literature

1997]   HAPPINESS AND ECONOMIC PERFORMANCE   1829

but probably still not well-known among economists. Innovative early work by economists includes Bjorklund (1985) and Edin (1988), who fail to find marked effects for Sweden. More recent research has uncovered large negative effects of joblessness upon wellbeing. The findings of Gerlach and Stephan (1996), Korpi (1997) and Winkelmann and Winkelmann (1997) seem particularly important. They control for person-specific fixed effects. The coefficient on unemployment in a panel well-being equation turns out to be fairly similar to that in a pure cross-section equation.

There are potential links between the happiness literature and the literatures on the quality of life and the Human Development Index, but they have yet to be forged. Nussbaum and Sen (1993) contains a set of essays on the border between philosophy and economics. Smith (1993) is a critical inquiry into HDI. Crafts (1997) is a recent application of HDI methods.

If well-being depends upon relative income, most of economists' optimal tax theory is incomplete or worse. The standard literature assumes that in setting taxes a government should pay no attention to people's feelings of how they compare with others: little or no role is assigned to personal notions of justice or relative deprivation. Some of the few attempts to change this are Boskin and Sheshinski (1978), Layard (1980) and Oswald (1983).

International comparisons using the multi-national *International Social Survey Programme* are given in Birdi *et al.* (1995), Blanchflower and Freeman (1997) and Curtice (1993). This paper focuses on well-being in developed countries. It seems likely that real income growth does buy a lot of happiness in a developing nation. Veenhoven (1991) presents evidence consistent with that.

REFERENCES

Andrews, F. M. (1991). 'Stability and change in levels and structure of subjective well-being: USA 1972 and 1988.' *Social Indicators Research*, vol. 25, pp. 1–30.
Andrews, F. M. and Inglehart, R. F. (1978). 'The structure of subjective well-being in nine western societies.' *Social Indicators Research*, vol. 6, pp. 73–90.
Andrews, F. M. and Withey, S. B. (1976). *Social Indicators of Well Being*, New York: Plenum Press.
Argyle, M. (1989). *The Psychology of Happiness*. London: Routledge.
Birdi, K. M., Warr, P. B. and Oswald, A. J. (1995). 'Age differences in three components of employee well-being.' *Applied Psychology: An International Review*, vol. 44, pp. 345–73.
Bjorklund, A. (1985). 'Unemployment and mental health: some evidence from panel data.' *Journal of Human Resources*, vol. 20, pp. 469–83.
Blanchflower, D. G. and Freeman, R. B. (1997). 'The legacy of communist labor relations, ' *Industrial and Labor Relations Review*, forthcoming.
Blanchflower, D. G. and Oswald, A. J. (1996). 'The rising well-being of the young.' Paper presented at an NBER Conference on Disadvantaged Youth, North Carolina, December.
Blanchflower, D. G. and Oswald, A. J. (1997). 'What makes an entrepreneur?' *Journal of Labor Economics*, forthcoming.
Blanchflower, D. G., Oswald, A. J. and Warr, P. B. (1993). 'Well-being over time in Britain and the USA.' Paper presented at an Economics of Happiness Conference, London School of Economics.
Boskin, M. and Sheshinski, E. (1978). 'Optimal redistributive taxation when individual welfare depends upon relative income.' *Quarterly Journal of Economics*, vol. 92, pp. 589–601.
Campbell, A. (1981). *The Sense of Well-Being in America*, New York: McGraw Hill.
Campbell, A., Converse, P. E. and Rodgers, W. L. (1976). *The Quality of American Life*, New York: Russell Sage Foundation.
Cantril, H. (1965). *The Pattern of Human Concerns*, New Brunswick: Rutgers University Press.
Charlton, J., Kelly, S., Dunnell, K., Evans, B., Jenkins, R., Wallis, R. (1992). 'Trends in suicide deaths in England and Wales', *Population Trends*, vol. 69, Autumn, Parts I and II.
Clark, A. E. (1992). 'Job satisfaction and gender: why are women so happy at work?' University of Essex, Economics Department Working Paper 415.
Clark, A. E. (1996a). 'Job satisfaction in Britain', *British Journal of Industrial Relations*, vol. 34, pp. 189–217.
Clark, A. E. (1996b). 'Working and well-being: some international evidence', mimeo, OECD, Paris.

Clark, A. E. and Oswald, A. J. (1994). 'Unhappiness and unemployment.' ECONOMIC JOURNAL, vol. 104, 648–59.

Clark, A. E. and Oswald, A. J. (1996). 'Satisfaction and comparison income.' *Journal of Public Economics*, vol. 61, pp. 359–81.

Clark, A. E., Oswald, A. J. and Warr, P. B. (1996). 'Is job satisfaction U-shaped in age?' *Journal of Occupational and Organizational Psychology*, vol. 69, pp. 57–81.

Crafts, N. F. R. (1997). 'Some dimensions of the "quality of life" during the British industrial revolution', mimeo, London School of Economics.

Curtice, J. (1993). 'Satisfying work – if you can get it.' In *International Social Attitudes and the Tenth BSA Report* (ed. R. Jowell *et al.*). London: Dartmouth.

Diener, E. (1984). 'Subjective well-being.' *Psychological Bulletin*, vol. 95, pp. 542–75.

Di Tella, R., MacCulloch, R. and Oswald, A. J. (1996). 'The macroeconomics of happiness', mimeo, Oxford and Warwick.

Dooley, D., Catalano, R., Rook, K. and Serxner, S. (1989). 'Economic stress and suicide: multi-level analysis', Parts 1 and 2, *Suicide and Life-Threatening Behaviour*, vol. 19, pp. 321–36 and 337–51.

Douthitt, R. A., MacDonald, M. and Mullis, R. (1992). 'The relationship between measures of subjective and economic well-being: a new look.' *Social Indicators Research*, vol. 26, pp. 407–22.

Durkheim, E. (1897). *Suicide: A Study in Sociology*, 1992 reprinting, London: Routledge.

Easterlin, R. (1974). 'Does economic growth improve the human lot? Some empirical evidence.' In *Nations and Households in Economic Growth: Essays in Honour of Moses Abramowitz* (ed. P. A. David and M. W. Reder). New York and London: Academic Press.

Easterlin, R. (1995). 'Will raising the incomes of all increase the happiness of all?' *Journal of Economic Behaviour and Organization*, vol. 27, pp. 35–48.

Edin, P.-A. (1988). 'Individual consequences of plant closures, Uppsala University, doctoral dissertation.

Fox, C. R. and Kahneman, D. (1992). 'Correlations, causes and heuristics in surveys of life satisfaction.' *Social Indicators Research*, vol. 27, pp. 221–34.

Frank, R. H. (1985). *Choosing the Right Pond.* New York and Oxford: Oxford University Press.

Gallie, D. and Russell, H. (1995). 'Unemployment, gender and life satisfaction', mimeo, Nuffield College.

Gerlach, K. and Stephan, G. (1996). 'A paper on unhappiness and unemployment in Germany', *Economics Letters*, vol. 52, pp. 325–30.

Hirsch, F. (1976). *The Social Limits of Growth*, Cambridge, Mass: Harvard University Press.

Humphry, D. (1992). 'Rational suicide among the elderly.' *Suicide and Life-Threatening Behaviour*, vol. 22, pp. 125–9.

Inglehart, R. (1990). *Culture Shift in Advanced Industrial Society.* Princeton: Princeton University Press.

Jackson, P. R., Stafford, E. M., Banks, M. H. and Warr, P. B. (1983). 'Unemployment and psychological distress in young people: the moderating role of employment commitment.' *Journal of Applied Psychology*, vol. 68, pp. 525–35.

Jahoda, M. (1982). *Employment and Unemployment: A Social Psychological Approach.* Cambridge: Cambridge University Press.

Kammerling, R. M. and O'Connor, S. (1993). 'Unemployment rate as predictor of rate of psychiatric admission.' *British Medical Journal*, vol. 307, pp. 1536–9.

Korpi, T. (1997). 'Is utility related to employment status?', *Labour Economics*, vol. 4, pp. 125–48.

Larsen, R. J., Diener, E. and Emmons, R. A. (1984). 'An evaluation of subjective well-being measures.' *Social Indicators Research*, vol. 17, pp. 1–18.

Layard, R. (1980). 'Human satisfactions and public policy.' ECONOMIC JOURNAL, vol. 90, pp. 737–50.

Morawetz, D. *et al.* (1977). 'Income distribution and self-rated happiness: some empirical evidence.' ECONOMIC JOURNAL, vol. 87, pp. 511–22.

Mullis, R. J. (1992). 'Measures of economic well-being as predictors of psychological well-being.' *Social Indicators Research*, vol. 26, pp. 119–35.

Ng, Y.-K. (1996). 'Happiness surveys: some comparability issues and an exploratory survey based on just perceivable increments.' *Social Indicators Research*, vol. 38, pp. 1–27.

Nussbaum, M. C. and Sen, A. (1993), eds. *The Quality of Life.* Oxford: Oxford University Press.

Oswald, A. J. (1983). 'Altruism, jealousy and the theory of optimal non-linear taxation.' *Journal of Public Economics*, vol. 20, pp. 77–87.

Pavot, W. (1991). 'Further validation of the satisfaction with life scale: evidence for the cross-method convergence of well-being measures.' *Journal of Personality Assessment*, vol. 57, pp. 149–61.

Platt, S. and Kreitman, N. (1985). 'Para-suicide and unemployment among men in Edinburgh 1968–82.' *Psychological Medicine*, vol. 291, pp. 1563–6.

Richman, J. (1992). 'A rational approach to rational suicide.' *Suicide and Life-Threatening Behaviour*, vol. 22, pp. 130–41.

Scitovsky, T. (1976). *The Joyless Economy.* Oxford: Oxford University Press.

Shin, D. C. (1980), 'Does rapid economic growth improve the human lot? Some empirical evidence.' *Social Indicators Research*, vol. 8, pp. 199–221.

1997]   HAPPINESS AND ECONOMIC PERFORMANCE   1831

Smith, P. (1993). 'Measuring human development.' *Asian Economic Journal*, pp. 89–104.
Smith, R. (1985). 'I can't stand it any more: suicide and unemployment.; *British Medical Journal*, vol. 291, pp. 1563–6.
Smith, T. W. (1979). 'Happiness: time trends, seasonal variation, inter-survey differences and other mysteries.' *Social Psychology Quarterly*, vol. 42, pp. 18–30.
Thomas, M. E. and Hughes, M. (1986). 'The continuing significance of race: a study of race, class, and quality of life in America, 1972–1985', *American Sociological Review*, vol. 5, pp. 830–41.
Veenhoven, R. (1991). 'Is happiness relative?' *Social Indicators Research*, vol. 24, pp. 1–34.
Veenhoven, R. (1993). *Happiness in Nations: Subjective Appreciation of Life in 56 Nations 1946–1992*. Rotterdam: Erasmus University Risbo.
Warr, P. B. (1978). 'A study of psychological well-being.' *British Journal of Psychology*, vol. 69, pp. 111–21.
Warr, P. B. (1987). *Work, Unemployment, and Mental Health*. Oxford: Oxford University Press.
Warr, P. B. (1990a). 'The measurement of well-being and other aspects of mental health.' *Journal of Occupational Psychology*, vol. 63, pp. 193–210.
Warr, P. B. (1990b). 'Decision latitude, job demands, and employee well-being.' *Work and Stress*, vol. 4, pp. 285–94.
Warr, P. B. (1992). 'Age and occupational well-being.' *Psychology and Aging*, vol. 7, pp. 37–45.
Warr, P. B., Jackson, P. and Banks, M. (1988). 'Unemployment and mental health: some British studies.' *Journal of Social Issues*, vol. 44, pp. 47–68.
Watson, D. and Clark, L. (1991). 'Self versus peer ratings of specific emotional traits: evidence of convergent and discriminant validity.' *Journal of Personality and Social Psychology*, vol. 60, pp. 927–40.
Weaver, C. N. (1980). 'Job satisfaction in the United States in the 1970s.' *Journal of Applied Psychology*, vol. 65, pp. 364–7.
Whelan, C. T. (1992). 'The role of income, life-style deprivation and financial strain in mediating the impact of unemployment on psychological distress: evidence from the Republic of Ireland.' *Journal of Occupational and Organizational Psychology*, vol. 65, pp. 331–44.
Winkelmann, L. and Winkelmann, R. (1997). 'Why are the unemployed so unhappy? Evidence from panel data.' *Economica*, forthcoming.

[11]

The Economic Journal, **104** (*May*), 648–659. © Royal Economic Society 1994. Published by Blackwell Publishers, 108 Cowley Road, Oxford OX4 1JF, UK and 238 Main Street, Cambridge, MA 02142, USA.

UNHAPPINESS AND UNEMPLOYMENT*

Andrew E. Clark† and Andrew J. Oswald

I. INTRODUCTION

Most people agree that unemployment in the Western economies is worryingly high. Before they can design economic policies to try to do something about it, however, politicians and economists have to decide the answer to an emotionally charged question. Are individuals effectively choosing to be unemployed? If the answer is yes, the State might wish to reduce the attractiveness of being without work, and to allow those in jobs to keep a larger share of the tax revenue that at present goes to cross-subsidize the jobless. If the answer is no, the State may have to look elsewhere for ways to tackle unemployment, and perhaps consider methods of directly raising the number of jobs[1] rather than reducing the number of benefit claimants. The tension between these opposing views is visible in most public debates about the nature of unemployment. Put loosely, the first of the two is the right-wing position that unemployment is predominantly voluntary,[2] and the second the left-wing position that unemployment is predominantly involuntary.

It might be thought that, as this is arguably the necessary starting question for any analysis of unemployment policy, economics journals would be full of studies that attempt to evaluate the voluntariness of unemployment. In practice, such studies hardly exist. The probable reason is that economists have traditionally been hostile to the notion that utility can be measured. A different attitude is found among psychologists (who might be thought to be better qualified than economists to judge such things). Thousands of papers in the psychology literature are concerned with the statistical analysis of subjective utility information.[3]

This paper, which is in the psychologists' tradition, uses data from the first sweep of the new British Household Panel Study to try to test whether, in the 1990s, unemployed people are relatively happy or unhappy. It does this by using mental well-being scores from a form of psychiatric evaluation known as the General Health Questionnaire. The paper also touches upon various related questions. Are young people less concerned than the old about being

† We are grateful to Danny Blanchflower, David Greenway, Barry McCormick and Peter Warr for useful discussions.

* This work was funded by the Economic and Social Research Council.

[1] A discussion of possible policies is contained in Clark and Layard (1993).

[2] An argument close to this can be found in Minford (1983).

[3] Warr (1987) and Argyle (1989) are readable introductions. Recent papers by economists include Blanchflower, Oswald and Warr (1993), Clark (1992, 1994) and Clark and Oswald (1993). Easterlin (1974) is a famous paper by an economist who wishes to argue that economic growth does not raise happiness. Veenhoven (1991) disputes the evidence. Technical discussions of the difficulties of measuring subjective well-being are contained in sources such as Bradburn (1969), Larsen, Diener and Emmons (1984), Pavot and Diener (1993) and Warr (1990).

[MAY 1994]   UNHAPPINESS AND UNEMPLOYMENT   649

unemployed? Is it easier, psychologically, to be unemployed in high-unemployment areas like the North? Does the distress from unemployment decrease with the duration of joblessness? Is joblessness worse for men or women, and for the highly educated or for those with low levels of education?

In cross-section analyses by social scientists, lines of causality are often open to debate. The same is true in this case. If, in the data, the unemployed appear to be less happy and to have poorer mental health than those in jobs, it could be that this is because such people are inherently less desirable as employees. In other words, psychological status might be the cause, rather than the effect, of joblessness. Although this objection is hard to overturn conclusively, there is longitudinal evidence, collected by psychologists from smaller samples, that sheds doubt on such an interpretation. A summary is provided by Warr, Jackson and Banks (1988). The paper refers to this form of evidence where it is relevant.

II. UNEMPLOYMENT AND UNHAPPINESS

The analysis draws upon data collected recently by an interdisciplinary research team. The first sweep of the British Household Panel Study provides information, for the year 1991, about a random sample of approximately six thousand working Britons. One way to assess these people's feelings of subjective well-being is to use their scores from the General Health Questionnaire (GHQ) section of the survey. Argyle (1989) argues that a GHQ assessment is one of the most reliable indicators of psychological distress or 'disutility'. In its simplest form this assessment weights the answers to the following set of questions.

Have you recently:
   *1. Been able to concentrate on whatever you are doing?
    2. Lost much sleep over worry?
   *3. Felt that you are playing a useful part in things?
   *4. Felt capable of making decisions about things?
    5. Felt constantly under strain?
    6. Felt you couldn't overcome your difficulties?
   *7. Been able to enjoy your normal day-to-day activities?
   *8. Been able to face up to your problems?
    9. Been feeling unhappy and depressed?
   10. Been losing confidence in yourself?
   11. Been thinking of yourself as a worthless person?
  *12. Been feeling reasonably happy all things considered?

People's answers to these questions are coded on a four-point scale running from 'disagree strongly' to 'agree strongly'. Starred items are coded in reverse, so that, for example, zero then corresponds to 'agree strongly'. These twelve are then combined into a total GHQ level of mental distress in which high numbers correspond to low feelings of well-being. The data provide a mental stress or, less accurately, 'unhappiness' level for each individual in the sample.

There are various ways to work with GHQ responses. This paper calculates so-called 'Caseness scores'. These are produced by taking people's answers to the twelve questions that are listed above and summing the number of times the person places himself or herself in the fairly stressed or highly stressed category. With this method, the lowest possible level of well-being corresponds to a caseness level of 12 (meaning that the individual felt stressed on every one of the twelve questions). The highest level of well-being corresponds to 0 (meaning that the individual felt stressed on none of the twelve questions). Individuals with high caseness levels are defined as people who would benefit from psychiatric treatment. To make the results easier to read, later statistics are described as measures of mental distress. More accurately, however, they are caseness levels.

If unemployment is voluntary, the jobless should presumably be just as contented, other things held constant, as those with jobs. It might be objected that the answers to a survey could be manipulated by unemployed workers. Such dissembling cannot be ruled out. Nevertheless, it is not easy to believe that, in the middle of a long interview and questionnaire, unemployed individuals – who like all other interviewees have been promised confidentiality – strategically lie to represent themselves as having low well-being scores on the GHQ questions summarised above. It is not obvious what the motive would be for deceit of this kind. Moreover, as explained below, some of the patterns found in the data have been discovered before on different samples under very different conditions.

The data reveal evidence of involuntary, rather than voluntary, un-employment. Unemployed Britons show high levels of mental distress. Using the scale just described, the mean levels are the following.

Labour market status	N	Average Mental Distress
Unemployed	522	2·98
Employee	4893	1·45
Self-employed	736	1·54

In other words, the 522 jobless people in the sample had approximately twice the mean mental distress score of those with jobs.[4] The difference between the employed and unemployed is statistically significant (with a t-statistic of over 10).

To understand the size of this effect, which is large, it is necessary to have some feel for the statistical distribution of the six thousand answers. In the full sample, taking everyone classified as in the labour force, more than half of all individuals report a mental distress score of zero. This is, by a large margin, the modal characteristic; it is also, by a narrow margin, the median characteristic. Just under one thousand other individuals have a distress level of 1, and approximately five hundred have a distress level of 2. The great majority of Britons, therefore, show low degrees of GHQ distress. Moving through the remaining scores from 3 to 12, the numbers of individuals become gradually smaller. The mean difference of approximately one-and-a-half points on an

---

[4] A causal interpretation of the correlation is made more plausible by longitudinal studies such as Warr (1978), who tracked jobless workers' declining mental well-being after the closure of a steelworks, and Jackson, Stafford, Banks and Warr (1983), who showed that movement from unemployment into paid work was accompanied by a rise in well-being.

unemployed person's distress level means that those without work appear to be substantially more stressed than people with jobs.[5]

The raw data also show that mental distress is found disproportionately among women,[6] among people in their thirties, and (though the effect is small) among those with high levels of education. For each sub-group, unemployed individuals report much lower well-being.

A cross-tabulation by education is a natural place to begin.

	N	Mental distress
High education (HNC up to degree)		
In work	1612	1·48
Unemployed	86	3·44
Medium education (GCSE up to A level)		
In work	2157	1·43
Unemployed	161	3·15
Low education (less or no qualifications)		
In work	1848	1·43
Unemployed	273	2·70

This shows that distress from joblessness is, at 3·44, greatest for those who are highly educated. Although it is impossible to be sure why this is, the result fits with the economist's presumption that, because of the greater foregone wage, the opportunity cost of unemployment should be larger for the highly-educated.

It is well known that in Britain the unemployment rate is much greater among young people than among the old. Is there anything to the idea that the young are somehow more content to be without a job? The following tabulation throws some light on this issue.

	N	Mental distress
Age less than 30		
In work	1582	1·43
Unemployed	248	2·69
Age 30–49		
In work	2941	1·56
Unemployed	168	3·42
Age over 50		
In work	1104	1·17
Unemployed	106	2·93

A powerful association between unemployment and mental distress is again apparent. For each of three age-bands, the well-being levels of the jobless are roughly half those of workers. The utility penalty attached to joblessness is smallest for those aged under thirty years old. The gap in mental distress for this

[5] There is longitudinal evidence consistent with these apparently big effects. Banks and Jackson (1982), using a sample of young people, studied GHQ scores before and after the subjects left school. Those who found jobs exhibited a large decline in mental distress; those who did not find work showed greatly increased distress scores.

[6] This contrasts with Clark's (1992) finding that women are happier at work.

group is 1·26 points (that is, 2·69–1·43). For those aged thirty to forty nine, the gap is larger at 1·86. It is 1·76 for those over the age of fifty. Unemployment does, it seems, worry the young the least.

The unemployment percentage among the youngest group is 14%, among the middle group is 5%, and among the oldest group is 9%. Hence there is a crude negative association between the utility penalty and the proportion unemployed. Although it is impossible to say anything definite about causality, it is conceivable, on the basis of these findings, that young people are unemployed more than the old because they find the state of unemployment less stressful than do the old. An alternative possibility is that young people worry less about unemployment because they recognise that it happens more to people like them.

Is it easier being unemployed once one has been without work for some time, or if one lives in a region with high unemployment? The answer to these questions is yes. The data are as follows.

	N	Mental distress
Unemployed in		
Region > average unemployment	262	2·81
Region < average unemployment	260	3·15
Unemployment duration		
> one year	197	2·74
< one year	323	3·13

However, the t-tests on these differences are insignificant at the five per cent level.

There is a relationship, in these data, between the rate of joblessness in a region and the average loss of well-being from being unemployed. A revealing check can be done by looking at the graph between the regional unemployment rate and the utility gap between working and not working. For example, in the region North–West, the average difference in mental distress between those working and those unemployed is − 1·1 (so the unemployed are worse off by this amount). This is the region with the second-smallest utility gap. The unemployment rate in the North–West in the year of the survey, namely 1991, was 9·8%. This was the second-highest unemployment rate across the regions. The Rest of the North region had a utility gap of − 0·9, and an unemployment rate of 10·4%. These are, respectively, the smallest loss in mental well-being from joblessness of any region, and the greatest unemployment rate of any region. If one had to be unemployed, this region was the least unpleasant to be unemployed in. Perhaps not coincidentally, it also had the greatest amount of joblessness. At the other end of the distribution, and of the country, unemployment is relatively more unpleasant, and there is less of it. In the South–East excluding London, for example, the unemployment rate in the data is 6·7% (the second-lowest regional level in Britain) and the utility gap is − 1·9 (second-highest). Although the relationship is not perfect, Figure 1 shows that for the eleven regions of Great Britain there appears to be a positive link

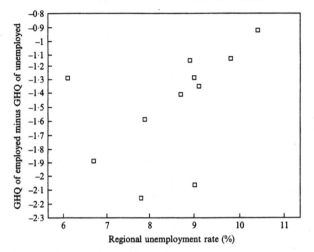

Fig. 1. Regional unemployment and individual utility loss.

Table 1

Proportion of People With Low Subjective Well-Being

(Those scoring 2 or worse on the mental distress scale)

	Number	Mean	Standard Error	t-statistic
All	5629	0·2992	0·006	9·94
	522	0·5249	0·022	
Men	2966	0·2664	0·008	8·47
	365	0·4986	0·026	
Women	2663	0·3357	0·009	6·18
	157	0·5860	0·039	
Age < 30	1582	0·3047	0·012	5·65
	248	0·4960	0·032	
Age 30–49	2941	0·3234	0·009	7·15
	168	0·6012	0·038	
Age 50+	1104	0·2274	0·013	4·86
	106	0·4717	0·049	
High education	1612	0·3176	0·012	6·03
	86	0·6395	0·052	
Medium education	2157	0·3032	0·010	5·52
	161	0·5280	0·039	
Low education	1848	0·2771	0·010	6·44
	273	0·4835	0·030	
Unemployed	262	0·4885	0·031	1·67
High unemployment region	260	0·5615	0·031	
Another u/e'd	84	0·4762	0·055	0·97
Person in h/h	438	0·5342	0·024	
Duration over one year	197	0·4924	0·036	1·16
	323	0·5449	0·028	

The second row in each case gives figures for the unemployed, the first row the rest of the sample.

Table 2
Mental Well-Being Equations
(Ordered probits on the full labour force sample)

Unemployed	−0·621	(0·049)	−0·689	(0·051)	−0·640	(0·051)	−0·642	(0·051)
Self-employed	−0·064	(0·044)	−0·129	(0·046)	−0·134	(0·046)	−0·135	(0·046)
Male	—	—	0·187	(0·030)	0·162	(0·030)	0·161	(0·030)
Age	—	—	−0·032	(0·007)	−0·031	(0·008)	−0·030	(0·008)
Age Squared	—	—	4.4E-4	(8.7E-5)	4·3E-4	(1·0E-4)	4·2E-4	(1·0E-4)
Region dummies								
Inner London	—	—	−0·145	(0·083)	−0·104	(0·085)	−0·103	(0·084)
Outer London	—	—	−0·190	(0·074)	−0·189	(0·075)	−0·195	(0·075)
South West	—	—	−0·127	(0·058)	−0·128	(0·059)	−0·130	(0·059)
East Anglia	—	—	−0·018	(0·069)	−0·020	(0·069)	−0·020	(0·069)
East Midlands	—	—	0·092	(0·091)	0·052	(0·092)	0·052	(0·092)
West Midlands conurbation	—	—	−0·087	(0·071)	−0·094	(0·071)	−0·095	(0·071)
Rest of West Midlands	—	—	−0·127	(0·084)	−0·101	(0·086)	−0·112	(0·085)
Greater Manchester	—	—	−0·101	(0·078)	−0·113	(0·079)	−0·112	(0·079)
Merseyside	—	—	−0·158	(0·085)	−0·135	(0·086)	−0·138	(0·086)
Rest of North West	—	—	−0·158	(0·108)	−0·220	(0·108)	−0·219	(0·108)
South Yorkshire	—	—	−0·070	(0·085)	−0·074	(0·085)	−0·076	(0·085)
West Yorkshire	—	—	−0·168	(0·097)	−0·187	(0·098)	−0·186	(0·098)
Rest of Yorkshire and Humberside	—	—	−0·213	(0·089)	−0·200	(0·090)	−0·203	(0·090)
Tyne and Wear	—	—	0·154	(0·098)	0·137	(0·099)	0·138	(0·099)
Rest of North	—	—	−0·087	(0·108)	−0·110	(0·109)	−0·113	(0·109)
Wales	—	—	−0·036	(0·089)	−0·063	(0·090)	−0·062	(0·090)
Scotland	—	—	−0·192	(0·082)	−0·203	(0·082)	−0·203	(0·082)
Education								
Higher	—	—	−0·055	(0·038)	−0·123	(0·039)	−0·123	(0·039)
A/O/Nursing	—	—	−0·028	(0·036)	−0·061	(0·036)	−0·060	(0·036)
Health								
Excellent	—	—	—	—	0·662	(0·042)	0·662	(0·042)
Good	—	—	—	—	0·398	(0·038)	0·397	(0·038)
Race								
Black	—	—	—	—	0·154	(0·116)	—	—
Asian subcontinent	—	—	—	—	0·211	(0·168)	—	—
Marital status								
Married	—	—	—	—	0·078	(0·049)	0·074	(0·049)
Separated	—	—	—	—	−0·265	(0·104)	−0·268	(0·104)
Divorced	—	—	—	—	−0·173	(0·069)	−0·175	(0·069)
Widowed	—	—	—	—	−0·161	(0·126)	−0·166	(0·126)
Number of children								
1	—	—	—	—	−0·130	(0·045)	−0·131	(0·045)
2	—	—	—	—	−0·045	(0·048)	−0·046	(0·048)
3+	—	—	—	—	−0·034	(0·068)	−0·036	(0·068)
Intercept	0·153	(0·018)	0·682	(0·142)	0·153	(0·193)	0·299	(0·158)
MU2	0·384	(0·012)	0·390	(0·012)	0·402	(0·013)	0·402	(0·013)
MU3	0·656	(0·016)	0·664	(0·016)	0·686	(0·016)	0·685	(0·016)
MU4	0·880	(0·018)	0·891	(0·018)	0·921	(0·019)	0·921	(0·019)
MU5	1·065	(0·020)	1·079	(0·021)	1·115	(0·021)	1·115	(0·021)
MU6	1·262	(0·023)	1·277	(0·023)	1·320	(0·024)	1·319	(0·024)
MU7	1·445	(0·026)	1·463	(0·026)	1·511	(0·027)	1·511	(0·027)
MU8	1·608	(0·029)	1·629	(0·029)	1·682	(0·030)	1·682	(0·030)
MU9	1·807	(0·033)	1·830	(0·034)	1·891	(0·035)	1·891	(0·035)
MU10	1·980	(0·038)	2·002	(0·038)	2·070	(0·040)	2·069	(0·040)
MU11	2·233	(0·047)	2·258	(0·048)	2·337	(0·050)	2·337	(0·050)
MU12	2·580	(0·068)	2·607	(0·068)	2·692	(0·070)	2·692	(0·070)
Number of observations	6151		6135		6117		6117	
Log Likelihood	−9965·87		−9880·34		−9700·97		−9701·98	

between the unemployment rate and the smallness of the utility loss from being without work.

As a further illustration of the spread of different well-being levels in the population, Table 1 gives the proportion of people in the labour force reporting mental distress levels of 2 or above. Also given is, in each category, the proportion for those who are unemployed. These numbers are presented in the row below each line. By way of illustration, of the total of 5,629 employed workers, 29·9% scored worse than a 2 on mental distress. Of 522 unemployed workers, 52·5% scored worse than a 2. This remarkable difference is an indication of the way that the distribution of the unemployed's mental well-being is heavily skewed to low levels of utility.

III. REGRESSION RESULTS

Although the previous section uses only elementary methods, the patterns found in the data are confirmed when more formal multivariate techniques are employed. This section describes the results of estimating ordered probit equations in which individuals' well-being levels are regressed on a set of personal characteristics.[7] Tests of the earlier hypotheses can then be performed in circumstances where other factors are held constant.

A number of ordered probit equations are given in Table 2. These are mental well-being equations in which the earlier GHQ distress measure has been multiplied by minus one. The dependent variable can be thought of as an ordered variable which takes values between zero and minus twelve (where minus twelve is the lowest possible level of subjective well-being).

Unemployment enters negatively in Table 2's four different specifications. Its coefficient is consistently close to $-0·6$, with a well-determined standard error of approximately $0·05$. Therefore the effect of being jobless is, at any conventional level, statistically significant and is negatively correlated with well-being. As can be seen, this effect is robust across varied specifications. The effect is quantitatively large. If these equations accurately capture a causal link, joblessness depresses well-being more than any other single characteristic (including important negative ones such as divorce and separation).

Table 2 builds up, by the gradual addition of extra regressors, to larger specifications. The fourth column is the preferred form. The Table reveals that, as in Clark, Oswald and Warr (1993), there is a U-shape in mental well-being with respect to age. On average, 'happiness' is lowest in a person's mid-thirties. Regional dummies are in a number of cases statistically significant. The self-employed show slightly lower mental distress than employees.[8] As in the cross-tabulations, highly-educated individuals show more distress than others. It

---

[7] This section can be omitted by readers unfamiliar with the statistical techniques, because the key patterns are visible in a rough way in the cross-tabulations set out in the previous section.

[8] Blanchflower and Oswald (1992) find, however, that job satisfaction is greatest among self-employed Britons and Americans.

656 THE ECONOMIC JOURNAL [MAY

Table 3
Mental Well-Being Equations: Further Experiments
(Ordered probits on the full labour force sample)

Unemployed						
Age < 30	−0·558	(0·074)	—	—	—	—
Age 30–49	−0·747	(0·085)	—	—	—	—
Age > 50	−0·656	(0·110)	—	—	—	—
Unemployed						
High u/e region	—	—	−0·563	(0·071)	—	—
Low u/e region	—	—	−0·720	(0·070)	—	—
Unemployed						
Duration < 6 months	—	—	—	—	−0·764	(0·074)
Duration 6–12 months	—	—	—	—	−0·633	(0·107)
Duration 1–2 years	—	—	—	—	−0·632	(0·129)
Duration 2+ years	—	—	—	—	−0·426	(0·099)
Self-employed	−0·139	(0·046)	−0·137	(0·046)	−0·134	(0·046)
Male	0·163	(0·030)	0·160	(0·030)	0·160	(0·030)
Age	−0·027	(0·009)	−0·030	(0·008)	−0·031	(0·008)
Age Squared	$3 \cdot 9\text{E-}4$	$(1 \cdot 1\text{E-}4)$	$4 \cdot 2\text{E-}4$	$(1 \cdot 0\text{E-}4)$	$4 \cdot 3\text{E-}4$	$(1 \cdot 0\text{E-}4)$
Region dummies						
Inner London	−0·101	(0·084)	−0·085	(0·084)	−0·109	(0·084)
Outer London	−0·195	(0·075)	−0·179	(0·076)	−0·193	(0·075)
South West	−0·130	(0·059)	−0·117	(0·059)	−0·125	(0·059)
East Anglia	−0·019	(0·069)	−0·004	(0·070)	−0·015	(0·069)
East Midlands	0·053	(0·092)	0·066	(0·092)	0·050	(0·092)
West Midlands constituency	−0·095	(0·071)	−0·079	(0·072)	−0·090	(0·071)
Rest of West Midlands	−0·111	(0·085)	−0·117	(0·085)	−0·116	(0·085)
Greater Manchester	−0·110	(0·079)	−0·113	(0·079)	−0·109	(0·079)
Merseyside	−0·138	(0·086)	−0·138	(0·086)	−0·140	(0·086)
Rest of North West	−0·223	(0·108)	−0·223	(0·108)	−0·228	(0·108)
South Yorkshire	−0·074	(0·085)	−0·076	(0·085)	−0·079	(0·085)
West Yorkshire	−0·191	(0·098)	−0·189	(0·098)	−0·187	(0·098)
Rest of Yorkshire and Humberside	−0·204	(0·090)	−0·202	(0·090)	−0·204	(0·090)
Tyne and Wear	0·140	(0·099)	0·140	(0·099)	0·133	(0·099)
Rest of North	−0·113	(0·109)	−0·110	(0·109)	−0·114	(0·109)
Wales	−0·061	(0·090)	−0·063	(0·089)	−0·060	(0·090)
Scotland	−0·202	(0·082)	−0·204	(0·082)	−0·202	(0·082)
Education						
Higher	−0·123	(0·039)	−0·123	(0·039)	−0·117	(0·039)
A/O/Nursing	−0·058	(0·036)	−0·061	(0·036)	−0·058	(0·036)
Health						
Excellent	0·662	(0·042)	0·662	(0·042)	0·668	(0·042)
Good	0·398	(0·038)	0·398	(0·038)	0·401	(0·038)
Marital status						
Married	0·073	(0·049)	0·0076	(0·049)	0·081	(0·049)
Separated	−0·267	(0·104)	−0·270	(0·104)	−0·260	(0·104)
Divorced	−0·171	(0·069)	−0·177	(0·069)	−0·175	(0·069)
Widowed	−0·161	(0·126)	−0·167	(0·126)	−0·157	(0·126)
Number of children						
1	−0·132	(0·045)	−0·131	(0·045)	−0·136	(0·045)
2	−0·047	(0·048)	−0·048	(0·046)	−0·052	(0·048)
3+	−0·034	(0·068)	−0·037	(0·068)	−0·042	(0·068)
Intercept	0·229	(0·164)	0·291	(0·159)	0·317	(0·159)
MU2	0·402	(0·013)	0·402	(0·013)	0·402	(0·013)
MU3	0·686	(0·016)	0·686	(0·016)	0·686	(0·016)
MU4	0·921	(0·019)	0·921	(0·019)	0·921	(0·019)
MU5	1·115	(0·021)	1·115	(0·021)	1·116	(0·021)
MU6	1·320	(0·024)	1·320	(0·024)	1·321	(0·024)
MU7	1·511	(0·027)	1·511	(0·027)	1·512	(0·027)

Table (cont.)

MU8	1·683	(0·030)	1·683	(0·030)	1·684	(0·030)
MU9	1·891	(0·035)	1·892	(0·035)	1·894	(0·035)
MU10	2·070	(0·040)	2·070	(0·040)	2·073	(0·040)
MU11	2·338	(0·050)	2·337	(0·050)	2·340	(0·050)
MU12	2·694	(0·070)	2·693	(0·070)	2·695	(0·070)
Number of observations	6117		6117		6117	
Log likelihood	−9700·54		−9700·69		9698·01	

may be that this is some kind of comparison effect caused by high aspirations.[9] Well-being is higher, as might be expected, among the healthy. Race is statistically insignificant. Married people have the lowest degree of mental distress. Having children (especially one) is associated with less contentment. Experiments with income as a regressor proved inconclusive: robust effects were not found. Although unexpected, this is not too serious a problem for the present analysis, because the aim is to chart the total disutility associated with joblessness. Entering income as a control, and then calculating the coefficient on unemployment status, would give the pure non-pecuniary loss from joblessness.

The ordered probit's threshold levels are denoted MU2 up to MU12. The coefficients on them, in Table 2, suggest that being unemployed is enough to change an individual's distress level from 0 to 2, or 1 to 4, or 4 to 8. As the possible values of mental distress range from 0 to 12, and the data are bunched at the bottom end of the distribution, it seems that joblessness has a large negative effect upon well-being.

Further results are given in Table 3, which reports another three well-being ordered probit equations. The first column includes an interaction between being unemployed and various age levels. The largest negative effect from joblessness mimics that in the cross-tabulations: it is for unemployed individuals aged between 30 and 49. The young suffer least from the loss of a job, but they still suffer. The second column of Table 3 interacts the state of being unemployed with the state of living in a region with above-average unemployment. Distress is greatest among those surrounded by low un-employment. The standard errors are individually well-determined, which sharpens the result from the cross-tabulation, but the F test that the coefficients are identical is not rejected at 5 %. This finding may merely indicate that it is harder to put up with unemployment if one lives in a place where few people are without a job. One piece of evidence consistent with such an interpretation is produced by Platt and Kreitman (1985). Their Edinburgh study reports that attempted suicide by unemployed men (relative to employed men) is less common in high-unemployment parts of the city. The third column of Table 3 uncovers a monotonic interaction effect between unemployment and duration

---

[9] Clark and Oswald, 1993, concludes that job satisfaction is a declining function of the person's level of educational qualification).

of unemployment.[10] The loss in well-being is estimated at -0.764 after less than six months of unemployment, gradually reducing to -0.426 after two years' unemployment duration. The F test that the coefficients on these interactions are all the same is rejected at the 5% level. Distress is greatest among those who have recently lost their job.

IV. CONCLUSIONS

As unemployment rises secularly over time, there is an increasing feeling among Western politicians that something must be done. A commonly expressed view is that, perhaps because of the generosity of financial aid to those without jobs, large numbers of people in Britain may be choosing to be unemployed. The implications of such thinking are stark.

With this kind of argument in mind, the paper uses data from the new British Household Panel Study in an attempt to assess the utility levels of the jobless. It explores, and rejects, the hypothesis that unemployment is voluntary. Unemployed people in Great Britain in 1991 have much lower levels of mental well-being than those in work. As a rough illustration, being unemployed is worse, in terms of lost 'utility' units, than divorce or marital separation. The results in this paper suggest that British policy measures aimed at cutting out supposedly high levels of voluntary joblessness would be misguided.

Nevertheless, there are signs in the data that high unemployment levels across regions and age-groups are correlated with relatively low disutility from joblessness.[11] First, distress from unemployment is less among the young and among workers in high-unemployment areas such as the North. Secondly, people who have been unemployed a long time show less distress than those who have recently lost their jobs. In this sense, the long-term unemployed are somewhat 'happier' than the short-term unemployed. Exactly what these correlations mean, and how a government should react to them, is a pressing matter for research.

CEREMAP, Paris and Centre for the Study of Micro Social Change,
University of Essex

Centre for Economic Performance, LSE

REFERENCES

Argyle, M. (1989). *The Psychology of Happiness*. London: Routledge.
Banks, M. H. and Jackson, P. R. (1982). 'Unemployment and risk of minor psychiatric disorder in young people: cross-sectional and longitudinal evidence.' *Psychological Medicine*, vol. 12, pp. 789–798.
Blanchflower, D. G. and Oswald, A. J. (1992). 'Entrepreneurship, happiness and supernormal returns: evidence from Britain and the USA.' NBER Working Paper no. 4228, Cambridge: Massachusetts.

[10] It is natural to wonder if this might just stem from the fact that those most averse to joblessness may be likely to leave the pool of unemployment most quickly. Longitudinal research, such as the study described in Warr and Jackson (1987), against suggests not.

[11] It may be worth recalling that in, for example, an efficiency-wage model such as Shapiro and Stiglitz (1984), it will be true both that unemployment is involuntary and that the level of unemployment benefit affects the equilibrium unemployment rate. If this is the correct general way to think about the labour market, governments face the difficult task of choosing the optimal compromise between having high benefits with high unemployment and having low benefits with much unhappiness among a smaller number of jobless.

Blanchflower, D. G., Oswald, A. J. and Warr, P. B. (1993). 'Well-being over time in Britain and the USA.' Paper presented at the November 1993 Happiness and Fairness Conference. London School of Economics.

Bradburn, N. M. (1969). *The Structure of Psychological Well-Being*. Chicago: Aldine.

Clark, A. E. (1992). 'Job satisfaction and gender: why are women so happy at work?' University of Essex, Economics Department Working Paper 415.

Clark, A. E. (1994). 'The economics of job satisfaction.' In *British Households Today*. (ed. N. Buck, D. Rose and J. Scott) (forthcoming).

Clark, A. E. and Layard, R. (1993). *UK Unemployment*. Oxford: Heinemann Educational.

Clark, A. E. and Oswald, A. J. (1993). 'Satisfaction and comparison income,' (mimeo), Centre for Economic Performance, London School of Economics.

Clark, A. E., Oswald, A. J. and Warr, P. B. (1993). 'Is job satisfaction U-shaped in age?' (mimeo), Centre of Economic Performance, London School of Economics.

Easterlin, R. (1974). 'Does economic growth improve the human lot? Some Empirical Evidence.' In *Nations and Households in Economic Growth: Essays in Honour of Moses Abramowitz*. (ed. P. A. David and M. W. Reder). New York and London: Academic Press.

Jackson, P. R., Stafford, E. M., Banks, M. H. and Warr, P. B. (1983). 'Unemployment and psychological distress in young people: the moderating role of employment commitment.' *Journal of Applied Psychology*, vol. 68, pp. 525–535.

Larsen, R. J., Diener, E. and Emmons, R. A. (1984). 'An evaluation of subjective well-being measures.' *Social Indicators Research*, vol. 17, pp. 1–18.

Minford, P. (1983). 'Labour market equilibrium in an open economy.' *Oxford Economic Papers*, vol. 35, (supplement) pp. 207–244.

Pavot, W. and Diener, E. (1993). 'Review of the satisfaction with life scales.' *Psychological Assessment*, vol. 5, pp. 164–172.

Platt, S. and Kreitman, N. (1985). 'Parasuicide and unemployment among men in Edinburgh 1968–82.' *Psychological Medicine*, vol. 15, pp. 113–123.

Shapiro, C. and Stiglitz, J. E. (1984). 'Equilibrium unemployment as a worker discipline device.' *American Economic Review*, vol. 74, pp. 433–444.

Veenhoven, R. (1991). 'Is happiness relative?' *Social Indicators Research*, vol. 24, pp. 1–34.

Warr, P. B. (1978). 'A study of psychological well-being.' *British Journal of Psychology*, vol. 69, pp. 111–121.

Warr, P. (1987). *Work, Unemployment and Mental Health*. Oxford: Oxford University Press.

Warr, P. (1990). 'The measurement of well-being and other aspects of mental health.' *Journal of Occupational Psychology*, vol. 63, pp. 193–210.

Warr, P. B. and Jackson, P. R. (1987). 'Adapting to the unemployed role: A longitudinal investigation.' *Social Science and Medicine*, vol. 25, pp. 1219–1224.

Warr, P. B., Jackson, P. R. and Banks, M. (1988). 'Unemployment and mental health: some British studies.' *Journal of Social Issues*, vol. 44, pp. 47–68.

[12]

Preferences over Inflation and Unemployment: Evidence from Surveys of Happiness

By RAFAEL DI TELLA, ROBERT J. MACCULLOCH, AND ANDREW J. OSWALD*

Modern macroeconomics textbooks rest upon the assumption of a social welfare function defined on inflation, π, and unemployment, U.[1] However, no formal evidence for the existence of such a function has been presented in the literature.[2] Although an optimal policy rule cannot be chosen unless the parameters of the presumed $W(\pi, U)$ function are known, that has not prevented its use in a large theoretical literature in macroeconomics.

This paper has two aims. The first is to show that citizens care about these two variables. We present evidence that inflation and unemployment belong in a well-being function. The second is to calculate the costs of inflation in terms of unemployment. We measure the relative size of the weights attached to these variables in social well-being. Policy implications emerge.

Economists have often puzzled over the costs of inflation. Survey evidence presented in Robert J. Shiller (1997) shows that, when asked how they feel about inflation, individuals report a number of unconventional costs, like exploitation, national prestige, and loss of morale. Skeptics wonder. One textbook concludes: "we shall see that standard characterizations of the policy maker's objective function put more weight on the costs of inflation than is suggested by our understanding of the effects of inflation; in doing so, they probably reflect political realities and the heavy political costs of high inflation" (Blanchard and Fischer, 1989 pp. 567–68). Since reducing inflation is often costly, in terms of extra unemployment, some observers have argued that the industrial democracies' concern with nominal price stability is excessive—and have urged different monetary policies.[3]

This paper proposes a new approach. It examines how survey respondents' reports of their well-being vary as levels of unemployment and inflation vary. Because the survey responses are available across time and countries, we are able to quantify how self-reported well-being alters with unemployment and inflation rates. Only a few economists have looked at patterns in subjective happiness and life satisfaction. Richard Easterlin (1974) helped to begin the literature. Later contributions include David Morawetz et al. (1977), Robert H. Frank (1985), Ronald Inglehart (1990), Yew-Kwang Ng (1996), Andrew J. Oswald (1997), and Liliana Winkelmann and Rainer Winkelmann (1998). More recently Ng (1997) discusses the measurability of happiness, and Daniel Kahneman et al. (1997) provide an axiomatic defense of experienced utility, and propose applications to economics. Our paper also borders on work in the psychology literature; see, for example, Edward Diener (1984), William Pavot et al. (1991), and David Myers (1993).

Section I describes the main data source and the estimation strategy. This relies on a regression-adjusted measure of well-being in a particular year and country—the level not explained by individual personal characteristics. This residual macroeconomic well-being measure is the paper's focus.

* Di Tella: Harvard Business School, Morgan Hall, Soldiers Field, Boston, MA 02163; MacCulloch: STICERD, London School of Economics, London WC2A 2AE, England; Oswald: Department of Economics, University of Warwick, Coventry CV4 7AL, England. For helpful discussions, we thank George Akerlof, Danny Blanchflower, Andrew Clark, Ben Friedman, Duncan Gallie, Sebastian Galiani, Ed Glaeser, Berndt Hayo, Daniel Kahneman, Guillermo Mondino, Steve Nickell, Julio Rotemberg, Hyun Shin, John Whalley, three referees, and seminar participants at Oxford University, Harvard Business School, and the NBER Behavioral Macro Conference in 1998. The third author is grateful to the Leverhulme Trust and the Economic and Social Research Council for research support.

[1] See, for example, Olivier Blanchard and Stanley Fischer (1989), Michael Burda and Charles Wyplosz (1993), and Robert E. Hall and John Taylor (1997). Early influential papers include Robert J. Barro and David Gordon (1983).

[2] N. Gregory Mankiw (1997) describes the question "How costly is inflation?" as one of the four major unsolved problems of macroeconomics.

[3] A recent contribution to this debate in the United States is Paul Krugman's piece, "Stable Prices and Fast Growth: Just Say No," *The Economist*, August 31, 1996.

In Section II we show, using a panel analysis of nations, that reported well-being is strongly correlated with inflation and unemployment. It should be emphasized that people are not asked whether they dislike inflation and unemployment. Instead, individuals are asked in surveys how happy they are with life, and the paper demonstrates that—possibly unknown to them—their en masse answers move systematically with their nation's level of joblessness and rate of price change.[4] Section III concludes.

I. Happiness Data and Empirical Strategy

Our main data source is the Euro-Barometer Survey Series. Partly the creation of Ronald Inglehart at the University of Michigan, it records happiness and life-satisfaction information on 264,710 people living in 12 European countries over the period 1975 to 1991. A cross-section sample of Europeans is interviewed each year. One question asks "Taking all things together, how would you say things are these days—would you say you're very happy, fairly happy, or not too happy these days?" Another elicits answers to a "life-satisfaction" question. This question, included in part because the word happy translates imprecisely across languages, is worded, "On the whole, are you very satisfied, fairly satisfied, not very satisfied or not at all satisfied with the life you lead?" We concentrate on the life-satisfaction data because they are available for a longer period of time—from 1975 to 1991 instead of just 1975–1986. Unsurprisingly, happiness and life satisfaction are correlated (the correlation coefficient is 0.56 for the available period 1975–1986), so a focus on life satisfaction may be sufficient. A companion paper, Di Tella et al. (2000), presents extra results using European happiness statistics.

We also study happiness data on 26,668 individuals from the United States General Social Survey (1972–1994). There the happiness question reads: "Taken all together, how would you say things are these days—would you say that you are very happy, pretty happy, or not too happy?" The question was asked in each of 23 years. There is no life-satisfaction question for the United

States. It would be ideal if the well-being questions' wordings were identical in the European and U.S. cases, but they are not. However, most of the paper's conclusions rest upon cross-Europe results, where the wording of questions is the same. For a data set on Great Britain, in which, unusually, both happiness and life-satisfaction answers are available from the same individuals, David Blanchflower and Oswald (2000) have shown that estimated happiness and life-satisfaction equations have almost identical structures.

A. *Estimation Strategy*

We study a regression of the form

$$\text{LIFE SATISFACTION}_{it} = \alpha \text{ INFLATION}_{it}$$

$$+ \beta \text{ UNEMPLOYMENT}_{it} + \varepsilon_i$$

$$+ \delta_t + \mu_{it}$$

where LIFE SATISFACTION is the average life satisfaction in country i in year t that is not explained by personal characteristics; UNEMPLOYMENT is the unemployment rate in country i in year t; INFLATION is the rate of change of consumer prices in country i and year t; ε_i is a country fixed effect; δ_t is a time effect (a year fixed effect); and μ_{it} is an error term. Life satisfaction has no natural units. It is measured here by assigning integers 1–4 to people's answers: 1 (to "not at all satisfied"), 2 (to "not very satisfied"), 3 (to "fairly satisfied"), and 4 (to "very satisfied"). We experimented with other cardinalizations; the paper's findings were unaffected. The data on unemployment and inflation are from the Organization for Economic Cooperation and Development (OECD). Some regressions also include a country-specific time trend.

A two-step methodology is employed. In the first stage, microeconometric OLS life-satisfaction regressions are estimated for each country in the sample. The mean residual life satisfaction is calculated for each nation in each year, which gives 150 observations in a second-stage regression. These country-by-year unexplained life-satisfaction components then become the dependent variable in a second-stage regression of the form given in the equation above. Three-year moving averages of the explanatory variables are used; the moving averages are

---

[4] Our analysis complements the survey approach of, for example, Shiller (1997), who uses questions regarding inflation.

centered on year $t - 1$. This smooths out some of the noise evident in the data (and, we found, produces succinct estimating equations while leaving the substantive conclusions unaffected when compared to equations with many lagged and autoregressive terms).

For three reasons, issues of simultaneity are ignored. First, it might be believed that "happiness" does not itself mold the levels of inflation and unemployment. Second, our aim is primarily to document correlations in the data. Third, it is unclear what kind of variable could serve as a persuasive instrument for macroeconomic variables in a well-being regression equation. Nevertheless, future research may have to return to this issue.

The building blocks of the analysis are thus well-being regressions for each of the countries in our sample. These are similar to emerging microeconometric work such as that of Blanchflower and Oswald (2000), who estimate the impact of personal characteristics on happiness responses for the United States and the United Kingdom.[5]

Although coefficients in our regressions do not have a ready cardinal meaning, a number of personal characteristics are positively associated with reported well-being, and are statistically significant, in every country in our sample. These characteristics include being employed, young, or old (not middle aged), and belonging to a high-income quartile. The microeconometric structure of well-being equations is similar across nations.

Table A1 in the Appendix presents a pooled microeconometric life-satisfaction regression for Europe. This is an ordinary least-squares regression; we checked that an ordered probit produces the same substantive conclusions. Greater family income increases the likelihood that a respondent reports a high level of well-being. This effect of income is monotonic and is reminiscent of the utility function of standard economics. The regression evidence is also consistent with the commonsense idea that unemployment is a major economic source of human distress (on psychiatric stress data, see Andrew Clark and Oswald, 1994). Our companion paper reports other well-being regressions.

The main data are as follows.

B. Data Definitions

LIFE SATISFACTION: The average of the residuals from a Life Satisfaction Ordinary Least-Squares regression on personal characteristics. The residuals are averaged for each country and year in the sample. (Mean $= -0.004$; standard deviation $= 0.082$.)

UNEMPLOYMENT: The unemployment rate (three-year moving average) from the OECD-Centre for Economic Performance data set. (Mean $= 0.086$; standard deviation $= 0.037$.)

INFLATION: The inflation rate (three-year moving average), as measured by the rate of change in consumer prices, from the OECD-Centre for Economic Performance data set. (Mean $= 0.081$; standard deviation $= 0.057$.)

Throughout the paper, unemployment and inflation are measured as fractions. For example, an 8-percent rate of inflation is entered in our data set as 0.08, and a 9-percent unemployment rate is represented as 0.09.

II. The Inflation-Unemployment Trade-Off in Well-Being Equations

Regression (1) of Table 1 studies the dependence of life satisfaction on the unemployment rate and the rate of inflation. The specification includes time and country dummies. The coefficients from regression (1) in Table 1 imply that higher unemployment and higher inflation both decrease life satisfaction.

The effects of unemployment and inflation, which in column (1) of Table 1 have coefficients -2.8 and -1.2 respectively, are significantly different from zero at conventional levels of statistical significance. It is necessary to be clear about the units of measurement in Table 1. The numbers -2.8 and -1.2 represent the effect upon well-being (as cardinalized) of a 1-percentage-point change in each of the two independent variables. As an example, consider the impact of an increase in the rate of unemployment from the mean of 9 percent by 1 percentage point to 10 percent. According to our estimate, this single-point rise in unemployment from 0.09 to 0.10 diminishes life satisfaction by 0.028 units. The number 0.028 is the product of 0.01 and 2.8. Consider instead an increase in the inflation rate from the mean of 8 percent by 1 percentage point to 9 percent. This single-point rise in inflation from 0.09 to 0.10

---

[5] Inglehart (1990) also documents the patterns in the micro data by looking at cross-tabulations.

338 THE AMERICAN ECONOMIC REVIEW MARCH 2001

TABLE 1—LIFE-SATISFACTION EQUATIONS FOR EUROPE 1975–1991

	(1)	(2)	(3) Pre 84	(4) Post 83	(5)
Unemployment t	−2.8	−2.0	−0.4	−2.0	−2.1
	(0.6)	(0.6)	(1.6)	(1.1)	(0.6)
Inflation t	−1.2	−1.4	−0.5	−2.0	−2.3
	(0.3)	(0.4)	(0.7)	(0.8)	(0.9)
Inflation^2 t					3.5
					(3.0)
Time trends	No	Yes	Yes	Yes	Yes
Country dummies	Yes	Yes	Yes	Yes	Yes
Year dummies	Yes	Yes	Yes	Yes	Yes
Number of observations	150	150	72	78	150
Adjusted R^2	0.27	0.54	0.57	0.66	0.55

Notes: Standard errors are in parentheses. Time trends are country specific. Three-year moving averages of the explanatory variables are used. This is a second-stage regression. It uses as a dependent variable the regression-corrected life-satisfaction levels from a first-stage OLS regression of the general kind given in the Appendix.

leads to a 0.012 reduction in units of life satisfaction. The number 0.012 is the product of 0.01 and 1.2.

Given that the inflation and unemployment data are in fractions, these effects of unemployment and inflation are not small. Consider the consequences of a rise in unemployment of 0.04 (namely, 4 percentage points of joblessness, which is equal to the standard deviation in the sample). This produces a decline in well-being of 0.04 times −2.8, which is −0.11. In our cardinalization, people's levels of satisfaction are coded in four categories from 1 (not at all satisfied) up to 4 (very satisfied). Hence a movement of −0.11 is not a trivial event for a society. It is equivalent to shifting 11 percent of the population downwards from one life-satisfaction category to another. An alternative way to make the same point is to note that 0.11 slightly exceeds the standard deviation of life satisfaction in our panel of countries.

The implicit utility-constant trade-off between inflation and unemployment can now be calculated. We make the assumption that, over the relevant range, utility is linear (so that the margin is equal to the average). As in conventional economic theory, what is done in the paper is to measure the slope of indifference curves. This leads to a measure of the marginal rate of substitution between inflation and unemployment. It is useful to explain what such correlations are likely to mean within a conventional natural-rate-of-unemployment analytical framework. The estimation describes preferences themselves. Standard

economic models suggest, of course, that there is no downward-sloping Phillips curve in the long run. Knowledge of iso-utility contours is then of use to policy makers primarily because it informs the choice of an optimal disinflationary path. Our estimates, and more broadly this kind of methodology, can be viewed as aiding central bankers concerned with the choice of policy trajectories.

Regression (2) in Table 1 shows that unemployment and inflation enter strongly even if country-specific time trends are introduced into the equations. The coefficients on the two variables are negative and significantly different from zero at normal confidence levels. They are now more similar than in the first column of Table 1. However, equality of the two coefficients, in regression (2), can still be rejected statistically. Life satisfaction is therefore not captured exactly by a simple linear misery function defined on the sum of inflation and unemployment, $W = W(\pi + U)$. Unemployment has a larger weight.

Regressions (3) and (4) in Table 1 divide the sample into two time periods: before 1984 and after 1983. The coefficients keep their signs, although, as is to be expected, they are not now as well defined. Degrees of freedom here are a source of potential concern; but this approach is primarily designed as a check on robustness. Column (5) adds into the equation a squared term in inflation—to test if inflation is particularly bad at high levels—but again the key result is left unaffected. If an additional squared term in unemployment is entered, its effect is negligible.

TABLE 2—CHECKS ON LIFE-SATISFACTION EQUATIONS FOR
EUROPE 1975–1991

	(6)	(7)	(8)
Life satisfaction $t - 1$	0.3		0.2
	(0.1)		(0.1)
Unemployment t	−1.7	−2.1	−1.8
	(0.7)	(0.6)	(0.7)
Inflation t	−0.7	−1.4	−0.8
	(0.5)	(0.4)	(0.5)
ΔUnemployment t		−1.0	−0.1
		(0.9)	(0.9)
ΔInflation t		−0.7	−0.5
		(0.4)	(0.4)
Time trends	Yes	Yes	Yes
Country dummies	Yes	Yes	Yes
Year dummies	Yes	Yes	Yes
Number of observations	140	150	140
Adjusted R^2	0.56	0.55	0.56

Notes: Standard errors are in parentheses. Time trends are country specific. Three-year moving averages of the explanatory variables are used. This is a second-stage regression. It uses as a dependent variable the regression-corrected life-satisfaction levels from a first-stage OLS regression of the general kind given in the Appendix.

Table 2 presents further tests of the relationship between inflation, unemployment, and well-being. Regression (6) in Table 2 controls for a lagged dependent variable. It finds that there is a little autoregression, with a lagged dependent variable coefficient of 0.3, but that life-satisfaction data continue to be correlated with macroeconomic variables.

Regression (7) in Table 2 tests whether well-being depends on changes in the two macroeconomic variables. We use the growth in inflation (or unemployment) from one year to the next. There is some evidence that these changes matter. Both enter with the expected negative sign. Regression (8) in Table 2 shows that the inclusion of a lagged dependent variable reinforces these findings. Nevertheless, the underlying ideas remain the same.

It could be argued that the above calculations underestimate the cost of unemployment. The reason is that the first-stage regressions have already controlled for the personal cost of being unemployed. Somehow a way has to be found to measure the two unpleasant consequences of a rise in unemployment: some people lose their jobs while at the same time everyone in the economy becomes more fearful.

There is a way to take account of the extra first-stage cost of joblessness, namely, to work out the sum of the aggregate and personal effects of unemployment. It is best to think of it as asking what happens if unemployment in the economy rises by 1 percentage point. We can calculate from regression (2) that an increase in the unemployment rate of a percentage point (namely, 0.01) has a cost in the chosen well-being units equal to approximately 0.02 for the average citizen. This number might be viewed as capturing a "fear of unemployment" effect for everyone. However, it is clear from our microeconomic data that the person who actually falls unemployed experiences a much larger cost. The loss from being unemployed is equal to 0.33 when measured in the same units. This number comes from the coefficient on being unemployed in a life-satisfaction micro regression, like the one in Appendix Table A1, estimated with OLS to keep the units consistent.

The entire well-being cost of a 1-percentage-point increase in the unemployment rate is therefore given by the sum of two components. One component is the 0.33 multiplied by the 1 percent of the population who have been unlucky enough actually to become unemployed. This is 0.33 times 0.01, which is 0.0033. The second component, which is more akin to higher fear of unemployment for everyone in society, is 0.02. Combining the two, we have 0.0033 + 0.02 = 0.0233 as society's overall well-being cost of a rise in unemployment by 1 percentage point.

To put this differently, in column (2) of Table 1 the well-being cost of a 1-percentage-point increase in the unemployment rate equals the loss brought about by an extra 1.66 percentage points of inflation. The reason is that 1.66 = 0.0233/0.014, where 0.0233 is the marginal effect of unemployment on well-being, and 0.014 is the marginal effect of inflation on well-being (where 0.014 is derived from 1.4 multiplied by 0.01). Hence 1.66 is the marginal rate of substitution between inflation and unemployment. Because this number is larger than unity, the well-known "misery index" is not an accurate representation of the data.

A. *Inflation, Unemployment, and Happiness in the United States*

Since there is no question on life satisfaction in the United States General Social Survey (GSS) (1972–1994), it was not possible to include the

United States in the panel regressions. Using GSS happiness data we estimated an OLS happiness regression—available upon request—on personal characteristics for the United States and obtained the mean residuals for each year. The year-to-year changes in the "happiness residuals" were negatively correlated with the corresponding year-to-year changes in the so-called "misery index." When viewed as two individual explanatory variables, the yearly changes in happiness were somewhat more strongly associated with changes in the unemployment rate than with inflation. Necessarily, the U.S. findings stem from a single time-series regression. The U.S. results are consistent with, though a little less well-defined than, the European results.

III. Conclusions

This paper studies reported well-being data on a quarter of a million people across 12 European countries and the United States. We show that people appear to be happier when inflation and unemployment are low. Consistent with the standard macroeconomics textbook's assumption that there exists a social objective function $W(\pi, U)$, randomly sampled individuals mark systematically lower in well-being surveys when there is inflation or unemployment in their country. The rates of price change and joblessness affect reported satisfaction with life even after controlling for the personal characteristics of the respondents, country fixed effects, year effects, country-specific time trends, and a lagged dependent variable. A function strongly reminiscent of the textbook $W(\pi, U)$ exists in the data.

A large literature in economics has tried to measure the losses from inflation. By examining the appropriate area under a money demand curve, Martin Bailey (1956) and Milton Friedman (1969) originally concluded that inflation has only small costs. Similarly, Fischer (1981) and Robert E. Lucas, Jr. (1981) find the cost of inflation to be low, at 0.3 percent and 0.5 percent of national income, respectively, for a 10-percent level of inflation. The numbers implied by our happiness-equation estimates seem consistent with larger welfare losses.

At the margin, unemployment depresses reported well-being more than does inflation. In a panel that controls for country fixed effects, year effects, and country-specific time trends,

the estimates suggest that people would trade off a 1-percentage-point increase in the unemployment rate for a 1.7-percentage-point increase in the inflation rate. Hence, according to these findings, the famous "misery index" $W(\pi + U)$ underweights the unhappiness caused by joblessness.

APPENDIX

TABLE A1—OLS LIFE-SATISFACTION MICRO EQUATION FOR EUROPE 1975–1991

Dependent variable: Reported life satisfaction	Coefficient	Standard error
Unemployed	−0.33	7e-3
Self-employed	0.04	5e-3
Male	−0.04	3e-3
Age	−0.02	1e-3
Age squared	2e-4	6e-6
Education to age:		
15–18 years	0.03	4e-3
≥19 years	0.06	4e-3
Marital status:		
Married	0.08	4e-3
Divorced	−0.18	0.01
Separated	−0.23	0.01
Widowed	−0.10	0.01
Number of children between 8 and 15		
years: 1	−0.02	4e-3
2	−0.03	0.01
3	−0.06	0.01
Income quartiles:		
Second	0.12	4e-3
Third	0.20	4e-3
Fourth (highest)	0.30	5e-3
Retired	0.05	6e-3
In school	0.04	7e-3
At home	0.03	5e-3

Notes: Number of observations = 264,710. Adjusted R^2 = 0.17. The regression includes country and year dummies from 1975 to 1991. The country dummies (standard errors) are: Belgium 0.315 (0.006), Netherlands 0.540 (0.006), Germany 0.242 (0.006), Italy −0.087 (0.006), Luxembourg 0.469 (0.009), Denmark 0.694 (0.006), Ireland 0.356 (0.007), Britain 0.328 (0.006), Portugal −0.171 (0.008), Greece −0.146 (0.007), and Spain 0.124 (0.008). The base country is France. The exact question is: "On the whole, are you very satisfied, fairly satisfied, not very satisfied, or not at all satisfied with the life you lead?" Answers were coded as follows: 1 to "not at all satisfied," 2 to "not very satisfied," 3 to "fairly satisfied," and 4 to "very satisfied." Microeconometric life-satisfaction equations are used as a first stage in the paper's analysis.

REFERENCES

Bailey, Martin. "The Welfare Cost of Inflationary Finance." *Journal of Political Economy*, February 1956, *64*(1), pp. 64–93.

Barro, Robert J. and Gordon, David. "A Positive Theory of Monetary Policy in a Natural Rate Model." *Journal of Political Economy*, August 1983, *91*(3), pp. 589–610.

Blanchard, Olivier and Fischer, Stanley. *Lectures on macroeconomics*. Cambridge, MA: MIT Press, 1989.

Blanchflower, David and Oswald, Andrew J. "Well-being Over Time in Britain and the USA." National Bureau of Economic Research (Cambridge, MA) Working Paper No. 7487, February 2000.

Burda, Michael and Wyplosz, Charles. *Macroeconomics: A European text*. Oxford: Oxford University Press, 1993.

Clark, Andrew and Oswald, Andrew J. "Unhappiness and Unemployment." *Economic Journal*, September 1994, *104*(5), pp. 648–59.

Diener, Edward. "Subjective Well-Being." *Psychological Bulletin*, 1984, *93*(3), pp. 542–75.

Di Tella, Rafael; MacCulloch, Robert J. and Oswald, Andrew J. "The Macroeconomics of Happiness." Unpublished manuscript, Harvard Business School, June 2000.

Easterlin, Richard. "Does Economic Growth Improve the Human Lot? Some Empirical Evidence," in Paul A. David and Mel W. Reder, eds., *Nations and households in economic growth: Essays in honour of Moses Abramovitz*. New York: Academic Press, 1974, pp. 89–125.

Fischer, Stanley. "Towards an Understanding of the Costs of Inflation: II." *Carnegie-Rochester Conference Series on Public Policy*, Autumn, 1981, *15*, pp. 5–41.

Frank, Robert H. *Choosing the right pond*. New York: Oxford University Press, 1985.

Friedman, Milton. *The optimum quantity of money and other essays*. Chicago: Aldine, 1969.

Hall, Robert E. and Taylor, John. *Macroeconomics*, 5th Ed. New York: Norton Press, 1997.

Inglehart, Ronald. *Culture shift in advanced industrial society*. Princeton, NJ: Princeton University Press, 1990.

Kahneman, Daniel; Wakker, Peter P. and Sarin, Rakesh. "Back to Bentham? Explorations of Experienced Utility." *Quarterly Journal of Economics*, May 1997, *112*(2), pp. 375–406.

Krugman, Paul. "Stable Prices and Fast Growth: Just Say No." *The Economist*, August 31, 1996.

Lucas, Robert E., Jr. "Discussion of: Stanley Fischer, 'Towards an Understanding of the Costs of Inflation: II'." *Carnegie-Rochester Conference Series on Public Policy*, Autumn 1981, *15*, pp. 43–52.

Mankiw, N. Gregory. *Macroeconomics*, 3rd Ed. New York: Worth Publishers, 1997.

Morawetz, David et al. "Income Distribution and Self-Rated Happiness: Some Empirical Evidence." *Economic Journal*, September 1977, *87*(3), pp. 511–22.

Myers, David. *The pursuit of happiness*. London: Aquarian, 1993.

Ng, Yew-Kwang. "Happiness Surveys: Some Comparability Issues and an Exploratory Survey Based on Just Perceivable Increments." *Social Indicators Research*, 1996, *38*(1), pp. 1–27.

_____ . "A Case for Happiness, Cardinalism, and Interpersonal Comparability." *Economic Journal*, September 1997, *107*(5), pp. 1848–58.

Oswald, Andrew J. "Happiness and Economic Performance." *Economic Journal*, September 1997, *107*(5), pp. 1815–31.

Pavot, William; Diener, Edward; Colvin, C. Randall and Sandvik, Edward. "Further Validation of the Satisfaction with Life Scale: Evidence for the Cross-Method Convergence of Well-Being Measures." *Journal of Personality Assessment*, 1991, *57*(1), pp. 149–61.

Shiller, Robert J. "Why Do People Dislike Inflation?" in Christina D. Romer and David H. Romer, eds., *Reducing inflation: Motivation and strategy*. Chicago: University of Chicago Press, 1997, pp. 13–65.

Winkelmann, Liliana and Winkelmann, Rainer. "Why Are the Unemployed So Unhappy? Evidence from Panel Data." *Economica*, February 1998, *65*(257), pp. 1–15.

[13]

The Economic Journal, 110 (October), 918–938. © Royal Economic Society 2000. Published by Blackwell Publishers, 108 Cowley Road, Oxford OX4 1JF, UK and 350 Main Street, Malden, MA 02148, USA.

HAPPINESS, ECONOMY AND INSTITUTIONS*

Bruno S. Frey and Alois Stutzer

Institutional factors in the form of direct democracy (via initiatives and referenda) and federal structure (local autonomy) systematically and sizeably raise self-reported individual well-being in a cross-regional econometric analysis. This positive effect can be attributed to political outcomes closer to voters' preferences, as well as to the procedural utility of political participation possibilities. Moreover, the results of previous microeconometric well-being functions for other countries are generally supported. Unemployment has a strongly depressing effect on happiness. A higher income level raises happiness, however, only to a small extent.

To discover the sources of people's well-being is a major concern in the social sciences. Many inquiries have been undertaken to identify the determinants of individual happiness. This paper analyses data on reported subjective well-being in order to directly assess the role of *democratic* and *federal institutions* on people's satisfaction with life. Thus, a new set of determinants is considered, which expands previous research results showing the effects on happiness of individual income and unemployment, as well as of aggregate unemployment, inflation and income growth (see Oswald, (1997) for a survey).[1]

We argue that institutional conditions with regard to the extent and form of democracy have systematic and sizeable effects on individual well-being, in addition to demographic and economic factors. Using recent interview data from 6,000 residents of Switzerland, we show that individuals are *ceteris paribus* happier, the better developed the institutions of direct democracy are in their area of residence. This also applies to a second institution, the degree of government decentralisation (federalism). Finally, we are able to support some of the earlier results for other countries and periods with new data also based on a survey with a large sample size. In particular, we find that the unemployed are much less happy than employed persons, and that a higher household income level only raises happiness to a small extent.

* We thank Matthias Benz, Iris Bohnet, Rafael Di Tella, Richard Easterlin, Reiner Eichenberger, Lars Feld, Douglas Hibbs, Reto Jegen, Marcel Kucher, Robert Lane, Robert Leu, Yew-Kwang Ng, Felix Oberholzer-Gee, Karl-Dieter Opp, Andrew Oswald, Marcel Savioz, Jean-Robert Tyran, Ruut Veenhoven, Rainer Winkelmann and two anonymous referees for helpful remarks, and Lorenz Götte for providing econometric support.
1 'Happiness' is, for simplicity's sake, in the following interchangeably used with the terms 'satisfaction with life' and 'reported subjective well-being'. We are aware that subjective well-being is a scientific concept rather than a specific measure of well-being, and that it contains affective components i.e. mood and emotions like joy, happiness or depression as well as cognitive evaluations of life satisfaction (see e.g. Lucas et al., 1996). However, most of these measures are substantially correlated. In the current study we use a measure of satisfaction with life.

1. Determinants of Happiness

It is useful to differentiate three sets of sources of individual well-being:

(1) *Personality and demographic factors.* These factors have for many decades been extensively studied by psychologists. Diener *et al.* (1999) provide a survey, extending and bringing up to date the earlier surveys by Wilson (1967) and Diener (1984). Monographs are by Argyle (1987) and Myers (1993).

(2) *Micro- and macroeconomic factors.* An early study of the effect of income on happiness is due to Easterlin (1974, see also 1995), but psychologists have also undertaken substantial work in this direction (see the survey by Diener and Oishi, 2000). In most nations, individuals belonging to the upper income groups report somewhat higher subjective well-being than persons with low income. The often dramatic increase in per capita incomes in recent decades has not raised happiness in general; the national indices for subjective well-being have virtually remained flat over time (see Blanchflower and Oswald, 2000). In contrast to these longitudinal findings for single nations, per capita income levels and happiness are more strongly positively related across nations (for further discussion see also Kenny, 1999).

The influence of the other two major economic variables, unemployment and inflation, is clear-cut. Unemployment is correlated with substantial unhappiness (Clark and Oswald, 1994; Winkelmann and Winkelmann, 1998). As the income level is kept constant, that influence is not due to lower revenue, but to non-pecuniary stress. In terms of a trade-off, 'most regression results imply that an enormous amount of extra income would be required to compensate people for having no work' (Oswald, 1997, p. 1821). Individuals also have a strong aversion towards inflation and are prepared to carry significant cost to evade it: 'one percentage point of inflation corresponds to a well-being cost of approximately two per cent of the level of income per capita' (Di Tella *et al.* 1997, p. 18).[2]

(3) The third set of influences on happiness relates to the *institutional* (or constitutional) *conditions* in an economy and society, of which democracy and federalism are of greatest importance. To our knowledge, the impact of the extent and design of democratic and federal institutions on subjective well-being has, at best, been alluded to, but has not been empirically analysed.

The determinants of happiness are usually investigated under the assumptions that subjective well-being is cardinally measurable and interpersonally

[2] These results provide welcome and important insights into a broader effort to measure empirically individuals' reaction to, and therewith evaluation of, the influence of macro-economic variables. Other approaches are (see more extensively Frey (1991)): (i) retreat from society, or at least from the official economy, e.g. by working in the shadow sector (e.g. Cowell, 1990; Thomas, 1992); (ii) popularity and election functions (surveys are given e.g. in Nannestad and Paldam (1994), Schneider and Frey (1988)); (iii) political preference functions derived from the behaviour of governments and central banks (see the survey and critique in Makin (1976)); (iv) non-conventional political participation ranging from demonstrations to publicly motivated strikes (see e.g. Hibbs, 1976; Opp, 1989); and (v) use of force, i.e. all sorts of revolutions and coups d'état (e.g. Hibbs, 1973; Opp *et al.*, 1995). The well-being functions, together with popularity and election functions, belong to the best defined and statistically most advanced efforts to measure the absolute and relative importance of macro-economic conditions for individuals.

comparable; i.e. two claims economists are likely to be sceptical about. To avoid problems in regard to a cardinal interpretation of subjective variables, it is often possible to treat the subjective data qualitatively in econometric analyses. In contrast, whether people associate the same degree of subjective experience with a certain score on a ladder for life satisfaction is more difficult to assess. However, there is a lot of indirect evidence that cardinalism and interpersonal comparability are much less of a problem practically than theoretically. The measures of subjective well-being have high consistency, reliability and validity. Happy people are e.g. more often smiling during social interactions (Fernández-Dols and Ruiz-Belda, 1995), are rated as happy by friends and family members (Sandvik *et al.*, 1993), as well as by spouses (Costa and McCrae, 1988). Furthermore, the measures of subjective well-being have a high degree of stability over time (Headey and Wearing, 1989) and are not systematically biased with regard to social desirability (Konow and Earley, 1999). But there is, of course, room for methodological concerns (e.g. Diener *et al.*, 1999, pp. 277–8). Moreover, as will be demonstrated in this paper, the main use of happiness measures is not to compare levels, but rather to seek to identify the determinants of happiness.

2. Effects of Institutions on Happiness

Most political *institutions* tend to be stable over time, so that a cross-sectional analysis of subjective well-being is appropriate. This has been done between countries (e.g. by Veenhoven (1993) on the basis of the World Values Survey, and by Diener *et al.*, (1995)).[3] It is, of course, difficult to isolate the effect of particular institutions on reported individual well-being because the countries differ in a great variety of aspects. This problem is less acute for institutional variations *within* a (federal) country. Therefore, we study the case of Switzerland and its institutions of direct democracy. Their wide dissemination is unique for a European country. As far as we know, this is the first paper using cross-regional variations in a happiness study. Cross-regional procedures have been used with good results to account for the share of government expenditures between governmental units with different degrees of direct participation possibilities for its citizens (as done for the United States,[4] as well as for Switzerland[5]).

There are two major reasons why a higher extent of direct political participation possibilities, or more strongly developed institutions of *direct democracy* (in

[3] The study of institutional differences is methodologically closely related to cross-country growth analysis (see e.g. Barro, 1997). However, this literature has not yet been incorporated into happiness research. There is also a relation to well-being measurement in research on economic development. Dasgupta (1993), for example, provides a measure of well-being that includes standard of living as well as indices of political and civil liberties.

[4] See e.g. Matsusaka (1995) or Rueben (2000) for general government expenditure, or Santerre (1989; 1993) for public education expenditures.

[5] See e.g. Schneider and Pommerehne (1983) and Feld and Kirchgässner (1999) for general government expenditures. The latter also study the effect on self-financing ratios, taxes, and debt. Pommerehne and Weck (1996) and Frey (1997) analyse the effect on tax evasion, and Feld and Savioz (1997) on per capita gross domestic product.

particular via popular referenda and initiatives) can be expected to raise citizens' subjective well-being (Cronin (1989), Budge (1996) or for an economic analysis Frey (1994)).

Firstly, due to the more active role of the citizens, (professional) politicians are better monitored and controlled. Government activity, i.e. public outlays as well as the many other decisions by the government, are closer to the wishes of the citizenry.[6] As a consequence, satisfaction with government output is reflected in a higher level of overall well-being.

Secondly, the institutions of direct democracy extend the citizens' possibilities to get involved in the political process. Experimental evidence (e.g. Tyler, 1990; Bohnet and Frey, 1999) suggests that this procedural effect is independent of the outcome of the political activity itself.

Federal decentralisation, and, in particular, local autonomy, is another constitutional element which can be hypothesised to positively affect citizens' happiness. Political decision making in municipalities is closer to relevant information about residents' preferences and also closer to direct control by its citizens (Frey and Eichenberger, 1999).

3. Data for Econometric Analysis

Our empirical work is based on the survey results of more than 6,000 residents of Switzerland, collected by Leu *et al.* (1997).[7] The dependent variable called 'happiness' is based on the answers to the following question: 'How satisfied are you with your life as a whole these days?' Simultaneously, the respondents were shown a table with a 10 point scale of which only the two extreme values ('completely dissatisfied' and 'completely satisfied') were verbalised. The survey found a high general life satisfaction in Switzerland with an average of 8.2 out of 10 points. No fewer than 29% of the interviewees reported a satisfaction level of 10 ('completely satisfied'), 17% of 9, and 27% of 8. The lower end of the happiness-scale, 'completely dissatisfied' (score 1), score 2 and score 3, were indicated only by 0.4%, 0.5%, and 0.9%, respectively. As these categories of great unhappiness are thinly populated, they are aggregated, leaving us with eight happiness categories.[8]

In this paper, the major explanatory variable focused on is the institutionalised rights of individual political participation, which vary considerably between the 26 Swiss cantons. Due to the federal structure of Switzerland, major areas of competence are kept by the cantons (states). As on the national level, there exist direct democratic instruments besides representative democratic parliaments and governments. The most important direct democratic instruments in cantons are the popular initiative to change the canton's constitution

---

[6] This statement is supported by considerable empirical (econometric) evidence, e.g. Pommerehne (1978; 1990) or Gerber (1999).

[7] The survey data were collected between 1992 and 1994 in order to investigate the problem of poverty in Switzerland. The information contained in the data set is based on personal interviews and tax statistics.

[8] The regrouping of the lowest categories does not change the qualitative results.

922   THE ECONOMIC JOURNAL   [OCTOBER

or laws, a compulsory and optional referendum to prevent new laws, or the changing of existing laws, and optional financial referenda to prevent new state expenditure. Citizens' access to these instruments differ from canton to canton. Thus, for example, the number of signatures required to launch an initiative or an optional referendum, or the time span within which the signatures have to be collected, varies. The referendum on public expenditures may be launched at different levels of additional outlays. For the 26 cantons, we constructed an index designed to reflect the extent of direct democratic participation possibilities (for details of the index construction, see the Appendix). This index is defined using a six point scale with 1 indicating the lowest, and 6 the highest degree of participation possibilities for the citizens. Fig. 1 provides an overview.

The purpose of our estimate is to show that the extent of direct democratic participation possibilities exerts a statistically significant, robust and sizeable effect on happiness *over and above* the demographic and economic determinants so far taken into account in the literature.

We also intend to demonstrate that institutional factors are relevant for happiness in general by analysing the impact of federalism. The division of competence between communities and the cantonal government reflects the federal structure of a canton or, from the municipalities' point of view, their autonomy. The extent of local autonomy is measured by an index (due to Ladner, 1994). The index over the 26 cantons is based on survey results. Chief local administrators in 1856 Swiss municipalities were asked to report how they perceive their local autonomy on a 10 point scale, with one indicating 'no autonomy at all', and 10 'very high' communal autonomy.

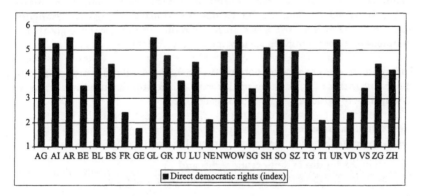

Fig. 1. *Direct Democracy in Swiss Cantons*
The figure shows the degree of direct democratic participation possibilities in the 26 Swiss cantons, namely Aargau (AG), Appenzell i. Rh. (AI), Appenzell a. Rh. (AR), Bern (BE), Basel Land (BL), Basel Stadt (BS), Fribourg (FR), Genève (GE), Glarus (GL), Graubünden (GR), Jura (JU), Luzern (LU), Neuchâtel (NE), Nidwalden (NW), Obwalden (OW), St. Gallen (SG), Schaffhausen (SH), Solothurn (SO), Schwyz (SZ), Thurgau (TG), Ticino (TI), Uri (UR), Vaud (VD), Valais (VS), Zug (ZG) and Zürich (ZH).

The estimation equations regress the indices of individual happiness on three sets of determinants:

(1) *Demographic variables*
They describe the personal attributes of the respondents and comprise

- age. Six age groups are explicitly accounted for, ranging from 30 years to 80 years and older (the constant term includes the reference group 'people younger than 30');
- gender (male/female);
- citizenship (national/foreigner);
- extent of formal education (middle/high education) (in the reference group are 'people with low education');
- family setting (single woman or man; couple with children; single parent, other, collective household) (in the reference group are 'couples') and
- individual employment status (self-employed or employee in one's own firm; housewife or houseman; other) (in the reference group are 'employed persons').

(2) *Economic variables*
Two influences are considered:

- Individual unemployment (the constant term includes the reference group 'employed persons');
- Income situation of the household (equivalence income). Total household income after taxes, social security expenditure, interest on debts and maintenance is divided through the equivalence scale of the Swiss Conference for Public Assistance. Four income groups are explicitly distinguished, ranging from Sfr. 2,000 to Sfr. 5,000 per month and more (in the reference group are 'people with a lower equivalence income than Sfr. 2,000').

The above two sets of variables are used as *controls*.[9] While they are of obvious interest in themselves, they mainly serve to isolate the unbiased influence of the third set of variables.

(3) *Political institutions*
The variables included in the estimation models are

- an index for direct democratic rights and
- an index for the extent of local (communal) autonomy.

The latter variables refer to the 26 cantons in Switzerland. The structure of Swiss cantons, however, does not only differ in respect of direct democracy and federal organisation, but also in other respects, such as the degree of urbanisation. Therefore, to control for further regional differences, we include five

---

[9] We cannot address the issue of how inflation affects reported subjective well-being, as our data set is a cross-section of individuals.

924 THE ECONOMIC JOURNAL [OCTOBER

variables for the size of community and seven variables for the type of community in the estimation equations.

4. Results and Discussion of the Econometric Analysis

We present the results of our econometric analysis in seven separate sections. In Sections 4.1 to 4.4, we discuss the effects of the three sets of demographic, economic and institutional variables on happiness. In Section 4.5 we perform several tests of robustness. Finally, Sections 4.6 and 4.7 indicate who benefits from direct democracy and that the benefits can be attributed to a favourable outcome as well as to a favourable direct democratic process itself.

4.1. *Microeconometric Happiness Functions*

Table 1 presents the estimated coefficients and marginal effects of two micro-econometric happiness functions, taking into account demographic and economic determinants as well as the institutional variable direct democratic rights. In the first equation, a weighted least squares model is estimated. In the second one, a weighted ordered probit model is used in order to exploit the ranking information contained in the originally scaled dependent variable. The weighting variable that is applied allows representative results on the subject level for Switzerland.[10] Throughout the paper, we use a robust estimator of variance because random disturbances are potentially correlated within groups or clusters. Here, dependence refers to residents of the same canton.[11]

The estimation results show statistically significant effects of several demographic factors, all the economic variables and, most importantly, the institutional determinant on individual happiness. The least squares estimation that treats happiness as a cardinal variable offers qualitatively very similar results to the ordered probit model, i.e the results are robust in regard to the estimation method. The coefficients of the former model can be interpreted in a simple way: people belonging to a certain category on average report happiness scores deviating from that of the reference group on the scale of the coefficient.[12] (For example, people of middle education on average report 0.23 score points more satisfaction with life than people with lower education.) In the ordered probit estimation, a positive coefficient indicates that the probability of stating

[10] Due to clustering and stratification in contrast to pure random sampling, weights are necessary to get approximately unbiased point estimates. Weights are proportional to the inverse of the probability of being sampled. In addition, the weights are adjusted to the demographic structure in 1992.

[11] Ignoring the clustering in the estimation model is likely to produce downward biased standard errors, due to the effects of aggregate variables on individual data (Moulton, 1990). To get unbiased standard errors for the aggregate variable 'direct democratic rights', the 26 cantons are used as sampling units. (Ignoring clustering, a t-value of 5.079 instead of 3.054 is estimated in Table 1.) Apart from clustering, stratification also has a downward effect on standard errors. The significance levels take into account the bias due to stratification, i.e. $p < 0.01$ for $|t| > 2.88$, $0.01 < p < 0.05$ for $2.17 < |t| < 2.88$ and $0.05 < p < 0.10$ for $1.81 < |t| < 2.17$.

[12] For a continuous variable, the coefficient indicates the increase in happiness scores when the independent variable increases by one unit.

© Royal Economic Society 2000

happiness greater than or equal to any given level increases. The marginal effect indicates the change in the share of persons belonging to a stated happiness level when the independent variable increases by one unit.[13] In the case of dummy variables, the marginal effect is evaluated in regard to the reference group. For simplicity, only the marginal effects for the extreme value of very high happiness (score 10) are shown in Table 1. (For example, being unemployed rather than employed lowers the probability of a person stating that he or she is completely satisfied by 21.1 percentage points.)

4.2. *Demographic and Economic Factors of Life Satisfaction*

Compared to the reference group, people older than 60 are happier. Women are not happier than men if the different employment status is considered separately. Furthermore, foreigners are subject to a significantly lower probability of reaching high happiness scores compared to the Swiss. People with higher education report significantly higher subjective well-being. Couples without children are happier than singles, single parents and people living in collective households.

Among the economic variables, higher income correlates with higher happiness in a statistically significant way. However, the differences in subjective well-being are rather small. Consider, for example, the highest income group with a monthly equivalence income above Sfr. 5,000. Compared to persons with low income, only a 6.8 percentage points larger share reports being 'completely satisfied'. As already alluded to above, unemployment has a very large negative influence on individual well-being. The coefficient of this variable is largest in comparison to the other significant coefficients mentioned.

The demographic and economic variables in the happiness equation thus yield very similar results for Swiss data as were previously found by Blanchflower and Oswald (2000) and Di Tella *et al.* (1997) for other countries, in particular the highly significant and large negative effect of being unemployed, and the small positive effect of income.[14]

4.3. *The Effect of Direct Democracy on Subjective Well-being*

Table 1 also shows the results for one of the institutional variables. The index for direct democratic rights has a highly significant positive effect on happiness. An increase in the index of direct democracy by one point raises the share of persons indicating very high satisfaction with life by 2.8 percentage points. This result is consistent with our hypothesis that the institutions of direct democracy raise the reported subjective well-being. In addition, the

---

[13] Alternatively, the marginal effect indicates the change of the probability belonging to a stated happiness level when the independent variable increases by one unit.

[14] Part of the correlation observed can, of course, be explained by reverse causation. For happy people, it is easier to find a partner. They probably less often lose their job and get jobs where they earn more money.

926   THE ECONOMIC JOURNAL   [OCTOBER

Table 1

Direct Democracy and Satisfaction with Life in Switzerland

	Weighted least squares Std. err. adjusted to clustering in 26 cantons		Weighted ordered probit Std. err. adjusted to clustering in 26 cantons		
Variable	Coefficient	t-value	Coefficient	t-value	Marginal effect (score 10)
(1) Demographic variables					
Age 30–39	−0.145	−1.064	−0.079	−0.865	−0.027
Age 40–49	−0.031	−0.270	−0.008	−0.106	−0.003
Age 50–59	−0.177	−1.898	−0.081	−1.275	−0.027
Age 60–69	0.258*	2.349	0.206**	2.903	0.073
Age 70–79	0.389*	2.866	0.295**	3.401	0.106
Age 80 and older	0.341*	2.519	0.273**	2.968	0.099
Female	0.039	0.765	0.043	1.211	0.015
Foreigner	−0.450**	−5.146	−0.284**	−5.048	−0.091
Middle education	0.232**	4.504	0.113**	3.143	0.039
High education	0.266**	3.387	0.119*	2.472	0.042
Single woman	−0.373**	−6.238	−0.258**	−6.294	−0.083
Single man	−0.295*	−2.557	−0.174*	−2.589	−0.057
Couple with children	−0.090	−1.440	−0.068	−1.777	−0.023
Single parent	−0.614**	−3.312	−0.372**	−3.602	−0.113
Other private household	−0.170	−1.499	−0.128	−1.664	−0.042
Collective household	−0.646**	−3.171	−0.413**	−3.432	−0.124
Self-employed	0.058	0.796	0.072	1.413	0.025
Housewife	0.155$^{(*)}$	2.065	0.123*	2.463	0.043
Other employment status	−0.216$^{(*)}$	−2.110	−0.129$^{(*)}$	−1.911	−0.044
(2) Economic variables					
Unemployed	−1.574**	−5.768	−0.841**	−5.814	−0.211
Equiv. income Sfr. 2,000–3,000	0.156*	2.697	0.084*	2.199	0.029
Equiv. income Sfr. 3,000–4,000	0.243**	3.747	0.143**	3.169	0.050
Equiv. income Sfr. 4,000–5,000	0.399**	5.646	0.258**	5.382	0.092
Equiv. income Sfr. 5,000 and more	0.302**	4.938	0.192**	4.277	0.068
(3) Institutional variable					
Direct democratic rights	0.116**	2.907	0.082**	3.054	0.028
Observations	6,134		6,134		
R^2	0.091				
Prob > F	0.049		0.001		

Notes: Dependent variable: level of satisfaction on an eight point scale (scores of 1, 2 and 3 were aggregated). White estimator for variance. In the reference group are 'people younger than 30', 'men', 'Swiss', 'people with low education', 'couples', 'employed people' and 'people with a lower equivalence income than Sfr. 2,000'. Additional control variables (not shown) for size of community (5 variables) and type of community (7 variables). Significance levels: $^{(*)}$ $0.05 < p < 0.10$, *$0.01 < p < 0.05$, **$p < 0.01$.
Data source: Leu *et al.* (1997).

effect itself is sizeable: (i) The marginal effect of direct democratic rights on happiness is as large as the effect of living in the second-bottom (Sfr. 2,000-3,000) instead of the bottom income category (< Sfr. 2,000). (ii) The effect is even larger when the full range of the institutional variable is considered, i.e. when individuals in canton Basel Land (with the highest democracy index of

2000]   HAPPINESS, ECONOMY AND INSTITUTIONS   927

5.69) are compared to citizens in canton Geneva (with the lowest direct participation rights of 1.75). The former state with an 11 percentage points higher probability that they are completely satisfied. (iii) The improvement affects everybody, i.e. the institutional factor is important in an aggregate sense. In comparison, getting a job 'only' raises the subjective well-being of the unemployed.

Do happy people choose direct democratic institutions? Or, in other words, does the causality between direct democracy and subjective well-being work in reverse? Direct democratic participation possibilities, in the form of referenda and initiatives in Switzerland, started to develop in the middle of the 19th century. The adoption of some of the instruments of direct popular participation reflects the spread of the spirit and ideas behind the American and the French revolutions. Equally important were political movements within the citizenry. Citizens fought for direct democratic instruments to gain political power against arbitrary decisions by parliaments and the influence of industrial pressure groups on these authorities in the cantons (see e.g. Kölz, 1998). This historic perspective suggests that the democratic institutions are not simply the result of happy and satisfied citizens. Especially during recent decades, institutional conditions in Swiss cantons have been quite stable,[15] which suggests that causality runs unambiguously from direct democratic rights to satisfaction with life.

4.4. *The Effect of Federalism on Happiness*

Table 2 focuses on federalism in the sense of 'devolution' as a second important political institution hypothesised to raise happiness. Therefore, the

Table 2

Local Autonomy and Satisfaction with Life in Switzerland

Variable	Weighted ordered probit Std. err. adjusted to clustering in 26 cantons			Weighted ordered probit Std. err. adjusted to clustering in 26 cantons		
	Coefficient	t-value	Marginal effect (score 10)	Coefficient	t-value	Marginal effect (score 10)
(1) Demographic variables	yes			yes		
(2) Economic variables	yes			yes		
(3) Institutional variables						
Local autonomy	0.098**	2.913	0.033	0.036	1.005	0.012
Direct democratic rights				0.071*	2.317	0.024
Observations	6,134			6,134		
Prob > F	0.003			0.001		

Notes: see Table 1.
Data sources: Ladner (1994) and Leu *et al.* (1997).

[15] The Spearman rank order correlation of the index for direct democratic rights between 1970 and 1996 is 0.803.

variable 'local autonomy' is added to the demographic and economic factors in the happiness equation. (For simplicity, only the coefficients for variables of interest are shown. However, they indicate the partial effects controlling for the demographic and economic variables included in Table 1. Moreover, the coefficients of the latter variables are almost unaltered.[16]) The estimate reveals a statistically significant positive effect on subjective well-being. For local autonomy, the proportion of persons indicating very high happiness increases by 3.3 percentage points, compared to a situation in which the communes are one index point less autonomous vis-à-vis their canton.

Local autonomy and direct democracy are not independent of each other, of course. On the one hand, direct democracy fosters federal structures on the national and state level because citizens – in contrast to politicians – are most interested in strong federalism (Blankart, 1998). On the other hand, the persons bearing the costs and benefits of government action are better identifiable in a decentralised system. Direct legislation, therefore, leads to better political decisions, and federalism thus preserves direct democracy. As a result, the indices for direct democratic rights and local autonomy are correlated ($r = 0.605$). This makes it impossible to separate the effects of the two variables in one model clearly. The second equation in Table 2 jointly includes the two constitutional factors, local autonomy and direct democratic rights. The coefficient for the variable measuring federalism is roughly one third as large as when it is taken alone and it loses its significance. The index for direct democracy has only a slightly smaller marginal effect on life satisfaction than estimated in Table 1, namely 0.024 instead of 0.028.[17] Direct democracy and federalism in Switzerland thus seem to be complements rather than economic substitutes. Local autonomy is one of the several 'transmission mechanisms' of direct democracy's beneficial effects. In the following paragraphs, we therefore focus on direct democracy.

4.5. *Sensitivity Analysis*

To check the reliability of the results, several tests of robustness are performed: (i) the influence of outliers is analysed with a DFBETA-test; (ii) an ordinal measure instead of a cardinal one is applied for the extent of direct democratic rights; (iii) the effect of the four sub-indices on happiness is tested; and finally (iv) four different aggregate control variables are used.

To investigate whether the positive correlation between direct democracy and happiness is largely driven by a single canton, a DFBETA-test is performed. A two-step approach is chosen. In the first step, a further weighted ordered probit model with a dummy variable for each canton is estimated. In preparation for the second step, the estimated coefficients are correlated with the index for direct democratic rights. Due to the problem of heteroskedasticity, a

---

[16] The full estimation results for all the equations are available from the authors on request.

[17] In an adjusted Wald test, the two institutional factors together are significant on the 5% level (Prob > F = 0.016).

weighted least square regression is estimated.[18] The result is as follows (t-values in parentheses):

$$\text{fixed effects for cantons} = \underset{(-2.653)}{-0.275^*} + \underset{(3.041)}{0.079^{**}}$$

$$\times \text{ index for direct democratic rights,}$$

$$\text{number of observations} = 26 \text{ and adjusted } R^2 = 0.248.^{[19]}$$

With the same estimation model, 26 equations are estimated, with a different canton omitted each time. For each equation, the estimated coefficient for the institutional variable is subtracted from the coefficient in the base equation (0.079) and divided by the estimated standard error. The resulting value is called DFBETA. If it is greater than 1.96 in absolute value, the omitted canton has a significant influence on the coefficient of the institutional variable. Table A3 in the Appendix shows that not one observation from a single canton has a significant influence. The maximum value of the DFBETA statistic is -0.829 for canton Ticino.[20] This shows that the positive effect of direct democracy on happiness is not the result of an influential outlier.

The measure applied for the extent of direct democratic participation possibilities is constructed as a cardinal index. However, the same results should be obtained if ordinal dummy variables for direct democratic rights are constructed. To test this claim, cantons were classified into three groups: cantons with an index score lower than four have low direct democratic rights, cantons with an index between four and five have medium direct democratic rights, and cantons with an index score above five are ranked highly with respect to direct democratic rights. The two dummy variables for cantons with a medium and a high ranking are included in the estimation equation presented in Table 3. As can be seen, satisfaction with life is higher for people living in cantons with medium and high direct democratic rights. The significant coefficient for the top category is 0.179. (In the reference group are people who live in cantons with low direct democratic rights).

The variable for direct democratic participation possibilities is a non-weighted composite index (see Appendix). This aggregation disregards various substitutive and complementary relationships between the single components of the index. Nevertheless, the components can be evaluated by themselves.

---

[18] Heteroskedasticity arises because the coefficients for the canton's dummy variables are based on samples with largely different size. Therefore, the weighting variable contains the number of observations per canton.

[19] The results for ordinary least squares are as follows:

$$\text{fixed effects for cantons} = \underset{(-2.277)}{-0.402^*} + \underset{(3.104)}{0.125^{**}} \times \text{ index for direct democratic rights,}$$

with adjusted $R^2 = 0.257$.

[20] If the fixed effect of this canton is omitted, the coefficient for direct democratic rights increases to 0.100.

However, the analysis faces the problem of multicorrelation.[21] Therefore, the influence of each component is evaluated separately (see Table 3).

All four sub-indices of direct democratic rights have a significantly positive effect on reported subjective well-being. The coefficients for the two sub-indices for the right to change the canton's law or the canton's constitution with a legislative or constitutional popular initiative are largest. Thus, the possibility of putting new questions on the political agenda is of special importance for the beneficial effects of direct democracy on citizens individual well-being.

In order to test for alternative explanations of the cross-regional differences in happiness, the effect of some aggregate control variables is estimated on its own as well as jointly with the institutional variable. Table 4 exhibits the results for the two macroeconomic variables 'national income per capita' and 'total tax burden', as well as for the two language variables 'French speaking canton' and 'Italian speaking canton'. Equations (1) and (2) indicate that national income per capita does not influence happiness significantly, whether it is controlled for institutional differences or not. The same holds for the variable total tax burden in (3) and (4). As can be seen, the introduction of these two macroeconomic variables does not (much) affect the size and significance of the direct democracy variable. In contrast, the variables for majority language are significantly correlated with reported satisfaction with life, i.e. living in a French speaking canton means significantly lower happiness, whereas living in the Italian speaking canton Ticino means significantly higher reported sub-

Table 3

Sensitivity Analysis: Ordinal Variable and Sub-Indices for Direct Democracy

Variable	Weighted ordered probit, std. err. adjusted to clustering in 26 cantons				
	(1)	(2)	(3)	(4)	(5)
(1) Demographic variables	yes	yes	yes	yes	yes
(2) Economic variables	yes	yes	yes	yes	yes
(3) Institutional variables					
Direct democratic rights index between 4 and 5	0.114 (1.733)				
Direct democratic rights index above 5	0.179* (2.308)				
Index for constitutional initiative		0.060* (2.311)			
Index for legislative initiative			0.072** (2.891)		
Index for legislative referendum				0.042(*) (1.945)	
Index for financial referendum					0.059** (3.075)
Observations	6,134	6,134	6,134	6,134	6,134
Prob > F	0.001	0.001	0.002	0.004	0.004

Notes: see Table 1. Coefficients with significance levels. t-values in parentheses. In the reference group in (1) are cantons with direct democratic rights lower than 4.
Data sources: Leu *et al.* (1997).

[21] The correlation between the four sub-indices is shown in Table A2 in the Appendix.

Table 4

Sensitivity Analysis: Aggregate Control Variables

Variable	Weighted ordered probit, std. err. adjusted to clustering in 26 cantons					
	(1)	(2)	(3)	(4)	(5)	(6)
(1) Demographic variables	yes	yes	yes	yes	yes	yes
(2) Economic variables	yes	yes	yes	yes	yes	yes
(3) Institutional variable						
Direct democratic rights		0.087**		0.084*		0.080*
		(3.223)		(2.698)		(2.806)
(4) Macroeconomic conditions						
National income per capita in canton (in 1,000) in 1992	-1.8×10^{-4} (−0.054)	−0.004 (−1.256)				
Total tax burden (index) in canton in 1992			−0.002 (−1.340)	2.7×10^{-4} (0.171)		
(5) Majority language						
French speaking canton					−0.213** (−3.554)	−0.076 (−1.123)
Italian speaking canton					$0.073^{(*)}$ (1.963)	0.252** (3.337)
Observations	6,134	6,134	6,134	6,134	6,134	6,134
Prob > F	0.005	0.007	2.0×10^{-4}	0.002	0.010	0.001

Notes: see Table 1. Coefficients with significance levels. t-values in parentheses.
Data sources: Leu *et al.* (1997) and Swiss Federal Statistical Office (1997).

jective well-being (5). However, the lower well-being in the French speaking cantons can to a large extent be explained by weaker direct democratic rights (6). In (6) the coefficient of the institutional variable is almost unchanged and still significant ($p < 0.05$). It can be concluded that the extent of direct democracy has a robust influence on happiness.

4.6. *Who Benefits from Direct Democracy?*

Are the beneficial effects of direct democracy restricted to some privileged groups? To investigate this important question of equality, we analyse the influence of direct democracy for groups of persons sharing common characteristics in regard to sex, education, employment status and income. Technically, interaction variables are included in the estimation equation, in addition to the demographic and economic variables. The interaction variables are the product of dummy variables for the personal characteristics and the index for direct democratic rights.

The benefits of direct democracy reaped by women are smaller than for men. However, the difference is not statistically significant. There is also no significant difference between the three levels of education and the five categories of employment status distinguished, i.e. the positive effect of direct

© Royal Economic Society 2000

democracy does not arise with the education classes and is not bound to a certain employment status. We have also analysed whether direct democracy raises the happiness of high income recipients, while not doing so for low income recipients. However, the interaction variables do not show any statistically significant differences. The positive effect of direct democracy on happiness applies to all income classes, and is not restricted to a particular one.

Overall, our analysis indicates that direct democracy is not used to discriminate against certain groups within society. The benefits are distributed rather evenly among social classes. However, as in other countries, a large proportion of residents is formally excluded from participation in the direct democratic process, namely foreigners. In the next paragraph, it is argued that they can reap only part of the utility derived from direct democracy.

4.7. *Direct Democracy and Procedural Utility*

Do citizens derive procedural utility from the possibility of participating in the directly democratic process? To answer this question, it is crucial to note that political participation in initiatives and referenda is restricted to Swiss nationals; only they can reap the respective procedural utility. Foreigners, in contrast, have in general no political participation rights. However, they cannot be discriminated from the favourable outcome of direct democracy (outcome utility). As foreigners cannot reap procedural utility from political participation, they are hypothesised to gain less from direct democracy than Swiss citizens. This can be tested either by considering an interaction effect between direct democracy and being a foreigner or by running separate equations for foreigners and Swiss.[22] The results for the latter test are shown in Table 5.[23]

In both equations, direct democratic rights have a positive effect on reported subjective well-being. However, a direct comparison of the two coefficients for direct democratic rights suggests that foreigners benefit less than Swiss citizens in cantons in which the institutions of direct democracy are well

---

[22] Two separate regressions allow different coefficients for the control variables of the sample for foreigners and for Swiss citizens and thus foster the *ceteris paribus* interpretation of the results of the institutional variable.

[23] The results for the former test (a weighted ordered probit estimation with clustering in cantons) are as follows:

$$\text{satisfaction with life} = \ldots \quad \underset{(-0.283)}{-0.042} \quad \text{being a foreigner} \ldots + \underset{(3.384)}{0.097^{**}}$$

$$\times \text{index for direct democratic rights} \quad \underset{(-1.699)}{-0.067}$$

$$\times \text{interaction term (index for direct democratic rights} \times \text{being a foreigner),}$$

with t-values in parentheses. The coefficient for the index of direct democracy is positive and statistically highly significant. This effect accounts for everybody, whether a Swiss citizen or a foreigner. The interaction variable shows that foreigners are *ceteris paribus* relatively less happy compared to Swiss citizens in cantons in which the institutions of direct democracy are well developed. However, the positive effect accounting for everybody is not compensated. This suggests, firstly, that foreigners are still better off in a more direct democratic canton and, secondly, that procedural utility, in addition to outcome utility, is an important source of satisfaction related to direct democracy.

Table 5

Satisfaction with Life of Foreigners and Swiss in Switzerland

Variable	Foreigners Weighted ordered probit Std. err. adjusted to clustering in 26 cantons			Swiss Weighted ordered probit Std. err. adjusted to clustering in 26 cantons		
	Coefficient	t-value	Marginal effect (score 10)	Coefficient	t-value	Marginal effect (score 10)
(1) Demographic variables	yes			yes		
(2) Economic variables	yes			yes		
(3) Institutional variable						
Direct democratic rights	0.035	0.951	0.010	0.098**	3.270	0.034
Observations	743			5,391		
Prob > F	0.002			0.006		

Notes: see Table 1.
Data source: Leu *et al.* (1997).

developed. Moreover, there is no evidence that the Swiss majority in more directly democratic cantons uses its institutional possibilities to exploit the minority of foreigners.

The size of the procedural utility gained from being able to participate in the direct democratic process can also be assessed. Comparing the positive marginal effect for direct democracy of 3.4 percentage points for Swiss citizens with the marginal effect of 1.0 percentage points for foreigners suggests that two thirds of the gain in well-being is due to the application of a favourable process in political decision-making.[24] Procedural utility, over and above outcome utility, is an important source of satisfaction due to direct democracy.

An alternative interpretation of these results can be advanced on the basis of the missing variables problem. Assuming that foreigners and Swiss citizens are equally affected by unobserved regional factors, the causal effect of direct democratic rights on happiness is identified by the difference in the coefficients for this variable between the two groups.[25] According to this interpretation, the marginal effect of direct democratic rights on subjective well-being is slightly smaller, namely 3.4 minus 1.0, i.e. 2.4 percentage points instead of 2.8 percentage points as estimated in Table 1.

5. Conclusions

With data from interviews of more than 6,000 Swiss residents, we have adduced strong evidence that institutional (or constitutional) factors exert a systematic and sizeable positive influence on reported happiness. The existence of

[24] Quantitatively very similar results are obtained if interaction terms for direct democratic rights and being Swiss and being foreigner, respectively, are included in one equation instead of estimating two separate regressions.
[25] This interpretation is analogous to the differences-in-differences estimator for time series as e.g. applied in Card (1990).

934 THE ECONOMIC JOURNAL [OCTOBER

extended individual participation possibilities in the form of initiatives and referenda, and of decentralised (federal) government structures raises the subjective well-being of people.

The influence of these political institutions on happiness is consistent with the hypothesis that politicians in a strongly developed direct democracy are forced to follow the preferences of the voters more than when direct popular participation rights are less well developed. Moreover, the citizens gain procedural utility from the fuller possibilities of directly participating in the political process. Foreigners living in Switzerland are more likely to benefit from the outcome than from the process (from which they are excluded). We find indeed that foreigners tend to reap systematically positive but lower satisfaction from living in a canton with strongly developed direct participation rights than do the Swiss.

These results, with respect to the institutional determinants of happiness, are obtained even if the 'standard' determinants of happiness due to demographic and economic factors are controlled for, and a number of robustness checks are undertaken.

In consonance with other happiness studies, unemployment is associated with a considerably lower level of subjective well-being. A higher equivalence income has a statistically significant positive but small effect on happiness.

University of Zurich

Date of receipt of first submission: March 1999
Date of receipt of final typescript: February 2000

References

Argyle, M. (1987). *The Psychology of Happiness*. London: Methuen.
Barro, R. J. (1997). *Determinants of Economic Growth: A Cross-Country Empirical Study*. Cambridge: MIT Press.
Blanchflower, D. G. and Oswald, A. J. (2000). 'Well-being over time in Britain and the USA.' NBER Working Paper No. 7487, Cambridge, M.A.: National Bureau of Economic Research.
Blankart, C. B. (1998). 'Politische Ökonomie der Zentralisierung der Staatstätigkeit.' Discussion Paper 108, Humboldt-Universität, Berlin.
Bohnet, I. and Frey, B. S. (1999). 'Social distance and other-regarding behavior in dictator games: comment.' *American Economic Review*, vol 89, no. 1, pp. 335–9.
Budge, I. (1996). *New Challenge of Direct Democracy*. Cambridge: Polity Press.
Card, D. E. (1990). 'The impact of the mariel boatlift on the Miami labor market.' *Industrial and Labor Relations Review*, vol. 43, no. 2, pp. 245–57.
Clark, A. E. and Oswald, A. J. (1994). 'Unhappiness and unemployment.' ECONOMIC JOURNAL, vol. 104, no. 424, pp. 648–59.
Costa, P. T. and McCrae, R. R. (1988). 'Personality in adulthood: a six-year longitudinal study of self-reports and spouse ratings on the NEO personality inventory.' *Journal of Personality and Social Psychology*, vol. 54, no. 5, pp. 853–63.
Cowell, F. A. (1990). *Cheating the Government. The Economics of Evasion*, Cambridge, M.A.: MIT Press.
Cronin, T. E. (1989). *Direct Democracy. The Politics of Initiative, Referendum and Recall*, Cambridge, M.A.: Harvard University Press.
Dasgupta, P. (1993). *An Inquiry into Well-being and Destitution*. Oxford, N.Y.: Oxford University Press.
Di Tella, R., MacCulloch, R. J. and Oswald, A. J. (1997). 'The macroeconomics of happiness.' Discussion Paper No. 19, Centre for Economic Performance, University of Oxford.
Diener, E. (1984). 'Subjective well-being.' *Psychological Bulletin*, vol. 95, no. 3, pp. 542–75.
Diener, E., Diener, M. and Diener, C. (1995). 'Factors predicting the subjective well-being of nations.' *Journal of Personality and Social Psychology*, vol. 69, no. 5, pp. 851–64.

Diener, E. and Oishi, S. (2000). 'Money and happiness: income and subjective well-being across nations.' Forthcoming in (E. Diener and E. M. Suh eds) *Subjective Well-Being Across Cultures.* Cambridge, M.A.: MIT Press.

Diener, E., Suh, E. M., Lucas, R. E. and Smith, H. L. (1999). 'Subjective well-being: three decades of progress.' *Psychological Bulletin,* vol. 125, no. 2, pp. 276–303.

Easterlin, R. A. (1974). 'Does economic growth improve the human lot? Some empirical evidence.' In (P. A. David and M. W. Reder eds) *Nations and Households in Economic Growth: Essays in Honour of Moses Abramowitz.* New York and London: Academic Press, pp. 89–125.

Easterlin, R. A. (1995). 'Will raising the incomes of all increase the happiness of all?' *Journal of Economic Behaviour and Organization,* vol. 27, no. 1, pp. 35–48.

Feld, L. and Kirchgässner, G. (1999). 'Public debt and budgetary procedures: top down or bottom up. Some evidence from Swiss municipalities.' In (J. M. Poterba and J. von Hagen eds) *Fiscal Institutions and Fiscal Performance.* Chicago: Chicago University Press, pp. 151–79.

Feld, L. P. and Savioz, M. R. (1997). 'Direct democracy matters for economic performance: an empirical investigation.' *Kyklos,* vol. 50, no. 4, pp 507–38.

Fernández-Dols, J.-M. and Ruiz-Belda, M.-A. (1995). 'Are smiles a sign of happiness? Gold medal winners at the Olympic games.' *Journal of Personality and Social Psychology,* vol. 69, no. 6, pp. 1113–9.

Frey, B. S. (1991). 'Forms of expressing economic discontent.' In (H. Norpoth, M. S. Lewis-Beck and J.-D. Lafay eds) *Economics and Politics. The Calculus of Support.* Ann Arbor: University of Michigan Press, pp. 267–80.

Frey, B. S. (1994). 'Direct democracy: politico-economic lessons from Swiss experience.' *American Economic Review,* vol. 84, no. 2, pp. 338–48.

Frey, B. S. (1997). 'A constitution for knaves crowds out civic virtues.' ECONOMIC JOURNAL, vol. 107, no. 443, pp. 1043–53.

Frey, B. S. and Eichenberger, R. (1999). *The New Democratic Federalism for Europe. Functional Overlapping and Competing Jurisdictions.* Cheltenham: Edward Elgar.

Gerber, E. (1999). *The Populist Paradox: Interest Group Influence and the Promise of Direct Legislation.* Princeton: Princeton University Press.

Headey, B. and Wearing, A. (1989). 'Personality, life events, and subjective well-being: toward a dynamic equilibrium model.' *Journal of Personality and Social Psychology,* vol. 57, pp. 731–9.

Hibbs, D. (1973). *Mass Political Violence: A Cross-National Causal Analysis.* New York: Wiley.

Hibbs, D. (1976). 'Industrial conflict in advanced industrial societies.' *American Political Science Review,* vol. 70, no. 12, pp. 1033–58.

Kenny, C. (1999). 'Does growth cause happiness, or does happiness cause growth?' *Kyklos,* vol. 52, no. 1, pp. 3–26.

Konow, J. and Earley, J. (1999). 'The hedonistic paradox: is homo economicus happier?' Mimeo, Department of Economics, Loyola Marymount University, Los Angeles.

Kölz, A. (1998). *Der Weg der Schweiz zum Modernen Bundesstaat. Historische Abhandlungen.* Chur and Zurich: Rüegger.

Ladner, A. (1994). 'Finanzkompetenzen der Gemeinden - ein Überblick über die Praxis.' In (F. Eng, A. Glatthard and B. H. Koenig eds) *Finanzföderalismus.* Bern: Emissionszentrale der Schweizer Gemeinden, pp. 64–85.

Leu, R. E., Burri, S. and Priester, T. (1997). *Lebensqualität und Armut in der Schweiz.* Bern: Haupt.

Lucas, R. E., Diener, E. and Eunkook, S. (1996). 'Discriminant validity of well-being measures.' *Journal of Personality and Social Psychology,* vol. 71, no. 3, pp. 616–28.

Makin, J. H. (1976). 'Constraints on formulation of models for measuring revealed preferences of policy makers.' *Kyklos,* vol. 29, no. 4, pp. 709–32.

Matsusaka, J. G. (1995). 'Fiscal effects of the voter initiative: evidence from the last 30 years.' *Journal of Political Economy,* vol. 103, no. 3, pp. 587–623.

Moulton, B. R. (1990). 'An illustration of a pitfall in estimating the effects of aggregate variables on micro units.' *Review of Economics and Statistics,* vol. 72, no. 2, pp. 334–8.

Myers, D. G. (1993). *The Pursuit of Happiness: Who Is Happy and Why?* New York: Avon.

Nannestad, P. and Paldam, M. (1994). 'The vp-function: a survey of the literature on vote and popularity functions after 25 years.' *Public Choice,* vol. 79, no. 3–4, pp. 213–45.

Opp, K.-D. (1989). *The Rationality of Political Protest, A Comparative Analysis of Rational Choice Theory.* Boulder: Westview Press.

Opp, K.-D., Voss, P. and Gern, C. (1995). *The Origins of a Spontaneous Revolution. East Germany 1989.* Ann Arbor: Michigan University Press.

Oswald, A. J. (1997). 'Happiness and economic performance.' ECONOMIC JOURNAL, vol. 107, no. 445, pp. 1815–31.

Pommerehne, W. W. (1978). 'Institutional approaches to public expenditure: empirical evidence from Swiss municipalities.' *Journal of Public Economics,* vol. 9, no. 2, pp. 225–80.

936   THE ECONOMIC JOURNAL   [OCTOBER

Pommerehne, W. W. (1990). 'The empirical relevance of comparative institutional analysis.' *European Economic Review*, vol. 34, no. 2–3, pp. 458–69.

Pommerehne, W. W. and Weck-Hannemann, H. (1996). 'Tax rates, tax administration and income tax evasion in Switzerland.' *Public Choice*, vol. 88, no. 1–2, pp. 161–70.

Rueben, K. (2000). 'Tax limitations and government growth: the effect of state tax and expenditure limits on state and local government.' Forthcoming in *Journal of Political Economy*.

Sandvik, E., Diener, E. and Seidlitz, L. (1993). 'Subjective well-being: the convergence and stability of self-report and non-self-report measures.' *Journal of Personality*, vol. 61, no. 3, pp. 317–42.

Santerre, R. E. (1989). 'Representative versus direct democracy: are there any expenditure differences?' *Public Choice*, vol. 60, no. 2, pp. 145–54.

Santerre, R. E. (1993). 'Representative versus direct democracy: the role of public bureaucrats.' *Public Choice*, vol. 76, no. 3, pp. 189–98.

Schneider, F. and Frey, B. S. (1988). 'Politico-economic models of macroeconomic policy: a review of the empirical evidence.' In (T. D. Willett ed.) *The Political Economy of Money, Inflation and Unemployment*. Durham and London: Duke University Press, pp. 240–75.

Schneider, F. and Pommerehne, W. W. (1983). 'Macroeconomia della crescita in disequilibrio e settore pubblico in espansione: il peso delle differenze istituzionali.' *Rivista Internazionale di Scienze Economiche e Commerciali*, vol. 33, no. 4–5, pp. 306–20.

Stutzer, A. (1999). 'Demokratieindizes für die Kantone der Schweiz.' Working Paper No. 23, Institute for Empirical Research in Economics, University of Zurich.

Swiss Federal Statistical Office (ed.) (1997). *Statistisches Jahrbuch der Schweiz*. Zürich: Neue Zürcher Zeitung.

Thomas, J. J. (1992). *Informal Economic Activity*. London: Wheatsheaf.

Trechsel, A. and Serdült, U. (1999). *Kaleidoskop Volksrechte: Die Institutionen der direkten Demokratie in den schweizerischen Kantonen 1970-1996*. Basel: Helbing and Lichtenhahn.

Tyler, T. R. (1990). *Why People Obey the Law*. New Haven: Yale.

Veenhoven, R. (1993). *Happiness in Nations: Subjective Appreciation of Life in 56 Nations 1946-1992*. Rotterdam: Erasmus University Press.

Wilson, W. (1967). 'Correlates of avowed happiness.' *Psychological Bulletin*, vol. 67, no. 4, pp. 294–306.

Winkelmann, L. and Winkelmann, R. (1998). 'Why are the unemployed so unhappy? Evidence from panel data.' *Economica*, vol. 65, no. 257, pp. 1–15.

Appendix

Index for Direct Democratic Rights and Local Autonomy in Swiss Cantons

Direct democracy is here defined in terms of individual political participation possibilities. In Switzerland, institutions for the direct political participation of citizens exist on the level of the federal state as well as on the level of cantons. However, the direct democratic rights on the level of cantons are very heterogeneous. Therefore, an index is constructed to measure the different barriers to citizens entering the political process, apart from elections in the year 1992. The index is based mainly on data collected in Trechsel and Serdült (1999) (for details see Stutzer, 1999).

The four main legal instruments directly influencing the political process in Swiss cantons are

   (a) the popular initiative to change the canton's constitution,
   (b) the popular initiative to change the canton's law,
   (c) the compulsory and optional referendum to prevent new law or changing law and
   (d) the compulsory and optional referendum to prevent new state expenditure.

Barriers are in terms of

   (a) the necessary signatures to launch an instrument (absolute and relative to the number of citizens with the right to vote),
   (b) the legally allowed time span to collect the signatures and
   (c) the level of new expenditure per head allowing a financial referendum.

   (Compulsory referenda are treated like referenda with the lowest possible barrier.)

Each of these restrictions is evaluated on a six point scale: 'one' indicates a high barrier, 'six' a low one. From the resulting ratings, a non-weighted average is calculated for each instrument (i.e. four sub-indices) and for the composite index, which represents the measure of direct democratic rights in Swiss cantons. The results are presented in Table A1.

The index for local autonomy is based on survey results by Ladner (1994). Chief local administrators in 1856 Swiss municipalities reported how they perceive their local autonomy on a 10 point scale, with one indicating 'no autonomy at all', and 10 'very high' communal autonomy. Average scores for each canton are also shown in Table A1.

Table A1
Index for Direct Democratic Rights and Local Autonomy in Swiss Cantons

Canton	Direct democracy					Local autonomy
	Index for constitutional initiative	Index for legislative initiative	Index for legislative referendum	Index for financial referendum	Composite index for direct demo-cratic rights	
Aargau	5.67	5.67	6.00	4.50	5.46	4.9
Appenzell i. Rh.	6.00	6.00	6.00	3.00	5.25	5.0
Appenzell a. Rh.	6.00	6.00	6.00	4.00	5.50	5.8
Bern	2.67	2.67	3.67	5.00	3.50	4.6
Basel Land	6.00	6.00	6.00	4.75	5.69	4.3
Basel Stadt	4.67	4.67	4.00	4.25	4.40	5.5
Fribourg	2.67	2.67	2.33	2.00	2.42	4.2
Genève	2.00	2.00	2.00	1.00	1.75	3.2
Glarus	6.00	6.00	6.00	4.00	5.50	5.6
Graubünden	4.00	5.00	6.00	4.00	4.75	5.8
Jura	4.67	4.67	3.00	2.50	3.71	4.0
Luzern	4.67	5.33	3.67	4.25	4.48	4.1
Neuchâtel	2.67	2.67	1.67	1.50	2.13	3.7
Nidwalden	2.67	6.00	6.00	5.00	4.92	5.5
Obwalden	5.33	6.00	6.00	5.00	5.58	6.0
Sankt Gallen	3.33	4.00	3.00	3.25	3.40	4.9
Schaffhausen	5.33	5.33	5.17	4.50	5.08	6.1
Solothurn	5.33	5.33	6.00	5.00	5.42	4.9
Schwyz	5.33	5.33	4.67	4.38	4.93	4.6
Thurgau	3.67	3.67	4.33	4.50	4.04	5.9
Ticino	1.33	2.67	1.67	2.75	2.10	4.3
Uri	5.67	5.67	5.33	5.00	5.42	5.4
Vaud	2.33	2.33	2.00	3.00	2.42	4.7
Valais	3.00	3.67	6.00	1.00	3.42	5.5
Zug	5.00	5.00	3.67	4.00	4.42	6.0
Zürich	3.33	3.33	6.00	4.00	4.17	5.4

Sources: Ladner (1994) and own calculations on the basis of Trechsel and Serdült (1999).

938   THE ECONOMIC JOURNAL   [OCTOBER 2000]

Table A2

Correlation of Sub-indices and Composite Index for Direct Democratic Rights and Local Autonomy in Swiss Cantons

	CI	LI	LR	FR	DDR	LA
Index for constitutional initiative (CI)	1.000					
Index for legislative initiative (LI)	0.871	1.000				
Index for legislative referendum (LR)	0.669	0.772	1.000			
Index for financial referendum (FR)	0.539	0.632	0.562	1.000		
Composite index for direct democratic rights (DDR)	0.888	0.943	0.877	0.767	1.000	
Local autonomy (LA)	0.410	0.506	0.646	0.531	0.605	1.000

Table A3

Sensitivity Analysis: DFBETA-Test for 26 Swiss Cantons

Independent variable: direct democratic rights

Omitted observation	$\hat{\beta}_0$	DFBETA	Omitted observation	$\hat{\beta}_0$	DFBETA
Aargau	0.078*	0.030	Nidwalden	0.079**	0.007
Appenzell i. Rh.	0.079**	−0.007	Obwalden	0.073**	0.264
Appenzell a. Rh.	0.073**	0.241	Sankt Gallen	0.082**	−0.108
Bern	0.081**	−0.072	Schaffhausen	0.083**	−0.161
Basel Land	0.088**	−0.325	Solothurn	0.081**	−0.049
Basel Stadt	0.078**	0.065	Schwyz	0.078**	0.062
Fribourg	0.073*	0.217	Thurgau	0.079**	0.025
Genève	0.080**	−0.035	Ticino	0.100**	−0.829
Glarus	0.080**	−0.027	Uri	0.077**	0.073
Graubünden	0.080**	−0.025	Vaud	0.058*	0.775
Jura	0.079**	0.002	Valais	0.080**	−0.024
Luzern	0.084**	−0.186	Zug	0.078**	0.042
Neuchâtel	0.075*	0.139	Zürich	0.082**	−0.117

Notes: A value of DFBETA greater than 1.96 in absolute value shows an influential observation. Weight: inverse of the number of observations per canton. Significance levels: *$0.01 < p < 0.05$, **$p < 0.01$.
Data source: Leu *et al.* (1997).

[14]

The Economic Journal, 111 (*July*), 465–484. © Royal Economic Society 2001. Published by Blackwell Publishers, 108 Cowley Road, Oxford OX4 1JF, UK and 350 Main Street, Malden, MA 02148, USA.

INCOME AND HAPPINESS: TOWARDS A UNIFIED THEORY*

Richard A. Easterlin

Material aspirations are initially fairly similar among income groups; consequently more income brings greater happiness. Over the life cycle, however, aspirations grow along with income, and undercut the favourable effect of income growth on happiness, although the cross-sectional happiness-income difference persists. People think they were less happy in the past and will be happier in the future, because they project current aspirations to be the same throughout the life cycle, while income grows. But since aspirations actually grow along with income, experienced happiness is systematically different from projected happiness. Consequently, choices turn out to be based on false expectations.

Life is a progress from want to want, not from enjoyment to enjoyment.

Samuel Johnson, 1776

The relationship between happiness and income is puzzling. At a point in time, those with more income are, on average, happier than those with less. Over the life cycle, however, the average happiness of a cohort remains constant despite substantial income growth. Moreover, even though a cohort's experienced happiness remains constant throughout the life span, people typically think that they were worse off in the past and will be better off in the future.

Can economic theory explain these paradoxical observations? Perhaps, with some amendment for systematic change in material preferences or aspirations. In what follows, after a brief discussion of the concept of happiness and the nature of these paradoxical relationships, I suggest a model to explain them, and present some supporting evidence.

1. Concept and Sources of Happiness

Throughout this article, I use the terms happiness, subjective well-being, satisfaction, utility, well-being, and welfare interchangeably. The measurement and analysis of these various notions of subjective well-being has a half century history in the social sciences (see the bibliographical survey by Veenhoven (1993) which contains about 2,500 references). In the past, contributions by economists have been relatively slim. Recent years, however, have seen a flowering of work, including a symposium on economics and happiness in this JOURNAL (see Dixon (1997), Frank (1997), Ng (1997), Oswald (1997) and the references in these articles). In work on quality of life and the standard of living, the use of subjective indicators such as happiness has also been

* I am grateful for the excellent assistance of Donna H. Ebata, Paul Rivera, and John Worth. For helpful suggestions I am indebted to Dennis Ahlburg, Richard H. Day, Nancy L. Easterlin, Stanley L. Engerman, Timur Kuran, Jim Martin, Bentley MacLeod, Vai-Lam Mui, Jeffrey Nugent, Andrew J. Oswald, Lynwood Pendleton, James Robinson, Alois Stutzer, participants in meetings at the California Institute of Technology, Oxford University, Penn State University, University of California Los Angeles, and the University of Southern California, and two anonymous referees. Financial support was provided by the Andrew W. Mellon Foundation and the University of Southern California.

receiving increasing attention (Blundell *et al.* 1994; Elster and Roemer, 1991; Nussbaum and Sen, 1993; Offer 1996).

The principal way in which subjective well-being is measured in this work is a direct question of the sort used since 1972 in the United States' General Social Survey (GSS): 'Taken all together, how would you say things are these days – would you say that you are very happy, pretty happy, or not too happy?' (National Opinion Research Center, 1999, p. 171). There are a large number of variations on this. For example, instead of happiness the respondent may be asked about his or her satisfaction with life as a whole. The wording and number of the response categories may also vary. Veenhoven (1993) provides a valuable classification of queries on well-being, their wording, and response groupings. As a general matter, people have little trouble answering such questions; in the GSS, for example, the average proportion of nonresponses was less than one percent in fourteen surveys conducted between 1972 and 1987.

Measurement issues such as the reliability and validity of the replies, whether respondents report their true feelings, and possible biases resulting from the context in which the question is asked, have been extensively studied in the literature (see Diener (1984) and Veenhoven (1993)). The general conclusion of such assessments is that subjective indicators such as those used here, though not perfect, do reflect respondents' substantive feelings of well-being – in the words of psychologist Ed Diener (1984, p. 551), the 'measures seem to contain substantial amounts of valid variance.'

In addition to meaningfulness there is the question of comparability of such measures. As phrased, the happiness questions typically leave each person free to define well-being as he or she pleases. How, then, can the happiness of persons be compared? The essence of the answer, suggested by responses to queries as to the sources of happiness, is this: in most people's lives everywhere the dominant concerns are making a living, family life, and health, and it is these concerns that ordinarily determine how happy people feel.

Because personal responses on the sources of happiness bear, not only on the issue of comparability, but also on the causes of happiness, it is worth noting some evidence. In the early 1960s, social psychologist Hadley Cantril (1965) carried out an intensive survey in fourteen countries with highly diverse cultures and at widely different stages of socio-economic development, asking open-ended questions about what people want out of life.[1] Economists may

---

[1] The specific countries are listed in the source note to Table 2. In each country in a face-to-face interview a respondent was asked to give his view of the best of all possible worlds for himself – 'his wishes and hopes as he personally conceives them and the realisation of which would constitute for him the best possible life' (Cantril, 1965, p. 22). A similar question elicited views on the worst possible life. A respondent could, and often did, name a variety of concerns. One example of the care with which the survey was conducted is Cantril's description of the problem 'of translating the original questions from English into the various languages used . . . [C]onsiderable time was spent with experts to be sure the translation contained the precise nuances wanted. One of the methods often utilised in this translation process was to have someone who knew the native language, as a native, for example, an Arab, and who also was completely fluent in English translate our questions into Arabic. Then someone whose native language was English but who had a perfect command of Arabic would translate the Arabic back into English so a comparison could be made with the original question and, through discussion and further comparisons, difficulties could be ironed out' (p. 26).

take some reassurance from the fact that in every country, material circumstances, especially level of living, are mentioned most often, being named, on average, by about three-fourths of the population (Cantril, p. 162). Next are family concerns – cited by about half – such as a happy family life and good relations with children and relatives. These are followed by concerns about one's personal or family health, which typically are named by about one-third of the people. After this, and about equal in importance, at around one-fifth of the population, are matters relating to one's work (a good job) and to personal character (emotional stability, personal worth, self-discipline, etc.). Perhaps surprisingly, concerns about broad international or domestic issues, such as war, political or civil liberty, and social equality, are not often mentioned, being named, on average, by less than one person in twenty. Abrupt changes in the latter circumstances do affect people's sense of well-being at the time they occur, but ordinarily they are taken as a given, and it is the things that occupy most people's everyday life, and are somewhat within their control, that are typically in the forefront of personal concerns. Results similar to Cantril's on the sources of happiness have been obtained by others (Andrews and Withey, 1976; Campbell, 1981; Campbell *et al.* 1976; Veroff *et al.* 1981).

Thus, although each individual is free to define happiness in his or her own terms, in practice the kinds of things chiefly cited as shaping happiness are for most people much the same – probably because most people everywhere spend most of their lives doing the same types of things. This is not to say that the happiness of any one individual can be directly compared with that of another. But if one is concerned with comparing the subjective well-being of sizable groups of people, such as social classes, this similarity in feelings about the sources of happiness gives credence to such comparison.

2. Empirical Relationships

Further testimony as to the meaningfulness of the data on subjective well-being is the empirical regularities that turn up, to which I now turn.

2.1. *The Cross Sectional Relationship*

I start with the simple point-of-time association between happiness and income. In the 1994 GSS, those reporting themselves very happy ranges from 16% in the lowest income class to 44% in the highest (Table 1, column 2). To avoid relying on only one happiness category, such as the percentage very happy, I have computed a mean happiness rating, which can vary from a minimum of zero to a maximum of four (the procedure is indicated in the table footnote).[2] By this measure, average happiness varies directly with income throughout the income range, from a low of 1.8 to a high of 2.8.

---

[2] Oswald (1997, p. 1817, fn. 5) is critical of the use of one happiness category, such as the percentage very happy. The present scoring technique is common in the literature (cf. Herzog *et al.* 1982; Veenhoven, 1993).

Table 1

Percent Distribution of Population by Happiness at Various Levels of Income, United States, 1994

Total household income (1994 dollars)	Mean happiness rating* (1)	Very happy (2)	Pretty happy (3)	Not too happy (4)	(Number of cases) (5)
All income groups	2.4	28	60	12	(2,627)
75,000 and over	2.8	44	49	6	(268)
50–74,999	2.6	36	58	7	(409)
40–49,999	2.4	31	59	10	(308)
30–39,999	2.5	31	61	8	(376)
20–29,999	2.3	27	61	12	(456)
10–19,999	2.1	21	64	15	(470)
Less than 10,000	1.8	16	62	23	(340)

Source: National Opinion Research Center (1999) Question 157. 'Don't know' and 'no answer' responses are omitted.
* Based on score of 'very happy' = 4, 'pretty happy' = 2, 'not too happy' = 0.

As far as I am aware, in every representative national survey ever done a significant positive bivariate relationship between happiness and income has been found (Andrews, 1986; p. xi; Argyle, 1999, pp. 356–7; Diener 1984, p. 533). The relationship holds for household income, both adjusted for family size and unadjusted as in Table 1. In recent work, there has been a tendency to discount this association between one's objective economic circumstances, as indexed by income, and subjective well-being (Diener and Lucas, 1999, p. 215; Lykken and Tellegen, 1996; Schwarz and Strack, 1999, pp. 79–80). Partly, this is because in individual data there is such a large amount of unexplained variance – the simple correlation, for example, between happiness and income in the individual data underlying Table 1, although highly significant, is only 0.20. Partly, it is because this modest happiness-income relationship is further weakened by the introduction of controls for other variables, such as unemployment and education (Frey and Stutzer 1999, Oswald 1997, Veroff *et al.* 1981). It is also sometimes argued that the happiness-income relation, such as it is, holds only in the lower part of the income range (Argyle, 1999, p. 356).

This is not the place for detailed discussion of these arguments, but several brief comments are in order. First, the use of controls depends on one's purpose. Education and unemployment affect well-being in part through their effect on income, and if one takes income as a proxy for an interrelated set of socio-economic circumstances, then the bivariate relation is important in its own right. Second, the supposed attenuation at higher income levels of the happiness-income relation does not occur when happiness is regressed on log income, rather than absolute income. Put differently – if the same proportional rather than absolute increase in income is assumed to yield the same increase in happiness, then income change at upper income levels causes the same increase in happiness as at lower. Finally, although the high degree of variance in individual data is indisputable – a situation common in bivariate correlations of individual data – to discount the happiness-income relationship is to discount the personal testimony of individuals in country after country who mention economic circumstances most frequently as a source of happiness. The positive happiness-income relation is consistent with this testimony.

2.2. *The Life Cycle Pattern*

When one turns to the life cycle change in happiness, however, a seeming contradiction arises to the positive happiness-income relationship. On average, income, and economic circumstances more generally, improve substantially up to the retirement ages; yet, there is no corresponding advance in subjective well-being (Fig. 1).[3] Nor does the levelling off and decline of income in the retirement years appear to be accompanied by any change in average happiness. The lack of a life cycle trend in happiness is supported by regressions of happiness on age for each of the cohorts in Fig. 1 – there is none with a statistically significant slope. A pooled regression with cohort dummy variables added also shows no significant coefficient.

It is possible, of course, that the seeming contradiction between the cross sectional and life cycle relation of happiness to income is because other factors

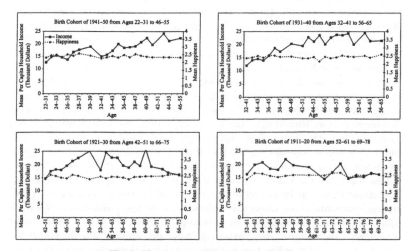

Fig. 1. *Happiness and Income over the Life Cycle*

[3] Household income in Fig. 1 has been converted to a *per capita* basis to give a better idea of the change in material living level over the life cycle; for a more refined adjustment see Easterlin and Schaeffer (1999).

overwhelm the effect of income on happiness over the course of the life cycle. Yet, the effect of income is certainly not overwhelmed by such factors in the cross section. Moreover, the top ranking of economic circumstances as a source of happiness persists at all points in the life cycle (Herzog *et al.*, 1982). Thus we are presented with a paradox: why at a point-in-time are happiness and income positively associated, but over the life cycle there is no relation?

The life cycle pattern here is obtained by following each of several birth cohorts over a twenty-four year segment of its life span linking appropriate age data for successive years – what is sometimes termed a 'synthetic cohort' approach (for further detail, see Easterlin and Schaeffer (1999)). This is the first time that this technique, originated by demographers a half century ago, has been used to study life cycle happiness. Previous generalisations are based almost entirely on cross sectional relations between happiness and age, and give no consistent picture. Some find a positive relation (Mroczek and Kolarz, 1998); others, a U-shaped relation (Oswald, 1997); and yet others, no relation at all (Myers, 1992). The only panel study covering a sizeable period (10 years) reports no relation, a result consistent with the results of the present longitudinal study (Costa *et al.*, 1987).

The mixed results from cross sectional studies should come as no surprise, because they fail to consider the possibility that the cross sectional relationship may vary over time. A survey of cross sectional studies by George (1992) finds that in the United States before the 1970s older persons were less happy than younger; in recent surveys, however, older persons are happier. This finding is consistent with the changing relative fortunes of older and younger cohorts since World War II (Easterlin, 1987). Hence, depending on the calendar year chosen, cross sectional studies may lead to quite different conclusions regarding the life cycle trend in happiness (cf. also Campbell, 1981, ch. 12).[4]

This is not to suggest that the present life cycle approach is without shortcomings. For one thing, it is not possible to follow the same individual from one year to the next, as can be done with panel data. Also, the composition of a synthetic cohort, unlike that in panel data, is altered somewhat by international migration. In addition, there may be period as well as cohort effects in the data. But for all its shortcomings, the life cycle measurement procedure used here seems considerably better for inferring life cycle change than cross sectional age data, because it follows essentially the same group of persons over sizeable segments of the life span.

Stability in the life cycle happiness of a cohort does not mean, of course, that at the individual level subjective well-being is simply a flat line over the life span. Significant changes in one's circumstances – life cycle events such as marriage, loss of a job, the birth of a child, retirement, and the death of a loved one – affect subjective well-being (McLanahan and Sorensen, 1985; Myers 1992). If the sample size here permitted finer calibration – for example, following single year birth cohorts – one might possibly observe the imprint of

---

[4] For further analysis of the relation of the cross sectional happiness-age patterns to the life cycle patterns in the United States, see Easterlin and Schaeffer (1999) pp. 289 ff.

such effects in the data, because some of them are age-related. For the 10 year birth cohorts and 24 year life span segments studied here, however, such effects, to the extent they exist, fail to alter the horizontal trend in happiness.

2.3. *Past and Prospective Happiness*

Based on the observed pattern of life cycle happiness, one would expect that individuals, when asked how their past and prospective happiness compares with the present, would report little change. As it turns out, this is not the case – people at any given point in the life cycle typically think that they will be better off in the future than at present, and that they are better off today than in the past. I am talking here of comparisons over periods of some length, say, five years or more, not very short intervals such as year or less. The most comprehensive evidence of this comes from the Cantril survey previously mentioned. Respondents, after indicating their present happiness level on an integer scale from zero to ten, were asked where on the scale they were five years ago, and where they think they will be five years hence. In every country in every age group from 18–29 to 50 and over, respondents, on average, rated their prospective happiness higher, and their past happiness less, with only a few trivial exceptions (Table 2). Younger respondents saw, on average, greater changes than older, and future changes were envisaged to be greater than past.

Time series data for the United States confirm the evidence of Cantril's international cross section. The same question as Cantril's was asked in 36

Table 2
*Past and Future Happiness Compared with Present Happiness, by Age,
14 Countries, 1965*

	(1)	(2)	(3)	(4)	(5)
		Past versus present happiness		Future versus present happiness	
Age group	Number of observations	Number rating past lower	Mean difference, present minus past	Number rating future higher	Mean difference, future minus present
18–29	14	14	1.0	14	2.2
30–49	22	22	0.8	22	2.0
50+	14	12	0.6	13	1.3
65+	4	2	0.1	4	0.4

Source: Cantril (1965), pp. 365–77. An observation is the mean happiness value for an age group in a country. In some countries age groups were more detailed than those given here, hence the number of observations exceeds the number of countries. The questioning procedure is of the following nature. Respondents indicate where they currently are on a ladder with rungs from zero to ten, where ten is 'completely happy' and zero is 'unhappy'. They then indicate where on the ladder they stood five years ago and where they think they will be five years hence (Cantril, 1965, p. 23). The countries included (with sample sizes) are: Brazil (2,170), Cuba (992, urban only), Dominican Republic (814), Egypt (499), India (2,366), Israel (1,170), Japan (972), Nigeria (1,200), Panama (642), Philippines (500), Poland (1,464), United States (1,549), West Germany (480), Yugoslavia (1,523).

surveys in the 26-year-period from 1959 to 1985 (Lipset and Schneider, 1987, pp. 130–1). In every survey respondents expected, on average, to be happier in the future, and felt that they had been worse off in the past, there being only three small exceptions in the present/past comparison. As in the international data, future changes were envisaged to be greater than past.[5] But in fact, over the entire period present happiness was, on average, constant.[6] Thus we have another paradox to explain – why people typically think that they were worse off in the past and will be better off in the future, although their reports on present happiness remain constant over time.

3. Explaining the Relationships: Theory

I have noted three empirical regularities that need to be explained. At a given time those with higher incomes are happier, on average, than those with lower. Also, at a point-in-time respondents typically feel that they were less happy in the past and will be more happy in the future. Finally, experienced happiness is, on average, constant over the life cycle. The tentative explanation, to which I now turn, involves taking account of both income and aspirations, and how they vary at a point in time as well as over time.[7] As has been seen, the sources of happiness reported by individuals range beyond purely material concerns, but I focus here on goods aspirations because of the pre-eminent importance of economic circumstances in reports on sources of happiness.

Assume that at the start of the adult life cycle people in different socio-economic circumstances have a fairly similar set of material aspirations, say, A_1. Those with higher income will then be better able to fulfill their aspirations and, other things equal, will, on average, feel better off (Fig. 2, compare points 1, 2, 3 on the utility function corresponding to the aspiration level, A_1). This is the point-of-time positive association between happiness and income.

If income rises and material aspirations remain constant, then individuals will move upward along the A_1 utility function in Fig. 2, increasingly realising their aspirations and experiencing rising levels of well-being – progressing, for example, from point 2 to point 3, with well-being rising from u_m to u_2. If, however, income remains constant and aspirations rise to, say, A_2, then the satisfaction associated with a given level of income would diminish. An individual whose income is, say, y_m, would experience a level of satisfaction u_m if she were on the utility function corresponding to aspiration level A_1

---

[5] Loewenstein and Schkade (1999, p. 90) report other instances in which future changes in well-being are systematically projected to be greater than past.

[6] This is, of course, the well-established finding that as the income of a nation rises, happiness typically remains unchanged (Blanchflower and Oswald, 1999; Diener and Oshi, forthcoming; Easterlin, 1974, 1995; Kenny, 1999). Life cycle well-being does not have to follow the national pattern of time series stability. Each cohort, for example, might have an identical life cycle pattern of rising well-being, but if each started at the same initial level, then the national average would be constant over time.

[7] See March and Simon's (1968) 'general model of adaptive motivated behaviour'. De la Croix (1998), building on Ramsey (1928), presents a formal economic model of well-being, using this approach. For similar models in psychology, see Michalos (1986, 1991).

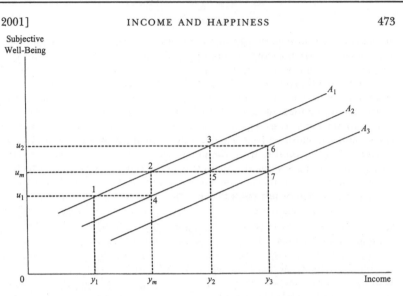

Fig. 2. *Subjective Well-Being* (u) *as a Function of Income* (y) *and Aspiration Level* (A)

(point 2), but a lower level of satisfaction, u_1, if she were on the utility function corresponding to the higher aspiration level, A_2 (point 4).

I conjecture that, in reality, material aspirations change over the life cycle roughly in proportion to income. Hence, individuals typically move from point 2, neither to point 3 nor point 4, but to point 5, because both aspirations and income rise, with roughly offsetting effects on well-being. This results in the observed stability during the working ages of life cycle well-being, a product of the countervailing effects of rising income and aspirations. The stability of well-being in the retirement ages suggests that this mechanism is reversible.

How does one explain the statements on past and prospective welfare? The key is to recognise that these are point-of-time responses and are consequently based on the aspirations that people have acquired at that point in time. Consider, for example, an individual who has moved from point 2 to point 5, with income growing from y_m to y_2 and aspirations rising from A_1 to A_2. When asked at point 5 how well off he was in the past, his judgment is based on his current higher level of aspirations (A_2), not on the lower level of aspirations (A_1) he actually had in the past. Because his aspirations have risen he evaluates his previous income, y_m, on the basis of his new utility function, A_2, and sees y_m as yielding the satisfaction level, u_1 (point 4). When he was actually at y_m, however, his material aspirations were lower, and he enjoyed the higher happiness level, u_m (point 2 on the utility function A_1).

The assessment of one's future well-being is similarly premised on one's material aspirations at the time the question is asked. A person at point 5 on the utility function A_2, who anticipates a growth in income to y_3 will envisage an improvement in welfare from u_m to u_2, that is, an upward movement along the A_2 function from point 5 to point 6. What she does not know is that when she gets to y_3 she will have, not just higher income, but higher material aspirations as well, and be on the utility function corresponding to the higher aspiration level, A_3. Thus, she will end up at point 7, not point 6, and experience about the same level of satisfaction, u_m, that she did at point 5.

The distinction drawn by psychologists between decision utility and experienced utility is illustrated clearly here (Kahneman *et al.* 1997; Tversky and Griffin, 1991). Decision utility is the perceived (*ex ante*) satisfaction associated with choice among several alternatives; experienced utility is the satisfaction realised (*ex post*) from the outcome actually chosen. When asked about well-being five years ago or five years hence, a person at point 5 with income y_2 on utility function A_2, can be thought of as telling us how she would feel *today* if she had the income y_m (worse off) or y_3 (better off). This is her *decision* utility. It explains, for example, why she says she would not want to go back to her old lower-paying job (point 4) and why she may take a new higher-paying job (point 6). However, if she does take the higher-paying job and her income goes up, her material aspirations too will rise. Hence, when asked how happy she is when she actually has income y_3, that is, what her *experienced* utility is, she turns out to be at point 7, not point 6.

Economists tend to assume that decision utility and experienced utility are the same. The present theory implies that there is a mechanism at work – aspirations rising in proportion to income – that makes them systematically different (see also Kahneman (1999), Rabin (1998)). If one's interest is solely in the choices determining behaviour, then decision utility is enough. But if one is interested in the welfare effects of behaviour, then the effect of the income-aspiration mechanism on experienced utility needs to be taken into account.

4. Explaining the Relationships: Evidence

It is one thing to speculate; it is another to give supporting evidence, particularly with regard to the central feature of the theory – differences and trends in material aspirations. There is virtually no systematic empirical work on changing aspirations on which to build, but in what follows, I present a few pieces of new data that I think are consistent with the theory just presented. I also note some supporting evidence from the psychological literature.

I first divide each cohort in Fig. 1 into two socio-economic groups whose composition remains largely the same over the life cycle – those with more than a high school education and those with a high school education or less. In effect, the educational system is seen as channelling persons into two different life cycle tracks, with the higher schooling group enjoying the benefit of higher income.[8] The analysis is necessarily more approximate than the

[8] For a review of recent studies of the relation between education and income, see Ashenfelter and Rouse (1999). The authors' survey concludes that education has an important causal impact on income independently of ability and family background.

previous one for several reasons: dividing a birth cohort by level of education results in a smaller sample size, misreporting of educational level may be a problem, and during the life cycle some individuals shift from the lower to the higher educational cohort as a result of ongoing education. In the happiness data below, I have tried to minimise these problems by using a three-year moving average, and confining the analysis to that segment of a cohort's life cycle for which the distribution by level of education remains fairly constant.[9]

The cohorts, when subdivided by level of education, present a microcosm of the cross-sectional and life cycle patterns already presented (Fig. 3). At any given point in the life cycle, happiness varies directly with socio-economic status as measured by education; over the course of the life cycle, however, there is no change in the happiness of either socio-economic group.

The persistent differential by socio-economic status underscores the impor-tance of objective circumstances for well-being. Essentially the same people are in each educational group throughout the life cycle, and those on the higher income track are consistently happier, on average, than those on the lower. Psychologists have sometimes pointed to the finding that over time the same individuals tend to be high (or low) on the happiness scale as evidence that personality or genetic differences are the source of differences in happiness, not 'external conditions' such as economic circumstances (Diener and Lucas, 1999, p. 214). This conclusion is contradicted by the present result. To dismiss the effect here of economic circumstances on well-being, one would have to

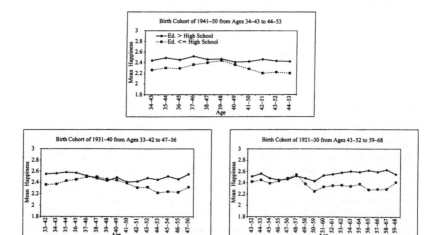

Fig. 3. *Life Cycle Happiness by Level of Education*

[9] For the cohort of 1941–50, the total sample size for the 3-year moving average is around 900 or more and the percentage of the cohort with a high school education or less fluctuates within a few percentage points of 44. For the cohort of 1931–40, the corresponding figures are 600 or more and 65; for that of 1921–30, 600 or more and 71.

make a very strong case that inherent genetic and personality traits are what lie behind the channelling of persons into the two educational tracks.

The theory I have presented makes three assumptions about material preferences: (1) early in the life cycle, preferences are fairly similar among income groups, (2) over the life cycle, preferences vary in proportion to income, and (3) in evaluating past or future happiness, people take their preferences to be the same as those held currently. Each of these will be taken up, in turn.

The desires of high school seniors (largely 18 year-olds) for big ticket consumer goods, as reported in surveys, provide striking evidence that people start out with very similar aspirations. The proportion naming each of twelve consumer goods as extremely or quite important is virtually the same for those who expect to attend a four-year college as for those who do not (Table 3). The average number of consumer goods named as extremely or quite important by the two groups is an identical 4.5 (see the bottom line of Table 3).

This does not mean that material aspirations, in general, are identical for the two groups. Although a number of important consumer goods are reported on here, the list is not exhaustive. Moreover, the responses do not indicate the specific characteristics of each good that the respondent has in mind. It is plausible to suppose that the characteristics of a 'house of my own' envisaged by those from higher status backgrounds differ systematically from those contemplated by persons from lower status backgrounds. Nevertheless, the similarity of the two lists is remarkable – who would have predicted, for

Table 3

Desires of High School Seniors for Big Ticket Consumer Goods, by Plans to Attend Four Year College, 1976

	(1)	(2)
Consumer good	College plans	No college plans
	(percent answering extremely or quite important)	
At least one car	76	80
A house of my own (instead of an apartment or condominium)	52	53
Lots of space around my house, a big yard	60	58
A well-kept garden and lawn	60	58
Major labour-saving appliances (washer, dryer, dishwasher, etc.)	51	51
A high quality stereo	45	44
Clothes in the latest style	41	40
A motor-powered recreational vehicle (powerboat, snowmobile)	15	16
At least two cars	14	14
A large (full-sized) car	14	13
A vacation house	12	11
A new car every 2–3 years	11	11
Mean number of goods per person extremely or quite important	4.5	4.5

Source: Bachman *et al.* (1980) pp. 139–41. The question asked is: Looking toward the future, how important would it be for you to have each of the following things? The number of cases in each column is about 1,400.

example, that the proportion naming 'major labour-saving appliances' as extremely or quite important would be the same 51% for each group?

Given the similarity in material aspirations at the start of the life cycle, initial differences in happiness by level of schooling must be due, according to the theory, to differences in income that make it possible for those with more schooling to attain their material aspirations better than those with less. Suggestive evidence that the happiness difference early in the adult life cycle is due to differences in income comes from survey questions that were asked of a nationally representative sample of the adult population in 1978. In this survey respondents were asked whether they considered each of ten consumer goods – much like those on which high school seniors reported – to be part of the 'good life', that is, 'the life you'd like to have', and also whether they actually had the items. For the youngest age group of respondents, those 18 to 29 years old, the bivariate correlation between material aspirations, measured by the number of big ticket consumer goods named as part of the good life, and income was −0.01, indicative again of the lack of difference in aspirations by socio-economic status early in the adult life cycle. The correlation between the number of big ticket consumer goods respondents actually had and income was a highly significant 0.21. Although there are no reports on happiness in this survey, it is noteworthy that the magnitude of the correlation with income of what one might call 'consumer wealth' is just about the same as that reported earlier for the correlation of happiness with income. These results are consistent with the view that the point-of-time positive association between happiness and income is due to the fact that higher income makes possible greater fulfillment of material aspirations.

The theory also postulates that over the life cycle material aspirations rise roughly in proportion to income. Again, the 'good life' data provide some support. If one follows cohorts over a roughly 15 year segment of the life span, one finds that within a cohort the increase in the number of consumer goods desired – that is, the number named as part of the good life – is greater for those with more schooling than for those with less (Table 4, column 1).[10] The increase in consumer wealth is also greater for the higher educational group (column 2). The greater growth in both material aspirations and consumer wealth for the higher schooling group is consistent with the hypothesis that growth in income is driving the growth in material aspirations.[11]

Further support for the hypothesis that income is behind the growth in aspirations comes from the changing correlation between aspirations and

---

[10] The approach here is to follow a 'synthetic cohort' as in the happiness analysis described in Section 2.2. The analysis is more approximate, however, because the Roper 'good life' question has been asked only intermittently, the sample size is smaller, and the age reporting in the data is usually for groups of five years or more. For the analysis reported in Tables 4 and 5, I have paired the 1978 data for ages 18–29 with the 1994 data for ages 30–44 (roughly the birth cohort of 1950–64) and the 1978 data for ages 30–44 with the 1994 data for ages 45–59 (roughly the birth cohort of 1935–49).

[11] Hirsch (1976, p. 61) discusses how the 'fulfilment of given wants generates new and higher order wants.' Cf. also Durkheim ([1930] 1952, p. 248), Leibenstein (1976, p. 197). Rainwater (1994) finds that in the United States the income perceived as necessary to get along rose between 1950 and 1986 in the same proportion as actual *per capita* income.

Table 4

Change between Specified Life Cycle Ages in Mean Number of Big Ticket Consumer Goods Desired and Owned for Persons with Specified Amount of Schooling

	(1)	(2)
	Change in number of consumer goods	
Cohort, age, and schooling	desired	owned
A. Cohort of 1950–64 between ages 18–29 and 30–4		
Persons with schooling greater than 12 years	1.4	1.6
Persons with schooling 12 years or less	1.0	1.1
Difference	0.4	0.5
B. Cohort of 1935–49 between ages 30–44 and 45–59		
Persons with schooling greater than 12 years	1.3	1.0
Persons with schooling 12 years or less	0.9	0.4
Difference	0.4	0.6

Source: Roper-Starch Organization (1979, 1995)

income over the course of the life cycle. If income is the cause of changing material aspirations, then one ought to observe the gradual emergence during the life cycle of a positive correlation between material aspirations and income, and this, in fact, is the case (Table 5).

Fig. 2 can be used to interpret these patterns by level of education. Early in the adult life cycle, those with more and less education are both on roughly the same utility function, sharing a common set of aspirations, A_1. Because those with more education earn a higher average income than those with less

Table 5

Correlation with Income of Number of Big Ticket Consumer Goods Desired, Specified Age in Life Cycle, Cohorts of 1950–64 and 1935–49

	(1)	(2)	(3)	(4)
	Age	Correlation coefficient	Age	Correlation coefficient
Cohort of 1950–64	18–29	−0.01	30–44	0.08*
Cohort of 1935–49	30–44	0.05	45–59	0.14*

* Significance levels are approximately as follows: 0.08 correlation is significant at 0.10 level; 0.12 at 0.01 level; and 0.15 at 0.001 level. The number of cases in the first row is 474 and 562; in the second row, 427 and 349.
Source: Same as Table 4.

– say, y_m compared to y_l – their subjective well-being is correspondingly greater, the differential equalling $(u_m - u_1)$. As each group progresses through the life cycle, incomes rise more for the higher schooling group from, say, y_m to y_3, while those of the lower schooling group rise from y_1 to y_m. But the greater growth of income of the higher schooling group causes their aspirations also to rise more – from, say, A_1 to A_3, compared to a growth in aspirations for the lower schooling group from A_1 to A_2. Hence, the higher schooling group moves from point 2 to point 7 while the lower schooling group moves from point 1 to point 4. As a result, the happiness differential enjoyed by the higher schooling group remains constant at $(u_m - u_1)$.

The psychological mechanism implicit in the view here of the determinants of material aspirations is suggested by the well-known ring toss experiment in which individuals – given free choice of how close to stand to the peg – are found to set their aspirations in proportion to their abilities. Then, as they get better at the ring toss, they tend to move farther away. Increasing skill is thus matched by increasing aspirations, in much the same way that increasing ability to get goods is matched by increasing material aspirations.

The third assumption about preferences is that people base their past or prospective happiness evaluations on their current preferences. The social science literature provides some support for this hypothesis. A cohort study of political attitudes by Markus (1986) found that respondents whose attitudes actually had changed tended to report that their past attitudes were the same as those currently held. Social psychologists Kahneman and Snell (1992), based on small group experiments, report that 'the dominant heuristic [to predict future tastes] is to consult current desires' and that 'there was little or no correlation between the predictions of hedonic change that individuals made and the changes they actually experienced' (pp. 187, 189). Rabin (1998), generalising from a survey of the social psychology literature, observes that 'we don't always accurately predict our own future preferences, nor even accurately assess our experienced well-being from past choices' (p. 12). Such statements, though not providing as specific support as one might like, are consistent with the current hypothesis.

The present model, however, leaves unanswered an important question – how to explain the similarity in material aspirations among those of different socio-economic status at the start of the life cycle? Those with more schooling typically come from more affluent backgrounds; hence, one would suppose that they would start out with higher material aspirations as well.

I believe that the explanation for the initial similarity and then growing divergence in aspirations by socio-economic status lies in the changing role over the life cycle of two factors determining aspirations – one's own past experience and social comparison. The importance of peer influences – that is, social comparison – in shaping the aspirations of the young is widely recognised. These peer influences, I believe, typically make for a commonality in the aspirations of young persons from different socio-economic origins. In the pre-adult ages, those from different backgrounds intermingle to a fair extent – at school, in sports, in recreational activities such as rock concerts, and at work, where they may hold the same jobs, such as fast food vendors. They see much the same television programmes, movies, and advertisements. These common experiences and social contacts make for more similar aspirations by socio-economic status than if family background were the only factor. However, once people enter the working ages, the experiences and contacts shared by those of different socio-economic status diminishes. Those who go on to college are embarked on a different career trajectory, and have limited contact in the workplace with those who do not share the same educational background. Their higher income also makes for residential segregation by socio-economic status. Although the experiences of others continue to influence aspirations, it seems likely that throughout the socio-economic spectrum, reference groups, over the course of the life cycle, become increasingly narrower than in the pre-adult years, and more confined to those of like status. As a result, the factors making in the pre-adult years for similarity in aspirations among those from different socio-economic backgrounds become progressively less salient over the course of the life cycle.

This reasoning can be tied to the more general theoretical literature in psychology and economics on the formation of preferences. In psychology, the two sets of factors identified here as influencing aspirations – one's past personal experience and the experience of others – correspond roughly to what is known as adaptation level theory and social comparison theory (Brickman and Campbell 1971, Frederick and Loewenstein 1999, Helson 1964, Myers 1992, Olson *et al.* 1986).[12] The counterparts in economics of these two theories are habit formation models and theories of interdependent preferences (Day, 1986; Duesenberry, 1949; Frank, 1985, 1997; Modigliani, 1949; Pollak, 1970, 1976; Tomes, 1985). Both the psychological and economic theories stress that judgments are formed by comparison – in the first case with one's past experience; in the second, with the experience of others.

I am suggesting that while both influences are at work in shaping material aspirations and hence judgments of well-being, their relative importance shifts over the course of the life cycle. In the pre-adult years social comparison over a wide socio-economic spectrum plays a relatively larger part than personal background in shaping aspirations. In the adult years, as individuals with different educational backgrounds embark on relatively segregated socio-economic tracks, past personal experience becomes more important and social comparison influences are increasingly confined to a reference group comprised of those of one's own socio-economic status. Hence, material aspirations start out much more alike among those from different socio-economic backgrounds than is true later in the life cycle, when one's personal income experience and that of others on the same track becomes the major driving force behind material aspirations.

---

[12] Kahneman (1999) points out that adaptation level and aspiration level are two different concepts. It seems likely, however, that they change in tandem. As one adapts to improved performance at the ring toss, aspirations correspondingly increase.

5. Summary

The pattern of change in material aspirations over the life cycle explains some of the paradoxical relationships between subjective well-being and income. At the start of the adult life cycle material aspirations are fairly similar throughout the population, but over the life cycle, aspirations increase in proportion to income. Utility functions shift inversely with material aspirations.

As a general matter, subjective well-being varies directly with income and inversely with material aspirations. At the start of the life cycle those with higher income are happier, because material aspirations are fairly similar throughout the population, and those with more income are better able to fulfill their aspirations. Income growth does not, however, cause well-being to rise, either for higher or lower income persons, because it generates equivalent growth in material aspirations, and the negative effect of the latter on subjective well-being undercuts the positive effect of the former. Even though rising income means that people can have more goods, the favourable effect of this on welfare is erased by the fact that people want more as they progress through the life cycle. It seems as though Emerson (1860) had it right when he said 'Want is a growing giant whom the coat of Have was never large enough to cover.'

Because the educational system channels people into two different life cycle tracks characterised by higher and lower income trajectories, those with more education are, on average, happier throughout the life cycle than those with less. Some psychologists have claimed that persistent interpersonal differentials in well-being over the life cycle are evidence that personality or genetic traits primarily determine relative well-being, not 'external' factors such as income. The present analysis makes clear that external factors are important, because the educational tracking of persons leads to persistent differences in well-being via its effect on relative incomes.

Judgments of well-being at any particular point in time are based on the material aspirations prevailing at that time. As a result, people tend to evaluate past lower incomes less favourably than they did when they were actually in that situation and had lower aspirations. Similarly, they judge prospective higher income situations more favourably than when they actually are in those situations, because they fail to anticipate the rise in material aspirations that will come with the growth in income. Choice among alternatives – decision utility – is based on the aspirations prevailing at the time of choice. The actual welfare effect of such choice – experienced utility – differs systematically from decision utility, because of unforeseen changes in aspirations. Thus, movement to a higher income situation is envisaged by a decision-maker as increasing happiness, because it is based on a projection of income growth with aspirations unchanged. But the increase in income itself engenders a corresponding rise in material aspirations, and experienced utility does not rise as expected.

University of Southern California

Date of receipt of first submission: April 1999

Date of receipt of final typescript: August 2000

References

Andrews, F. M. ed. (1986). *Research on the Quality of Life*. Ann Arbor, MI: Survey Research Center, Institute for Social Research, University of Michigan.

Andrews, F. M. and Withey, S. B. (1976). 'Developing measures of perceived life quality: results from several national surveys', *Social Indicator Research* I (1974), pp. 1–26.

Argyle, M. (1999). 'Causes and correlates of happiness', in (D. Kahneman, E. Diener, and N. Schwarz eds.), *Well-Being: The Foundations of Hedonic Psychology*, New York: Russell Sage Foundation, pp. 353–73.

Ashenfelter, O. and Rouse, C. (1999). 'Schooling, intelligence, and income in America: cracks in the bell curve', National Bureau of Economic Research, Working Paper No. 6902.

Bachman, J. G., Johnston, L. D., and O'Malley, P. M. (1980). *Monitoring the Future: Questionnaire Responses from the Nation's High School Seniors, 1976*. Ann Arbor, MI: Survey Research Center, Institute for Social Research.

Blanchflower, D. G. and Oswald, A. J. (1999). 'Well-being over time in Britain and the USA', unpublished manuscript, November.

Blundell, R., Preston, I. and Walker, I. eds. (1994). *The Measurement of Household Welfare*. Cambridge: Cambridge University Press.

Brickman, P. and Campbell, D. T. (1971). 'Hedonic relativism and planning the good society', in (M. H. Appley, ed.), *Adaptation Level Theory: A Symposium*, New York: Academic Press.

Campbell, A. (1981). *The Sense of Well-Being in America*, New York: McGraw-Hill.

Campbell, A. Converse, P. E. and Rodgers, W. L. (1976). *The Quality of American Life: Perceptions, Evaluations, and Satisfactions*. New York: Russell Sage.

Cantril, H. (1965). *The Pattern of Human Concerns*. New Brunswick, NJ: Rutgers University Press.

Costa, P. T. Jr., Zonderman, A. B., McCrae, R. R., Cornoni-Huntley, J., Locke, B. Z. and Barbano, H. E. (1987). 'Longitudinal analyses of psychological well-being in a national sample: stability of mean levels', *Journal of Gerontology*, vol. 42(1), pp. 50–5.

Day, R. H. (1986). 'On endogenous preferences and adaptive economising', in (R. H. Day, ed.), *The Dynamics of Market Economies*, Amsterdam: North Holland, pp. 153–70.

de la Croix, D. (1998). 'Growth and the relativity of satisfaction', *Mathematical Social Sciences*, vol. 36, pp. 105–25.

Diener, E. (1984). 'Subjective well-being', *Psychological Bulletin*, vol. 95(3), pp. 542–75.

Diener, E. and Lucas, R. E. (1999). 'Personality and subjective well-being', in Kahneman, *et al.* (1999)

Kahneman, D., Diener, E. and Schwarz N. eds. (1999). *Well-Being: The Foundations of Hedonic Psychology*, New York: Russell Sage Foundation.

Diener, E. and Oshi, S. (forthcoming) 'Money and happiness: income and subjective well-being across nations', in (E. Diener and E. M. Suh, eds.), *Subjective Well-Being Across Cultures*, Cambridge, MA: MIT Press.

Dixon, H. D. (1997). 'Controversy: economics and happiness', ECONOMIC JOURNAL vol. 107 (November), pp. 1812–4.

Duesenberry, J. S. (1949). *Income, Savings, and the Theory of Consumer Behaviour*. Cambridge, Mass.: Harvard University Press.

Durkheim, E. ([1930] 1952). *Suicide: A Study in Sociology*. New York: Free Press.

Easterlin, R. A. (1974). 'Does economic growth improve the human lot?' in (P. A. David and M. W. Reder, eds.), *Nations and Households in Economic Growth: Essays in Honour of Moses Abramovitz*. New York: Academic Press Inc.

Easterlin, R. A. (1987). *Birth and Fortune: The Impact of Numbers on Personal Welfare*. 2nd edition, Chicago: University of Chicago Press.

Easterlin, R. A. (1995). 'Will raising the incomes of all increase the happiness of all?' *Journal of Economic Behavior and Organization*, vol. 27, pp. 35–47.

Easterlin, R. A. and Schaeffer, C. M. (1999). 'Income and subjective well-being over the life cycle', in (C. D. Ryff and V. W. Marshall, eds.), *The Self and Society in Aging Processes*. New York: Springer, pp. 279–301.

Elster, J. and Roemer, J. E. eds. (1991). *Interpersonal Comparisons of Well-Being*. New York: Cambridge University Press.

Emerson, R. W. (1860). 'Wealth', in (R. W. Emerson), *The Conduct of Life*, Boston: Ticknor and Fields.

Frank, R. H. (1985). 'The demand for unobservable and other nonpositional goods', *American Economic Review*, vol. 75 (March), pp. 279–301.

Frank, R. H. (1997). 'The frame of reference as a public good', ECONOMIC JOURNAL vol. 107 (November), pp. 1832–47.

Frederick, S. and G. Loewenstein (1999). 'Hedonic adaptation', in Kahneman, *et al.* (1999), pp. 302–29.

Frey, B. S. and Stutzer, A. (1999). 'Measuring preferences by subjective well-being', *Journal of Institutional and Theoretical Economics*, vol. 155, pp. 1–24.

George, L. K. (1992). 'Economic status and subjective well-being: a review of the literature and an agenda for future research' in (N. E. Cutter, D. W. Grigg, and M. P. Lawton, eds.), *Aging, Money, and Life Satisfaction: Aspects of Financial Gerontology.* New York: Springer Publishing Co.

Helson, H. (1964). *Adaptation-Level Theory,* New York: Harper and Row.

Herzog, A. R., Rodgers, W. L. and Woodworth, J. (1982). *Subjective Well-Being Among Different Age Groups,* Ann Arbor, MI: Institute for Social Research, University of Michigan.

Hirsch, F. (1976). *Social Limits to Growth.* Cambridge, Mass: Harvard University Press

Kahneman, D. (1999). 'Objective happiness', in Kahneman, *et al.* (1999) pp. 3–25.

Kahneman, D. and Snell, J. (1992). 'Predicting taste change: do people know what they will like?' *Journal of Behavioral Decision-Making,* vol. 5, pp. 187–200.

Kahneman, D., Wakker, P. P. and Sarin, R. (1997). 'Back to Bentham? explorations of experienced utility', *Quarterly Journal of Economics,* vol. 112(2) (May), pp. 375–405.

Kenny, C. (1999). 'Does growth cause happiness or does happiness cause growth?' *Kyklos,* vol. 52(1), pp. 3–26.

Leibenstein, H. (1976). *Beyond Economic Man.* New York: Harvard University Press.

Lipset, S. M. and Schneider, W. (1987). *The Confidence Gap: Business, Labor, and Government in the Public Mind,* revised edition. Baltimore, MD: Johns Hopkins University Press.

Loewenstein, G. and Schkade, D. (1999). 'Wouldn't it be nice? Predicting future feelings', in Kahneman, *et al.* (1999) pp. 85–105.

Lykken, D. and Tellegen, A. (1996). 'Happiness is a stochastic phenomenon', *Psychological Science,* vol. 7(3) (May), pp. 180–9.

March, J. G. and Simon, H. A. (1968). *Organizations.* New York: John Wiley.

Markus, G. B. (1986). 'Stability and change in political attitudes: observed, recalled, and explained', *Political Behavior,* vol. 8(1), pp. 21–44.

McLanahan, S. and Sorensen, A. B. (1985). 'Life events and psychological well-being over the life course', in (G. H. Elder, Jr., ed.), *Life Course Dynamics: Trajectories and Transitions, 1968–1980.* Ithaca, NY: Cornell University Press, pp. 217–38.

Michalos, A. C. (1986). 'Job satisfaction, marital satisfaction, and the quality of life: a review and a preview', in (F. M. Andrews, ed.), *Research on the Quality of Life.* Ann Arbor, MI: Survey Research Center, Institute for Social Research, University of Michigan, pp. 57–83.

Michalos, A. C. (1991). *Global Report on Student Well-Being: Vol. I: Life Satisfactions and Happiness.* New York: Springer-Verlag.

Modigliani, F. (1949). 'Fluctuations in the saving-income ratio: a problem in economic forecasting', in Conference on Research in Income and Wealth, *Studies in Income and Wealth,* Vol. 11, New York: National Bureau of Economic Research, pp. 371–443.

Mroczek, D. K. and Kolarz, C. M. (1998). 'The effect of age on positive and negative affect: a developmental perspective on happiness', *Journal of Personality and Social Psychology,* vol. 75(5), pp. 1333–49.

Myers, D. G. (1992). *The Pursuit of Happiness: Who Is Happy and Why.* New York: William Morrow.

National Opinion Research Center (1999). *General Social Surveys, 1972–1998: Cumulative Codebook.* Chicago: National Opinion Research Center.

Ng, Y. K (1997). 'A case for happiness, cardinalism, and interpersonal comparability', ECONOMIC JOURNAL, vol. 107 (November), pp. 1848–58.

Nussbaum, M. C. and Sen, A. eds. (1993). *The Quality of Life.* Oxford: Clarendon Press.

Offer, A., ed. (1996). *In Pursuit of the Quality of Life.* New York: Oxford University Press.

Olson, J. M., Herman, C. P. and Zanna, M. P. eds. (1986). *Relative Deprivation and Social Comparison. The Ontario Symposium.* Vol. 4, Hillsdale, NJ: Erlbaum.

Oswald, A. J. (1997). 'Happiness and economic performance', ECONOMIC JOURNAL vol. 107 (November), pp. 1815–31.

Pollak, R. A. (1970). 'Habit formation and dynamic demand functions', *Journal of Political Economy,* vol. 78(4) (July/August), pp. 745–63.

Pollak, R. A. (1976). 'Interdependent preferences', *American Economic Review,* vol. 66(3) (June), pp. 309–20.

Rabin, M. (1998). 'Psychology and economics' *Journal of Economic Literature,* vol. 36 (March), pp. 11–46.

Rainwater, L. (1994). 'Family equivalence as a social construction', in (O. Ekert-Jaffe, ed.), *Standards of Living and Families: Observation and Analysis,* Montrouge, France: John Libbey Eurotext, pp. 23–39.

Ramsey, F. (1928). 'A mathematical theory of savings', ECONOMIC JOURNAL vol. 38, pp. 543–59.

Roper-Starch Organization (1979). *Roper Reports 79–1.* Storrs, CT: University of Connecticut, The Roper Center.

Roper-Starch Organization (1995). *Roper Reports 95–1.* Storrs, CT: University of Connecticut, The Roper Center.

Schwarz, N. and Strack, F. (1999). 'Reports of subjective well-being: judgmental processes and their methodological implications', in Kahneman, *et al.* (1999) pp. 61–84.

Tomes, N. (1985). 'Income distribution, happiness, and satisfaction', *Journal of Economic Psychology*, vol. 7, pp. 425–46.

Tversky, A. and Griffin, D. (1991). 'Endowment and contrast in judgments of well-being', in (F. Strack, M. Argyle and N. Schwarz, eds.), *Subjective Well-Being: An Interdisciplinary Perspective*. Oxford: Pergamon Press, pp. 101–18.

Veenhoven, R. (1993). *Happiness in Nations, Subjective Appreciation of Life in 56 Nations 1946-1992*. Rotterdam: Erasmus University.

Veroff, J., Douvan, E. and Kulka, R. A. (1981). *The Inner American: A Self-Portrait from 1957 to 1976*. New York: Basic Books.

[15]

Amartya Sen

RATIONALITY, JOY AND FREEDOM

ABSTRACT: *In* The Joyless Economy, *Tibor Scitovsky proposes a model of human behavior that differs substantially from that of standard economic theory. Scitovsky begins with a basic distinction between "comfort" and "stimulation." While stimulation is ultimately more satisfying and creative, we frequently fall for the bewitching attractions of comfort, which leads to impoverished lives. Scitovsky's analysis has far-reaching implications not only for the idea of rationality, but for the concept of utility (by making it plural in nature) and, perhaps most importantly, for the importance of freedom (including the freedom to change our preferences).*

When *The Joyless Economy* was published more than two decades ago, even a seasoned admirer of Tibor Scitovsky's writings (as I have always been) could not but marvel at the elegance and reach of this unusual book. It was the middle 1970s. Growing conservatism in social thought (following the radical 1960s) was being accompanied by some hardening of methodological inertia in economics. Amidst all this arrived *The Joyless Economy*, questioning with great style the very foundations of established economic thinking, and doing so, I might add, in quite a joyful way. A combination of stimulating insights and entertaining arguments, combined with remarkable seriousness, distinguished this altogether unusual monograph.

Critical Review 10, no. 4 (Fall 1996). ISSN 0891-3811. © 1996 Critical Review Foundation.

Amartya Sen, Lamont University Professor and Professor of Economics and Philosophy, Harvard University, Cambridge, MA 02138, telephone (617) 495-1871, telefax (617) 496-5942, is the author of, *inter alia, Inequality Reexamined* (Harvard, 1992), (with Jean Drèze) *Hunger and Public Action* (Oxford, 1989), and *On Ethics and Economics* (Blackwell, 1987).

Behavior and Its Scientific Study

More than 20 years later, we have good reason to ask: what did the book do? What are its lasting contributions? And where do we go from here? I shall propose some answers to these questions. But before I try to do that, let me clarify the nature of the radicalism I associate with Scitovsky's book, since I began with a reference to the resurgence of conservatism—an inherently ambiguous concept.

In the Preface to *The Joyless Economy*, Scitovsky says (commenting on the reception of the ideas underlying this book): "Economists are deeply divided into the Establishment and radical-left critics, but they were like a harmonious and happy family in the unanimous hostility to my ideas" (1976, xi). Paranoia? Not so, I think. The nonconformism that characterizes Scitovsky's work involves asking questions that had been—and alas, still largely are—ignored by all the dominant economic schools, irrespective of their political positioning. The need for a change in investigative analysis and in practical reason that emerges from Scitovsky's inquiry has disturbing implications, but there was—and is—great reluctance to go the way that Scitovsky wanted economics to go.

What did Tibor Scitovsky think he was doing? His starting point clearly was a deep skepticism about the "science" of economics, as it was practiced by the dominant schools. Indeed, a far-reaching scientific ambition lies at the very root of *The Joyless Economy*. The policy lessons that emerge arise from—and are entirely derivative on—his attempt to develop a more scientific approach to the subject matter of human behavior and satisfaction.

Scitovsky's prime target was the use of the idea of rationality in economics in predicting and explaining behavior. He begins by noting that "economists assume that the consumer is rational; in other words, they assume that whatever he does must be the best thing for him to do, given his tastes, market opportunities, and circumstances, since otherwise he would not have done it." He points out that "many of the economists' arguments, conclusions, recommendations" are based on this assumption. It is this approach that Scitovsky found "unscientific," to be contrasted with what he took to be the "scientific approach": "to observe behavior—different people's behavior in similar situations and the same person's behavior in different situations—in order to find, contained in those ob-

servations, the regularities, the common elements, the seeming contradictions and the resolution of those contradictions which then
become the foundations of a theory to explain behavior" (1976,
vii–viii).

If science is Scitovsky's first concern, the practical relevance of
his work lies no less in its implications for policies, actions, and decisions, based on a different understanding of the nature of our behavior. Part of the exercise in practical reason is geared to the individual, and is a modern revival of the Socratic question: "How
should one live?" But there are lessons also for public policy, involving group behavior as well as the instruments of the state.

Comfort and Stimulation

The scientific as well as applied conclusions that Scitovsky draws
involve many complexities and qualifications, but it would not be, I
think, unfair to give the pride of place to his basic distinction between "comfort" and "stimulation" as two aspects of enjoyment
that are quite different from each other and that can, to a great extent, compete with each other for our attention, time, and
resources.

At the end of the analysis, in the last chapter of the book, Scitovsky arrives at the firm conclusion that "we overindulge in comfort." Furthermore, "the economies of scale impose the majority's
tastes on the whole society, and when the majority chooses to sacrifice the stimulus of novelty for the sake of comfort, the creation
of novelty and the minority's seeking new ways of attaining the
good life are both impeded." This impoverishes the lives of the minority restrained from seeking departures from the merely comfortable, but also makes the mundane and joyless existence of the majority durable and self-sustaining. Not only does the irrational
neglect of systematic and cultivated stimulation lead to reduced
lives, it also makes us respond to this lacuna with feverish thought-
lessness. Scitovsky even argues that "our dearth of the conventional
forms of stimulation" makes us more vulnerable to destructive
forms of stimulation that may come our way, whether in real life or
in entertainment, leading to "great tolerance of crime, violence, and
threats to life and property" (1976, 282-83).

Life Style and Public Policy

How can we get out of this rut? Scitovsky points to different possibilities, but focuses particularly on changing the cultural dimensions
of our lives.

> The remedy is culture. We must acquire the consumption skills that
> will give us access to society's accumulated stock of past novelty and
> so enable us to supplement at will and almost without limit the cur-
> rently available flow of novelty as a source of stimulation. Different
> skills of consumption open up different sources of stimulation, and
> each gives us greatly enhanced freedom to choose what we person-
> ally find the most enjoyable and stimulating, holding out the
> prospect of a large reservoir of novelty and years of enjoyment.
> Music, painting, literature, and history are the obvious examples.
> (1976, 235)

Scitovsky's scrutiny of educational and cultural policy, and other social influences in developing our skill for constructive stimulation,
provide some of the most important practical lessons to emerge
from this book. Scitovsky went on to pursue some of these issues
further in his collection of essays, *Human Desire and Economic Satisfaction* (1986).

Do these issues remain as relevant today as they were 20 years ago?
I would argue that they are, if anything, more so. Scitovsky saw his
work as the beginning of a different line of analysis, but unfortunately not many economists have followed the course he opened up.
However, two decades is not a long time in the development of a
discipline. As the overdue reexamination of the behavioral foundations of economics and the other social sciences gathers more mo-
mentum (as I am sure it will), Scitovsky's analyses, hypotheses, and
counsel will no doubt have the influence they richly deserve. In the
rethinking of public policy, too, the directions towards which Scitovsky points remain to be fruitfully explored and pursued.

So far, in interpreting the relevance of Scitovsky's work, I have
tried to follow him faithfully and have retained the emphases that
he has himself suggested. I want now to move a little further in a
somewhat different direction, but draw heavily on his work and the
illumination that he has provided. In particular, I want to reexam-
ine three of the basic concepts of social and economic philosophy

on which *The Joyless Economy* has a clear bearing: (1) *rationality*, (2) *utility*, and (3) *freedom*.

Rationality of Choice

Scitovsky's criticism of the presumption of rational behavior was, as we saw, the starting point of the analysis of *The Joyless Economy*. There are two different issues here:

(1) Do people behave in the way that standard economic theory characterizes rational behavior?
(2) Does the characterization of "rational behavior" in standard theory provide an adequate understanding of rationality?

Scitovsky was primarily occupied with the first question, which he answered in the negative. He put emphasis, in particular, on his diagnosis that what people do may very often not be in their respective best interests. In particular the rational pursuit of creative and sustainable stimulation may be hampered by a variety of problems, including the bewitching attraction of comfort and the neglect of skill formation in generating and enjoying stimulation.

I referred earlier to the Socratic question about how one should live. The related Socratic claim that the "unexamined life" is not worth living has some affinities with Scitovsky's diagnosis.[1] If constructive stimulation is neglected in actual behavior, this is not because people have examined the alternatives and the range of choices that are in fact within their command, and have come to the considered conclusion that they really do want comfort rather than stimulation. Had that been the case, it would have been harder for Scitovsky to press stimulation on them, "in their own best interest." The last thing that can be said about *The Joyless Economy* is that it is paternalistic in spirit.

Scitovsky's theory turns to a considerable extent on our unwillingness or reluctance to examine and explore the real options we have. Another way of understanding Scitovsky's thesis, then, is to see it as the identification of the need for more *self-examination* of what it is that we really want, rather than considering it simply as an external diagnosis that what people will profit from most is stimulation rather than comfort. In this way of seeing the problem, which is implicit in Scitovsky's own analysis (if not stated in quite this form), the real departure from orthodox economic theory is Scitovsky's emphasis on critical reflection about what one wants, rather than on making cunning choices in line with given preferences. Critique may or may not be in itself stimulating, but it is critique—not just stimulation—that must emerge as the point of practical departure in this line of analysis.

At this point we may move over to the second question. Is it sensible to characterize rational behavior in terms of intelligently pursuing given preferences and thereby promoting one's own welfare? There are many weaknesses in this characterization, some of which I have tried to discuss elsewhere.[2] The deficiency that is closest to Scitovsky's concern relates to what was just discussed: the lacuna of seeing rationality in terms of attempting the best fulfilment of what one wants (even in the absence of critical examination of what is wanted).

Scitovsky's theory of rationality does not, ultimately, involve denying the necessity—for rationality—of attempting to get what one really wants, but this wanting is considered, as it were, at a higher level. A person may really want creative stimulation—without being reflectively clear that this is what she does want—and then mistakenly pursue a life style that does not promote what would most satisfy her. In this sense, Scitovsky's thesis can be seen as being broadly within the conventional framework of rationality in terms of what a person *really* desires: much of the sophistication of the concept takes the form of providing a deeper characterization of what is really desired. This congruence with individuals' own judgments (in the form of deliberate, scrutinized and skilled conclusions) is worth stressing, since social influences are discussed by Scitovsky with such care and penetrating insight that it might be tempting to think that he is irreconcilably anti-individualist in a deeper sense as well, which would be a mistake.

This distinction between actual desires (for commodities and life styles) and scrutinized desires (taking full note of the need for constructive stimulation) has bearing on some of the most basic concepts of social analysis. I shall come presently to the implications of this distinction for the ideas of freedom and utility, but there is a further remark to be made about Scitovsky's suggestion that human beings often fail to conform to the notion of rationality postulated by standard theory.

As argued already, this claim is indeed correct in one sense: if the concept of rationality is to include doing things that are "best" for the person, then a chasm does clearly exist between that notion of rational behavior and the way in which Scitovsky describes how people actually behave. But Scitovsky also describes standard theory as requiring that a person's "actual behavior is a faithful reflection of his preferences." This is, of course, a different requirement, since a person's preferences may or may not correspond to what would be best for him. Scitovsky is right to see standard theory as demanding behavior that reflects both one's interests and one's preferences, and indeed it is the simultaneous insistence on these very different requirements that gives orthodox theory its peculiarly extensive reach.[3]

However, not all of the demands made by orthodox theory are equally central to its program (1976, vii-viii). Scitovsky refers to "the theory of revealed preference" (on which "are based many of the economists' arguments, conclusions, recommendations") and sees it as reflecting this structure of presumptions. It can, however, be argued that the theory of "revealed preference" in itself does not say anything about a person's pursuing what is in his best interest. Rather, if a person were to act consistently in the sense of satisfying the axioms of revealed preference, then a ranking relation (called "revealed preference" only out of courtesy) can be constructed from his actual choices such that he can be seen *as if* he were consistently pursuing that preference. Then of course, the person's "actual behavior" will be, definitionally, "a faithful reflection of his preferences" (taking preferences to be what the choices themselves have yielded). In this sense revealed preference theory is only a demand for internal consistency of choice.[4] Any further conclusion that the person is actually doing things that are "best for him" does not, strictly speaking, belong to the theory of revealed preference.

If we take the theory of revealed preference in this limited form, the behavior patterns to which Scitovsky draws attention need not involve any violation of the axioms of revealed preference and can be seen as being quite consistent with rational behavior according to that theory. People may not be acting in their best interest, they may not be able to defend their choices under scrutiny, and they may not be sensibly pursuing their higher-level desire for stimulation, but still their actual choices can be fully in line with the permissible behavior patterns under the theory of revealed preference.

In this sense, Scitovsky's empirical conclusions do not, in fact, contradict revealed-preference theory.

This qualification of one of Scitovsky's remarks is not meant to suggest that his analysis does not hit at the very root of the use of standard theory; it does. In standard economic analysis, the empty shell of "revealed preference theory" is actually combined with substantive assumptions about what is in the person's best interest (to wit, what he or she can be seen as pursuing), as well as with other presumptions, and thus the full characterization of behavior and its implications in that analysis can indeed be criticized for precisely the reasons that Scitovsky identifies.

Scitovsky's general critique remains, therefore, on target, despite the possibility of disputing his remark about the theory of revealed preference. But this entails that in terms of the two questions presented earlier, Scitovsky should be seen as answering No to question (2), not question (1). It is not so much, on this interpretation, that people do not behave in the way that standard revealed-preference economics characterizes rational behavior, but that this characterization of rational behavior is deeply inadequate and unilluminating. This interpretational shift does nothing to weaken the force of Scitovsky's critique of standard theory, nor of course to reduce the importance of his analysis for practical reason and policy.

Utility

Scitovsky does not explicitly invoke a theory of utility. It is not a concept for which he has indicated any special fondness, and indeed, the subject index of neither *The Joyless Economy* nor of *Human Desire and Economic Satisfaction* betrays any interest in this idea. However, insofar as the theory of utility concerns what a person values and how this affects her choices, there is an implicit theory of utility behind Scitovsky's behavioral analysis.

It may be useful to bring in a comparison here with what has been called "the new theory of consumption behavior," as developed by W. M. (Terence) Gorman (1956, 1975) and Kevin Lancaster (1966, 1971). In that theory (which is no longer particularly "new"), each commodity is seen as having certain "characteristics," and the consumer is understood to be in hot pursuit of these characteristics, rather than the commodities as such. For example, rice may offer some calories, some protein, some vitamins, some hunger-satisfying potential, some means of entertaining others, and so on. Even when one's demand for a collection of underlying characteristics is given, that demand can be fulfilled through different commodity baskets which all yield that very collection of characteristics. Different goods are substitutes for each other since they may be offering, at least partly, the same characteristics. This characteristics-based analysis has been an enriching departure in the theory of consumption.

Could we see Scitovsky's concepts of "stimulation" and "comfort" as being characteristics of this kind? To some extent, we can: the Scitovsky program shares with the Gorman-Lancaster program a search for something that lies behind the demand for commodities. But there are dissimilarities as well. Stimulation is not a characteristic of a commodity as such; it is more a question of what we are able to make of commodities. Stimulation and comfort result from the combination of commodities with our motivations and skills, and while we can still make use of the Gorman-Lancaster formulations, this may not be the most useful way of exploring Scitovsky's theory.

Indeed, it is the role of motivational and decisional variability on which Scitovsky concentrates. As he points out, we can get stimulation, to varying extents, from such diverse activities as "going to a colorful market or shopping center, browsing in a good bookshop, reading a Sears catalog, looking at the latest fashions in elegant department stores or inspecting next year's models of automobiles" (1976, 232-33). The production of stimulation is a "relational" activity, involving both the nature of the commodity or action and what we are motivated—and trained—to make out of it.

Another formulation of utility theory with which Scitovsky's theory has affinity is the view of utility as irreducibly diverse. In standard utility theory, utility is seen either in classical Benthamite terms, as mental satisfaction (as Alfred Marshall and A.C. Pigou saw it), or in terms of the overall fulfilment of felt desires (as Frank Ramsey viewed it), or as a representation of choice behavior (as revealed preference theory sees it). These variants of standard utility theory differ from each other, but they do share the general characteristic of seeing utility as basically a homogeneous magnitude, representable by a real number. In contrast, Aristotle saw "eudaemonia" as being constitutively diverse, leading to a heterogeneous view of fulfilment. John Stuart Mill also argued for accepting the diversity of different kinds of utilities (the pleasure from gambling not being the same as the joy from reading poetry).

To some extent, the distinctions drawn by Scitovsky follow the Aristotle-Mill path in denying the usefulness of some homogenized magnitude of utility, proceeding instead in the direction of a structured diversity of joys, including comfort and stimulation. This analogy is worth bearing in mind, since the Aristotelian and Millian perspectives have been well explored (particularly in the philosophical literature), and Scitovsky's particular characterization of heterogeneity in fulfilment can profit from similar investigation and scrutiny. I shall not pursue this suggestion further here, but the richness of Aristotelian and Millian structures can be, I believe, both enhanced and utilized by combining them with Scitovsky's penetrating partitioning of forms of joy and joylessness.

Freedom

Finally, I come to freedom—a subject in which orthodox economics does not take an overwhelming interest. Scitovsky does not go much into this concept, but his work is ultimately also about freedom. In particular, he analyzes how we can enhance our freedom to get what we have reason to value (such as stimulation) through reflective examination as well as by developing skills. And indeed at one place, he mentions this aspect of his thesis explicitly: "Different skills of consumption open up different stores of sources of stimulation, and each gives us greatly enhanced freedom to choose what we personally find the most enjoyable and stimulating" (1976, 235).

There are at least two ways of seeing substantive freedom: (1) *instrumentally*, as a means of getting what we want, and (2) *intrinsically*, as something we value in itself (over and above its instrumental role).[5] Scitovsky's reference to freedom in the quotation above is primarily instrumental. But it is not absurd to claim that our interest in freedom cannot be only instrumental. For example, suppose we choose some option x from a set S of alternatives. If we are concerned only with the instrumental view, it would appear that nothing is lost if all alternatives other than x were to be removed from S, since x is what I chose (I can still choose that even after the reduction of the set S). If, however, freedom is valued in itself, we can argue that my freedom is significantly reduced if these other alternatives are removed from the available set, even if my choice remains the same (to wit, x) in both the cases. It is "up to me," I can argue, to choose what I like, and even if the selected alternative is the same, there is a loss of freedom in my being given the reduced set from which to choose, and this I can, with reason, resent.

This is a subject on which there is a considerable literature.[6] A question that has to be asked is: Why do we seek freedom? The instrumentalist view tends to suggest that this may be related to uncertainty about our own preferences, so that having more options can be useful. (David Kreps [1979] has presented the classic formulation of this approach, developing some suggestions of Tjalling Koopmans.) In contrast, the intrinsic view suggests that even if we do not have any uncertainty about our own preferences, we may still value freedom for its own sake, for one of various interrelated reasons: (1) because it may be valuable to be able to *choose freely*, or (2) because it may be important that the *agent* of choice be the person whose life would be most affected, or (3) because we have reason to value the *freedom to change our mind*.[7]

On this literature, Scitovsky's analysis has a considerable bearing. If we have some basic motivations (such as stimulation and comfort) and also, at any moment, some preference over commodity bundles that link up with those motivations, one source of variability arises precisely from the possibility that a person can alter her preferences in trying a different—and possibly more fruitful—way of advancing the basic motivations. The dichotomy between preferences over commodities (the meat and potatoes of standard economics) and more basic motivations (for example, in generating stimulation) points to a significant source of variability in preferences, and this is directly relevant to the valuation of freedom. I may not use the public park that exists, and yet may have good reason to resent that facility being withdrawn, since I could otherwise have pursued my basic motivations differently (by choosing to go to the park), after using my freedom to change my mind through self-critique.

The integration of *volitional* elements into the literature on preference variation and valuation of flexibility can lead to some significant enrichment of ongoing studies of freedom. The value of freedom and flexibility does not depend only on *given* uncertainty about our preferences. It is also a matter of being free to undertake a *critique* of our own preferences and being free to change our minds. Thus, the importance of freedom and the relevance of preference revision relate closely to the analysis of preference, behavior and self-critique presented by Tibor Scitovsky.

*   *   *

The Joyless Economy will continue to stimulate us and will go on enriching our understanding of the nature of the economy and of the society. In his concluding chapter, Scitovsky notes: "The novelty of the book lies in introducing novelty as an object of desire and a source of satisfaction" (1976, 282). I have tried to argue that the novelty that this rich monograph has presented to us goes well beyond the particular ideas on which the author himself has focused. I suppose one characteristic of a great work is that the author underestimates its reach. The reach, in this case, is remarkably extensive.

NOTES

1. For an important interpretation and pursuit of that task, see Nozick 1989.
2. In particular in Sen 1973 and 1977. See also Hirschman 1982, Mansbridge 1990, and Walsh 1996.
3. This insistence on the congruence of a set of diverse requirements also makes the individual, as seen in standard theory, something of a "rational fool" (I have tried to argue in Sen 1977). This postulated creature is terribly neat and consistent in thought and action, but unable to depart from a pervasive conformity that identifies—of necessity—several distinct and sometimes conflicting motivations, such as (1) acting according to one's actual preference, (2) going by one's scrutinized and corrected preference, (3) pursuing best one's self-interest, (4) doing what one thinks would be the right thing to do, and so on.
4. There is a different issue as to whether "internal consistency" is a viable concept for *choice behavior* over commodity bundles, and whether something additional has to be brought in—from "outside" observed choices (such as motivations and reasoning)—to make any sense of the idea of consistency. It can be shown, in particular, that *every* set of choices—whatever—can be claimed to be free from internal tension through a suitable account of motivations and strategies. Revealed preference theory, as developed by Paul Samuelson, avoids this difficulty by imposing some consistency "axioms," which amounts in effect to ruling out of court certain types of possible motivations. The thesis that the idea of a purely "internal consistency of choice" is methodologically unsustainable has been analyzed in Sen 1993.

5. There is, of course, also a procedural view of freedom, which brings in other concerns, such as the nature of rules and the operation of constraints that bind our action; see Nozick 1974.
6. Some alternative lines of analysis can be found in Kreps 1979, Suppes 1987, Arrow 1995, and in the literature cited in these works.
7. I have tried to address these issues in my Kenneth Arrow Lectures on "Freedom and Social Choice," given at Stanford University in 1992; to be published.

REFERENCES

Arrow, Kenneth. 1995. "A Note on Freedom and Flexibility." In Basu et al. 1995.
Basu, Kaushik, Prasanta Pattanaik, and Kotaro Suzumura, eds. 1995. *Choice, Welfare and Development*. Oxford: Clarendon Press.
Elster, Jon, ed. 1986. *Rational Choice*. Oxford: Blackwell.
Gorman, W.M. 1956. "The Demand for Related Goods." Journal paper J3129. Ames: Iowa Agricultural Experimental Station.
Gorman, W.M. 1975. "Tricks with Utility Functions." In Michael Artis and A.R. Nobay, eds., *Essays in Economic Analysis*. Cambridge: Cambridge University Press.
Hahn, Frank, and Martin Hollis, eds. 1979. *Philosophy and Economic Theory*. Oxford: Oxford University Press.
Hirschman, Albert. 1982. *Shifting Involvements: Private and Public Action*. Princeton: Princeton University Press.
Kreps, David. 1979. "A Representation Theorem for 'Preference for Flexibility.'" *Econometrica* 47: 565–78.
Lancaster, Kelvin. 1966. "A New Approach to Consumer Theory." *Journal of Political Economy* 74.
Lancaster, Kevin. 1971. *Consumer Demand: A New Approach*. New York: Columbia University Press.
Mansbridge, Jane J., ed. 1990. *Beyond Self-Interest*. Chicago: University of Chicago Press.
Nozick, Robert. 1974. *Anarchy, State and Utopia*. New York: Basic Books.
Nozick, Robert. 1989. *The Examined Life*. New York: Simon & Schuster.
Scitovsky, Tibor. 1976. *The Joyless Economy: An Inquiry into Human Satisfaction and Consumer Dissatisfaction*. New York: Oxford University Press.
Scitovsky, Tibor. 1986. *Human Desire and Economic Satisfaction: Essays on the Frontiers of Economics*. Brighton: Wheatsheaf Books.
Sen, Amartya. 1973. "Behaviour and the Concept of Preference." *Economica* 45: 241–59. Reprinted in Elster 1986.
Sen, Amartya. 1977. "Rational Fools." *Philosophy and Public Affairs* 6: 317–44. Reprinted in Hahn and Hollis 1979 and Mansbridge 1990.

Sen, Amartya. 1993. "Internal Consistency of Choice." *Econometrica* 61: 495–521.

Suppes, Patrick. 1987. "Maximizing Freedom of Decision: An Axiomatic Approach." In G. Feiwel, ed., *Arrow and the Foundations of the Theory of Economic Policy.* New York: New York University Press.

Walsh, Vivian. 1996. *Rationality, Allocation, and Reproduction.* Oxford: Clarendon Press.

Name Index

The International Library of Critical Writings in Economics

Future titles will include:

New Developments in Exchange Rate
Economics
Lucio Sarno and Mark P. Taylor

Long Term Trends and Business Cycles
Terence C. Mills

The Economics of Migration
Klaus F. Zimmermann and Thomas Bauer

The Economics of Language
Donald M. Lamberton

The Economics of Budget Deficits
*Charles Rowley, William F. Shughart and
Robert D. Tollison*

The Economics of Structural Change
*Harald Hagemann, Michael Landesmann
and Roberto Scazzieri*

Cost-Benefit Analysis
Arnold C. Harberger and Glenn P. Jenkins

Alternative Theories of the Firm
*Richard Langlois, Tony F. Yu and Paul
Robertson*

International Financial Integration
*Sylvester C.W. Eijffinger and Jan J.G.
Lemmen*

The Economics of Poverty and Inequality
Frank A. Cowell

Recent Developments in Labor Economics
Orley C. Ashenfelter and Kevin F. Hallock

Imperfect Competition, Nonclearing
Markets and Business Cycles
Jean-Pascal Bénassy

The Economics of Project Appraisal
David L. Bevan

Recent Developments in Transport Economics
Kenneth Button

Recent Developments in Urban and
Regional Economics
Paul C. Cheshire and Gilles Duranton

Path Dependence
Paul David

Global Capitalism
John Dunning

The Economics of Transfer Pricing
Lorraine Eden

Cognitive Economics
Massimo Egidi and Salvatore Rizzello

The Economics of Crime
Isaac Ehrlich

The Distribution of Tax Burdens
Don Fullerton and Gilbert E. Metcalf

Comparative Law and Economics
Gerrit de Geest and Roger Van Den Bergh

The International Economic Institutions of
the Twentieth Century
David Greenaway and Robert C. Hine

Intra-Industry Trade
Herbert Grubel and Peter Lloyd

The Economics of Schooling
Eric A. Hanushek

The Economics of Conflict
Keith Hartley and Todd Sandler

The Economics of Organisation and
Bureaucracy
Peter M. Jackson

The Economics of Networks
Michael Katz and Carl Shapiro

The Economics of Business Strategy
John Kay

The Economics of Natural Hazards
Howard Kunreuther and Adam Rose

Personnel Economics
Edward P. Lazear and Robert McNabb

Economics and Religion
Paul Oslington

Forms of Capitalism: Comparative
Institutional Analyses
Ugo Pagano and Ernesto Screpanti

The Economics of Public Utilities
Ray Rees

The Economics of Modern Business
Enterprise
Martin Ricketts

Complexity in Economics
J. Barkley Rosser, Jr.

New Developments in Public Choice
Charles Rowley

Recent Developments in International
Investment
Alan M. Rugman

Cartels
Stephen Salant and Margaret Levenstein

The Economics of Free Trade
Robert W. Staiger

The Economics of Contracts
Lars A. Stole

The Economics of Leisure and Recreation
Clem Tisdell

The Economics of the Mass Media
Glenn Withers

Recent Developments in Evolutionary
Economics
Ulrich Witt

Multinational and Public Policy
Stephen Young

Time in Economic Theory
Stefano Zamagni